# Oracle8*i*
# Tips & Techniques

# About the Authors

### Douglas Scherer

Douglas is president of Core Paradigm (www.coreparadigm.com), a firm providing consulting, mentoring and formal training solutions primarily for Oracle database application and management environments. He is a frequent speaker at conferences and user-group meetings internationally and has appeared in *Visions of the New Millennium,* a series seen on PBS and its affiliates. He is also contributing editor to the *Oracle Designer Handbook,* second edition (Osborne/McGraw-Hill) and chairs the database track at Columbia University's Computer Technology and Applications program. He holds an M.S. from Columbia University.

### William Gaynor, Jr.

William is a senior Oracle DBA and database modeler. He has designed, implemented, and maintained transactional and analytical systems for financial-services companies, educational institutions, and airlines, among others. He holds a Ph.D. in economics from Montréal's McGill University. William can be reached at wbgaynor@hotmail.com.

### Arlene Valentinsen

Arlene is assistant vice president in Deutsche Bank's Global Technology Services Group, where she is a senior database administrator for a number of major Oracle-based systems central to the bank's worldwide banking operations. Earlier she worked for the New York State Department of Transportation as an Oracle database administrator and developer, specializing in traffic safety decision support systems. She also was a consultant for CMA, Inc., a software development firm headquartered in Albany, NY, that develops large-scale systems in Oracle and other development environments. Arlene has an M.S. in computer science and a B.S. in applied mathematics and computer science from the State University of New York, at Albany.

### Xerxes Cursetjee

Xerxes is senior technical lead for data warehousing and distributed components at ASI Financial Services. Adept in Oracle, SQL Server, C++, and Java, he works on customer profitability systems for large banks such as Chase Manhattan and Citibank. He also teaches database courses at Columbia University's Computer Technology and Applications program. In his free time he enjoys playing jazz piano and reading. Xerxes can be contacted by e-mail at cursetjee@hotmail.com.

ORACLE®  *Oracle Press*™

# Oracle8*i*
# Tips & Techniques

Douglas Scherer
William Gaynor, Jr.
Arlene Valentinsen
Xerxes Cursetjee

Osborne/**McGraw-Hill**

Berkeley  New York  St. Louis
San Francisco  Auckland  Bogotá  Hamburg  London  Madrid
Mexico City  Milan  Montreal  New Delhi  Panama City
Paris  São Paulo  Singapore  Sydney  Tokyo  Toronto

Osborne/**McGraw-Hill**
2600 Tenth Street
Berkeley, California 94710
U.S.A.

For information on translations or book distributors outside the U.S.A., or to arrange bulk purchase discounts for sales promotions, premiums, or fund-raisers, please contact Osborne/**McGraw-Hill** at the above address.

### Oracle8*i* Tips & Techniques

1234567890 AGM AGM 019876543210

ISBN 0-07-212103-3

| | |
|---|---|
| **Publisher**<br>Brandon A. Nordin | **Proofreader**<br>Stefany Otis |
| **Associate Publisher and Editor-in-Chief**<br>Scott Rogers | **Indexer**<br>Rebecca Plunkett |
| **Acquisitions Editor**<br>Jeremy Judson | **Computer Designers**<br>E. A. Pauw<br>Gary Corrigan<br>Dick Schwartz<br>Jim Kussow |
| **Project Editor**<br>Betsy Manini | |
| **Editorial Assistant**<br>Monika Faltiss | **Illustrator**<br>Robert Hansen<br>Brian Wells<br>Beth Young |
| **Technical Editor**<br>Leslie Tierstein | |
| **Copy Editor**<br>Stacey Sawyer | **Series Design**<br>Jani Beckwith |

This book was composed with Corel VENTURA™ Publisher.

**Dedicated in memory to my uncle, Dr. George P. Annes**
Douglas Scherer


**To my mother and father for their never-failing support
and generosity—oh, and for use of the car**
William Gaynor


**To my father, Eugene Galick. I wish you were here to see this**
Arlene Valentinsen


**To my parents**
Xerxes Cursetjee

# Contents at a Glance

PART III
# Application Development

# Contents

## PART I
## Overview

## PART II
## Server Administration

## PART III
## Application Development

# Foreword

## Oracle8*i*, the Internet Platform

Oracle8*i* is the most complete and comprehensive platform to develop and deploy Internet applications, and to manage all Internet-based content. Oracle8*i* changes the way information is managed and accessed to meet the demands on the Internet, while at the same time providing significant new features for traditional OLTP and data warehouse applications. Oracle8*i* has the performance and scalability needed to support today's large Internet sites and other mission-critical applications with high quality of service. Oracle8*i* is also the lowest cost development and deployment platform, making it the platform to choose for enabling business on the Internet.

Oracle relational database technology is already the foundation of the Internet. Every major Web site and all of the top ten e-commerce sites use Oracle. Oracle8*i* is the Internet platform designed for:

- ■ Developing Applications for the Internet

- ■ Deploying Applications for the Internet

- ■ Managing Internet Content

- ■ Enabling Business Online

# Java, the Language of the Internet

Until the advent of the Java programming language, it was difficult to manage Internet content, to build and deploy applications that accessed this content, and to run these Internet applications with excellent service.

Application developers were required to learn a variety of languages, tools, types of servers, and middleware in order to build Internet applications. Now, Java is becoming the standard language of the Internet.

With the release of Oracle8i, Oracle provides Java developers with a robust infrastructure on which to build and deploy multi-tier applications and to program the client, middle-tier, and database-tiers, all in Java. Now developers need only learn a single language and a single tool set to develop their complete Internet applications.

Oracle's Java Platform provides a complete, integrated set of products to enable the development, debugging, and deployment of database applications for the Internet. This solution consists of:

- Oracle8i, the platform for Internet computing.

- Oracle JServer, a server-side Java engine for the Oracle8i database.

- Oracle Application Server, an open, standards-based platform for deploying transactional business and commerce applications on the Web.

- Oracle8i Lite, a small footprint, Java-enabled database for mobile and embedded devices.

- Oracle JDeveloper, a powerful visual IDE for developing, debugging and deploying Java Internet applications.

Featured in Oracle JServer is a Java Virtual Machine which is completely compliant with Java standards and provides the fastest, most scalable, reliable, portable and manageable environment in which to run Java applications. Oracle's Java VM, enables developers to write, store and execute Java code within the database.

Also provided is support for Enterprise JavaBeans (TM) and communication via the CORBA communication standard, IIOP. Distributed Java objects can connect directly to Java objects in an Oracle Data Server via native CORBA protocols.

Oracle offers two programming interfaces for Java programs to access SQL: JDBC and SQLJ. JDBC is the Java equivalent of ODBC or OCI and is an industry standard way to connect to a database from Java. SQLJ is a powerful and easy to use interface between relational databases and Java. It is an open standard being developed by Oracle, IBM, and Sun. Using SQLJ, SQL can easily be embedded in client or server Java code for communication with a relational database.

# *inter*Media, for Managing Documents and Multimedia Content

Web applications require advanced data management services that support the rich data types used in Web repository, e-commerce, and other Internet applications. Oracle *inter*Media adds support that enables Oracle8*i* to manage multimedia content, both for Internet, and traditional applications that need access to image, audio, video, text, and location information in an integrated fashion with structured enterprise information. Oracle *inter*Media is a building block that can be used with Java for the development of scalable, performant, and attractive multimedia applications.

Oracle *inter*Media includes the following:

- Award-winning text services to deliver the powerful text retrieval capabilities fundamental to Web applications.

- Audio, Image and Video services to support integrated management of audio, image and video information within an Oracle8*i* database.

- Geometric locator services to support the development of Internet applications that help users locate information, such as stores, distribution points, and events, based on their location or distance from a given address.

# Oracle8*i* Tips and Techniques

Oracle8*i* is perhaps the most significant new release of the Oracle server ever. It is the first system to fully embrace the core technologies required for Internet applications – JAVA, XML, CORBA, rich media types, etc. This book will help you unlock the power of Oracle8*i*, the perfect choice for Internet based and other business applications. Included in this book is information about the newest features in the world's most powerful and popular platform for application development.

Sue Mavris
*inter*Media Audio, Image, Video Development Manager
Oracle Corporation

# Acknowledgments

*Shakespeare in Love* is a movie in which the play Romeo and Juliet receives its first performance. At one point in the action, the play's worried investor threatens, literally, to put the theater owner's feet to the fire. The theater owner, in an attempt to reassure the investor, offers a brief explanation about the theater business. "The natural condition is one of insurmountable obstacles on the road to imminent disaster." The theater owner continues to assuage the investor by telling him that all will turn out well. "How?" the investor asks. "I don't know," the theater owner replies. "It's a mystery."

There is no mystery, though, about how this book came to be. It was from the dedication and hard work of many individuals. No other way could this book, which represents the compilation of so much new information, receive such a productive treatment in so little time.

As lead author, my first task was to gather a team of co-authors. In William Gaynor, Arlene Valentinsen and Xerxes Cursetjee I found three exceptional co-authors with the rare combination of strong technical background and the skill to translate those technical capabilities onto paper. William Gaynor, the first to join, worked with me early in the process to develop the book's outline and overall scope. He took charge of the Installation and PL/SQL chapters, and with Xerxes Cursetjee co-authored the Java Enabling Infrastructure chapter. Arlene Valentinsen, the next member to join, was charged with the System Management, Performance, and Data Warehousing chapters. The final team member, Xerxes Cursetjee, took on the job of producing the SQLJ and JDBC and Enterprise JavaBeans chapters, as well as co-authoring the

Java Enabling Infrastructure chapter. I have respected the work of these individuals for years and am grateful that they were able to bring their expertise and insight to the material.

Beyond the work of my co-authors, the most significant contribution was that of technical editor Leslie Tierstein, whose work in preparing the material went far beyond that of technical expertise. Leslie's responsibilities spanned the broad spectrum of topics in all the chapters. Her careful, critical, and highly skilled reviews, along with her clear and thoughtful comments, helped us greatly in preparing an integral and meaningful work.

The interMedia chapters utilized the input of many individuals. Steve Buxton and Roger Ford of Oracle Corporation's interMedia Text Product Management and Technical Marketing Group provided highly valuable insight into interMedia Text. William Beauregard, Marco Carrer, David Diamond, Susan Kotsovolos, Joe Mauro, Sue Mavris, Dan Mullen, Simon Oxbury, Mike Rubino, Marion Smith, James Steiner, and Rodney Ward at Oracle Corporation's New England Development Center generously contributed to the interMedia: Multimedia chapter. Scott Geffert and Howard Goldstein of the Center for Digital Imaging, Inc. also provided assistance in the creation of the interMedia: Multimedia chapter. Their answers to my ad hoc questions about multimedia data, and the information I've learned working with them—designing and building digital image databases—were valuable contributions.

Carol Brennan, Rachel Carmichael, Arthur Lopatin, Maryann O'Leary, Sudheer Marisetti of Abacus Concepts, Nélida Quintero, Govind Rabindran, and Allen Riberdy provided additional help in reading the chapters during their final stages. These individuals provided great assistance in acting as critics and as a surrogate audience, and in contributing technical tidbits of their own.

Jeremy Judson, the Osborne acquisitions editor, and Monika Faltiss, the editorial assistant, helped bring this book together with good humor. They, along with Betsy Manini, the production editor, and Stacey Sawyer, the copyeditor, made sure that all of the many pieces fit together during the production process.

Peter Koletzke of Millennia Vision Corporation and co-author of the *Oracle Designer Handbook* and *Oracle Developer Advanced Forms and Reports* has been my instructor, mentor, colleague, and friend for many years. When you find moments of my writing in this book that are helpful, interesting and fun, you are probably experiencing much of that from the brand of inspiration and the desire to share information that was inspired by Peter's example. Without his presence, the opportunity for me to participate in this project would not have existed.

From my family I learned some important qualities that were brought to bear on this material. My mother and father—Bernie and Helene—wisely convinced me to go on in higher education in case the music thing didn't pan out. My aunt Jackie helped me find a balanced way to sustain such different areas of interest. My brother and sister, Bob and Renee, showed me by example the kind of growth process required to become one's own person.

Finally, I owe my greatest thanks to Nélida, who somehow maintains the energy and patience to accompany and support me on the front lines during projects like this and who daily helps me remember the things that are important in life.

Douglas Scherer
New York, New York

First, Douglas Scherer is to be thanked for asking me to join him in writing this book. Initially it was not clear if there was light at the end of the tunnel as the projected contents of the book kept growing. But with Xerxes Cursetjee and Arlene Valentinsen joining Douglas and me, light eventually came into sight. Both Xerxes and Arlene are to be thanked for lending us their considerable expertise as our co-authors.

Several people at Oracle Corporation deserve my sincere thanks for helping me resolve questions that arose during the writing of my chapters: Harlan Sexton, Kant Patel, Steve Harris, Bill Kemp, and Ian Stocks.

The chapters that became my responsibility as the writing progressed were Chapter 3 on installing, configuring, and the initial tuning of Oracle8i, and Chapter 8 on Oracle8i's PL/SQL enhancements. I would be happy to hear comments from readers on the content of these chapters. I can be reached at wbgaynor@hotmail.com.

Finally, but very importantly, I would like to thank Elisabeth for letting yet one more of our summer vacations slip by not taken. Elisabeth, on the next book I'll hang on to the movie rights and we can sail into a long vacation.

William Gaynor, Jr.
Zurich, Switzerland

I would like to thank my co-authors and Osborne/McGraw-Hill for the opportunity to participate in this project. The insights of my colleagues Douglas, Bill, and Xerxes, and the constructive comments from technical editor Leslie Tierstein and others at Osborne improved both the quality and relevance of my sections of the book.

I also want to acknowledge my many co-workers at Deutsche Bank for their support and encouragement during the project. In particular, I want to thank my colleagues in the Database Administration Group: Vinayak Chintapally, James Zhu, Rupali Anjaria, Vivian Lee, Rachel Qi, John Sun, Craig Rapley, and Paul Agnew. Their great breadth and depth of knowledge of Oracle is inspiring.

I also want to thank my "in-house" clients Klaus Sommer, Andrew Pugliese, Joe DiMaria, Adelino Stifanic, Hanns Ewald, and Gino Composto. Not only have they always challenged me to apply my knowledge in new and innovative ways, they have also taught me the value of a good cognac and a fine cigar after dinner.

In addition, I want to acknowledge my former colleagues at the New York State Department of Transportation. Al Karoly and Bob Kuzniar, from the Department's Traffic Engineering and Safety Division, were among the first in state government to use Oracle as a development tool and they gave me the opportunity to learn the power of Oracle.

I also want to thank Al Kronenberg for encouraging me to make the transition from public sector to private and for showing me where to find all the good steak houses in New York City.

Finally, I want to acknowledge my husband, Barry, without whose support, encouragement, and patience I would not have been able to finish this project.

Arlene Valentinsen
New York, New York


I am greatly indebted to Douglas Scherer for inviting me to contribute to this book. I also want to thank the experts from Oracle Corporation—William Kemp, Moe Fardoost, Harlan Sexton, and Jeremy Lizt—for answering my technical questions. In addition, I owe thanks to Govind Rabindran and Marc Schiffrin, who gave generously of their time in reading the material for technical accuracy; and to Ghada Captan and Mark Nazimova, whose suggestions performed magic in improving my organization and content. Praises are due Elizabeth Erskine, Katia Kubicek, Jay Miller, and Dr. G. Uswatte-Aratchi for deftly reviewing my chapters. Finally, thanks to my wife, Kumudini Uswatte-Aratchi, for her patience and inspiration.

Xerxes Cursetjee
New York, New York

# Introduction

What is Oracle8i; an upgrade to the database containing 150 new features, an application server with an embedded JVM and CORBA ORB, a secure multimedia repository? All are equally true. One thing is for certain. In this new release of the Oracle server, rich with features both fully developed and others in the process of maturation—there is something interesting and useful to everyone who cares to investigate.

The list of new offerings is so rich that it is difficult to find a starting point. Lines of database administration, design, and development blur as Oracle becomes an all-in-one repository for application logic and data. It also becomes difficult to clearly categorize the new features. For example, transportable tablespaces—a new feature that allows you to copy a tablespace from one database and weld it onto another—could be considered as a topic under each and all of the following categories: data warehousing, backup and recovery, replication, system management, application development, and multimedia.

## The Focus of Oracle8i Tips & Techniques

As the title *Oracle8i Tips & Techniques* implies, this work provides tips and techniques that evolved from use with the Oracle8i server. Covering so much ground required tough choices to be made about what material to include and at what depth. With so much information to discuss, the book could not be a comprehensive treatment of Oracle8i, but rather it is comprised of selected topics to assist in the work you're doing and to get you going with new Oracle8i features. For readers seeking something more, there are suggested readings from the Oracle Documentation set throughout the text.

The book provides a fairly equal number of tips as there are techniques. The chapters often flow in such a way that each successive tip or technique builds upon ones just presented. Thus, if you have prior information about a topic, you can go directly to the tip or technique. If the topic is new to you, you can read the chapter from the beginning and work your way into the tip or technique.

## Areas of Consideration

*Oracle8i Tips & Techniques* groups issues into three general areas: Overview, Server Administration, and Application Development. Each chapter brings together study and experimentation with the information held in many hundreds of pages of Oracle documentation, white papers, marketing literature, and Oracle programmers' insights.

- **Overview**   This first area includes a review of Oracle database architecture (Chapter 1, "Oracle ORDBMS Overview") and an overview and introduction to the new concepts concerning the Oracle8i Java component (Chapter 2, "Java Enabling Infrastructure"). These chapters provide a basis from which to move forward into the Tips & Techniques.

- **Server Administration**   This second area discusses features dealing with configuring the database and keeping it running well. The five chapters "Installation," "Security," "Server Management," "Performance," and "Data Warehousing" cover new and improved ways of dealing with those issues.

- **Application Development**   This third area includes the chapters "PL/SQL," "SQLJ and JDBC," "Enterprise JavaBeans," "interMedia Text," and "interMedia: Multimedia." These chapters present practical issues regarding additions and changes to the Oracle applications development environment.

Even though it seems as if the newest features are concentrated in the realm of application development, this is not the case. The common-sounding chapter titles such as "Security" and "Installation" are surely important and integral to the work done with the application development components. The "Security" chapter, for example, focuses on the Virtual Private Database feature, which can be used strategically to support the varying ways in which multiple types of users, logging on from the Web or client/server applications, are allowed to see data. The "Installation" chapter includes Tips that are essential to the proper configuration of the server, including those important for use with Oracle JVM.

# Getting Ready

The examples in the book are almost all built upon the schemas SCOTT and DEMO, which are supplied with the default database installation. If the accounts do not exist in your database, you can create them with the scripts ORACLE_HOME/rdbms/admin/utlsampl.sql and ORACLE_HOME/rdbms/admin/demo.sql respectively. The scripts to create the DEMO schema are not provided on all platforms. If you need them, you can download them from the Osborne Web site.

As always, before you try a new technique, you should make sure you have a backup of whatever schema or application you will affect with the techniques. And, of course, you should never try a technique for the first time in a production database! Since the examples often require augmentation to the sample schemas, you may wish to use the scripts to create the sample objects in your own test schema.

# Where to Begin

The numerous options for this new product can create confusion about how the components interact. Even so, you no doubt know what needs to be done, what you want to accomplish, and what new scenarios you want to experiment with. Use that focus as an entry point to this book.

Review the Tips & Techniques and imagine how they can work within your activities. Some of the features are so wildly new to the Oracle environment that you may find them hard to resist even though you don't have an immediate application for them. Others will be the answers to your wish lists.

# More Oracle8i Resources

More information, software, and examples are available on several Web sites. Oracle Technet is a Web site that provides access to code snippets, documentation, and discussion groups. It is also the site from which you will download the newest components of the server, such as those found in interMedia. The Technet Web site—which can be found at http://technet.oracle.com—is run by Oracle Corporation.

The Osborne Web site—which is at http://www.osborne.com—also has code samples and additional information that can accompany this book.

# PART
# I

# Overview

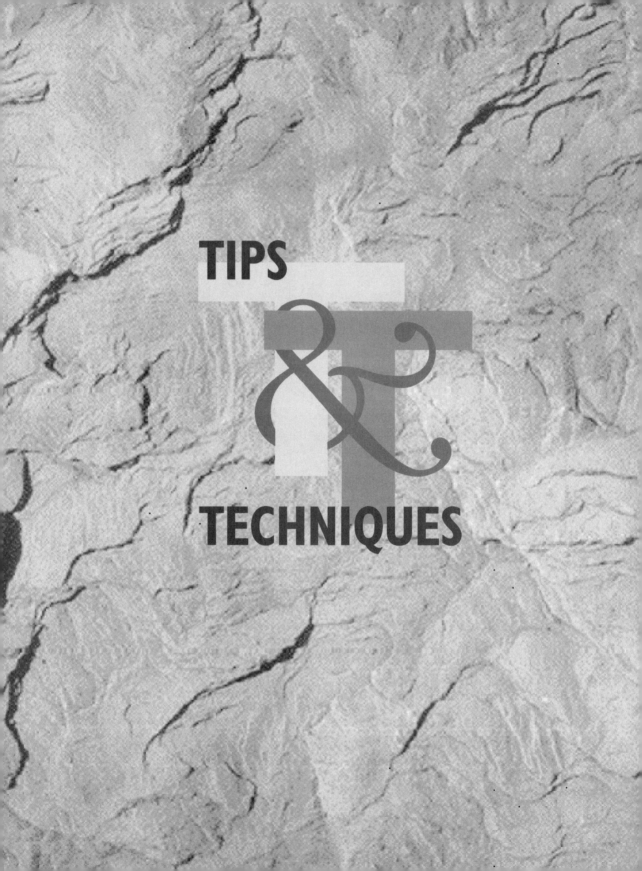

TIPS
&
TECHNIQUES

# CHAPTER

# 1

## Oracle ORDBMS
## Overview

Oracle8i provides a tremendous amount of new functionality and the means for administering it. This book will discuss many of the new features of Oracle8i and how they can assist your applications and database development and administration work. The basis of much of that functionality is built on the Relational Database Management System (RDBMS) product. This chapter will review the core architecture of the Oracle RDBMS. The new functionality will be reviewed in Chapter 2. The concepts described in both chapters provide a foundation for the remainder of the material in this book. Topics reviewed in this chapter fall into the following general categories:

- Instance (including memory area, and background processes)

- Database (covering datafiles, redo log files, control files, archived redo log files, and configuration files)

- Using the database system (with sections on starting a database, and shutting down a database)

- Database objects

- Tablespaces

- Segments (covering storage parameters, and rollback segments)

- Database connections

- Backup and recovery

- Security

- Tuning

## Instance

The word *database* is overloaded with different meanings. In the Oracle architecture, a *Database* (distinguished in this book with an uppercase "D") is the set of physical files required to manage storage (datafiles), behavior (control files), and data integrity (redo logs). An *instance* is a memory area and a set of background processes that make up the kernel. The RDBMS services are provided by the cooperative efforts of the database and the instance. This concept was expanded in Oracle8 with the addition of the PL/SQL Object option, which allowed the Oracle RDBMS to be an

ORDBMS, or Object Relational Database Management System. ORDBMS will be used in this book to refer to the Oracle Database management system, since the PL/SQL Object option is provided as part of the standard Oracle8i database product.

Some confusion can result from the colloquial manner in which the word *database* is typically used. For example, a DBA may hear that a user cannot "connect to the database." This expression, of course, means that the user cannot connect to the ORDBMS, not that the user is having trouble locating the physical files that store the data. Figure 1-1 shows an overview of an Oracle instance.

Looking at this overview, you can see how an instance resides on a host machine and consists of the SGA and background processes.

## Memory Area

The memory area allocated to an instance at startup is called the *System Global Area (SGA)*. When the instance is stopped, the memory area is given back to the operating system (OS). The information in the SGA is used by the Oracle Database engine for such purposes as maintaining locking information, passing information between database sessions via database pipes, and holding the response and request queues that participate in multithreaded server configurations. It also contains information that is shared more directly by multiple users. This information is divided between the Database Buffer Cache and the Shared Pool.

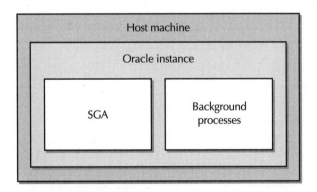

**FIGURE 1-1.**   *Overview of an Oracle instance*

The three main areas in the SGA are as follows:

■ The *Database Buffer Cache* holds data that has been read from datafiles for use in updates or result sets.

■ The *Shared Pool* is divided into two areas:

  ■ The *Library Cache* holds parsed SQL and PL/SQL statements, as well as control structures such as locks.

  ■ The *Dictionary Cache* holds information read from the Oracle data dictionary; This information is used for such purposes as query optimization and security checking.

■ The *Redo Log Buffer* holds all changes made to data that has been read into the Database Buffer Cache. This information is later used in many recovery scenarios.

■ The Java Pool, which is new to Oracle8i, holds session-specific Java code and data used by the *Java Virtual Machine (JVM)*.

**NOTE**
*The Java Pool size cannot be seen in the dynamic performance (V$) views in Oracle8.1.5. There is more information on this new SGA area in Chapter 3.*

## Background Processes

The *background processes* are programs that are loaded into memory and run when you start an Oracle instance. These programs make up the kernel of the database product.

**NOTE**
*The background processes actually create sessions in the instance, which can be seen in the dynamic performance view V$SESSION with the following query. Dynamic performance views are structures that can be queried to obtain information about the current status of the database. For queries against dynamic performance views, you need to be logged on as a DBA or have been granted SELECT permission for these by the user SYS. These views are prefixed with V$.*

```
SELECT *
  FROM v$session
 WHERE username IS NULL;
```

Ten background processes are available in Oracle8i. Five always begin running with the start of an instance on all platforms. The others will run depending on the operating system and options you choose in the init.ora file (the instance configuration parameter file). Table 1-1 shows information about the five default background processes.

You can find a list of the running background processes in most operating systems by using an operating system command that shows the process list. In UNIX, you would use some form of the ps command. In NT, Oracle is seen by the operating system as one process—oracle.exe. To find out which background processes are running on any platform, you can issue the following SELECT statement:

```
SELECT vb.name NAME, vp.program PROCESSNAME,
       vp.spid THREADID, vs.sid SID
  FROM v$session vs, v$process vp, v$bgprocess vb
 WHERE vb.paddr != '00'
   AND vb.paddr = vp.addr
   AND vp.addr = vs.paddr;
```

| Abbreviated Name | True Name | Description |
| --- | --- | --- |
| CKPT | Checkpoint | Signals DBW*n* at checkpoints and writes checkpoint information into the control files and datafiles. |
| DBWR / DBW*n* | Database Writer | Writes dirty/modified blocks from the database buffer cache to disk. You can have multiple database writers per instance; hence the DBW*n* designation. |
| LGWR | Log Writer | Writes entries in the redo log buffer to the redo log files on disk. |
| PMON | Process Monitor | Cleans up transactions and resources after disconnected sessions. |
| SMON | System Monitor | Performs automatic recovery at startup, and performs free space coalescing. |

**TABLE I-I.**  *The Five Compulsory Background Processes and Their Usage*

# Database

Unlike the Oracle instance, the Oracle Database consists of a set of physical files on disk. On a logical level, the data is stored in tables, but it is truly stored in the physical database files.

There are three types of database files—datafiles, redo log files, and control files—along with some additional files that support the ORDBMS, as shown in Figure 1-2.

These files are used by the instance to provide access to and integrity of the data. The two main reasons for the separation of the instance and database in Oracle's architecture are:

■ To provide a level of administering with the database system that is separate from the data storage. This can be important, for example, during database creation or recovery.

■ To allow for the optional placing of the ORDBMS in a parallel server configuration, which uses two or more instances—usually on two clustered machines—working with the same Oracle Database. The Oracle parallel server can be used to support load balancing and high availability.

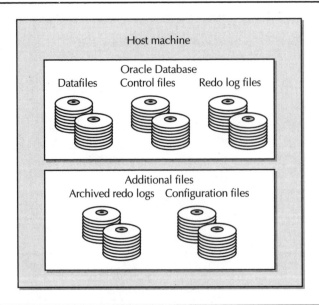

**FIGURE 1-2.**   *The Oracle Database and additional files*

## Datafiles

Data in the database system is stored in the datafiles. Blocks in the Database Buffer Cache that were modified by transactions, are periodically flushed from the Database Buffer Cache to the datafiles by the DBW*n* background process. A datafile can reside on a raw device or in a file system. At the time of their creation, datafiles do not contain any data but rather are areas of allocated disk space that have the potential to store data. When data is queried from the database and it is not found in the Database Buffer Cache, it is read from the datafiles into the cache.

When a database is created, one or more datafiles are created to store the *data dictionary*—the set of database objects that hold the database system's metadata. Throughout the life of the database, you will use Oracle commands to add more datafiles as needed. Other commands will assist you in renaming, enlarging, and moving datafiles, and enabling them to automatically extend in size. Similarly, you can reduce the size of a datafile as long as doing so will not destroy existing data. If a datafile is lost or becomes corrupted, the Oracle ORDBMS allows you to take it offline for recovery while the rest of the database remains online and available to users.

## Redo Log Files

For performance and recoverability, Oracle does not immediately write committed data to the datafiles. Committing data is actually the act of writing it—in the form of redo entries—to the redo log files. The LGWR background process performs this action. The Oracle database manages the redo log files in redo log groups. In other words, multiple copies of redo log files can be maintained, with each redo log file in the group being called a member. All members of the same redo log group are the same size. The redo log files can be renamed and moved by using ALTER DATABASE commands. You can also add and remove members from the log file group.

Redo log files are critical in recovering the database from media failure. You will want to have at least two members in each redo log group even if the redo log files reside on mirrored devices. If a member in a redo log group becomes corrupted, then the data can be read from another member. If the redo log file is mirrored solely by the operating system, then any corruption will be mirrored as well. The list of current redo log files can be seen with the following SQL statement:

```
SELECT group#, status, member
  FROM v$logfile
 ORDER BY group#;
```

## Control Files

Control files contain information about the state of the database. For example, they record the database structure (that includes a list of datafiles and redo log files) and timestamps that help confirm whether the datafiles are properly synchronized. The control files may also include information used by RMAN (recovery manager).

When a database is started, the control file contents are checked to see that all of the files that were associated with the database at the last shutdown are in place. This and the timestamp information tell the instance whether it needs to perform recovery on the database. Control files are written to by the ARC*n* process and CKPT process.

Other information that is stored in the control files includes the name and creation date of the database. Like redo log files, control files can and should be multiplexed; that is, the database should maintain multiple control files. This acts as a safeguard against database failure when, for example, one control file is accidentally deleted. The list of current control files can be seen with the SQL statement:

```
SELECT name
  FROM v$controlfile;
```

## Archived Redo Log

Several other background processes can be configured to start with the instance. One of them is the Archiver process (denoted as ARC*n,* since several Archiver processes can be running simultaneously). The Log Writer (LGWR) writes Redo Buffer Cache entries to the redo log files. A log switch is the moment when LGWR stops writing to one redo log group and begins writing to another. At that time, ARC*n* makes copies of the redo log files of the redo log group that's no longer being written to, so that they can later be used for recovery. Redo log files can also be copied manually. Backup copies of used redo logs are called *archived redo logs.* Archived redo logs are uniquely named according to a format mask set in the init.ora configuration file.

The archived redo logs in Figure 1-2 are shown in the area of Additional files. It is depicted this way because configuring your database to create archived redo logs is optional. Archived redo logs are needed for point-in-time recovery from media failure, but they are not essential for the database to function. As a DBA, however, you will never want to run a production online transaction processing system (OLTP)—one that supports the daily activities of your business—without creating archived redo logs.

## Configuration Files

Another set of files that falls outside the strict definition of database files is the set of configuration files. You will often see references to the init.ora file. The init.ora file contains the configuration parameters that an instance uses at startup time to determine, for example, the size of the SGA.

One of the parameters in the init.ora file, ifile, is a reference to another configuration file. This file—by default named config*instance_name*.ora—

simply holds additional instance configuration. The ifile parameter and the config*instance*_name.ora files are used together to support the Oracle parallel server configuration, where the file named by the ifile parameter holds additional parameters that are common to all instances participating in the parallel server configuration. For instances not participating in parallel server configuration (which are more common), the ifile is not necessary, but on some platforms it is included by default in the init.ora file. Thus, you should be careful to look for the ifile parameter in the init.ora file to make sure that all instance parameters are correct.

**NOTE**
*Even though the configuration files and the archived redo logs are not technically part of the Oracle Database, they are important files to include in any backup scenario that you devise.*

# Using the Database System

All the core database components interact to provide the ORDBMS. Figure 1-3 represents only the key relationships and interactions between an instance and its database.

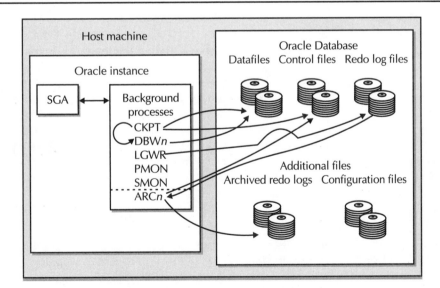

**FIGURE I-3.**   *Interaction between the core components*

You can see that the background processes use information from the SGA. The DBW*n* writes to datafiles whereas CKPT writes to the control files and the datafiles and interacts with DBW*n*. LGWR writes the redo entries from the Redo Log Buffer in the SGA to the redo log files. ARC*n* copies the redo log files to archived redo logs and then can write to the control files.

## Starting a Database

For administrative and application programs to create database sessions, the database must already be started. There are three modes of starting the database:

- **NOMOUNT**   Starts the instance without mounting the database. This step includes locating and reading the init.ora file, allocating the SGA, and starting the background processes. This mode is used for administrative purposes such as creating a new database or backing up a control file. Application programs will still not be able to access a database started in NOMOUNT mode.

- **MOUNT**   Starts the instance and mounts the database to the instance. This process includes locating the control files as specified in the init.ora file and reading the control files for the names of the redo log files and datafiles. In this mode, you can perform such actions as database recovery and datafile renaming. The database does not yet allow connections by user applications, and the data dictionary is not yet available.

- **OPEN**   Starts the instance, mounts the database, and opens the database for use by client applications—making access to the datafiles and redo log files available to the users through the database kernel. It is during this phase that missing or out-of-date redo log file and datafile problems are detected. It is also at this point that automatic crash recovery is performed if necessary.

You can bring the database up one level at a time or simply issue the command STARTUP, which defaults to STARTUP OPEN. One way to start an Oracle8i database is to connect to the database as an administrator through SQL*Plus and issue the STARTUP command. Figure 1-4 shows SYS as SYSDBA logging on and starting up the database using the default startup mode—open.

**CAUTION**
*You can also perform a STARTUP FORCE. FORCE is not a mode, but rather an option that performs several steps. If you perform a STARTUP FORCE on a running database, the server aborts the instance (uncleanly stops the running instance) and then performs a STARTUP OPEN.*

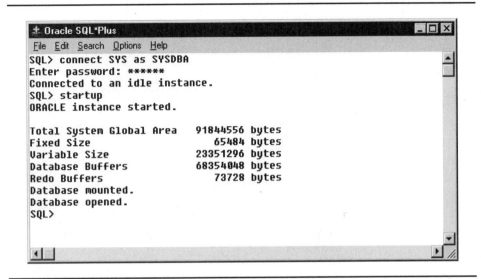

```
± Oracle SQL*Plus                                          _ □ ✕
File  Edit  Search  Options  Help
SQL> connect SYS as SYSDBA
Enter password: ******
Connected to an idle instance.
SQL> startup
ORACLE instance started.

Total System Global Area      91844556 bytes
Fixed Size                       65484 bytes
Variable Size                 23351296 bytes
Database Buffers              68354048 bytes
Redo Buffers                     73728 bytes
Database mounted.
Database opened.
SQL>
```

**FIGURE 1-4.**   *A SQL*Plus session of instance and database startup*

**NOTE**
*To connect administratively through SQL*Plus, it
is best to run in NOLOG mode. NOLOG mode
allows you to start SQL*Plus without first connecting
to the database. You start SQL*Plus in NOLOG mode
from the command line by issuing the command:*
`sqlplus /nolog`. *To start in NOLOG mode
from the Windows version of SQL*Plus, create
a new shortcut based on ORACLE_HOME\
bin\sqlplusw.exe. Open the shortcut's properties
window and click on the Shortcut tab. In the Target:
field add* `/nolog` *to the end of the executable string.
While you're at it, you should also change the value
in the Start in: field so that your SQL*Plus default
directory will not be ORACLE_HOME\bin. Figure 1-5
shows the necessary alterations to the Windows
SQL*Plus shortcut.*

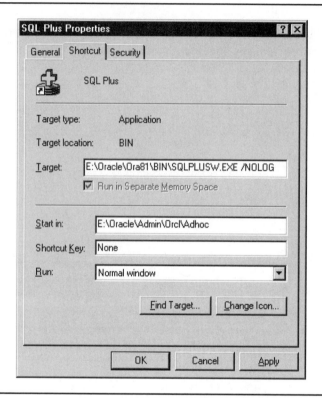

**FIGURE 1-5.** *NOLOG alterations to the Windows SQL\*Plus shortcut*

## Shutting Down a Database

There are four modes for shutting down the database. Your choice will depend on how rapidly you need to shut down and what your maintenance agenda is for the closed database. The four shutdown modes are as follows:

- **Normal**   The cleanest of all the shutdown modes. When this shutdown mode is used, no new users may connect to the database, and the database will wait until all current users have disconnected.

- **Immediate**   Prevents new users from creating database sessions, rolls back any uncommitted transactions, ceases all active transactions, and disconnects any sessions. This mode can be used if you must shut down the database quickly but can still allow some time for a cleaner termination of the instance.

- **Transactional** Similar to immediate, except that it allows active transactions to be completed before the database is shut down.

- **Abort** The quickest shutdown mode, but it is also the dirtiest. Use of this mode will cause instance recovery to be performed during the next startup open.

# Database Objects

Within the database you can define many types of objects. You can list the types of objects that have previously been created in the database by issuing the following SELECT statement:

```
SELECT DISTINCT object_type
  FROM dba_objects;
```

Some of the database object types you see listed are ones that store data. For example, tables and indexes are database objects that store data. Even though you do not usually add data directly into an index (an index-organized table straddles this line), data is still being stored in the index.

Other database objects listed in the query's result set do not store data. When you create a synonym (a database object name alias), it simply stores the definition of the synonym, not the data held in the database object to which it refers. The main way that you can tell if an object stores data or not is by seeing whether or not the object has a corresponding *segment*. You can check this by issuing a query against the DBA_SEGMENTS data dictionary view, where the segment_name is the same as the database object name that you want to check, as in the query shown here.

```
SELECT owner, segment_name, segment_type
  FROM dba_segments
 WHERE segment_name = 'EMP';


OWNER SEGMENT_NAME SEGMENT_TYPE
----- ------------ ------------
SCOTT EMP          TABLE
```

# Tablespaces

Tablespaces are represented on disk as one or more datafiles and hold zero or more segments. There is a one-to-one relationship between a database object and its segment. Here finally is the connection between the logical construct of a table and its physical representation in the operating system. Table data is ultimately held in the datafile(s) that support the tablespace holding the table's segment.

# Segments

Starting from a database object that stores data, a table, for example—we see that a segment is the next step closer to physical storage (that is, the datafile). There are four main types of segments:

- **Table/Data** Stores table data
- **Index** Stores index data
- **Rollback** Stores rollback/undo data, which is used to roll back a transaction, and for read consistency
- **Temporary** Used for the sorting needs, such as ORDER BY clauses in queries and index creation

Figure 1-6 shows an overview of the hierarchical relationship between database objects that store data down to the level of the row.

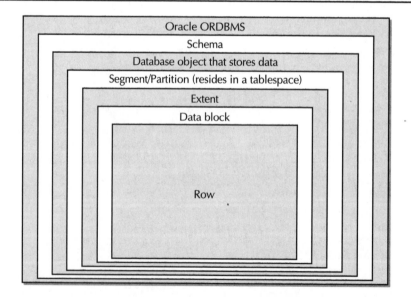

**FIGURE 1-6.** *Hierarchy of database objects that store data to their rows*

## Reading a ROWID

In Oracle8i, the physical location cannot easily be read by selecting the pseudocolumn ROWID from a table. This is because since Oracle8, Oracle uses extended ROWIDs, which store the restricted ROWID data (block.row.file) plus a data object number. The data object number is an identification number assigned to every database segment and is used in support of partitioning.

To decipher the ROWID pseudocolumn, you can use the Oracle built-in package DBMS_ROWID. The three functions you will use to find the block, row, and file—the combination uniquely identifies the row and its physical storage location—are:

- DBMS_ROWID.ROWID_BLOCK_NUMBER*(rowid)*

- DBMS_ROWID.ROWID_ROW_NUMBER*(rowid)*

- DBMS_ROWID.ROWID_TO_ABSOLUTE_FNO*(rowid, schema, object name)*

For example, you could issue the following query to get the physical location of a particular row. Note that row numbers start counting at zero.

```
SELECT DBMS_ROWID.ROWID_BLOCK_NUMBER(ROWID) "BLOCK",
       DBMS_ROWID.ROWID_ROW_NUMBER(ROWID) "ROW",
       DBMS_ROWID.ROWID_TO_ABSOLUTE_FNO
         (ROWID, 'SCOTT', 'EMP') "FILE"
  FROM scott.emp
 WHERE empno = 7934;


BLOCK      ROW        FILE
---------- ---------- ----------
      263         13          2
```

You could then issue a command to get the name of the file.

```
SELECT file_name
  FROM dba_data_files
 WHERE file_id = 2;


FILE_NAME
-------------------------------------
E:\ORACLE\ORADATA\ORCL\USERS01.DBF
```

There is also a function, DBMS_ROWID.ROWID_TO_RESTRICTED that returns the ROWID in *restricted* format (block.row.file).

From this diagram, you can see that the schema owns a database object and that if the object is one that stores data it is manifested as a segment. That segment, which is stored in one and only one tablespace, is created in multiples of *extents*. Those extents are manifestations of groups of contiguous data blocks. Data blocks—the smallest unit of Oracle database storage—contain rows that can be represented in a SELECT statement with the pseudocolumn ROWID. The size of the data blocks is set at database creation time. ROWID contains a unique combination of object number, file id, block id, and row number and can be used, for example, to see how a table is organized or to see the physical location of a table's rows to assist in striping decisions. Tables and indexes can be partitioned, breaking them into smaller tables and indexes that can be managed individually. For partitioned objects, each partition is considered a segment and will be seen as such in a query against the DBA_SEGMENTS view.

## Storage Parameters

An Oracle database allows control over how to allocate physical storage. Although you can use the default parameters, for a production system you will definitely want to do some resource planning to make sure that your storage capacity is sufficient and that performance needs are met. For example, a database object that stores data will be created by default in the default tablespace of the user that owns the object. The default tablespace can be set when the user account is created and may be changed afterward. Tablespaces have default storage parameters that are applied to segments when the CREATE <object> statement does not contain its own storage parameters.

There are scripts provided with the database installation that create objects in the SCOTT/TIGER account, one of the sample schemas provided by Oracle. With the sample *CREATE TABLE scott.emp* statement as a base, the following SQL statement shows how parameters can be added to support the physical and logical manifestation of the table and its associated indexes. The following statement is an excerpt from the scott.sql script provided by Oracle. The lines in boldface, which contain storage parameters, have been added for the storage clause example.

```
CREATE TABLE EMP
   (EMPNO                 NUMBER(4) NOT NULL,
    ...
     CONSTRAINT EMP_PRIMARY_KEY PRIMARY KEY (EMPNO)
       USING INDEX
       PCTFREE 2
       STORAGE (INITIAL 1M MAXEXTENTS UNLIMITED PCTINCREASE 0)
       TABLESPACE INDX
   )
   STORAGE (INITIAL 2M MAXEXTENTS UNLIMITED PCTINCREASE 0)
   TABLESPACE users;
```

In the Data Definition Language (DDL) statement above, you can see that storage parameters are specified for the index supporting emp's primary key and are also specified for the emp table itself. Storage parameters can be specified at the segment level (expressing the allocation of the segment's extents) and the block level (expressing the management of data blocks within the segment's extents). Table 1-2 shows the segment level storage parameters and their use.

| Storage Parameter | Default | Description |
|---|---|---|
| INITIAL | 5 data blocks | Size in bytes of the first extent to be created for the segment. Note: With a default block size of 2K or 4K (depending on the operating system), five data blocks are usually not enough to hold the data of most tables. Make sure to do proper sizing. |
| NEXT | 5 data blocks | Size in bytes of the next extent that gets created if needed. NEXT is used in two ways. First it is the actual size of the extent that will be created after the INITIAL extent (i.e., the segment's second extent). Second, and thereafter, it represents the size of the next extent that will be created by calculating the size of the most recently allocated extent times (1 + PCTINCREASE/100) |
| MINEXTENTS | 1 | The total number of extents to be allocated for the segment at creation time. |
| MAXEXTENTS | 2K block size: 121<br>4K block size: 249<br>8K block size: 505<br>16K block size: 1017<br>32K block size: 2041 | The maximum number of extents that you allow a segment to have. If you specify UNLIMITED, then the segment will be allowed to grow until it runs out of space in the datafiles supporting its tablespace. Some DBAs prefer to use a limited number of extents to assist them in monitoring growth of the data. The default is dependent on the database block size. |

**TABLE 1-2.**  *Segment Level Storage Parameters*

| Storage Parameter | Default | Description |
|---|---|---|
| PCTINCREASE | 50 (percent) | You set this if you want every extent that is created to be larger than the last one. If the value is not set to 0, then each new extent will equal the size of the most recently allocated extent times (1 + PCTINCREASE/ 100). A non-zero value for a tablespace's default allows SMON to periodically coalesce the tablespace's free space, (unused extents that are available for INSERTs and UPDATEs). Note: Many DBAs set PCTINCREASE to 0 to prevent runaway growth and tablespace fragmentation. |
| INITRANS | 1 for tables<br>2 indexes and clusters | During a transaction, a *transaction entry* is made in the data blocks of tables, indexes, and clusters. INITRANS represents how many concurrent transactions you wish to reserve space for in each data block. |
| MAXTRANS | Operating System Specific (will not exceed 255) | The maximum number of concurrent transaction entries that you want to allow per data block. You may wish to limit this, since space that is allocated beyond INITRANS remains permanently allocated in the data block. |

**TABLE 1-2.** *Segment Level Storage Parameters* (continued)

Whereas the segment parameters control how the segment allocates its extents, block parameters determine how space is managed at the data block level. Table 1-3 shows the block level parameters and their use.

| Storage Parameter | Default | Description |
|---|---|---|
| PCTFREE | 10 | Allows you to reserve space in a data block for rows to grow during an UPDATE statement. A PCTFREE of 10 saves 10 percent of the space in the data block. You can insert new rows into the block until the PCTFREE point is reached. |
| PCTUSED | 40 | After new rows have been disallowed in the block because of the PCTFREE, you need to specify when to allow INSERTs to occur again in the block. When you set PCTUSED, you are saying, "allow the amount of space used in the block to drop—via deletes—below 40 percent before allowing UPDATEs to occur again in the block." |

**TABLE I-3**   *Block Level Storage Parameters*

**NOTE**
*PCTFREE and PCTUSED added together cannot be greater than 100. The defaults for these two block level storage parameters are rarely correct for a production database. A quick rule of thumb is as follows: For a high-transaction database, use a larger PCTFREE. For more static data (such as you might find in a data warehouse), use a smaller PCTFREE. The concern with PCTUSED is that you not set it so close to PCTFREE that blocks are constantly moved on and off the freelist yet not set it so low that block space is wasted.*

## Rollback Segments

Rollback segments have two main purposes. The first is to provide an undo or rollback mechanism. The second is to support read consistency. When you issue a *Data Manipulation Language (DML)* statement, the data to be changed—if not found in the Database Buffer Cache—is read into the cache and is changed there. When a change is made to data in the cache, one of the many events that occur is that a copy of the old version of the data is stored in a rollback segment. The copy is held in the rollback segment until it is overwritten by the modifications of another transaction. It is not flushed immediately upon a COMMIT or ROLLBACK since it may be needed for read consistency.

In Oracle, when you issue a SELECT statement you are guaranteed to receive a result set that is entirely unchanged from the time at which you issued the statement. In other words, if another user changes any data that is in your result set—regardless of whether they commit, roll back, or have not closed the transaction—your data set will not include those changes. Oracle is very efficient in the way it implements this functionality. If your query needs data that it finds has been changed by another session after your query started, it will look in the rollback segments for the copy that was made in support of the other user's transaction. This mechanism provides read consistency.

As long as the other user has not completed (committed or rolled back) his or her transaction, the data will assuredly be found in the rollback segments. If the other user has completed the transaction, a problem known as "ORA-01555: snapshot too old (rollback segment too small)" could possibly occur. This is because once the other user completes the transaction, the data copy is released so that rollback segment space can be used by other transactions. The deleterious situation that this presents can be avoided by carefully setting the rollback segment storage parameters.

**NOTE**
*There is an additional segment level storage parameter for rollback segments known as OPTIMAL. OPTIMAL allows space used in the rollback segment to be deallocated in order to create space in the rollback segment's tablespace for other rollback segments in the same tablespace to grow in support of additional transactions.*

# Database Connections

There are many methods by which a connection to the database can be created. Some of them will be presented throughout the book. The more established and conventional methods involve the use of dedicated and/or shared servers. It will help to take a brief historical look of how Oracle client/server database connection methods have evolved.

At all stages of this evolution, there has always been a database client (front end, batch program, application) and a server (the Oracle Database server). Early on, it was typical for the client and the server to be on the same machine. The client could be programmed in a number of languages. Each client program had bound within it a standard set of server routines to connect and interact with the Oracle database. Figure 1-7 shows the relationship between client and server in this *single task* configuration.

In the next evolution, Oracle allowed application-specific routines to be bound into the client while a *dedicated server* performed the server routines of interacting with the database. This relationship between client and server shown in Figure 1-8 depicts how the dedicated server can be used whether the application is running on the same machine as the database or on a separate machine. In both connections, the applications are interacting with the database via a dedicated server. In one case, the application is running on the same machine as the database, communicating directly with its dedicated server (via IPC, bequeath, or the like). In the second case, the application is running on the client's machine, communicating with its dedicated server remotely via SQL*Net. Each dedicated server interacts with the database in the same way whether the application is running on the host machine or on the client's machine.

This configuration allowed for a truly distributed client/server environment. This development continued from SQL*Net v.1 and v.2 through Oracle8, where SQL*Net is called Net8.

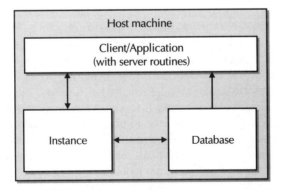

**FIGURE 1-7.**   *Single task client application*

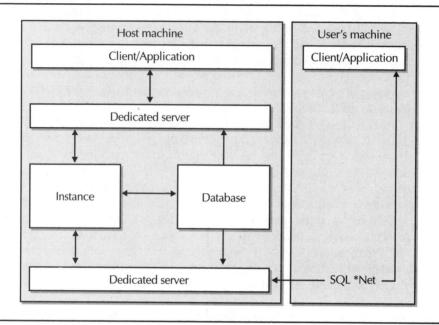

**FIGURE 1-8.**  *Dedicated server configuration*

Starting with SQL*Net v.2, client applications were allowed to connect to the database server in a *multithreaded server (MTS)* configuration. This supports a shared server implementation in addition to the dedicated server implementation. This is useful, for example, in an OLTP environment, where there may be many users logged on concurrently but only a few issuing database requests at a time. You can envision a sales desk at which the salesperson retrieves information about the customer, then talks for a while to that customer, then issues another database request to see more of their information. The database requests in this case are small and infrequent, even though the salesperson remains connected to the database the entire time. MTS is required in Oracle8i in order to use the Java Virtual Machine (described in Chapter 2).

The MTS configuration adds additional background processes to the instance. They are the *shared server* (S000) and the *dispatcher* (D000). A typical scenario consists of the user making a remote connection request to the database. The request is sent to the database from the client's machine via Net8. A *listener* process waiting for requests on the host machine takes the connection request and sends it to the dispatcher. The dispatcher interacts with the shared server through areas in the SGA called the *response and request queues*. The response to the request is routed back to the client application through the dispatcher.

Figure 1-9 shows applications interacting with the database via dedicated and shared servers (MTS).

All the pieces fit together in an architecture that presents the data in an efficient way. You can see how a user application connects through a dedicated or shared server. That server is responsible for reading the datafiles and passing information back through the SGA to the client.

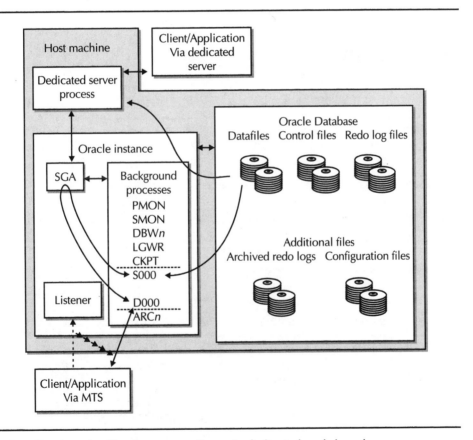

**FIGURE 1-9.** *Application connections via dedicated and shared servers*

The configuration files used by the Net8 components can usually be found in the ORACLE_HOME/net8/admin directory. Some of the better-known configuration files are as follows:

- **tnsnames.ora**  Maps connection-routing information to a user-friendly service name. A tnsnames.ora file can be found on the client and server machines.

- **listener.ora**  Provides configuration to the listener, which resides on the server machine.

- **sqlnet.ora**  Contains preferences for how a client or server will use Net8 features.

# Backup and Recovery

Any production system needs a backup and recovery strategy to protect against data loss in case of system failure. Failures can be one of five types:

- **Statement failure**  A logical error that can occur, for example, when your program contains a SQL statement that cannot be parsed. In this case, the effects of the statement will simply be undone.

- **Process failure**  An error that can occur when a client application terminates abnormally (for example, the user turns off his or her machine without first disconnecting from the database). In this case, the PMON background process will handle the rolling back of uncommitted transactions associated with the session and perform any other cleanup that is needed.

- **Instance failure**  A type of failure that occurs if something causes the instance to stop (for example, power is lost on the host machine). This is similar to a shutdown abort in that modified blocks in the Database Buffer Cache do not get written back to the datafiles. Oracle will perform automatic recovery the next time the database is started.

- **User or application error**  Occurs, for example, when a user mistakenly deletes data that is still needed.

- **Media failure**  Revolves around the inability for a database file to be read. This could result, for example, from a damaged disk or corrupted data file.

For each of these failure types, there is a specific method of recovery. A user or application error, for example, can be rectified through the use of a logical database backup that was created with Oracle's export program. It can also be handled using

*point-in-time* database recovery, which involves reading the information in the
archived redo logs back into the database up to the moment when the error occurred.
Problems resulting from instance failure will in most cases be remedied automatically.
Media failure will almost assuredly require the intervention of the DBA.

# Security

Oracle database security can be configured for each user down to the row level.
Using roles (groups of user privileges) and profiles (resource limits), you can define
the level of access users have in the database and which objects they have the
ability to see and affect. You may also use Oracle's auditing functionality on user
sessions to keep a history of, for example, which tables they've affected or for how
long their typical user session is connected to the database.

# Tuning

A key feature of the Oracle database is its configuration flexibility. Placement of the
database files, fine-level tuning of SQL statements, and manipulation of the Oracle's
memory area are just a few examples of the combinations of techniques that are
available to you as a DBA and applications programmer to make the database
perform at acceptable levels.

Oracle provides scripts and tools to assist with these tasks. Using the SET
AUTOTRACE ON command in SQL*Plus, you can see the access path of SQL
statements. SQL Trace and TKPROF used together can reveal an application's
queries and their access paths. Reviewing an access path can lead to the discovery
of what is impeding the query's performance. The scripts utlbstat.sql and utlestat.sql
report on overall configuration problems. *Oracle Enterprise Manager (OEM)* can
assist in proactively identifying performance problems such as whether the
Database Buffer Cache has been set too small.

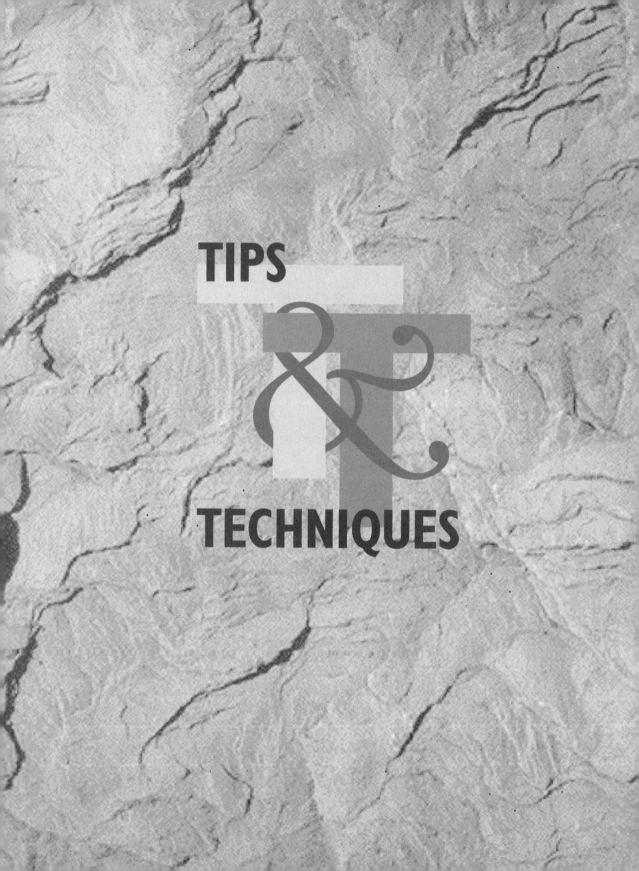

TIPS

&

TECHNIQUES

# CHAPTER
## 2

## Java Enabling
## Infrastructure

Oracle has made Oracle8i the key piece of its Internet strategy by integrating a Java Virtual Machine (JVM), a Java Database Connectivity (JDBC) driver, and an Object Request Broker (ORB) directly into the database engine. This new infrastructure allows you to easily develop dynamic database-driven intranet and Web applications using two different programming models: stored procedures and component-based modeling.

Stored procedures can be written in Java or PL/SQL. Java programs can access data via JDBC or SQLJ (a standard way of embedding SQL in Java that is simpler to use than JDBC). Java stored programs reap performance benefits from an embedded native compiler and the tight integration of the JVM with the database.

Component-based programs can be written using two models. Common Object Request Broker Architecture (CORBA) is a standard way of building distributed applications. Enterprise JavaBeans (EJB) is a server-side component model for Java. Both models help you construct applications rapidly by assembling components from different vendors.

JDBC and SQLJ programming tips are presented in Chapter 9, and an overview of EJB programming is presented in Chapter 10. This chapter presents a technical overview of the new Java-enabling architecture of Oracle8i. You will see how the infrastructure components—JVM, JDBC drivers, and ORB—can be harnessed using JDBC, SQLJ, CORBA, and EJB in a number of deployment scenarios. The topics in this chapter fall into the following categories:

- JVM
- SQLJ support in Oracle8i
- Java stored procedures
- CORBA ORB
- Distributed component support in Oracle8i
- Choosing a programming model
- Choosing the right JDBC Driver
- Deployment scenarios using Oracle8i

# JVM

Oracle8i's JVM supports all standard Java Development Kit (JDK) libraries and APIs in the 1.1.7 JDK specification except the Java Abstract Windowing Toolkit (AWT). The AWT is excluded because it makes little sense to use windows inside a JVM embedded in the database.

The JVM (see Figure 2-1) runs in the same address and process space as the database kernel. It uses the same memory page size used by the database engine for its memory structures. And it directly accesses the SQL memory cache. The net result is optimized memory use and increased throughput. You will find tips on how to tune the JVM in Chapter 3.

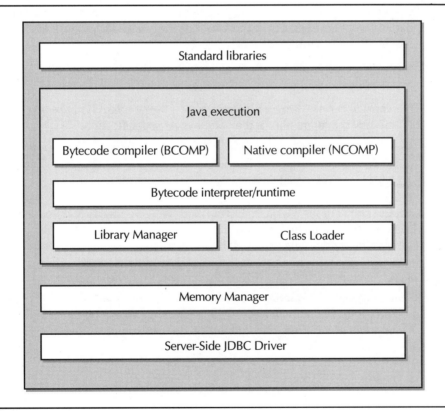

**FIGURE 2-1.**  *Oracle8i's JVM*

Oracle8i's JVM consists of the following components:

- **Bytecode compiler (BCOMP)**   Translates Java programs into Java .class binaries.

- **Bytecode interpreter and runtime**   Executes standard Java binaries.

- **Native code compiler (NCOMP)**   Converts standard Java bytecodes into C source code. The C source code is then compiled with a platform-dependent C compiler, resulting in significant execution performance improvements over interpreted Java bytecode.

- **Library Manager**   Imports and exports Java objects into and out of the database.

- **Class Loader**   Finds, loads, and initializes Java classes (in Java binary or native compiled form) out of the local database store in response to requests from the runtime.

- **Memory Manager (and garbage collector)**   Manages memory allocation and deallocation.

- **Standard libraries**   Provides support for all the standard libraries (except for the AWT) that are part of the core Java API specification.

- **Server-Side JDBC Driver**   Includes all of the 1.22 JDBC specification for relational database support and parts of the 2.0 specification that extend 1.22 to object-relational types, collections, and LOBs.

In addition, Oracle8i comes with a SQLJ Translator which converts SQLJ programs to pure Java code that can then be run with the SQLJ runtime. The following sections discuss these components in detail.

## Compilers

Oracle8i embeds JavaSoft's standard bytecode compiler (BCOMP) to transform Java source programs into Java .class binaries. The binaries are executed by Oracle's bytecode interpreter at run time. The interpreter supports Java threads and exceptions.

   Oracle8i also embeds a native compiler (NCOMP) that converts the standard Java .class binaries into C source code. The C code can then be compiled with a platform-dependent C compiler to native dynamic libraries that can be stored in the database and then dynamically loaded by the JVM at run time. Oracle claims that the native compilation approach results in dramatically better performance than any just-in-time (JIT) approach. Oracle itself has used NCOMP in its implementation of the bytecode compiler, the Java-to-C compiler, the ORB, the JDK class libraries, and the SQLJ Translator.

**NOTE**
*As of release 8.1.5 of Oracle8i, NCOMP is available only to Oracle internal developers. Oracle intends to open NCOMP for general use in future releases.*

**NOTE**
*You cannot use the Java Native Interface (JNI) to call C and C++ programs from the database. Use of JNI in Oracle8i is restricted to Oracle internal developers. The restriction ensures that applications that run in the database do not compromise the integrity of the data or the availability of the database server.*

## Library Manager

The Library Manager loads and manages Java programs in the database. The programs are stored in *library units* in the database rather than in operating system files. There are three kinds of library units, corresponding to the three types of Java files (source, binary, and archive). Here are the key responsibilities of the Library Manager:

■ **Import**   You can use the Library Manager to import Java source, binary, and archive files into library units in the database.

■ **Namespace management**   The Library Manager maps Java names to database names. This is required because Java names are global, case sensitive, and of arbitrary length, whereas database names are relative (resolved in relation to a schema), case insensitive, and restricted to 30 characters.

■ **Name resolution**   The Library Manager is also responsible for resolving library units. A library unit is considered resolved when all of its external references to Java classes are bound.

**NOTE**
*JavaSoft's JVM uses a CLASSPATH environment variable (which contains a list of file directories) to search for class libraries, including user-defined class libraries.*

*You cannot use CLASSPATH with Oracle8i's JVM since Java code is stored in library units in the database rather than in operating system files. Instead, you use a RESOLVER specification containing a list of SQL schemas that tells the Library Manager where to search for library units.*

■ **Bytecode verification**   The Library Manager verifies that imported binaries were compiled with a compliant compiler.

■ **Dependency maintenance**   The Library Manager automatically tracks dependent class binaries and recompiles them when source code changes are made.

■ **Export**   You can use the Library Manager to export Java programs as source, binary, or archive files. You can export from one Oracle8i database to another or from Oracle8i to other JVMs.

## Java Class Loader

The Java Class Loader finds, loads, and initializes Java classes (in Java binary or Java-to-C compiled form) out of the library units stored in the database in response to calls from the Java runtime. Here are the key aspects of the Loader:

■ It initializes the immutable components of Java objects (bytecode vectors, metadata, and constant pool data) once into shared memory, where they are shared among users. This serves to reduce per-session memory usage, thereby increasing scalability.

■ It is not network-configurable and cannot download Java applets over a network. This limitation is in place to ensure the integrity of the local database by making it impossible to download unknown bugs and security incursions.

■ It supports two forms of authentication and authorization: traditional *definer rights* and a new model called *invoker rights*.

**NOTE**
*Prior to Oracle8i, a stored PL/SQL code executed with definer-rights—that is, it executed under the authority of the definer (owner) of the program. A definer-rights program is bound to the schema in which it is defined. It executes at the defining site in the definer's schema and accesses database objects with the definer's visibility and permissions. Oracle8i introduced a new privilege mechanism called invoker-rights that allows stored PL/SQL code to be executed under the authority of the invoker (caller). An invoker-rights program is not bound to a specific schema. It executes at the calling site and accesses database objects with the caller's visibility and permission. Definer- and invoker-rights are elaborated in Chapter 8.*

## Memory Manager and Garbage Collector

Java applications are well known for their ability to transparently manage memory and clean up after themselves. Java programmers need not concern themselves with memory leaks or memory corruption thanks to Java's built-in garbage-collection mechanism and Java's restriction on creating and modifying pointers in arbitrary ways. The safety provided by Java allows Oracle to integrate the JVM directly into the database kernel.

Oracle8i's Memory Manager, an enhancement of JavaSoft's standard JVM, conforms to and is tuned to Oracle's multithreaded server's shared memory model. It allocates memory for Java objects in standard chunks called *object memories*. There are two types of object memories, representing different object lifetimes and degrees of sharing of objects among users:

■ **Call memory**   Java objects that are newly called or newly loaded go into call memory. Call memory cannot be paged or cached to disk; it does not persist and therefore does not contain application state information.

Call memory is divided into *new space* and *old space*. Java objects that are newly allocated go into new space. Objects that survive multiple garbage collections are moved from new to old space. Old space is garbage-collected less frequently than new space. Garbage-collection performance is, thus, enhanced because the garbage collector for new space has to check fewer objects.

■ **Session memory**  Session memory can persist with "static" data. Objects that are long-lived—typically representing the "conversational" state of a Java application—are moved to session memory at the end of a call. The garbage collector handles the migration of objects between new space and old space and between call memory and session memory.

The net result of this memory management mechanism is increased scalability and better performance.

# SQLJ Support in Oracle8i

SQLJ is a standardized Java programming extension for embedding *static SQL* statements in Java that is easier to program than traditional JDBC. Operations in static SQL are predefined: they do not change in real-time, although the transmitted data values may change dynamically. By contrast, operations in dynamic SQL are not predefined: they change in real-time. In most applications, the bulk of the SQL statements consist of static SQL.

You can use a variety of static SQL statements in SQLJ, including the following:

■ **Data Definition Language (DDL)** statements such as CREATE, ALTER, and DROP

■ **Data Manipulation Language (DML)** statements such as INSERT, UPDATE, DELETE, and SELECT

■ **Data Control Language (DCL)** such as GRANT and REVOKE

■ **Transaction control language** such as COMMIT and ROLLBACK

■ **Session control statements** such as ALTER SESSION

■ **PL/SQL blocks**

**NOTE**
*Only static SQL may be used in SQLJ. Dynamic SQL requires the use of JDBC. However, you can mix SQLJ code and JDBC code in the same source file.*

### SQLJ Translator and SQL Runtime

The SQLJ development process is illustrated in Figure 2-2. The SQLJ Translator converts SQLJ programs to pure Java code and replaces the embedded SQL statements with calls to the SQLJ runtime. The generated Java code can be compiled using any Java compiler and then executed against the Oracle database. The SQLJ Runtime Library is a thin layer of pure Java code that uses a JDBC driver for database access.

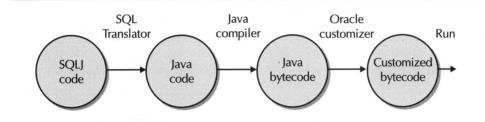

**FIGURE 2-2.** *The SQLJ development process*

**NOTE**
*SQLJ is similar to Oracle's pre-compiler PRO\*C.
PRO\*C permits embedded SQL in C programs. SQLJ
can be thought of as a PRO\*Java.*

## SQLJ Benefits

SQLJ is a simpler and more productive alternative to JDBC for static SQL. The major benefits from using SQLJ include the following:

- **Conciseness** SQLJ code is more succinct than JDBC. In SQLJ, you embed a SQL statement directly into Java code by simply prefacing the SQL statement with #sql. SQLJ handles JDBC connections and calls transparently for you. You can also embed Java variables and expressions as bind (host) expressions directly into the SQL statement by prefacing them with a colon, as shown in the following example:

```
float newSalary = 100000;
#sql {UPDATE emp SET sal = :newSalary WHERE empno = 598};
```

Here the bind expression is :newSalary. More complex bind expressions are also supported.

- **Compile-time checking** Unlike JDBC, SQLJ supports compile-time instead of run-time checking of SQL statements. Compile-time (often called translation-time) checking leads to earlier detection of errors and thus more robust code. The SQLJ Translator performs three types of checking at compile-time to detect syntax and semantic errors in the embedded SQL:

  - *Syntax checking* of the SQL statements

  - *Type checking* to ensure that Java host variables are type-compatible with the SQL statements in which they are used

■ *Schema checking* to ensure that the SQL constructs are well formed and are valid in relation to the definitions of the schema objects—such as tables, views, and stored procedures—that are accessed

■ **Portability**    Oracle, IBM, Compaq-Tandem, Sybase, Informix, JavaSoft, and others have jointly authored a standard language specification of SQLJ with a Reference Implementation of the SQLJ Translator that permits compatibility and interoperability between the different vendors' database products. SQLJ programs and applications can be made vendor independent by adhering to the ANSI/ISO-approved standards for SQLJ, which prescribes the SQL92 entry-level standard for embedded SQL. Both SQLJ Java source code and binaries can be moved between vendor platforms regardless of where the translation will be done or has been done. The call-level API between the SQLJ Runtime Library and the database is open to vendor choice.

Vendor-specific customizations are addressable through *SQLJ profiles.* A SQLJ Java binary program contains a set of SQLJ profiles that describes SQL operations contained in the SQLJ source. The binary may contain a profile for a given vendor's customizations and contain multiple profiles for multiple vendors. The same binary can then run against different databases and take advantage of vendor-specific features. Profile sets lead to binary portability, across not only operating systems (owing to Java's portability), but also proprietary databases.

### Deploying SQLJ

To deploy SQLJ programs, a platform must have a JVM, a SQLJ Runtime Library, and, in Oracle's case, a JDBC driver. You can use Oracle8i's embedded SQLJ Translator and SQLJ runtime with any JDBC driver, including the following:

■ Oracle's Thin JDBC Driver

■ Oracle's JDBC-OCI (Oracle Call Interface) Driver

■ Oracle's embedded (Server-Side) JDBC Driver

You will learn more about these JDBC drivers and how to choose the driver best suited for your specific deployment situation in the section "Choosing the Right JDBC Driver" in this chapter.

# Java Stored Procedures

With Oracle8i, database stored procedures, functions, and triggers traditionally written in PL/SQL can now be written in Java. Java stored code offers the advantage of portability across different databases.

Java stored code can interoperate with SQL and PL/SQL. In order to make a Java method callable from SQL, you must publish the Java method to SQL with a call specification (*call spec* for short). Here is a simple Java class to illustrate how call specs work.

```
public class MyClass {
    public static String fullName(String first, String last) {
        return first + " " + last;
    }
}
```

The following call spec publishes the Java method fullName to SQL.

```
CREATE FUNCTION full_name(first VARCHAR2, last VARCHAR2)
  RETURN VARCHAR2
AS
LANGUAGE JAVA
NAME
'MyClass.fullName(java.lang.String, java.lang.String) return
java.lang.String';
```

The keyword LANGUAGE JAVA informs Oracle that the JVM must be invoked whenever the function full_name is called. The method signature (following the keyword NAME) specifies how the Java method name, parameter types, and return types are to be converted to their SQL counterparts. Once published to SQL, you can invoke full_name from within SQL statements, PL/SQL blocks, and CALL statements—as if full_name were a PL/SQL function.

**NOTE**
*For calls from SQL or PL/SQL to Java stored programs, Oracle8i uses the same mechanism that allows SQL to call PL/SQL: Inter-Language Method Services (ILMS). ILMS handles trans-language calls running from SQL and PL/SQL to Java or external C programs.*

Java stored procedures can be accessed by the following:

- Java clients through JDBC or SQLJ
- Net8 clients, including Oracle Call Interface, Pro*, and Oracle Developer clients

# CORBA ORB

CORBA is an outgrowth of the Object Management Group (OMG). It defines a language- and platform-independent object bus called the Object Request Broker

(ORB). The ORB provides the mechanism for distributed objects written in various languages to communicate with each other. Using an ORB, a client can call a method on a remote object as if it were a local call. It is the ORB's responsibility to find the object implementation, transparently activate it if necessary, deliver the request to the object, and return the response to the client.

CORBA 2.0 added a protocol called *Internet Inter-ORB Protocol (IIOP)*—mandatory for all ORB vendors—to guarantee a minimum level of interoperability among different ORBs. IIOP uses TCP/IP as the underlying transport protocol.

### NOTE
*Java programmers may notice that there are both similarities and differences between CORBA-IIOP and Remote Method Invocation (RMI), a technology developed by JavaSoft. RMI is intended for Java-to-Java communications across JVMs; CORBA-IIOP allows distributed objects written in various languages to communicate. Most CORBA ORBs, unlike RMI, provide connection pooling and load balancing features.*

## How ORBs Work

Here is a simplified explanation of how CORBA ORBs work. A client requests an object's services through a well-defined interface specified in a language called *Interface Definition Language (IDL)*. An IDL compiler transforms IDL definitions into the target programming language. Target code produced by the IDL compiler occurs in pairs: a client-side mapping called a *stub* and a server-side mapping called a *skeleton.*

The server object is where the actual execution of the code takes place. Before compilation, the implementation code for each method (represented by the skeleton) must be fleshed out. Stubs do not need to be fleshed out since they simply represent the mapping between the client's implementation language and the ORB. The client can be written in any language as long as the implementation of the ORB supports this mapping.

To invoke a method on the remote object, the client simply calls the method in the stub as if the object resided locally. The ORB accomplishes this feat under the covers through a process of *marshaling* (the translating of a remote method call into network format) and the reverse process, *unmarshaling.* The stub *marshals* any parameter data and sends them across the network to the skeleton on the remote object. In turn, the skeleton *unmarshals* the parameter data and *upcalls* (calls the proper method) to the object's container. The object executes the method. Return values are sent back to the client, using a process in which the skeleton and the stub switch roles—the skeleton marshals and the stub unmarshals.

**NOTE**

*CORBA competes with a similar strategy from Microsoft called the Distributed Component Object Model (DCOM). CORBA objects can communicate with DCOM objects through bridges.*

# Distributed Component Support in Oracle8i

Oracle8i includes a CORBA 2.0 compliant Java ORB (Inprise's VisiBroker) in the database. The ORB and the JVM included in the Oracle8i database provide a compelling alternative to procedural programming: component-based development. Component-based development holds promise of rapid application development from vendor components, code reuse, ease of maintenance, deployment flexibility, and scalability.

Oracle8i supports two different component development paradigms: CORBA and EJB. CORBA is a model for the development of multi-tier applications that allow interoperability between programming languages, networks, and operating systems. EJB extends the JavaBean component framework to server-side components.

CORBA objects (written in Java) and EJBs can be deployed directly into the Oracle8i database. They can be invoked from an applet in a Netscape browser or from any other CORBA ORB compliant application over IIOP. Moreover, Oracle8i can also be a CORBA client. For example, Java stored procedures and EJBs can invoke ORB compliant objects residing elsewhere.

## CORBA Support in Oracle8i

Various infrastructure elements come together to provide CORBA support in Oracle8i:

- **JVM**   Provides a scalable engine to run CORBA servers implemented in Java.

- **CORBA ORB**   Provides IIOP protocol interpretation. IIOP can be used to both call-into and call-out from the database. The EJB specification specifies Java RMI as the transport protocol. Oracle8i implements RMI over IIOP.

- **Embedded JDBC Driver and SQLJ Translator**   Provides efficient access to object-relational data.

■ **COSNaming service** Provides a naming service to publish and look up CORBA objects. CORBA server objects publish their Interoperable Object References (IOR) to the COSNaming service. CORBA clients invoke methods on the server objects after connecting to the COSNaming service and getting their IORs.

**NOTE**
*Java programmers may prefer to access the COSNaming service through Oracle's Java Naming and Directory Interface (JNDI).*

■ **Oracle multithreaded server** Provides support for persistence, security, transactions, and scalability. The Oracle server must be configured as a multithreaded server to activate CORBA objects or EJBs.

**CAUTION**
*Do not configure Oracle8i as a dedicated server if you want to use CORBA or EJB features.*

In addition to the infrastructure elements, Oracle8i provides a number of features and tools to assist you in programming CORBA servers in Java:

■ **Object-by-value support** Oracle8i allows Java objects to be passed by value as CORBA structs.

■ **Caffeine** This set of tools includes java2rmi_iiop and java2idl. The java2rmi_iiop generates the infrastructure required for EJBs to call other remote objects. The java2idl compiles Java interfaces to IDL code, eliminating the need for writing IDL definitions.

## Enterprise JavaBeans (EJB) Support in Oracle8i

EJB is a cross-platform, server-side component model for Java. The EJB specification is an industry initiative led by Sun, with the participation of many vendors. Oracle8i supports the standard EJB 1.0 specification and provides a number of additional features to ensure high scalability, performance, availability, application throughput, and interoperability among Java, SQL, and PL/SQL.

While JavaBeans are typically client-side components for GUI development, EJBs are typically server-side components. A JavaBean could encapsulate a button on a user interface. An EJB, on the other hand, could encapsulate the business logic of a client session that transfers funds between two bank accounts.

An EJB runs in an EJB container. The container provides a thread or a process for the EJB to execute and provides transaction services, synchronization services, and security.

The EJB specification categorizes EJBs into Session Beans and Entity Beans, as follows:

## SESSION BEANS

A session bean is a logical extension of the client's session, running processes on the client's behalf remotely on the server. To develop a session bean, you must define the *home* and *remote interfaces* that represent the client view of the bean. You must also create a class that implements the *SessionBean* interface (and optionally the *SessionSynchronization* interface), as well as methods corresponding to those in the bean's home and remote interfaces.

The tools for a container generate additional classes for a session bean at deployment time. These tools get information from the EJB at deployment time by introspecting its classes and interfaces. This information is used to dynamically generate two classes, implementing the home and remote interfaces of the bean. These classes enable the container to intercede in all client calls on the session bean. The container also generates a serializable *Handle* class, providing a way to identify a session bean instance within a specific life cycle.

There are two types of session beans:

- **Stateless session beans**   These do not maintain state across method calls and transactions. They are intended to perform individual operations atomically. Stateless beans are also *amorphous:* any client can use any instance of a stateless bean at any time, at the container's discretion.

- **Stateful session beans**   These maintain state across method calls and transactions. Stateful session beans often maintain a cache of database information. To maintain data consistency, the cache must be synchronized with the database when transactions are started, committed, or aborted. To keep informed of transaction status changes, the bean implements the SessionSynchronization interface. The EJB container calls methods of this interface whenever transaction status changes.

Session beans, whether stateful or stateless, are not designed to be persistent. The data maintained by a stateful session bean is intended to be transitional, solely for the purpose of a particular session with a particular client. A stateful session bean instance typically cannot survive system failures. While a session bean has a container-provided identity (its handle), that identity passes when the session bean is removed by the client at the end of a session. If a client needs to revive a stateful session bean that has disappeared, it must provide its own means to reconstruct the bean's state.

### ENTITY BEANS

Entity beans (also known as persistent beans) represent specific data or collections of data, such as a row in a relational database. Entity bean methods provide operations for acting on the data represented by the bean. An entity bean is persistent; it survives as long as its data remains in the database.

**NOTE**
*Container support for Entity Beans is optional in release 1.0 of the Enterprise JavaBeans specification. Support will become mandatory with release 1.1 of the EJB specification. Oracle8i does not support Entity Beans. However, you can explicitly save the state of an Oracle session bean in tables in the database and manage the bean's persistent state via SQLJ or JDBC.*

## Implementing EJBs in Oracle8i

Here are the key concepts of EJBs you should grasp before you start programming EJBs. (EJB programming is covered in Chapter 10.)

### EJB REMOTE INTERFACE

The bean's remote interface specifies the methods that you want to expose to clients. The signature for each method you expose in the remote interface must match the signature of the *bean class* (also called the *bean implementation*). For the bean class you implement business logic using standard Java.

**NOTE**
*If you are familiar with PL/SQL, it might be helpful to think of a remote interface as a PL/SQL package without public variables. A remote interface is like a package spec; a remote interface implementation is like a package body.*

### EJB HOME INTERFACE

A client creates a bean instance through the home interface. The home interface specifies one or more `create` methods. A `create` method can take parameters that are passed in from the client when the bean is created. For each `create` method in the home interface, you must specify a corresponding `ejbCreate` method in the remote interface with the same signature. When a client invokes `create` on the home, the container interposes whatever services are required at that point and then calls the corresponding `ejbCreate` method in the bean itself.

### EJB DEPLOYMENT DESCRIPTOR AND THE "DEPLOYEJB" TOOL

The EJB Deployment Descriptor—a Java serialized class that extends the base Deployment Descriptor class—allows you to specify transaction and security attributes declaratively rather than procedurally. The "deployejb" tool verifies the bean interfaces, generates and compiles the required classes for the bean, loads the classes into the databases, and then publishes the bean home interface in the database so that clients can access it.

### INVOKING BEAN METHODS

Client access to an EJB takes several steps. First, the client must be authenticated against Oracle8i. (Chapter 10 discusses the different authentication methods that are available.) Second, the client must locate the EJB by looking up the class that implements its home interface by name through JNDI. Finally, the client uses methods of the home interface to acquire access to an instance of the class implementing the remote interface.

Once the client has access to the instance of the class implementing the remote interface, the client can invoke the bean methods. This is done through the ORB proxy-skeleton mechanism discussed in the section "How ORBs Work." The client sends a message through the stub. The skeleton unmarshals the message and upcalls it to the bean container. At this point, the bean container interposes the services that are required by the context. Typically, the bean container would do the following:

- Authenticate the client on the first method call

- Perform transaction management

- Call synchronization methods in the bean itself

The container then delegates the method call to the bean. After the bean executes, the thread of control returns to the bean container, which interposes services that are required by the context. (In a transaction context, for example, the bean container might perform a commit operation.) The bean container calls the skeleton, which marshals the data and returns it to the client stub. These system-level steps are hidden from you as an EJB developer. In fact, to implement an EJB in Oracle8i you only need to do the following:

- Define the remote and home interface

- Write the bean implementation

- Define the deployment descriptor

- Compile and package the bean

- Deploy the bean into the database using the "deployejb" tool

This ease of programming and many other EJB benefits are outlined in the next section.

## EJB Benefits

The following are the key benefits of EJBs:

- **Ease of programming**  Java programmers will find EJBs easier to program than CORBA or DCOM, for several reasons. First, EJBs offer a higher level of abstraction than CORBA. Low-level system programming issues, such as session management, remote invocation, transaction, security, and multithreading, have been abstracted into higher-level constructs, allowing you to focus on business logic instead of the underlying "plumbing."

  Second, EJBs are written entirely in Java. With CORBA and DCOM components, you must define interfaces in IDL. With EJBs, on the other hand, you define all interfaces in Java.

  Third, EJB transaction and security semantics are defined declaratively rather than procedurally. Transaction semantics can be defined at application assembly or deployment time. Transactions happen automatically when JavaBean's methods are executed. The EJB server automatically manages the start, commit, and rollback of transactions on behalf of the EJB, according to the transaction attribute you specify in the deployment descriptor. You may choose from a rich set of transaction policies: TX_BEAN_MANAGED, TX_NOT_SUPPORTED, TX_SUPPORTS, TX_REQUIRED, TX_REQUIRES_ NEW, and TX_MANDATORY (see Chapter 10).

- **Client independence of server implementation**  EJB clients implement server-independent interfaces. As a result, they disregard the specific EJB server implementation chosen.

- **Scalability**  EJBs allow server applications to scale with limited developer effort, since the EJB definition was specifically restricted to allow server scalability.

- **Portability across servers**  EJBs were designed for portability across JVMs and EJB servers that comply with the standard EJB specification in three ways. First, all EJB servers, Oracle8i included, accept EJBs in a standard format, called the *ejb-package format*. Second, a client's view of EJBs remain the same regardless of the container it is deployed in, since all containers present the same interfaces to the client. Third, since EJBs specify transactions declaratively, no explicit transaction code is required within the application itself. As a result, EJBs are portable across different transaction managers.

# Choosing a Programming Model

A rich variety of programming models (PL/SQL, Java stored procedures, EJBs, and CORBA objects) can be used in Oracle8i. Selecting one model over another can be a daunting task. Your choice will often boil down to the programming style with which you are most comfortable: stored procedures if you are most familiar with database programming; CORBA or EJBs if you are most familiar with distributed component development. You should also consider each model's strengths and weaknesses for a particular task. This section presents some points to consider when selecting a programming method.

### Component-Based Development versus Stored Procedures

Component-based programming is rapidly becoming the preferred method of developing applications. It holds promise of rapid-application development by wiring components from different vendors, better reuse, ease of maintenance, simplified deployment across tiers, and improved scalability. Applications that are good candidates for component-based development include the following:

- **Computation-intensive applications**   Applications that are logic- and computation-intensive can often benefit from third-party components and component reusability.

- **Complex multi-tier applications**   EJB and CORBA components running in Oracle8i can be easily invoked from internet browsers, CORBA clients, and pure Java clients via RMI over IIOP. DCOM clients (such as Visual Basic applications running in Microsoft Transaction Server) can access CORBA servers running in the database through a DCOM-to-CORBA bridge.

Applications that are good candidates for stored procedures include the following:

- **SQL-intensive applications**   Stored procedures are tightly integrated with the database and thus are well adapted for applications that access data frequently with SQL.

- **Traditional two-tier applications**   Stored procedures offer a direct and simple programming paradigm for traditional two-tier applications. Stored procedures in Oracle8i can be easily invoked from database clients including JDBC, SQLJ, ODBC, OCI, and Oracle Developer clients.

## Component Development-Based: EJB versus CORBA

EJB technology makes it easier to build Java applications on top of a CORBA infrastructure. As detailed in the "EJB Benefits" section in this chapter, EJBs augment CORBA by overlaying a higher-level programming interface; EJBs are written entirely in Java, requiring no IDL; EJB transaction and security policies can be specified declaratively rather than procedurally.

CORBA objects can be written in cases when fine-grained functionality is required. The Caffeine tools provided with Oracle8i can decrease some of the complexity of developing CORBA servers in Java.

**NOTE**
*While CORBA objects can be written in any language, only objects written in Java may be deployed into Oracle8i.*

## Stored Procedures: PL/SQL versus Java

PL/SQL is tightly integrated with the database and offers the following benefits:

- **Automatic visibility to SQL**   In PL/SQL, all procedures and functions are automatically visible to SQL. In Java, however, you must publish those methods that you want to be visible to SQL by writing call specs.

- **Efficient access to SQL**   PL/SQL should perform better than Java stored procedures in SQL-intensive applications (that is, where there are frequent reads/writes to tables) since PL/SQL supports the same native datatypes as SQL. Oracle does not provide native Java-type support within the database itself. Only SQL types and object-relational types can be stored in the database. Consequently, whenever you access the database from a Java stored procedure, Oracle must convert Java types to SQL datatypes (and vice-versa). There is efficiency overhead, and in certain cases, loss of precision as a result of this conversion.

**NOTE**
*You should see improvements in efficiency and precision when using SQL data with oracle.sql data types (rather than standard Java types) in your Java stored procedures as described in Chapter 9. The drawback: your Java code will no longer be portable since oracle.sql types are Oracle-specific.*

Java is rapidly becoming the language of choice for developing Internet and intranet applications. In addition, Java is becoming the language of choice for stored procedure development. With Oracle8i, Java and PL/SQL stored procedures can interoperate, so that your investment in existing PL/SQL code is not wasted.

Attributes that make Java a good choice as a stored procedure language for Oracle8i include the following:

- **Portability**   Java stored procedures are portable across databases from multiple vendors. PL/SQL, on the other hand, is specific to Oracle. In principle, you can port Java stored procedures from another database vendor to Oracle quite easily: you load the Java source or binaries into the database and publish them to SQL.

- **True object-oriented support**   Java was designed as a true object-oriented language from the onset. PL/SQL, originally a procedural language, is tightly integrated with the database, and has now been augmented with object-oriented features.

- **Availability of libraries and tools**   Java has a greater selection of libraries and third-party development tools than PL/SQL does.

- **Single language for all tiers**   With Java, you have a single language that can be used on all tiers: applications and applets on the front-end, servlets and database stored procedures on the back-end. This could reduce training and development costs.

- **Natively compiled libraries**   In applications that are computation-intensive and that contain few database reads/writes, Java stored code will run faster than equivalent PL/SQL code. This is because the java.lang package and other sys-owned packages are natively compiled. Natively compiled code that Java stored procedures call will run faster than equivalent code that is interpreted in the PL/SQL engine.

# Choosing the Right JDBC Driver

The three JDBC drivers offered by Oracle—OCI, Thin, and Server-Side—support the same syntax and APIs. All three support the 1.2.2 JDBC specification for relational databases and parts of the 2.0 specification that extend 1.2.2 to object-relational types, collections, and LOBs. However, they differ in how they connect to the database and how they transfer data, as follows:

■ **Thin JDBC Driver** This driver is a 100 percent Java, Type 4 driver that is small (only 300K). It connects directly to Oracle (without the need for an Oracle client installation) by emulating Net8 and TTC (the wire protocol using OCI) on top of Java sockets.

**NOTE**
*The Thin Driver cannot be used with non-TCP/IP protocols. Moreover, the JDBC Thin Driver can connect to a database only if a TNS Listener is up and listening on TCP/IP sockets on the server.*

*Because the Thin Driver is 100 percent Java, it is platform independent and can be used in applets. In fact, the JDBC Thin Driver provides the only way to access Oracle from an applet. A typical scenario in which the Thin Driver is put to use in an applet is as follows. A user selects a URL from an HTML page that contains a Java applet tag. A Java applet is downloaded into the browser, along with the Thin Driver and the SQLJ Runtime. The driver could then connect to the database using Java sockets, allowing the applet to access Oracle through JDBC or SQLJ over TCP/IP.*

■ **JDBC OCI Driver** This driver may offer a performance advantage over the Thin JDBC Driver. However, you must have Net8 installed and working to use the OCI Driver. Also, you cannot use the JDBC-OCI Driver in an applet because it uses native methods.

**NOTE**
*Firewalls could limit the use of both client-side (the Thin and the JDBC-OCI) drivers.*

■ **Server-Side Driver** This embedded driver is optimized to directly access SQL and PL/SQL. Use this driver for Java stored procedures, EJBs, or Java CORBA objects in the database.

# Deployment Scenarios Using Oracle8i

With Oracle8i's Java-enabling components—ORB, JVM, and embedded JDBC Driver—you have a wealth of powerful technologies at your disposal. You now

have a choice of several programming models—PL/SQL, JDBC, SQLJ, CORBA,
and EJB; a choice of JDBC drivers—OCI, Thin, and Server-Side; and a choice of two
protocols—Net8 and CORBA-IIOP.

As shown in Figure 2-3, Net8 is SQL-centric: it is optimized to retrieve data from
the database via SQL. Net8 clients can call Java stored procedures if you publish
the procedures to SQL. CORBA-IIOP, in Oracle's implementation, is Java-centric.
CORBA clients can access EJBs and CORBA servers stored in the database. Using
IIOP, you can both call-into and call-out of Oracle8i.

How do you harness these technologies? The following sections explore a range
of deployment possibilities, from simple two-tier client/server configurations to
complex configurations involving HTTP, Java Applets, and CORBA IIOP.

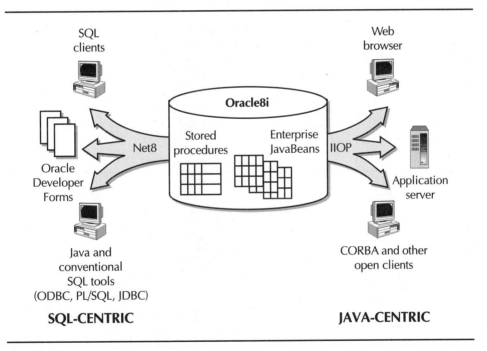

**FIGURE 2-3.**   *SQL-centric and Java-centric access in Oracle8i*

### Traditional Two-Tier Using JDBC-OCI

A traditional two-tier client/server configuration is shown in Figure 2-4. A Java application is deployed on each client. The Java application (since it is not a Java applet) can freely access the client machine's resources, such as printers and local files.

In addition to the Java application with SQLJ code, each client must have the SQLJ Runtime Library, the JDBC-OCI Driver, Net8 client, and any Oracle client libraries needed to support OCI and Net8. The Java application issues SQL using JDBC via Net8 over TCP/IP. Since this configuration requires deploying the Net8 client, Oracle's JDBC-OCI Driver, and both their supporting libraries, it is suitable for intranet and extranet applications only.

### Browser-Based Client Running SQLJ Using Thin JDBC

A three-tier configuration is shown in Figure 2-5. A Java applet tag in an HTML page loads the SQLJ applet, the SQLJ Runtime Library, and Oracle's Thin JDBC Driver into the client browser. The browser already contains a JVM as a browser-shipped component. The client SQLJ applet bypasses the application server and communicates directly with the database engine over TCP/IP. The main advantage of this configuration is that the application logic is deployed centrally.

This configuration is suitable mainly for intranet applications. Remember that the Thin JDBC Driver could be subject to firewall restrictions in this configuration. Also, due to Java sandbox security issues, an applet may not open a network connection to an Oracle database running on a different machine as the Web

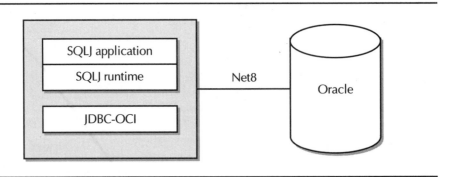

**FIGURE 2-4.** *Traditional two-tier configuration*

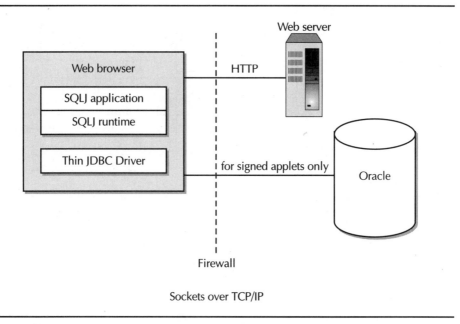

**FIGURE 2-5.**   *Browser-based client running SQLJ using the Thin JDBC Driver*

server. Techniques of working around the applet restriction are described in the "Applet Security Restrictions" section in this chapter.

## Browser-Based HTML Client with Java-Based Middle-Tier

Figure 2-6 shows a three-tier configuration that could be used for Internet, intranet, and extranet applications. Web browsers run on the clients. Oracle Application Server (OAS) runs on the middle-tier. The application server is the home of the SQLJ application, JVM, the SQLJ Runtime Library, the JDBC-OCI Driver, Net8 client, and any Oracle client libraries needed to support OCI and Net8.

The Web browsers connect via HTTP to OAS, which in turn uses the JDBC-OCI Driver to communicate over Net8 with the database engine. The client can invoke the Java application (including SQLJ) by calling a *Common Gateway Interface (CGI)* script. CGI enables Web servers to route the contents of HTML pages to back-end server applications.

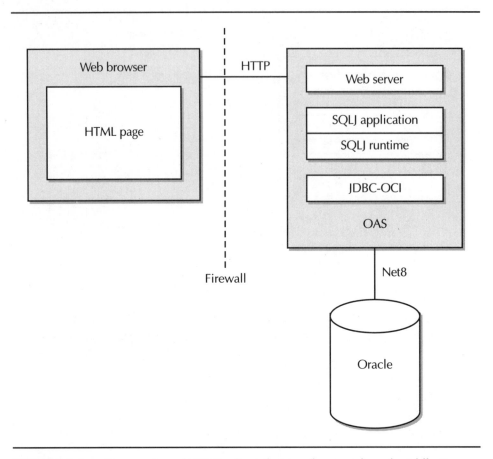

**FIGURE 2-6.** *Browser-based HTML client that invokes Java-based middle-tier*

## Browser-Based Client Invoking EJB and CORBA Objects via IIOP

Several problems arise as a result of using HTTP/CGI in the previous configuration:

- It is difficult to preserve state between invocations, since HTTP is a stateless protocol. Preserving state during a user's session is vital for many business applications. For example, in an online shopping application that provides a shopping cart, the user's within-session changes must be made to persist at least for the duration of the session.

■ Overall performance suffers because CGI launches a new process for each incoming client request.

There are many ways of working around the HTTP/CGI limitations, notably using Microsoft's *Active Server Pages (ASP)* and JavaSoft's *Servlets*. For example, the Java application in the previous configuration could run on the middle-tier as a *servlet*.

**NOTE**
*A servlet is Java code that a Web server loads to handle client requests. Servlets offer efficiency and security gains over CGI. Servlet code stays alive in memory when the request ends. A servlet can connect to a database when it is initialized and retain its connection across requests.*

The main drawback with both ASP and servlet approaches is that they require HTTP and the Web server to mediate between the client and the server objects. HTML forms must be used for client/server interaction, and HTML must be dynamically generated for each response.

With Oracle8i, true object-to-object interaction is possible using the embedded ORB. Using IIOP, the Web browser can become a CORBA client and the application server a CORBA server. The configuration in Figure 2-7 shows one such scenario. It is suitable for Internet, intranet, and extranet applications. Here the Web browser first downloads an HTML page that has references to embedded Java applets. The browser then retrieves the Java applet from the Web server. The applet contains client stubs that enable it to invoke EJB and CORBA objects on the Oracle server through IIOP.

Two security issues—firewall restrictions (related to Java clients over IIOP) and applet restrictions—must be overcome for this configuration to work. Once these issues are handled properly, the reward from this scheme is compelling: the need to generate HTML pages dynamically for each response is reduced. A typical application on the client would be a single HTML page with embedded CORBA components that interact with the server-side CORBA objects, including EJBs.

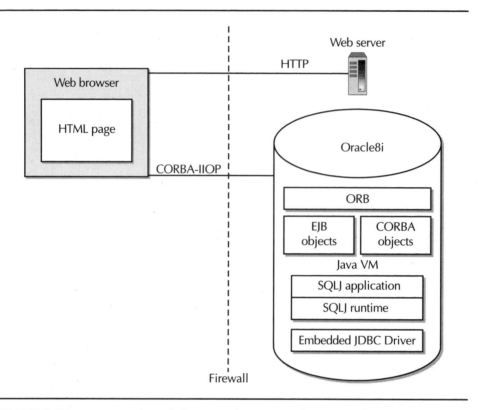

**FIGURE 2-7.** *Browser-based client invoking EJB and CORBA objects via IIOP*

## Applet Security Restrictions

Due to Java sandbox security restrictions, an applet may only open a TCP/IP sockets connection to a database that is running on the same host as the Web server that served the applet. You have two approaches to work around this restriction:

■ Use signed applets if your browser supports JDK 1.1.

■ Use a gateway process on the Web server machine. Oracle8 Connection Manager, for example, can be used to receive Net8 packets on the Web server machine and re-transmit them to the machine where the Oracle database is running.

Both Figure 2-5 and Figure 2-7 show an applet connecting to an Oracle database running on a machine other than the one which the Web server runs. Either the signed applet approach or the gateway approach can be taken with the configuration in Figure 2-5. The signed applet approach would have to be taken in the configuration in Figure 2-7.

Of course, you could convert these three-tier configurations into two-tier configurations by placing the Web server and database engine on the same physical server. However, this is not a very scalable approach since a Web server and an Oracle database both require significant resources.

# PART
# II

## Server Administration

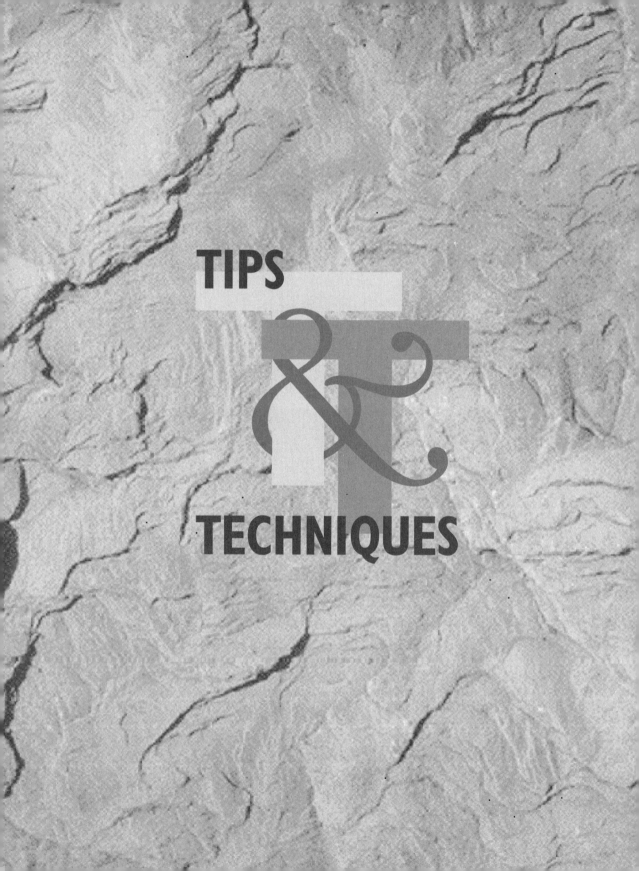

# TIPS

# T

# TECHNIQUES

# CHAPTER
# 3

## Installation

With Oracle8i, Oracle has changed the architecture of the database engine. This is particularly true with the addition of the Java Virtual Machine (JVM) or JServer. The JVM has added new considerations and elements to the installation process and has revised the interpretation of old elements. Connectivity issues are also raised with the advent of the embedded JVM. New tools include a new Oracle Universal Installer (OUI) and the Database Configuration Assistant (DBCA), each with a set of options. In addition, Oracle has made some new recommendations on database server configuration and tuning. This chapter describes some of the installation, configuration, connectivity, and tuning issues raised with the new Oracle8i database server:

- Implementing the Optimal Flexible Architecture (OFA)

- Converting a non-OFA Oracle8i install to OFA with a previous version of Oracle installed on Windows NT

- Converting a non-OFA Oracle8i install to OFA on UNIX

- Creating the Oracle Starter Database with a DB_BLOCK_SIZE greater than 2K

- Creating a database create script using Oracle Database Configuration Assistant

- Validating: some simple post-creation database tests

- Creating an additional rollback segment in the System tablespace

- Determining the number of user rollback segments

- Installing the Java Virtual Machine

- Tuning the Java Virtual Machine: the Shared Pool and the Java Pool

- Enabling the multithreaded server (MTS)

- Setting the LARGE_POOL_SIZE and SHARED_POOL_SIZE with MTS

- Reducing contention for MTS dispatcher and server processes

- Using one Net8 listener to connect to multiple Oracle Homes

# Oracle8i Installation and Database Creation

Oracle's Optimal Flexible Architecture (OFA) has been with the Oracle community since 1993, when it was documented in Cary Millsap's *The OFA Standard—Oracle7 for Open Systems*. This paper in turn reflected a presentation given at International Oracle User Week in 1991. Oracle8i gives added emphasis to OFA architecture, using it for the install of its Starter Database. The Starter Database can now be created with a DB_BLOCK_SIZE greater than 2K.

## Implementing the Optimal Flexible Architecture

In configuring new installs and databases and in reorganizing existing installation and databases so that they reflect OFA structure, you will make them transparent to administrators and developers. OFA enforces a consistent naming convention—the separation of Oracle homes and their executables for different software versions, the separation of the datafiles of different databases, and the separation of the administrative files of different databases. For administrators and developers needing access to Oracle8i's operating system files, the bottom line is that they will know where things are as they move from one database to the next and from one server to the next. OFA eases Oracle executable upgrades by separating Oracle homes and eases migrations by separating the files of different databases. (See Figure 3-1.)

The ORACLE_BASE directory, often labeled Oracle, has four branches. Two of the four branches, Ora81 and Ora82, are ORACLE_HOMEs. Their subdirectories hold different releases of the database engine into which the Oracle executables are installed. A third branch of the ORACLE_BASE is Admin, which contains subdirectories for each database on the system. Under the database specific subdirectories are standard subdirectories: Bdump, Cdump, and Udump, for background, core, and user alert and trace files; Create for the database create scripts; Pfile for the database's init.ora and config.ora files; Adhoc for SQL*Plus and operating system administration scripts, and Exp for database export files.

**CAUTION**
*On the NT operating system, Oracle8i does not use the Cdump (core dump) directory. Operating system core dumps are written to the Bdump directory. Oracle Technical Support claims this is due to the small size of NT core dumps. The init.ora parameter file for an Oracle8i instance on NT does not specify a core dump directory. If the parameter CORE_DUMP_DEST is specified in the init.ora file on NT, an error message—"LRM-00101: unknown parameter name 'core_dump_dest'"—will be generated on attempted startup, and the instance will not come up, issuing the message "ORA-01078: failure in processing system parameters."*

```
/Oracle (Oracle_Base)
 /Ora81 (Oracle_Home1)
  /Bin
  /Network
  /Rdbms
  /Doc
  /....etc
 /Admin
  /Acct_dev
   /Adhoc
   /Bdump
   /Cdump
   /Create
   /Exp
   /Pfile
   /Udump
  /Acct_test
   /Adhoc
   /Bdump
   /Cdump
   /Create
   /Exp
   /Pfile
   /Udump
 /Oradata
  /Acct_dev
   /Control01.ctl
   /Control02.ctl
   /Data01.dbf
   /System01.dbf
   /Rbs01.dbf
   /Redo01.log
   /Redo02.log
   /Index01.dbf
   /Users01.dbf
   /Temp01.dbf
  /Acct_test
   /Control01.ctl
   /Control02.ctl
   /Data01.dbf
   /System01.dbf
   /Rbs01.dbf
   /Redo01.log
   /Redo02.log
   /Index01.dbf
   /Users01.dbf
   /Temp01.dbf
 /Ora82 (Oracle_Home2)
  /Bin
  /Network
  /Rdbms
  /Doc
  /...etc
```

**FIGURE 3-1.** *A purist's Optimal Flexible Architecture*

The fourth branch is Oradata, in which subdirectories hold the actual database files for different databases. Thus, for example, under Oradata you might find an Acct_dev and an Acct_test subdirectory. Acct_dev would hold the database files for the accounting development environment, such as system01.dbf, control01.ctl, control02.ctl, redo01.log, redo02.log, rbs01.dbf, data01.dbf, index01.dbf, users01.dbf, and temp01.dbf. A similar set of database files would be present under Acct_test for the test environment.

**NOTE**

*Add a subdirectory under each database's subdirectory under Admin called logbook—for example, ORACLE_BASE/ admin/ORACLE_SID/logbook, where the ORACLE_BASE is usually Oracle and ORACLE_SID is the database's SID. Use the logbook to track all changes made to the database after creation. Include the scripts used, date the files according to when the changes were made, and record what issues motivated the modifications. If the modification is pending, mark the file as such. Use the logbook to track all Technical Assistant Requests (TARs) to Oracle Technical Support, devising a manner to mark the files with date, TAR number, and status. Track what was sent to Technical Support and any correspondences. Alternatively, create a separate subdirectory called tar at the same level as logbook, and manage the TARs separately. Further, add a subdirectory under each database's subdirectory under Admin called ctl, short for control—for example, ORACLE_BASE/admin/ ORACLE_SID/ctl, where ORACLE_BASE is often Oracle and ORACLE_SID is the database's SID. Use the ctl as the destination directory for a backup of the database control file(s). Use the command ALTER DATABASE BACKUP CONTROLFILE TO 'filename' REUSE, where filename is the full path to ctl plus the file to be used for the backup—for example, on NT, f:\oracle\ admin\ acct_dev\ctl\acct_dev_bk.ctl. Incorporate the ctl directory and its contents into your backup strategy. If you have multiple control files, as you should, only one backup in ctl is necessary, since they all have the same contents and the backup can be copied and renamed.*

Some variation on the OFA structure may become necessary. The point is to keep distinct the Oracle engine executables, the different administration files of the databases, and the different datafiles of the databases. For performance it would be expected that a database's files would be spread over multiple disks. Keeping rollback tablespaces and their files on different disks from redo log files is standard physical design practice, as is keeping data tablespaces and their files separate from index tablespaces and their files. In such cases, Oradata could be broken out from under the ORACLE_BASE into multiples, appearing as Oradata01 and Oradata02, and so on. Similarly, because of their size and the need for special handling, the actual database export files might be broken out from under their respective database Admin subdirectories under ORACLE_BASE. Figure 3-2 shows these variations.

```
/Oracle (Oracle_Base)
  /Ora81 (Oracle_Home1)
    /Bin
    /Network
    /Rdbms
    /Doc
    /....etc
  /Admin
    /Acct_dev
      /Adhoc
      /Bdump
      /Cdump
      /Create
      /Exp
      /Pfile
      /Udump
    /Acct_test
      /Adhoc
      /Bdump
      /Cdump
      /Create
      /Exp
      /Pfile
      /Udump
  /Ora82 (Oracle_Home2)
    /Bin
    /Network
    /Rdbms
    /Doc
    /....etc
  /Oradata01
    /Acct_dev
      /Control01.ctl
      /Control02.ctl
      /Data01.dbf
      /System01.dbf
```

**FIGURE 3-2.**   *Variation on the Optimal Flexible Architecture*

```
                    /Users.dbf
                    /Rbs01.dbf
                /Oradata02
                  /Acct_dev
                    /Redo01.log
                    /Redo02.log
                    /Index01.dbf
                    /Temp01.dbf
                /Oradata03
                  /Acct_test
                    /Control01.ctl
                    /Control02.ctl
                    /Data01.dbf
                    /System01.dbf
                    /Users.dbf
                    /Rbs01.dbf
                /Oradata04
                  /Acct_test
                    /Redo01.log
                    /Redo02.log
                    /Index01.dbf
                    /Temp01.dbf
                /Oraexp
                  /Acct_dev
                    /Acct_dev.dmp
                  /Acct_test
                    /Acct_test.dmp
```

Implementing the Optimal Flexible Architecture

**FIGURE 3-2.** *Variation on the Optimal Flexible Architecture* (continued)

**NOTE**
*The Starter Database is OFA compliant. It can be created in various ways. Accepting the Typical Installation Type with the Oracle Universal Installer will automatically install a Starter Database. Running the installer for a Minimal Installation Type and accepting the Starter Database option will also install it. When running the installer under the Custom option for an Oracle Server Installation, saying Yes to the Oracle Database Configuration Assistant, and accepting the Typical option will install the Starter Database. Finally, invoking the Oracle Database Configuration Assistant at any time after the Oracle executables are installed and accepting the Typical option will install the Starter Database.*

## Converting a Non-OFA Oracle8i Install to OFA with a Previous Version of Oracle Installed on NT

In an OFA-compliant installation, ORACLE_HOME directories lie under the ORACLE_BASE directory. The Oracle Universal Installer (OUI) will prompt you for values of the ORACLE_HOME name and the ORACLE_HOME path and will allow you to enter any values, provided that sufficient space is available in the specified file system. For example, when you install the Oracle8i engine executables on the F drive, f:\oracle\ORA81 would be the OFA-compliant ORACLE_HOME path, where the ORACLE_HOME name is ORA81 and the ORACLE_BASE is f:\oracle. Figure 3-3 shows these entries on the OUI screen.

Be sure to enter an OFA-compliant ORACLE_HOME path. If, for example, an ORACLE_HOME name of ORA81 was specified, but the path was simply entered as F: (not F:\oracle), the Oracle8i executables subdirectories would be installed at the same directory level as the Admin subdirectory. Oradata for the Starter Database would also be at the same level.

With this installation, problems will arise with upgrades, and with multiple ORACLE_BASEs some tools and the databases will not find all the required files.

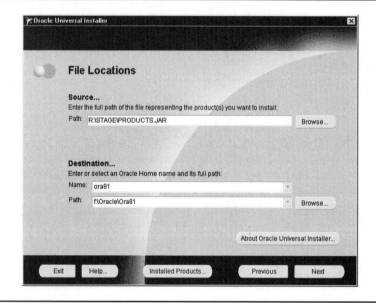

**FIGURE 3-3.** *ORACLE_HOME path and ORACLE_HOME name for an OFA installation*

Removing executables from the previous release will also be problematic, since their subdirectories share the same level as the Admin and Oradata subdirectories, which are to be preserved on upgrade.

The solution to this problem is to catch it early and redo a non-OFA-compliant installation after using the OUI to deinstall all Oracle8i products previously installed. If you must preserve the data already in the database, use the Export utility first to capture the data and import it after you have reconfigured. The problem with this approach is that the NT Registry has recorded the values for the ORACLE_HOME, the ORACLE_HOME name, and the ORACLE_BASE on the initial false install. When you try to rerun the OUI, it will read these values and not let you change the ORACLE_BASE. To prevent this, you must manually alter the Registry.

**NOTE**
*It is advisable to back up or export the NT Registry before and after installing any new software. Exporting before installation eases any clean-up operations that might be needed, and exporting after an install is a good backup and recovery practice. Use the regedit command to Export Registry File, with an Export range of All. Creating a NT Emergency Repair Disk also captures the information necessary to restore, an alternative to a Registry export.*

The *Release Notes* for Oracle8i describe how to create a clean NT machine by removing all Oracle entries in the Registry. This solution is not viable if you have an existing Oracle release installed and want to preserve it. The problem posed here is to keep the previous release and prepare for a refresh install of Oracle8i in an OFA-compliant manner.

**NOTE**
*In regedit, the folders that appear are correctly referred to as keys. To minimize confusion in terms, they will be referred to as folders—which is what they look like, though not what they are.*

1. If you need to preserve the database contents, use the Oracle Export utility to export your Oracle8i databases. Move the export and any create-database scripts to a directory outside the Oracle8i ORACLE_HOME or ORACLE_BASE.

2. Back up the listener.ora, tnsnames.ora, sqlnet.ora, and any other Net8 and connectivity files found under ORACLE_HOME/admin/network/admin. This

Converting from a Previous Install of Oracle on NT

will save time when reconfiguring connectivity, since the files can act as templates that simply need the correct path for the ORACLE_HOME changed.

**3.** Stop all Oracle services running by going to Control Panel | Services, highlight the services labeled with Oracle, and select Stop. Some services are dependent on others. When selecting a parent service, you will be asked if you want to stop the child service; select OK.

**4.** Use the Oracle Universal Installer to remove all Oracle8i installed products.

**5.** Use Windows NT Explorer to remove all directories related to the Oracle8i non-OFA-compliant ORACLE_BASE, such as Admin and Oradata, and the directories under the Oracle8i non-OFA-compliant ORACLE_HOME. Be careful to preserve the ORACLE_BASE of the installation(s) that remain.

**6.** Run regedit by selecting Start | Run | enter regedit, and then select OK. Go to HKEY_LOCAL_MACHINE\SOFTWARE\ORACLE. Under this folder (registry key), you will find a list of the installed ORACLE_HOMEs labeled HOME0, HOME1, and so on, in which the most recently installed ORACLE_HOME has the highest number. Opening each HOME folder will display its details. Figure 3-4 shows the Registry for ORACLE and HOMEs. After verifying it is the HOME that represents the ORACLE_HOME of Oracle8i, delete the HOME folder.

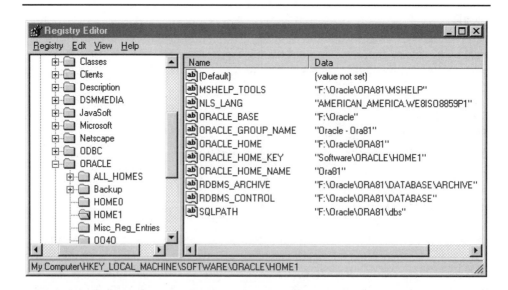

**FIGURE 3-4.** *Registry contents for HOME1 representing an OFA-compliant Oracle8i installation*

7. Open the ALL_HOMES folder under ORACLE in the same Registry area and reduce the value for LAST_HOME by one, so that if it was "1," now make it "0." The count of HOMEs begins with zero, and the LAST_HOME value should reflect the total number of HOMEs minus one that will remain after the Oracle8i HOME is removed. If the value of HOME_COUNTER is greater than the number of HOMEs that will exist after the Oracle8i HOME is removed, then reduce the value of HOME_COUNTER by one; otherwise leave the value of HOME_COUNTER unchanged. Figure 3-5 shows the Registry for ALL_HOMES after the HOME_COUNTER value has been modified.

8. While you are still in the Registry, remove all folders under \HKEY_LOCAL_MACHINE\SYSTEM\CurrentControlSet\Services that contain the ORACLE_HOME name given during the Oracle8i install, such as OracleOra81TNSListener, OracleOra81Agent, OracleOra81ClientCache, and OracleOra81DataGather, where Ora81 in these folder labels is the ORACLE_HOME name given on install. Figure 3-6 shows the Registry for Services belonging to Oracle. Those folders that do not contain the ORACLE_HOME name for the Oracle8i install should remain untouched; here they represent an Oracle7.3.4 installation on the same machine.

Converting from a Previous Install of Oracle on NT

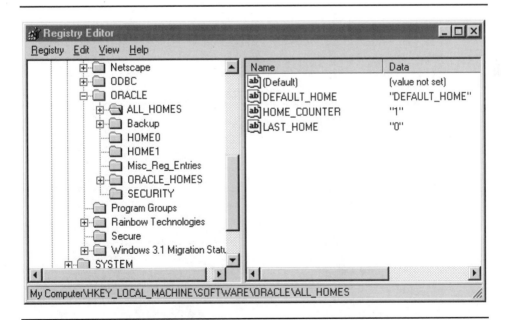

**FIGURE 3-5.** *Correct values for ALL_HOMES when HOME1 of Oracle8i will be removed*

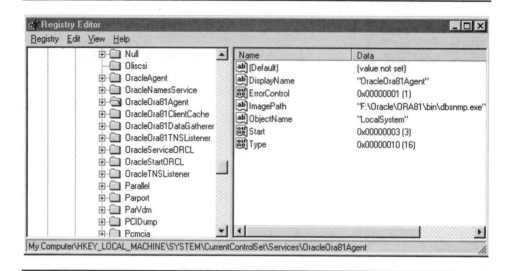

**FIGURE 3-6.** *Oracle8i and Oracle7.3.4 services folders in the NT Registry*

9. Still in the Registry under \HKEY_LOCAL_MACHINE\SYSTEM\
   CurrentControlSet\Services, drill deeper to \HKEY_LOCAL_MACHINE\
   SYSTEM\CurrentControlSet\Services\EventLog\Application. Explore the
   contents of any folder beginning with Oracle or ORACLE, and remove
   those folders that reference the Oracle8i installation. Figure 3-7 shows the
   contents of OracleAgent referencing ORA81 and the Oracle8i install path.
   The ORACLE7.orcl folder, if explored, would show it is related to the
   Oracle7.3.4 installation.

10. Reboot the computer.

11. Reinstall Oracle8i, specifying an OFA-compliant ORACLE_HOME path,
    such as f:\oracle\ORA81, with an ORACLE_BASE of f:\oracle and an
    ORACLE_HOME of ORA81.

12. Reconfigure connectivity from the backups made of the listener.ora,
    tnsnames.ora, sqlnet.ora. Place these files in ORACLE_HOME/admin/
    network/admin after the correct path for ORACLE_HOME has been
    entered in them.

13. After rebuilding the database instance, use the Oracle Import utility to
    import the previously exported database.

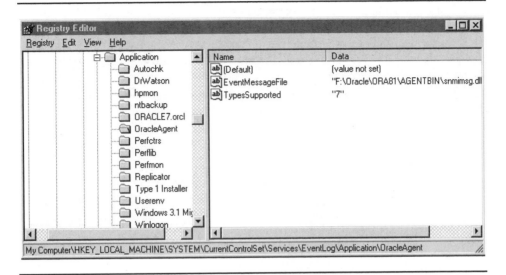

**FIGURE 3-7.**    *Oracle8i and Oracle7.3.4 application folders in the NT Registry*

## Converting a Non-OFA Oracle8i Install to OFA on UNIX

On UNIX, the .profile or .cshrc login files of the Oracle software owner fill the role of the NT Registry in identifying the ORACLE_BASE, ORACLE_HOME, and UNIX PATH. It is easier to reinstall in an OFA-compliant manner by going through the following steps:

1. Export the database and preserve the export dump file and any create-database scripts necessary to rebuild the instance, if a rebuild is required.

2. Back up the listener.ora, tnsnames.ora, sqlnet.ora, and any other Net8 and connectivity files found under ORACLE_HOME/admin/network/admin. This will save time when connectivity is reconfigured, since the files can act as templates that simply need the correct path for the ORACLE_HOME changed.

3. Remove the Oracle products installed with the Oracle Universal Installer.

4. Remove the directories created.

5. Recreate the mount points and file systems in an OFA-compliant manner. See the first Tip, "Implementing the Optimal Flexible Architecture," and the operating system–specific *Oracle Server Installation Guide*.

6. Redefine the correct UNIX environment variables for the ORACLE_BASE, ORACLE_HOME, and PATH, and any variables that rely on them, in the .profile or the .cshrc of the user that owns the Oracle executables, usually named Oracle. Details on all the required UNIX environment variables can be found in the operating system–specific *Oracle Server Installation Guide*.

7. Reinstall the Oracle8i engine. Check that the correct values of the ORACLE_BASE and ORACLE_HOME are now (a) entered into the oratab file and other server shutdown and startup scripts, such as rc.local and rc.shutdown, and (b) entered into oraenv or coraenv of the user's environmental scripts, if used.

8. Reconfigure connectivity from the backups made of the listener.ora, tnsnames.ora, sqlnet.ora. Place these files in ORACLE_HOME/admin/ network/admin after the correct path for ORACLE_HOME has been entered in them.

9. If necessary, rebuild the instance with the create-database scripts and import the database.

## Creating the Oracle Starter Database with a DB_BLOCK_SIZE Greater than 2K

In the past, the Starter Database has been thought to be of little use particularly because of its small 2K DB_BLOCK_SIZE and because of the fact that it is impossible to change the DB_BLOCK_SIZE after the database has been created. The init.ora parameter DB_BLOCK_SIZE influences the amount of data that can be read and written to disk by a database server process in one I/O pass. Together with the number of DB_BLOCK_BUFFERS, it determines the size of the data block buffer cache in the SGA. The higher the DB_BLOCK_SIZE, the greater the amount read. Only in an application in which a complete transaction reads and writes exclusively in 2K or smaller blocks would there be no performance gain with a greater block size. Such an application would be one that never did table or index scans on more than 2K of data, for example. Performance gains are generally experienced with a larger DB_BLOCK_SIZE. A DB_BLOCK_SIZE of 4K to 8K is usual for OLTP systems, and 16K is usual for OLAP systems. Oracle8 supports at least a maximum DB_BLOCK_SIZE of 16K on all operating systems and up to 32K on some. See the installation guide for specific operating systems.

Prior to Oracle8i, the default database was installed with a 2K DB_BLOCK_SIZE. Now when you are invoking the Oracle Database Configuration Assistant (DBCA) and accepting the option to Create New Database instead of the option to Copy Existing Database from the CD, a Starter Database will be created that assesses the resources of your system and modifies the DB_BLOCK_SIZE. On NT Workstations with 64M to 128M of RAM, this option was found to create Starter

Databases with a DB_BLOCK_SIZE of 8K. Furthermore, the Starter Database creates an OEM_REPOSITORY tablespace designed for Oracle Enterprise Manager. With a non-2K DB_BLOCK_SIZE and the OEM_REPOSITORY tablespace, the Starter Database is potentially useful. If the Copy Existing Database from CD option is taken instead, the default Starter Database will be installed with a 2K DB_BLOCK_SIZE.

To install the Starter Database with the DB_BLOCK_SIZE other than 2K, do not select the Typical option from the OUI. This option will install the Starter Database automatically but with a 2K DB_BLOCK_SIZE. Two other options are available when you are doing an initial installation of the Oracle8i executables. One method is to choose the Minimal option from the OUI and do not say Yes to the Select Starter Database option. Instead, complete the install and invoke the DBCA after installation. A second method is to select the Custom option, install the Oracle8i Server and any other desired products, and select Yes when asked to run the DBCA. Of course, you could complete the Custom install without invoking the DBCA, and the DBCA could be invoked later.

1. To invoke the DBCA, select Start | OracleOra81 | Database Administration | Database Configuration Assistant, in which Ora81 is the ORACLE_HOME name chosen on the initial install of Oracle8i.

2. Select Create A Database.

3. Select Typical.

4. Select Create New Database File. Do not select Copy Existing Database Files From The CD; this option builds a database with a 2K DB_BLOCK_SIZE.

5. Select from among Online Transaction Processing (OLTP), Decision Support System (DSS), or Hybrid.

6. Enter the number of Concurrently Connect Users according to your license and needs. This option sizes the rollback segment tablespace. It also generates one rollback segment for every ten users with the OLTP option and one rollback segment for every fifty users with the DSDS option. If the number of users is twenty or more, the multithreaded server option will be configured.

7. Select the options to be installed. Oracle JServer will install the JVM, for example.

8. Enter a global database name and SID (System Identifier), such as OEM.BigBusiness.com and OEM, respectively. A global database name is in the form of DB_NAME.DB_DOMAIN; both are init.ora parameters. The DB_NAME does not have to be the same as the SID.

**9.** Select Create Database Now to create the database.

The DBCA will then create the database—say OEM. The database files will be placed under ORACLE_BASE/oradata/database_name, such as f:\oracle\oradata\ OEM on NT, and a set of administrative subdirectories will be created under ORACLE_BASE/admin/database_name, such as f:\oracle\admin\OEM on NT. Under the ORACLE_BASE/admin/database_name/create, the database creation log files and the JVM log file will be created, if the JServer option was selected. Under ORACLE_BASE/admin/database_name/pfile, the init.ora file will be created. The database creation process also automatically updates the Net8 connectivity files listener.ora and tnsnames.ora, using the SID and the global database name supplied earlier.

## Creating a Database Create Script Using Oracle Database Configuration Assistant

The Oracle DBCA allows for the creation of a set of database creation scripts without your having to immediately and automatically create the database. In the creation of the scripts, options are presented to add the Oracle8i JServer or JVM components, the Advanced Replication components, or the interMedia demos. These scripts can be created on one platform and then modified for other ports. They can be generated once and then modified for other databases or modified to exclude components, such as the SCOTT/TIGER and DEMO/DEMO schemata. In the process of creating the scripts, you must enter the type of application (online transaction processing, decision support system, or hybrid) and the number of concurrent users. These choices will affect the configuration of the database in terms of the size of tablespaces, number of rollback segments, and init.ora parameters generated. In effect, then, the DBCA is doing some initial database tuning.

**1.** Follow Steps 1 through 8 exactly as if you wanted the DBCA to create the database as outlined in the previous Tip.

**2.** Select Save Information To A Batch File to have the database scripts created. You will be prompted for the name of the directory in which to create the file(s).

**3.** The DBCA will create under ORACLE_HOME/admin a subdirectory named after the database SID entered in Step 8. This subdirectory contains a subdirectory called Pfile, which has the init.ora file for this particular database.

A set of files will be generated into the chosen directory. When the JServer option is chosen, the files are <SID>run.sql, <SID>run1.sql, <SID>java.sql, and sql<SID>.bat. <SID>run.sql contains the CREATE DATABASE statement for the initial build, creating redo logs and the System tablespace. <SID>run1.sql builds the tablespaces RBS for rollback segments, USERS for user data and objects, INDX for user's indexes, TEMP for temporary usage, and OEM_REPOSITORY for the Oracle Enterprise Repository. <SID>run1.sql then creates rollback segments, builds the data dictionary, and creates the Oracle7 export utilities for backward compatibility and the PL/SQL engine. <SID>java.sql installs the Java Virtual Machine. Sql<SID>.bat calls the other three scripts and is not necessary for the database creation process, assuming the ORACLE_SID is set for the operating system session from which the creation will occur. The appropriate ORACLE_SID is the one for the database being created. The scripts generated do not alter the default or temporary tablespace of the SYSTEM user. The tablespace assigned to both is the System tablespace, and it is recommended that this be changed. This is to minimize the creation of database objects that are not strictly needed for the database engine in the System tablespace and to avoid any contention that might arise.

```
ALTER USER system
  DEFAULT TABLESPACE users
  TEMPORARY TABLESPACE temp
  QUOTA UNLIMITED ON users;
```

This command sets the default tablespace and temporary tablespace for SYSTEM user to the Users and Temp tablespaces, respectively. (Both tablespaces are created by the scripts generated by the DBCA.) In addition, the SQL command grants to user SYSTEM an unlimited space allocation in Users. An alternative to using the tablespace Users is to create one expressly for the user SYSTEM.

Minor changes are necessary to port the DBCA-generated scripts to other operating systems and/or to use them to create other instances, as follows:

- Change the file paths in all the scripts to reflect the naming convention of the operating system. At the same time, modify the SID for the new instance—say from acct_dev to acct_tst.

- Follow specific operating system conventions for setting the ORACLE_SID environment variable in the batch file—for example, in the UNIX Korn shell, make sure that the following lines

```
#!/bin/ksh
export ORACLE_SID=acct_tst
```

are first in the batch script and that

```
set ORACLE_SID=acct_tst
```

appears first on NT, where acct_tst is the SID

Creating a Database Create Script with Oracle DBCA

■ If a batch file generated on NT is to be ported to UNIX, remove the two lines that invoke the Oracle Oradim utility. The Oradim utility is used to create, delete, and modify a NT service for a database instance. Here the two commands create the NT service for the instance and then set it to automatically start on reboot.

■ You may want to change the suffix on the batch file to reflect your operating system convention, such as from sqlacct_tst.bat to sqlacct_tst.sh, if you are going from NT to UNIX. As mentioned, the .bat file is not essential to the creation process.

■ Eliminate actions that are not required from the code in <SID>run1.sql. If the SCOTT/TIGER schema is of no interest in the Starter Database, remove the call to scott.sql. If the DEMO/DEMO schema is of no interest, remove the call to demo.sql; also remove the connect INTERNAL statements that immediately precede them. If you are not using OEM or already have the repository in another database, remove the portion of the script that creates the OEM_REPOSITORY tablespace.

## Validating: Some Simple Postcreation Database Tests

Once a database and an instance are created, you can run a few simple tests to check its components. To check that you are in the correct instance before you run these tests, query V$INSTANCE through SQL*Plus logged in as the SYSTEM user:

```
SELECT *
  FROM v$instance;
```

This query will return the instance name, the host name, and the version of the Oracle engine installed, as well as other information. Now log in to SQL*Plus as SYSTEM and check that all tablespaces are online:

```
SELECT tablespace_name, status
  FROM dba_tablespaces;
```

This will return a status of "ONLINE" for each tablespace created, if the creation process was successful:

```
TABLESPACE_NAME                      STATUS
------------------------------------ ----------
SYSTEM                               ONLINE
RBS                                  ONLINE
USERS                                ONLINE
TEMP                                 ONLINE
INDX                                 ONLINE
OEM_REPOSITORY                       ONLINE
```

If a tablespace is missing or marked "OFFLINE," check the database creation logs, which should always be generated whether the database is created manually or automatically. In the automatic case, the log or logs will be found in the ORACLE_BASE/admin/<SID>/create subdirectory. A tablespace can be brought online with

```
ALTER TABLESPACE <tablespace_name> ONLINE;
```

Some of the tablespace creation scripts may need to be checked for typos and syntax and then rerun.

Log in to a SQL*Plus session as SYSTEM and check that the rollback segments are "ONLINE."

```
COLUMN segment_name FORMAT a16
COLUMN tablespace_name FORMAT a16
SELECT segment_name, tablespace_name, status
  FROM dba_rollback_segs;
```

The output from this query will show the status of the rollback segments:

```
SEGMENT_NAME      TABLESPACE_NAME   STATUS
----------------  ----------------  ----------------
SYSTEM            SYSTEM            ONLINE
SYSROL            SYSTEM            OFFLINE
RB0               RBS               ONLINE
RB1               RBS               ONLINE
```

The rollback segment Sysrol is "OFFLINE." To bring it online, issue an ALTER ROLLBACK statement:

```
ALTER ROLLBACK SEGMENT sysrol ONLINE;
```

Again log in to a SQL*Plus session as SYSTEM and check for any database objects marked "INVALID." Database objects include all Oracle8i database engine packages, such as PL/SQL and Import/Export utilities, as well as all other database objects: tables, views, indexes, sequences, Java classes, and so on.

```
SELECT object_name, object_type, status
  FROM dba_objects
 WHERE status = 'INVALID';
```

"No rows selected" is the anticipated response. If some objects are marked "INVALID," check the database logs as before. The catalog.sql, catexp7.sql, catproc.sql, or caths.sql under ORACLE_HOME/rdbms/admin may have to be run again in that order. If a Java class or Java resource is marked "INVALID," rerun initjvm.sql found under ORACLE_HOME/javavm/install. All of these scripts can be

**Validating: Some Simple Postcreation DB Tests**

run through Oracle Server Manager, svrmgrl; connect as INTERNAL or as SYS AS SYSDBA.

To further check the PL/SQL package installation, log in as any user to SQL*Plus and type the following lines, entering a return after each:

```
BEGIN
  NULL;
END;
```

"PL/SQL procedure successfully completed" is the expected result. If the errors occur and the syntax of this test was entered correctly, then rerunning catproc.sql should solve the problem by rebuilding the Oracle PL/SQL procedural option. The script catproc.sql can be found under ORACLE_HOME/rdbms/admin and is run as SYS AS SYSDBA through svrmgrl.

Finally, you can query V$OPTION as SYSTEM to view all options that have been installed:

```
SELECT *
  FROM v$option
 WHERE parameter = 'Java';
```

This query will return a value field with the value of 'TRUE,' if the JVM option has been installed. All options can be viewed by removing the where clause.

# Rollback Segments

Rollback segments, the database structures that are used for holding undo information and to support read consistency acquired some interesting characteristics in Oracle8i. These lead to differences in the way they are managed and acquired. These are especially important to be aware of when performing a migration from an earlier

## Connecting as INTERNAL

Oracle states that with Oracle8.2 connecting as INTERNAL will no longer be supported. Instead, those users that need to perform tasks done in the past with INTERNAL should now use SYSDBA. SYSDBA is a set of privileges that can be granted as a role to any users so they can connect to an instance as SYS using their own password. Thus, when granted SYSDBA, user PATDBA could issue at the Server Manager prompt *CONNECT PATDBA AS SYSDBA*; he or she would then be prompted for his or her password. Alternatively, a DBA could issue *CONNECT SYS AS SYSDBA* and be prompted for the SYS user's password.

version of Oracle, when creating a database without the use of the Oracle Database Configuration Assistant and when defining values for init.ora parameters.

## Creating an Additional Rollback Segment in the System Tablespace

With Oracle8i, Oracle is recommending that an additional rollback segment be created in the System tablespace. The Starter Database created on install or with the Oracle Database Configuration Assistant will do this automatically, but the additional segment may need to be brought online. The reason for the additional rollback segment lies in how Oracle acquires rollback segments for user transactions that are either modifying data with update and delete DML statements or issuing DDL statements against the database. An instance on startup will acquire the system rollback segment and use it for system transactions. Nonsystem-rollback segments outside of the System tablespace will also be acquired, if they exist, according to the rule CEIL(TRANSACTIONS/TRANSACTIONS_PER_ROLLBACK_SEGMENT), where CEIL is the SQL function that returns the smallest integer greater than or equal to the value in parentheses. The init.ora parameter TRANSACTIONS is an estimate of the maximum number of concurrent transactions for the instance, and TRANSACTIONS_PER_ROLLBACK_SEGMENT is the number of concurrent transactions allowed per rollback segment; they default to 66 and 5, respectively. In the default configuration, on instance startup, Oracle will attempt to acquire 14 nonsystem rollback segments. If they do not all exist, the instance will start up without error.

**CAUTION**
*New with Oracle8i, and different from previous releases of the Oracle database server, on instance startup the database will attempt to acquire the number of user rollback segments as just calculated. These rollback segments do not need to be listed in the init.ora parameter ROLLBACK_SEGMENTS. To start up the instance having more rollback segments online than the number calculated, you must list the segment names in the ROLLBACK_SEGMENTS parameter.*

The nonsystem rollback segments will be used for user transactions, unless the user transactions overflow the space available for nonsystem rollback segments. Then Oracle will allocate the overflow to the system rollback segment. Adding the extra rollback segment to the System tablespace will make space available in the event of nonsystem overflow. The following statement will create the rollback segment sysrol in the System tablespace; 'sysrol' is the default name for the extra system rollback segment created with the Starter Database:

```
CREATE ROLLBACK SEGMENT sysrol
  TABLESPACE system
  STORAGE (INITIAL 128K NEXT 128K);
```

To bring the new rollback segment online, immediately issue an ALTER ROLLBACK statement:

```
ALTER ROLLBACK SEGMENT sysrol ONLINE;
```

If the initial and next extents are not multiples of the data block size of the operating system, then both will be rounded up to exact multiples.

**NOTE**
*Better use and reuse of disk space is possible, if all objects created in a database are exact multiples of the data block size of the operating system. Ask your system administrator for the block size information.*

To have the new rollback segment come online automatically when the instance is restarted, modify the init.ora file of the instance adding or modifying the parameter ROLLBACK_SEGMENTS. For example, add or modify

```
rollback_segments = (sysrol, rb0, rb1, rb2, rb3, rb4, rb5, rb7)
```

to reflect the new sysrol system rollback segment. The additional system rollback segment must be listed in the ROLLBACK_SEGMENTS parameter for it to come online at startup. Only user rollback segments are included in the set of rollback segments that Oracle8i will bring online automatically.

When implementing an extra system rollback segment, make sure there is adequate disk space on the disk(s) that holds the System tablespace, and set the database file holding the System tablespace to autoextend. Use an ALTER DATABASE statement to set autoextend on:

```
ALTER DATABASE DATAFILE 'file specification' AUTOEXTEND ON;
```

The file specification is placed in single quotes and gives the full path and system database filename—on NT, for example, 'F:\ORACLE\ORADATA\ACCT_DEV\ SYSTEM01.DBF', where acct_dev is the database SID.

## Determining the Number of Oracle8i User Rollback Segments

Oracle8i has significantly changed the way in which the number of user rollback segments is estimated. On startup, an instance will acquire the system rollback segment and use it for system transactions. User or nonsystem rollback segments outside of the System tablespace will also be acquired, if they exist, according to the rule CEIL(TRANSACTIONS/TRANSACTIONS_PER_ROLLBACK_SEGMENT), where

CEIL is a SQL function that returns the smallest integer greater than or equal to the value in parentheses. The init.ora parameter TRANSACTIONS is an estimate of the maximum number of concurrent transactions for the instance, and TRANSACTIONS_ PER_ROLLBACK_SEGMENT is the number of concurrent transactions allowed per rollback segment; they default to 66 and 5, respectively. In the default configuration, Oracle will attempt to acquire 14 nonsystem rollback segments. If they do not all exist, the instance will start up without error. On the face of it, the implication is that, with Oracle8i, Oracle is recommending the creation of 14 user rollback segments in the RBS (rollback segment) tablespace. In Oracle7.3.4, the default values for TRANSACTIONS and TRANSACTIONS_PER_ROLLBACK_SEGMENT are 66 and 30, respectively, implying that three user rollback segments are created.

**NOTE**

*Even more rollback segments can be acquired at instance startup than calculated here. Those rollback segments listed in the init.ora parameter ROLLBACK_SEGMENTS will also be acquired. For ease of management, you should list all rollback segments except the initial system rollback segment in the init.ora parameter ROLLBACK_SEGMENTS. New with Oracle8i, and different from previous releases of the Oracle database server, on instance startup the database will attempt to acquire the number of user rollback segments as calculated earlier. These rollback segments do not need to be listed in the init.ora parameter ROLLBACK_SEGMENTS. If the number of rollback segments exceeds the calculation, then to have them online at instance startup they must be listed in the ROLLBACK_SEGMENTS parameter.*

Digging a little deeper, you see that the value of TRANSACTIONS is derived from the value of another init.ora parameter SESSIONS, which in turn is derived from the value of yet another init.ora parameter, PROCESSES.

Look at the last parameter first. The maximum number of operating system Oracle user processes plus the Oracle background processes constitute the value of PROCESSES. User processes span server processes when a user connects to Oracle. If it is a dedicated connection, the relationship is one-to-one; if it is a multithreaded connection, user processes share server processes. It is the server processes spanned by user connections that are included in PROCESSES, since it is the server processes that interact with the database instance and generate rollback activity. PROCESSES also include background processes, such as PMON and SMON, as well as Parallel

Server inter-instance locking processes, Job Queue processes, and Parallel Query or Parallel Execution server processes.

A user session is defined as a user connection to an instance via a user process. The value of SESSIONS is the total number of user and system sessions and is calculated as ((1.1 * PROCESSES) + 5). The value of SESSIONS is higher than PROCESSES to allow for recursive sessions. Finally, TRANSACTIONS, the estimated maximum number of concurrent transactions for the instance, is calculated as (1.1 * SESSIONS), and it is higher than SESSIONS to allow for recursive transactions.

For example, if the number of PROCESSES equals 50, the default value for the Starter Database, then the value of SESSIONS equals 60 and the value of TRANSACTIONS equals 66. The number of rollback segments to create is 14, using CEIL(TRANSACTIONS/TRANSACTIONS_PER_ROLLBACK_SEGMENT), where TRANSACTIONS_PER_ROLLBACK_SEGMENT equals 5, the value recommended by Oracle for Oracle8i.

> **NOTE**
> *Since the init.ora parameters SESSIONS and TRANSACTIONS are both ultimately derived from the number of PROCESSES, when the number of PROCESSES in the init.ora file is modified, both these parameters should also be modified, if they are explicitly set in the init.ora file. If they are not explicitly set, they will automatically be adjusted when the number of PROCESSES is changed. SESSIONS equals ((1.1 * PROCESSES) + 5) and TRANSACTIONS equals (1.1 * SESSIONS). In general, these parameters should be synchronized. ENQUEUE_RESOURCES and DML_LOCKS may also need to be changed, depending on your configuration. If the Parallel Server option also is in use, then LM_PROCS may also need modification—see the Oracle8i Reference Manual.*

It is the estimate of the number of processes that will determine the number of rollback segments created. The number of processes depends on several factors. One is the number of users concurrently connected and whether they use the multithreaded server option (MTS), which lowers the number of processes. Another is whether Parallel Execution is enabled, which will raise the number of processes as parallelism spans "helper" server processes. If the Parallel Server option is used, it will raise the number of processes. If Job Queuing is used, it will raise the number of processes.

Lock contention or transactions waiting for rollback segments will have to be monitored to judge the adequacy of the number of rollback segments. Three V$ views are useful to this end—V$WAITSTAT, V$ROLLNAME, and V$ROLLSTAT:

```
SELECT class, count
  FROM v$waitstat
 WHERE class IN ('undo header', 'undo block');

CLASS                          COUNT
------------------  ---------
undo header                        0
undo block                         0
```

In this query, a count greater than zero implies transactions are waiting owing to rollback segment contention. A value close to zero is desired for optimum performance. Add user rollback segments to reduce the count if required. Zero waits are ideal, as are hit ratios of 100 percent in the following query:

```
COLUMN NAME FORMAT a10
SELECT name, gets, waits,
       ((gets-waits)*100)/gets "HIT RATIO",
       xacts "ACTIVE TRANSACTIONS"
  FROM v$rollstat a, v$rollname b
 WHERE a.usn = b.usn;
```

| NAME | GETS | WAITS | HIT RATIO | ACTIVE TRANSACTIONS |
|------|------|-------|-----------|---------------------|
| SYSTEM | 40 | 0 | 100 | 0 |
| SYSROL | 24 | 0 | 100 | 0 |
| RB0 | 22 | 0 | 100 | 0 |
| RB1 | 63 | 0 | 100 | 0 |

When any user rollback segment (not the system rollback segments System or Sysrol in the example) shows waits greater than zero, add one user rollback segment. Follow this up with further monitoring. The exception to this zero waits rule is when the DBA must factor in the influence of long-running update transactions, such as overnight batch updates. Perfect performance may not be an issue with such "exceptional" events in a database tuned for relatively small OLTP transactions. A large rollback segment can be created and specified for large batch transactions, using the SET TRANSACTION USE ROLLBACK SEGMENT <segment_name> command.

**Determine the Number of User Rollback Segments**

# The Java Virtual Machine

Introduced in Oracle8i, the embedded Java Virtual Machine is a key server component for the support of Java stored procedures and CORBA/EJB objects.

## Installing the Java Virtual Machine

After an upgrade or a migration of a pre-Oracle8i database or after the creation of an Oracle8i database without the Java Virtual Machine (JVM) option, the JVM can be installed. The JVM option is also referred to as the JServer option. Installing the JVM prepares the database for handling and running Java stored procedures, JDBC, SQLJ, and CORBA/EJB objects. It is easier and less demanding of system resources if the JVM is installed when the database is initially created. For a manual install, the init.ora parameters SHARED_POOL_SIZE and JAVA_POOL_SIZE must be adjusted, an adequate number of rollback segments must be available, and sufficient space must be available in the System tablespace for the 4015 Java objects that are installed with release 8.1.5. The install script loads a set of Java classes required to support Java and initializes some instance tables for CORBA usage. In addition, for CORBA/EJB use, the Multithreaded Server (MTS) option must be enabled. The MTS option is covered in the Tip "Enabling the Multithreaded Server Option."

To check if the JVM has been installed into an existing database, run the following query:

```
SELECT COUNT(*)
  FROM dba_objects
 WHERE object_type LIKE '%JAVA%';
```

A count of zero implies that the JVM is not installed. If you establish that the JVM is not installed, take the following steps to install it:

1. Modify the init.ora file of the database into which the JVM is to be installed by increasing the SHARED_POOL_SIZE to 50M and adding a JAVA_POOL_SIZE parameter equal to 20M:

   ```
   shared_pool_size = 52428800 # for jserver install
   java_shared_pool = 20971520 # for jserver install
   ```

2. Installing the JVM will require about 17M of rollback segments. Two methods are available to ensure the Rbs tablespace is prepared for these segments. You can set the operating system file that contains the Rbs tablespace to autoextend. Or you can create additional rollback segments in the Rbs tablespace. Both methods can be combined, creating additional rollback segments while setting the operating system file to autoextend. If new rollback segments are created, update the init.ora parameter ROLLBACK_SEGMENTS

to add the new segment names. Use some combination of the following ALTER DATABASE and CREATE ROLLBACK SEGMENT commands. The file specification is in the form of ORACLE_BASE/oradata/SID/filename—for example, on UNIX it is /oracle/oradata/acct_dev/rbs01.dbf and on NT it is F:\ORACLE\ORADATA\ACCT_DEV\RBS01.DBF, where the SID is acct_dev and the rollback segment operating system file is rbs01.dbf. Segment name is in the form of RBx, where x is the next number from the existing rollback segment list. Set the INITIAL and NEXT size storage clause to conform with the existing rollback segments, and query DBA_ROLLBACK_SEGS for details on sizing.

```
ALTER DATABASE DATAFILE 'file specification' AUTOEXTEND ON;
CREATE PUBLIC ROLLBACK SEGMENT <segment name> TABLESPACE RBS
   STORAGE (INITIAL 128K NEXT 256K)
```

3. Running the JVM install scripts loads Java objects into the System tablespace. With release 8.1.5, there are 4015 Java objects installed. To ensure that there is adequate room in the System tablespace, be sure to set the datafile holding the System tablespace to autoextend. Datafiles that are AUTOEXTENSIBLE have a value of YES in this column in the DBA_DATA_FILES view. Check the available disk space for the datafile holding the System tablespace at the operating system level. On NT, for example, the following will set the data filesystem 01.dbf to autoextend; on UNIX, change the file specification to /oracle/oradata/acct_dev/system01.dbf, continuing the example from Step 2.

```
ALTER DATABASE DATAFILE
'F:\ORACLE\ORADATA\ACCT_DEV\SYSTEM01.DBF'
   AUTOEXTEND ON;
```

4. Set the ORACLE_SID to the SID of the database into which the install will occur. For example, in the UNIX Korn shell, set the ORACLE_SID in the .profile of the Oracle8i executable owner and reinitialize the Oracle owner's environment. On NT as the administrator and at the MSDOS prompt type, *set* ORACLE_SID=<SID>. To check that the SID is set, you can enter *env* on UNIX or *set* on NT.

5. Invoke Server Manager and bounce the database to capture the changes made.

6. The script that installs the JVM is called initjvm.sql and can be found in ORACLE_HOME/javavm/install. While connected to Server Manager, as in Step 5, start a spool file to log the installation. Spool the log to ORACLE_BASE/admin/ORACLE_SID/create/jvminst.log as a Starter Database would. After you spool the log file, run the install script.

Installing the Java Virtual Machine

Depending on the system resources, the installation may take 10 to 20 minutes. The installation loads Java classes and builds public synonyms on them to allow user access. If the install succeeded, the Java objects created in the System tablespace will have a status of 'VALID.' This can be verified by running the following query to check for invalid objects:

```
SELECT object_name, status, object_type
  FROM dba_objects
 WHERE object_type LIKE '%JAVA%' AND status = 'INVALID';
```

The install log created in Step 6 can also be checked for any unusual Oracle error messages. In the install log, the ORA- errors generated by the SQL DROP commands can be ignored, such as ORA-00942, ORA-01432, ORA-01918, ORA-01919, or ORA-02289. If errors are detected, check that each previous step was completed, particularly that the SHARED_POOL_SIZE and the JAVA_POOL_SIZE were set correctly and adequate space was available for System tablespace and rollback tablespace growth. If RAM or CPU system resources are a problem, try shutting down other Oracle instances on the server. The JVM install has been successfully completed on a minimal NT Workstation with 64M of RAM and a 166 MHz processor. Here the trick was to shut down other instances and expand the NT virtual paging space to 200M.

After installation is completed, the SHARED_POOL_SIZE init.ora parameter can be adjusted. The Tip "Tuning the Java Virtual Machine: the Shared Pool and the Java Pool" covers the SHARED_POOL_SIZE and other init.ora parameters relevant to JVM tuning.

## Tuning the Java Virtual Machine: the Shared Pool and the Java Pool

Two parts of the Shared Global Area (SGA) are the Shared Pool and, with Oracle8i, the Java Pool. The other components of the SGA are the database buffer cache, the redo buffer cache, and the Large Pool. The Shared Pool—sized by the SHARED_POOL_SIZE—is used by the JVM for nonsession-specific Java code and data. It is used when the loadjava utility loads Java classes and jars, but loadjava does not hold Shared Pool memory resources caching the classes; the Shared Pool is used "transiently." Up to 50M of Shared Pool may be needed when particularly large Java classes (jars) are loaded and resolved during development and application implementation. The Shared Pool also requires roughly 8K per loaded class at run time as Java call specifications are created and for dynamically tracking used Java classes. In a Java development environment, a Shared Pool of 50M is recommended by Oracle. The estimate may need adjustment depending on the amount of Java development taking place and the concurrent use of SQL and PL/SQL. Further adjustment will be necessary if the multithreaded server (MTS) is implemented either for use with CORBA and EBJs or with Java stored procedures, SQL, and PL/SQL, as described in the following Tip, "Enabling the Multithreaded Server Option," and the boxed text accompanying this Tip. In a small production system, 15M may be enough, whereas in a large system, 60M or more may be needed.

To view the current size and memory usage of the Shared Pool, the V$PARAMETER and V$SGASTAT dynamic views can be queried:

```
COLUMN name FORMAT A20
COLUMN value_bytes FORMAT A20
SELECT name, TO_CHAR(bytes) value_bytes
  FROM v$sgastat
 WHERE pool ='shared pool'
   AND name = 'free memory'
 UNION
SELECT name, value
  FROM v$parameter
 WHERE name = 'shared_pool_size';
```

This query will return the 'free memory' currently available out of the allocated 'shared pool size' set by the similarly named init.ora parameter.

The Java Pool portion of the SGA is used by the JVM to hold session-specific Java code and data. If the instance is running in MTS mode, the SGA holds User

## MTS, GIOP, and TTC

With dedicated server processing, each user process connecting to a database instance is assigned a server process for his or her exclusive use. The multithreaded server (MTS) architecture allows a small number of server processes to handle a larger number of user processes, reducing system resource usage.

To implement CORBA and EJB applications, MTS is required, using the General Inter-ORB Protocol (GIOP). The Internet Inter-ORB Protocol (IIOP) is how Oracle has implemented GIOP over the TCP/IP protocol. When used for Java stored procedures, SQL, and PL/SQL, a MTS implementation uses a Two-Task Common (TTC) layer, not GIOP. The management of character set, format, and data type conversions is performed by TTC in a client/server environment, while GIOP must be used for CORBA and EJB applications.

The Shared Pool
and the Java Pool

Global Areas (UGAs). UGAs hold session information and are created with each session. MTS mode is required for the use of CORBA/EJB applications and can be used with Java stored procedures, SQL, and PL/SQL. In MTS mode, the UGAs are split, allocated in part to the Shared Pool and in part to the Java Pool.

**NOTE**

*To add a complication, if the LARGE_POOL_SIZE init.ora parameter is set, then that portion of the UGA allocated to the Shared Pool will instead be allocated to the Large Pool, relieving the Shared Pool of its UGA tasks. See the following Tip, "Setting the LARGE_POOL_SIZE and SHARED_POOL_SIZE with the Multithreaded Server."*

The portion of the UGA allocated to the Java Pool holds session state information for each Java session. The read-only portions of currently used Java classes that are shared across sessions are also held in the Java Pool but not in its Java session-specific UGAs.

**CAUTION**

*In release 8.1.5 of Oracle8i, the command SHOW SGA reports on the Total System Global Area. The figure presented does not include the Java Pool. Similarly, the Variable Size reported from SHOW SGA and SELECT * FROM v$sga does not include the Java Pool. Oracle anticipates that these figures will be corrected with release 8.1.6.*

If the instance is running in dedicated server mode, life is simpler. The UGAs are not in the SGA but are part of the Program Global Areas (PGAs) created for each dedicated server process. The read-only portions of currently used Java classes that are shared across sessions are still held in the Java Pool. The session state information for each Java session held in UGAs is now created in the PGAs. The PGA is variable in size, changing with the requests generated by server and user processes.

The init.ora parameter JAVA_POOL_SIZE determines the size of the Java buffer pool. Unlike the influence of Java on the size of the Shared Pool, which is relatively static, the Java Pool is dynamic. The read-only portions of currently used Java classes that are shared across sessions and held in the Java Pool are roughly 4K to 8K each. The read-only portions are held in the Java Pool whether MTS or dedicated server mode is used. The read-only portions are user-shared Java method and class definitions. The Java Pool also holds the individual nonshared JVM of each concurrent session, requiring roughly 40K per session. With CORBA and EJBs requiring MTS or Java stored procedures using MTS, the Java Pool holds additional concurrent session-specific nonshared Java objects in its UGAs. CORBA and EJB applications require the most memory resources at run time; roughly 200K will be used for each concurrent session.

The Java buffer pool is used during run-time Java execution and at compile-time, if the Java objects are compiled on the server. Except for EJB code, developers can compile Java code on their client machines and reduce the JAVA_POOL_SIZE allocation on the server. EJB application deployment requires server compilation. The default value for the JAVA_POOL_SIZE is 20M. 20M is the suggested size of the Java buffer for a development environment, but it may need to be increased, especially when CORBA and EJBs are implemented. Oracle posits that very large multiuser Java applications may require more than a gigabyte of memory allocated to the Java Pool.

**NOTE**
*The Oracle8i Reference Manual states that the JAVA_POOL_SIZE has a default value of 10M. However, if this init.ora parameter is not set explicitly, querying its value from the V$PARAMETER view returns a value of 20M. The readme.txt for the JVM found under ORACLE_HOME/javavm/doc correctly states the default is 20M—reminding us to follow Oracle's advice and read the Release Notes and Readme texts.*

With release 8.1.5 of Oracle8i, there is no way to monitor the current usage of the Java Pool in an instance. One would expect to see a column for 'java pool' in the V$SGASTAT view, along with the current values of 'shared pool' and 'large pool.' According to Oracle, release 8.1.6 of Oracle8i will fix this oversight. In release 8.1.6, the query

```
SELECT pool, name, bytes
  FROM v$sgastat
 WHERE pool = 'java pool';
```

will return under the name column the values of 'free memory' and 'memory in use,' and the bytes column will aid in correctly sizing the Java Pool.

**The Shared Pool and the Java Pool**

**CAUTION**
*Without reinstallation of the Oracle8i executables, the JAVA_POOL_SIZE has a minimum value of 1 million bytes regardless of whether the JVM has been installed into an instance. Setting its value below 1 million bytes results in an "ORA-01078: failure in processing system parameters" message on attempted instance startup. The instance startup will fail. Reinstalling the Oracle8i server executables during a custom installation that does not choose the JServer option will allow the JAVA_POOL_SIZE to be set to zero. This also requires that in the init.ora file of each instance the GIOP or SGIOP MTS_DISPATCHERS must be removed and in the listener.ora file the GIOP or SGIOP listeners must be removed. MTS, GIOP, and SGIOP are discussed in the next Tip, "Enabling the Multithreaded Server Option."*

Indications of a shortage of space for the Java Pool are given by two messages. An *ORA-04031: unable to allocate bytes of shared memory* is generated during compilation with the loadjava or deployejb utilities. The message text includes reference to the Shared Pool, but it is the JAVA_POOL_SIZE that should be increased. An ORA-00600 error with 26599 as the first argument will be raised during export of Java components, if there is not sufficient memory allocated to the Java Pool.

Oracle8i and the JVM introduce two other init.ora parameters: JAVA_SOFT_SESSIONSPACE_LIMIT with a default value of 1M and JAVA_MAX_SESSIONSPACE_SIZE with a default value of 4G. If a user's session exceeds the size of JAVA_SOFT_SESSIONSPACE_LIMIT, a warning is written to a trace file (.trc file) and the DBA is allowed to monitor excessive session usage. Setting this parameter to a very low value allows a Java application to be monitored and evaluated for initial JAVA_POOL_SIZE sizing. To avoid this overhead in production, set its value back to the default or higher. JAVA_MAX_SESSIONSPACE_SIZE places a hard limit on memory usage for a session, killing a user's session that exceeds this limit. It can guard against runaway sessions. Its default value is set extremely high, making it effectively unlimited. Its actual value will depend on the application deployed and memory resources available.

# The Multithreaded Server

With dedicated server processing, each user process connecting to a database instance is assigned an exclusive-use server process. The assigned server process remains idle when the user is not submitting requests to the database, but the server process holds memory and requires process management. The multithreaded server (MTS) architecture allows a small number of shared server processes to handle the same number of user processes, reducing system resource usage. One server process can be shared by many user processes.

**NOTE**
*On NT, the user processes and the server processes are not separate processes but actually separate threads. On UNIX, they are separate processes.*

## Enabling the Multithreaded Server Option

To implement CORBA and EJB applications, you will need MTS using the General Inter-ORB Protocol (GIOP). The Internet Inter-ORB Protocol (IIOP) is an implementation of GIOP, using TCP/IP as the transport layer; IIOP is how Oracle has implemented GIOP. GIOP is also known as a presentation layer, managing character set, format, and data type conversions between different sources and destinations. Java stored procedures, SQL, and PL/SQL can use either MTS or a dedicated server configuration. When used for Java stored procedures, SQL, and PL/SQL, MTS is implemented, using a Two-Task Common (TTC) presentation layer, not GIOP. TTC manages character set, format, and data type conversions between clients and servers and is the default presentation layer for Net8.

To implement MTS, the global database name must be specified in the listener.ora file. In each SID_DESC section of the SID_LIST_LISTENER portion of the listener.ora, the GLOBAL_DBNAME parameter must be set for the multithreaded server (MTS) option to work. Without it, clients will connect via dedicated servers. This is new to the configuration of Oracle8i and differs from both Oracle7.*x* and Oracle8.0.*x*. The relevant part of a listener.ora file is shown in the following listing; this file was taken from a NT instance.

```
SID_LIST_LISTENER =
  (SID_LIST =
    (SID_DESC =
       (GLOBAL_DBNAME = or8i.testnt)
       (ORACLE_HOME = F:\Oracle\ORA81)
       (SID_NAME = OR8I)
    )
  )
```

A global database name is in the form of DB_NAME.DB_DOMAIN. The DB_NAME does not have to be the same as the SID. The DB_DOMAIN here is the server name and is often something like BigBlahBlah.com. In the listener.ora text, it is testnt. Both DB_NAME and DB_DOMAIN are init.ora parameters.

In the case of the GIOP implementation of MTS for CORBA and EJBs, it is also necessary to further modify the listener.ora file. This will be addressed when you consider the forthcoming GIOP case. You will see the TTC and GIOP cases separately, and then you will be presented with several scenarios showing combinations of dedicated server and MTS implementations.

### Two-Task Common MTS Implementation

Four init.ora parameters are used to configure a MTS implementation: MTS_DISPATCHERS, MTS_MAX_DISPATCHERS with a default value of 5, MTS_SERVERS with a default value of 1, and MTS_MAX_SERVERS with a default value of 20. Accepting the default values for the last three, MTS can be implemented for TTC by adding the MTS_DISPATCHERS parameter to the init.ora file and bouncing the database engine.

```
mts_dispatchers = "(protocol=TCP)(DISP=1)"
```

The defaults for the other three parameters can be made explicit by adding them:

```
mts_max_dispatchers = 5
mts_servers = 1
mts_max_servers = 20
```

The flag "DISP" in the MTS_DISPATCHERS string stands for dispatchers, and 1 is its default value. A ratio of one dispatcher for every 250 concurrent connections is recommended. The number of dispatchers does not increase dynamically at run time but can be modified with an ALTER SYSTEM command. For example, the following command increases the number of dispatchers to four:

```
ALTER SYSTEM SET MTS_DISPATCHERS = 'TCP, 4';
```

MTS_MAX_DISPATCHERS does need to be coordinated with the value of MTS_DISPATCHERS for the latter to be increased.

The number of shared server processes is dynamically altered at run time; thus, to conserve resources, MTS_SERVERS does not need to be set overly high when you are determining the number of shared server processes to spawn at instance startup. One shared server per ten concurrent connections is recommended. MTS_SERVERS can be changed dynamically by issuing an ALTER SYSTEM command. For example, the following command increases the number of shared servers to 100:

```
ALTER SYSTEM SET MTS_SERVERS = 100;
```

MTS_MAX_SERVERS sets a hard limit to the number of shared servers that may be dynamically started, and its value cannot be changed without shutting down the instance, altering its value in the init.ora file and issuing a startup command. Its default value is 20 and is suitable for an application with 200 concurrent user connections.

> **NOTE**
> *See the forthcoming section "Reducing Contention for MTS Dispatcher and Server Processes" for a further discussion on tuning the MTS_DISPATCHERS and MTS_MAX_SERVERS init.ora parameters.*

## CORBA and EJB MTS Implementation

For the required use of MTS with CORBA and EJBs, Oracle8i supplies a session-based IIOP/GIOP connectivity string used with a MTS_DISPATCHERS init.ora parameter. The session-based connection is the most scalable option utilizing the listener to load balance users' requests to dispatchers. The session-based method can handle 1,000-plus concurrent users. It requires that the listener through the listener.ora file be configured to handle session-based GIOP connections and that a MTS_DISPATCHERS parameter be added to the init.ora of the instance. The alternative is to have the user's sessions connect to the database instance through a dedicated port and directly to dispatcher processes, bypassing the listener. The dispatcher-based method is easier to configure but less scalable. Oracle recommends that the session-based method be used. The session-based method will be addressed here. For information on the alternative, see the *Net8 Administrator's Guide*.

Set the value of the instance's init.ora parameter MTS_DISPATCHERS to:

```
"(PROTOCOL=TCP)(DISP=4)(PRE=oracle.aurora.server.SGiopServer)"
```

The protocol must be TCP, 'PRE' stands for presentation layer, and 'aurora' in the presentation layer string is the name Oracle sometimes uses for the JVM. If a value for 'DISP' is not specified and the flag does not appear, it is implicitly set to one. If the dispatcher-based method were used, the PRE string would be oracle.aurora.server.GiopServer. The differences is the 'S' in 'Sgiop.' In the listener.ora file, found under ORACLE_HOME/network/admin, a new description must be added to the description list. The first DESCRIPTION in the following listing is the GIOP addition:

```
LISTENER =
  (DESCRIPTION_LIST =
    (DESCRIPTION =
      (PROTOCOL_STACK =
        (PRESENTATION = GIOP)
        (SESSION = RAW)
      )
```

```
        (ADDRESS = (PROTOCOL = TCP)(HOST = testnt)(PORT = 2481))
    )
    (DESCRIPTION =
        (ADDRESS_LIST =
            (ADDRESS = (protocol=tcp)(host=testnt)(port=1521))
            )
        )
    )
```

The fields in the GIOP description have the following meanings. Protocol_stack defines the presentation layer for a connection. Presentation defines the GIOP/IIOP standard that supports either oracle.aurora.server.SGiopServer or oracle.aurora.server.GiopServer using TCP/IP. Session defines the session layer, but for GIOP/IIOP clients there is no session layer, and a value of 'RAW' signifies this. Address specifies the protocol, host or server, and port on which the listener is listening. The port number for the GIOP protocol is a "well known" port number, meaning an Oracle8i standard port for GIOP session-based connectivity. Port number 2481 is the default and standard port number; if this port number cannot be used, see "Configuring a Non-Default Listener" in the *Net8 Administrator's Guide.*

The listener.ora will, of course, also contain a description for the TTC protocol to capture non-CORBA and non-EJB client connection requests. The TTC protocol is captured in the second description in the code sample just listed.

The configuration of the MTS_MAX_DISPATCHERS, the MTS_SERVERS, and the MTS_MAX_SERVERS is the same as that previously outlined in the "Two-Task Common MTS Implementation" section. As the following discussion shows, it is possible to have multiple MTS_DISPATCHERS parameters defined in an init.ora parameter file. This will occur if the MTS is being used for both TTC and CORBA/EJBs. The number of concurrent sessions from both sources must be considered when you are calculating the values of the MTS_MAX_DISPATCHERS, the MTS_SERVERS, and the MTS_MAX_SERVERS parameters.

**CAUTION**
*If multiple MTS_DISPATCHERS parameters are defined in the same init.ora file, they must immediately follow each other with no other parameters intervening, though comments set off with pound signs may intervene.*

## Multiple Connectivity Methods for an Instance

It is possible to combine connectivity methods in an instance. A dedicated server method could be used for Java stored procedures, SQL, and PL/SQL, while MTS is used for CORBA and EJBs. Alternatively, all connections could use MTS, and if the application requires both TTC and GIOP methods, they would have to be separately defined in the init.ora. To reiterate the cautionary note, if multiple MTS_DISPATCHERS parameters are defined in the init.ora of an instance, then they must immediately follow each other, with no other parameters intervening, though comments set off with pound signs may intervene.

If the combination is dedicated server processing for Java stored procedures, SQL, and PL/SQL and MTS for CORBA and EJBs, then only the GIOP MTS_DISPATCHERS needs to be defined in the init.ora file, since dedicated server processing is the default behavior for client connectivity with Oracle8i. Only one MTS_DISPACHERS is needed, the value of which is:

```
= "(PROTOCOL=TCP)(DISP=1)(PRE=oracle.aurora.server.SGiopServer)"
```

Because this is the GIOP protocol, the listener.ora file needs to be modified, as was outlined in the previous subsection. If the combination is MTS for both TTC and GIOP, then two MTS_DISPATCHERS parameters must appear in the init.ora file of the instance. The additional MTS_DISPATCHERS parameter is:

```
mts_dispatchers = "(protocol=TCP)(DISP=2)"
```

Again, use of the GIOP protocol requires modification of the listener.ora file.

### Viewing the Configuration

When modifications are made to both the listener and the init.ora parameters, the listener must be restarted and the instance bounced. The commands lsnrctl stop and lsnrctl start will restart the listener, and Server Manager can be used to bounce the instance. The status of the listener, whether started or not, can be viewed with the command lsnrctl status, and the number of dedicated servers and MTS dispatchers started can be viewed with lsnrctl services LISTENER, where LISTENER is the default listener name. For example, this LSNRCTL for 32-bit Windows:

```
Version 8.1.5.0.0 - Production on 18-MAY-99 10:59:36
(c) Copyright 1998 Oracle Corporation.  All rights reserved.
Services Summary...
ORA81        has 6 service handler(s)
   DEDICATED SERVER established:0 refused:0
     LOCAL SERVER
   DEDICATED SERVER established:0 refused:0
     LOCAL SERVER
   DISPATCHER established:0 refused:0 current:0 max:254 state:ready
```

```
   D000 <machine: TESTNT, pid: 187>
   (ADDRESS=(PROTOCOL=tcp)(HOST=testnt)(PORT=1037))
   Presentation: oracle.aurora.server.SgiopServer
 DISPATCHER established:0 refused:0 current:0 max:254 state:ready
   D001 <machine: TESTNT, pid: 201>
   (ADDRESS=(PROTOCOL=tcp)(HOST=testnt)(PORT=1038))
   Presentation: oracle.aurora.server.SgiopServer
 DISPATCHER established:0 refused:0 current:0 max:254 state:ready
   D002 <machine: TESTNT, pid: 205>
   (ADDRESS=(PROTOCOL=tcp)(HOST=testnt)(PORT=1039))
 DISPATCHER established:0 refused:0 current:0 max:254 state:ready
   D003 <machine: TESTNT, pid: 86>
   (ADDRESS=(PROTOCOL=tcp)(HOST=testnt)(PORT=1040))
The command completed successfully
```

The listing shows four MTS dispatchers, with two for GIOP—D000 and D001—and two for TTC—D002 and D003. The MTS dispatchers are distinguishable by the Presentation line included with them: Presentation: oracle.aurora.server.SgiopServer. Aurora is another name used for the JVM. Behind the listing are settings of DISP=2 in the MTS_DISPATCHERS strings for GIOP and TTC. Two dedicated servers have also been started by default.

## Setting the LARGE_POOL_SIZE and SHARED_POOL_SIZE with the Multithreaded Server

The Shared Pool and the Large Pool memory buffers are both part of the System Global Area (SGA). When the MTS is used, within the Shared Pool there are two areas holding shared and private SQL representations; in addition, the Shared Pool holds information tracking user processes, dispatchers, and servers. The shared SQL areas and the tracking information are able to be shared across user sessions. With MTS, the private SQL area or the User Global Area (UGA) of the Shared Pool holds session data, including bind variable information, run-time buffers, and PL/SQL session-specific variables. This session information is also referred to as user state information. Without the use of the MTS, and with a dedicated server configuration, this session information would be held in UGA structures within the Program Global Area (PGA). The total amount of SGA memory increases with MTS, but compared to dedicated server mode, total memory usage falls, since there are fewer server processes and less PGA.

Oracle8 introduced the LARGE_POOL_SIZE as an optional init.ora parameter and memory area. Setting the Large Pool buffer allows session memory for UGA structures that would otherwise be allocated to the Shared Pool in MTS mode, to be allocated to the Large Pool. In this manner, the Shared Pool is not reduced by the private UGA structures with MTS, and the allocated memory is available to hold shared SQL representations available across sessions.

The next two queries help size the large buffer pool. They should be run at peak usage and return the current total usage and maximum total usage of the SGA for the private SQL area or the UGA structures.

```
SELECT SUM(value)
  FROM v$sesstat a, v$statname b
 WHERE a.statistic# = b.statistic#
   AND name ='session uga memory';
```

```
SELECT SUM(value)
  FROM v$sesstat a, v$statname b
 WHERE a.statistic# = b.statistic#
   AND name ='session uga memory max';
```

The value returned is in bytes. The second may be a better estimate of the space to be allocated to the parameter LARGE_POOL_SIZE; even then, it's advisable to pad it by an extra 25 percent. Oracle recommends 5K per concurrent user connecting via MTS. The LARGE_POOL_SIZE is an optional parameter and an optional memory allocation in the SGA, but if it is set, it will be used for session memory. If not enough space is allocated, then an *ORA-04031: unable to allocate <xxx> bytes of shared memory* error message will be generated. There is no aging mechanism to ageout session memory for active sessions. Even with the LARGE_POOL_SIZE parameter set, a small amount of memory will be allocated per session to the Shared Pool. This allocation is called the "fixed UGA" and may have an impact on the value of the SHARED_POOL_SIZE.

**CAUTION**
*As of Oracle8.1.3, the init.ora parameter LARGE_POOL_MIN_ALLOC has become obsolete. This parameter was a companion to the LARGE_POOL_SIZE parameter. On instance startup, an ORA-25138 warning will state that the parameter is obsolete, but the database will mount and open.*

An additional approach to aid sizing the current allocations to the Shared Pool and Large Pool buffers is to run the following two queries. They should be run in peak usage periods.

```
SELECT *
  FROM v$sgastat
 WHERE pool = 'large pool'
   AND name = 'free memory';
```

```
SELECT *
  FROM v$sgastat
```

Setting LARGE_POOL_SIZE and SHARED_POOL_SIZE

```
WHERE pool = 'shared pool'
  AND name = 'free memory';
```

These queries return the current free memory. The query results can be compared against the values for the LARGE_POOL_SIZE and SHARED_POOL_SIZE parameters of the instance to determine the accuracy of previous estimates.

**NOTE**

*If the database instance is running parallel query or parallel execution and the Oracle8i init.ora parameter PARALLEL_AUTOMATIC_TUNING is TRUE, then the database will automatically determine the LARGE_ POOL_SIZE to accommodate the parallel execution buffer pool and MTS buffers. The determination is based on the number of CPUs available and the value of the init.ora parameter PARALLEL_THREADS_ PER_CPU. If PARALLEL_AUTOMATIC_TUNING is FALSE and parallel query is in use, then the LARGE_POOL_SIZE will need increasing for the parallel execution buffer pool in addition to sizing for MTS use. Oracle recommends setting the PARALLEL_AUTOMATIC_TUNING parameter to TRUE, if parallel execution is in use, allowing automatic determination. Setting it to TRUE also allows Oracle to automatically determine the parameters PARALLEL_ADAPTIVE_MULTI_USER, PROCESSES, SESSIONS, PARALLEL_MAX_SERVERS, and PARALLEL_EXECUTION_MESSAGE_SIZE. See Chapter 26 of the Oracle8i Tuning Guide for further details.*

## Reducing Contention for MTS Dispatcher and Server Processes

Contention for either dispatcher or server processes will inhibit performance of a MTS implementation. Adjustments can be made to the init.ora parameters MTS_DISPATCHERS and MTS_MAX_SERVERS based on the busy or wait rates of sessions. For dispatchers, the busy rate for all types of dispatchers—TTC and GIOP—can be determined via the V$DISPATCHER dynamic performance view. At peak periods, the following query can be run:

```
SELECT SUBSTR(network,1,23) "Network",
       (SUM(busy)/(SUM(busy) + SUM(idle))) * 100 "% of Time Busy"
  FROM v$dispatcher
 GROUP BY SUBSTR(network,1,23);
```

The measurement is cumulative from instance startup. Prior to Oracle8, the SUBSTR() function was not necessary; removing the SUBSTR() function returns a row for each dispatcher. With a 50 percent or greater Time Busy rate, it is recommended that the number of dispatcher processes be increased by increasing the value of DISP in the MTS_DISPATCHERS init.ora parameter or by issuing an ALTER SYSTEM command. For example, the following command raises the number of TTC dispatchers to four:

```
ALTER SYSTEM SET MTS_DISPATCHERS = 'TCP, 4';
```

The wait time for all dispatcher processes in their queues can be determined through the V$QUEUE dynamic performance view in conjunction with the V$DISPATCHER view:

```
SELECT SUBSTR(network,1,23) "Network",
       DECODE(SUM(totalq), 0, 'No Responses',
       ROUND(SUM(wait)/SUM(totalq),2) || ' 100ths of secs')
       "Average Response Queue Wait"
  FROM v$queue a, v$dispatcher b
 WHERE a.type = 'DISPATCHER'
   AND a.paddr = b.paddr
 GROUP BY SUBSTR(network,1,23);
```

Again, the measurement is cumulative from instance startup, and the SUBSTR() function must be used to compute the sum for all dispatchers. An Average Response Queue Wait of one second should be adequate. If a faster response is required, you should raise the value of DISP in the MTS_DISPATCHERS init.ora parameter.

To differentiate between TTC and GIOP dispatchers, the dispatcher names must be determined and the previous two queries modified. To determine the dispatcher names, issue the command lsnrctl services LISTENER at the command prompt and view the Services Summary:

```
Services Summary...
ORA81     has 8 service handler(s)
   DEDICATED SERVER established:0 refused:0
     LOCAL SERVER
   DEDICATED SERVER established:0 refused:0
     LOCAL SERVER
   DISPATCHER established:1 refused:0 current:1 max:254 state:ready
     D003 <machine: TESTNT, pid: 217>
     (ADDRESS=(PROTOCOL=tcp)(HOST=testnt)(PORT=1036))
   DISPATCHER established:0 refused:0 current:0 max:254 state:ready
     D004 <machine: TESTNT, pid: 85>
     (ADDRESS=(PROTOCOL=tcp)(HOST=testnt)(PORT=1037))
   DISPATCHER established:0 refused:0 current:0 max:254 state:ready
     D005 <machine: TESTNT, pid: 213>
```

Reducing Contention for MTS Dispatcher/Server Processes

```
      (ADDRESS=(PROTOCOL=tcp)(HOST=testnt)(PORT=1038))
   DISPATCHER established:0 refused:0 current:0 max:254 state:ready
      D000 <machine: TESTNT, pid: 211>
      (ADDRESS=(PROTOCOL=tcp)(HOST=testnt)(PORT=1033))
      Presentation: oracle.aurora.server.SgiopServer
   DISPATCHER established:0 refused:0 current:0 max:254 state:ready
      D001 <machine: TESTNT, pid: 222>
      (ADDRESS=(PROTOCOL=tcp)(HOST=testnt)(PORT=1034))
   DISPATCHER established:0 refused:0 current:0 max:254 state:ready
      D002 <machine: TESTNT, pid: 212>
      (ADDRESS=(PROTOCOL=tcp)(HOST=testnt)(PORT=1035))
```

In this listing, D000 is a GIOP dispatcher, since it has a Presentation string and the string refers to Sgiop. One GIOP dispatcher is running. The MTS_DISPATCHERS init.ora parameter for GIOP has either the flag DISP=1 set or it has taken the default value for the DISP flag. More GIOP dispatchers may be set by changing the DISP flag. Modifying the two queries with an additional where clause to include or exclude D000 will differentiate the dispatcher types:

```
SELECT SUBSTR(network,1,23) "Network",
       DECODE(SUM(totalq), 0, 'No Responses',
       ROUND(SUM(wait)/SUM(totalq),2) || ' 100ths of secs')
       "Average Response Queue Wait"
  FROM v$queue a, v$dispatcher b
 WHERE a.type = 'DISPATCHER'
   AND a.paddr = b.paddr
   AND name IN ('D000')
 GROUP BY SUBSTR(network,1,23);
```

In this listing, the second query is modified to show the Average Response Queue Wait for the GIOP dispatcher. If instead AND name IN ('D001', 'D002', 'D003', 'D004', 'D005') were added to the query, it would return a value for all TTC dispatchers.

The wait time for server processes in their queues can also be determined through the V$QUEUE dynamic performance view:

```
SELECT DECODE(totalq, 0, 'No Requests',
       ROUND(wait/totalq, 2) || ' 100ths of secs')
       "Average Request Queue Wait"
  FROM v$queue
 WHERE type = 'COMMON';
```

An Average Request Queue Wait of a second should be fast enough, but if a faster server response is required, then you should raise the value of MTS_MAX_SERVERS in the init.ora file. Like MTS_MAX_DISPATCHERS, which is a hard limit, MTS_MAX_SERVERS is a hard limit on the number of server processes spawned for the MTS, and it is the parameter that needs adjustment. MTS_SERVERS determines the number of server processes to start at instance startup, and server processes will be spawned dynamically as needed up to the MTS_MAX_SERVERS limit.

The number of currently running shared-server processes can be queried through the V$SHARED_SERVER dynamic view:

```
SELECT COUNT(*) "Shared Servers"
  FROM v$shared_server
 WHERE status != 'QUIT';
```

As was explained earlier, the number of shared servers can be adjusted through the init.ora parameter MTS_MAX_SERVERS.

# Multiple Homes Connectivity

The ORACLE_HOME location acts as the top level for an Oracle product line. For example, two versions of the database may run on a single machine, but their software installations cannot be located under the same ORACLE_HOME. Two Oracle home directories may also be used to separate Oracle Tools executables from the database executables.

When setting up two ORACLE_HOMEs for the two versions of the database, issues evolve regarding the configuration of the listener, the Net8 component that initially receives a request for database connections. This section includes some tips to help make those configuration choices.

## Using One Net8 Listener to Connect to Multiple Oracle Homes

To lower resource overhead and ease connectivity management, Oracle recommends the use of one listener to connect to all database instances spread over multiple ORACLE_HOMEs on a server. For example, you could have one listener connect to both a new Oracle8i instance and a legacy Oracle7.3.4 instance. The listener for Oracle7.3.4 would no longer be used, and if used, then a port number conflict will occur when the same port number is used for the TCP/IP protocol. Implementing a single listener making TCP/IP network connections requires that alterations be made in the listener.ora and tnsnames.ora files.

**NOTE**
*Of course, the same listener used for TTC-TCP/IP connections can be configured both for the GIOP protocol used with CORBA and EJBs and for external procedure calls.*

The Oracle8i listener.ora is found at ORACLE_HOME/network/admin. The SID_LIST must include a SID_DESC for both the legacy instance and the Oracle8i instance. In the following list, the second SID_DESC is the addition for the legacy instance (which is non-OFA-compliant):

```
SID_LIST_LISTENER =
  (SID_LIST =
    (SID_DESC =
       (GLOBAL_DBNAME = or8i.testnt)
       (ORACLE_HOME = F:\Oracle\ORA81)
       (SID_NAME = OR8I)
    )
    (SID_DESC =
       (GLOBAL_DBNAME = orcl.testnt)
       (ORACLE_HOME = G:\Orant)
       (SID_NAME = ORCL)
    )
  )
```

The GLOBAL_DBNAME parameter must be set for the use of the multithreaded server (MTS). Without it, clients will connect via dedicated servers. This marks a change in configuration between Oracle8i and both Oracle7.*x* and Oracle8.0.*x*. The GLOBAL_DBNAME is in the form DB_NAME.DB_DOMAIN. In the preceding list, testnt is the DB_DOMAIN, and or8i is the DB_NAME for the Oracle8i database instance and orcl is the DB_NAME for the Oracle7.3.4 instance. In both cases, the DB_NAMEs are the same as the SIDs of the instances, but this need not be the case.

The tnsnames.ora file is found on both server and client machines at ORACLE_HOME/network/admin, except for Oracle8.0.*x* client machines, where the tnsnames.ora is found at ORACLE_HOME/net80/admin. An entry for a Net8 service or Net8 alias must be entered for the legacy database instance. Continuing the preceding example, note that an entry is created for the legacy Oracle7.3.4 instance, with a SID of orcl and an ORACLE_HOME of g:\orant. The aliases OR8I and ORA734 are arbitrary strings that can be up to 64 characters long.

```
OR8I =
  (DESCRIPTION =
    (ADDRESS_LIST =
      (ADDRESS = (PROTOCOL = TCP)(HOST = TESTNT)(PORT = 1521))
    )
    (CONNECT_DATA =
      (SERVICE_NAME = OR8i.TESTNT)
    )
  )
ORA734 =
  (DESCRIPTION =
    (ADDRESS_LIST =
```

```
      (ADDRESS = (PROTOCOL = TCP)(HOST = TESTNT)(PORT = 1521))
  )
  (CONNECT_DATA =
    (SID = ORCL)
    (ORACLE_HOME = G:\ORANT)
  )
)
```

Notice that the CONNECT_DATA portion of the entries has changed between Oracle7.*x* and Oracle8i. Under Oracle7.3.4, the string ORA734 was referred to as the "service name;" with Oracle8i, these strings are referred to as "net service names." The term service name is used in the CONNECT_DATA portion for an Oracle8i instance; its value is DB_NAME.DB_DOMAIN. While in the CONNECT_ DATA portion for the Oracle7.3.4 instance, the SID and ORACLE_HOME define its content as in the past.

After making these modifications to the Oracle8i listener.ora and the tnsnames.ora, stop the Oracle8i or current listener. From the UNIX or DOS prompt the command lsnrctl stop will stop the current listener. Before restarting the listener, make sure the environment variable PATH has ORACLE_HOME/bin for the Oracle8i ORACLE_HOME before the ORACLE_HOME/bin for the Oracle version of the legacy instance. This ensures that the Oracle8i listener is started.

On UNIX, make the PATH adjustment in the .profile or .cshrc login files. Also, be sure to modify the rc.local and rc.shutdown scripts, if they are used to stop and start the listener. Log out and back in on UNIX or bounce the login files.

On NT, select Start | Settings | Control Panel | System | Environment. Under System variables, select PATH and check that the Oracle8i ORACLE_HOME/bin precedes the legacy ORACLE_HOME/bin. Disable the legacy listener by selecting Start | Settings | Control Panel | Services, highlighting the legacy listener—for example, OracleTNSListener, selecting Startup and selecting Disable and OK. Disabling the legacy listener ensures it does not start automatically when the computer is rebooted.

To check that the PATH variable is properly set, issue the command env $PATH on UNIX or set PATH at a DOS prompt on NT. Now restart the listener with the command lsnrctl start at the UNIX or DOS prompt. Whether the listener is started or stopped can be checked with the command lsnrctl status.

Having started the listener and with it a service for the Oracle7.3.4 orcl SID, you can now make connections to the Oracle7.3.4 instance through server-side Oracle8i tools such as SQL*Plus. After the tnsnames.ora on each Net8 client machine is modified to reflect both the Oracle8i and Oracle7.3.4 instances, they can be connected through the Oracle8i listener to the Oracle7.3.4 instance and the Oracle8i instance. SQL*Net2.*x* clients from the Oracle7.*x* era will address Oracle8i database instances through their customary CONNECT_DATA configuration of SID and ORACLE_HOME.

**Using One Net8 Listener for Multiple Oracle Homes**

TIPS

REVIEW

# Tips Review

Implementing the Optimal Flexible Architecture (OFA) is the recommended method to install Oracle8i. Initial NT or UNIX installations that are not OFA compliant can be converted to OFA compliant installations. With the Database Configuration Assistant, an Oracle Starter Database instance with a DB_BLOCK_SIZE greater than 2K can be created, and database-create scripts can be created. With some simple postcreation database tests, the installation and instance creation can be validated. Oracle recommends that an additional rollback segment be created in the System tablespace. Determining the number of Oracle8i user rollback segments is different than their determination with earlier releases. Installation and tuning of the Java Virtual Machine is new with Oracle8i; here the issue of sizing the SHARED_POOL_SIZE and the JAVA_POOL_SIZE parameters must be considered. Further issues to be resolved with the installation of the JVM and Oracle8i concern the multithreaded server (MTS), including enabling MTS, setting the LARGE_POOL_SIZE and SHARED_POOL_SIZE for MTS, and reducing contention for MTS dispatcher and server processes. Oracle recommends with Oracle8i using one Net8 listener to connect to multiple Oracle Homes.

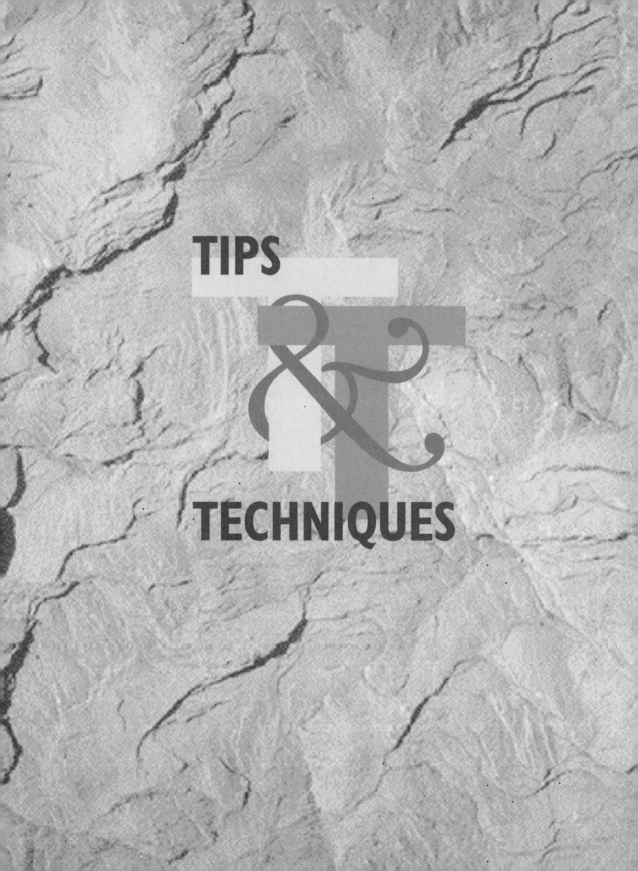

TIPS

&

TECHNIQUES

# CHAPTER
# 4

## System Management

Oracle8i introduces several features that simplify the management of the ORDBMS and make it easier to use. Online index rebuilds minimize downtime by allowing users to access table data while its indexes are being rebuilt. Locally managed tablespaces provide better space management, reduced fragmentation, and increased reliability. Columns can now be dropped to easily reclaim space from unused columns. With the advent of the LOB data type, the LONG data type is becoming obsolete. Oracle8i provides a new function to convert LONGs to LOBs. The LogMiner feature allows the DBA to tap into the wealth of information contained within log files. This chapter provides the following tips and techniques for taking advantage of these new system management features:

- Creating an index online
- Using locally managed tablespaces
- Dropping columns
- Converting LONG columns to LOBs
- Using the LogMiner to view the contents of redo log files

# Manageability Improvements

Oracle continues to make enhancements that reduce the amount of time and effort required to maintain the database while providing maximum availability to users. The features described in this section address several of the issues associated with managing an ORDBMS.

## Creating an Index Online

You can now create or rebuild an index on a table without interfering with transactions going on against the table. Before Oracle8i, creating an index on a table placed a DML S-lock (read-shared) on the table. Although the table could be queried, DML operations could not be performed while the index was being built. Creating an index with the online option, while allowing DML operations to take place during an online index rebuild, will still cause a shared DDL lock to be placed on the table so that DDL operations cannot be performed during the online index rebuild.

The following examples show how the online option is used:

```
CREATE INDEX emp_no ON emp (empno)
   TABLESPACE index1
   PCTFREE 10
```

```
  STORAGE (INITIAL 1M NEXT 1M PCTINCREASE 0)
  ONLINE;


ALTER INDEX emp_no REBUILD ONLINE;
```

**NOTE**
*Even though you can UPDATE a table during an online
index build, Oracle recommends that you not perform
DML operations that would affect a large percentage of
the table's rows while the index is being built.*

## Using Locally Managed Tablespaces

Unlike regular tablespaces that rely on data dictionary tables to track used and
free space, locally managed tablespaces use bit maps to track all extent information
within the tablespace itself. As a result, locally managed tablespaces manage space
more efficiently, provide reduced fragmentation, and increase reliability.

   When creating a locally managed tablespace, you can choose to have extent sizes
determined automatically by the system using the AUTOALLOCATE parameter, or
you can specify that all extents be uniformly sized using the UNIFORM parameter. If
you specify AUTOALLOCATE, users will not be able to specify an extent size when
creating objects in the tablespace. If you specify UNIFORM, you can use the SIZE
parameter to control the size of the extents. The following examples demonstrate
how you can create locally managed tablespaces using each of these parameters:

```
CREATE TABLESPACE data_01 DATAFILE '/u02/oradata/dev/data_01.dbf'
  SIZE 100M EXTENT MANAGEMENT LOCAL AUTOALLOCATE;


CREATE TABLESPACE data_02 DATAFILE '/u02/oradata/dev/data_02.dbf'
  SIZE 500M EXTENT MANAGEMENT LOCAL UNIFORM SIZE 1280K;
```

   You cannot specify values for the DEFAULT storage clause, TEMPORARY, or
MINIMUM EXTENT when you create a locally managed tablespace. The MINIMUM
EXTENT parameter is new in Oracle8i and is used to control tablespace fragmentation
by ensuring that each used or free extent is at least the size specified by MINIMUM
EXTENT or a multiple of MINIMUM EXTENT.

   You can have a combination of locally managed tablespaces and dictionary
managed tablespaces in the same database. However, if you create the System
tablespace as a locally managed tablespace, you must create all rollback segments
in locally managed tablespaces. The EXTENT MANAGEMENT LOCAL clause can
also be used with the CREATE TEMPORARY TABLESPACE command.

## Dropping Columns

You can drop a column that is no longer needed by using the ALTER TABLE command with the DROP COLUMN clause. This clause gives you several ways to drop a column. You can drop a column immediately or you can mark a column as unused, which treats a column as though it had been dropped but doesn't actually remove it. It also allows you to drop any referential integrity constraints that rely on the dropped columns, and it provides some control over how the transaction is processed. The following examples use the tables in the DEMO account to demonstrate how this clause can be used:

To directly drop a column:

```
ALTER TABLE customer DROP COLUMN credit_limit;
```

**CAUTION**

*Issuing the preceding command will also cause any columns previously marked as unused to be dropped.*

To mark one or more columns as unused:

```
ALTER TABLE customer SET UNUSED (credit_limit, salesperson_id);
```

To drop all columns in the table that are currently marked as unused:

```
ALTER TABLE customer DROP UNUSED COLUMNS;
```

To drop all referential integrity constraints that refer to the primary and unique keys defined on the dropped columns:

```
ALTER TABLE department DROP COLUMN department_id CASCADE CONSTRAINTS;
```

Issuing the preceding command will also cause the foreign key constraint on department_id in the employee table to be dropped.

To specify that a checkpoint for the operation is to be applied after 100 rows are processed:

```
ALTER TABLE sales_order DROP COLUMN ship_date CHECKPOINT 100;
```

You should use the CHECKPOINT option when dropping a column from a very large table so that you don't run out of rollback segment space. Checkpointing minimizes the amount of undo logs accumulated during the drop column operation. However, if the command is interrupted after a checkpoint has been applied, the table will be in an unusable state. If this occurs, you can bring the table back to a usable state by continuing the drop column operation as follows:

```
ALTER TABLE sales_order DROP COLUMNS CONTINUE;
```

## Converting LONG Columns to LOBs

In a future release, Oracle will be discontinuing support for LONG columns. However, you can use the TO_LOB function to convert LONG values to LOB values. The most efficient way to convert a LONG column to a LOB column is to create a new table and populate it by selecting data from the old table, using the TO_LOB function on the LONG column. The following example shows how this could be done for the customer table in the DEMO schema:

```
CREATE TABLE new_customer AS
   SELECT customer_id, name, address, city,
          state, zip_code, area_code, phone_number,
          TO_LOB(comments) comments
     FROM customer;
```

Once you are satisfied that the data has been properly copied, the original table can be dropped; however, you must be sure to preserve all of the indexes, integrity constraints, triggers, and grants so they can be created on the new table. After the table is dropped, the new table can be renamed to the original table name, or a synonym can be created. All applications that referred to the LONG column must be modified to use the LOB column.

**NOTE**
*You can use TO_LOB to convert both LONG and LONG RAW values. When you convert LONGs, the LOB column type must be CLOB or NCLOB. When you convert LONG RAWs, the LOB column type must be BLOB.*

## Using the LogMiner to View the Contents of Redo Log Files

The redo log files contain a great deal of information that you can use for a number of purposes, including the following:

■ Tracking changes to the database

- Determining when and where corruption occurred
- Tuning and capacity planning

Analyzing archived redo logs involves creating a dictionary file and running a LogMiner session. The dictionary file is a special file containing information about the log files and the database that generated the log files. The dictionary file is optional, but if you don't create it, Oracle internal object IDs will be generated instead of object names, and column values will be in hex. The dictionary file is created by mounting and opening the database and then executing the DBMS_LOGMNR_D.BUILD PL/SQL procedure, as shown in the following example:

```
BEGIN
  DBMS_LOGMNR_D.BUILD
    (DICTIONARY_FILENAME => 'dict.ora',
     DICTIONARY_LOCATION => '/u01/app/oracle/admin/dev/adhoc'
    );
END;
```

**NOTE**
*Some of the procedures, including the BUILD procedure, make calls to the UTL_FILE procedure, so you must set the UTL_FILE_DIR parameter in the init.ora file to enable writing to the directory where files will be located.*

A LogMiner session involves the following steps:

1. Start an Oracle instance, with the database either mounted or unmounted.

2. Execute the DBMS_LOGMNR.ADD_LOGFILE procedure with the NEW option. This will begin the session and add the first log file.

3. Execute the DBMS_LOGMNR.ADD_LOGFILE procedure with the ADDFILE option for each additional log file that you want to analyze.

4. Execute the DBMS_LOGMNR.START_LOGMNR procedure. This will extract data from the log files and bring it into the database, where it can be analyzed.

5. Query V$LOGMNR_CONTENTS to display information about each redo entry that was extracted.

The following example demonstrates a typical LogMiner session:

```
BEGIN
  DBMS_LOGMNR.ADD_LOGFILE
    (LOGFILENAME => '/u03/oraback/dev/log1.arc',
     OPTIONS => DBMS_LOGMNR.NEW
    );
  DBMS_LOGMNR.ADD_LOGFILE
    (LOGFILENAME => '/u03/oraback/dev/log2.arc',
     OPTIONS => DBMS_LOGMNR.ADDFILE
    );
  DBMS_LOGMNR.START_LOGMNR
    (DICTFILENAME => '/u01/app/oracle/admin||
     'dev/adhoc/dict.ora'
    );
END;
```

In the preceding example, the entire contents of the log files will be processed. If you don't want to analyze all of the records, you can use the STARTSCN and ENDSCN parameters of the DBMS_LOGMNR.START_LOGMNR procedure to filter the records by SCN, or you can use the STARTTIME and ENDTIME parameters to filter the records by time. The following example shows how to use the STARTSCN and ENDSCN parameters:

```
BEGIN
  DBMS_LOGMNR.START_LOGMNR
    (DICTFILENAME => '/u01/app/oracle/admin'||
     '/dev/adhoc/dict.ora',
     STARTSCN => 50025, ENDSCN => 50030
    );
END;
```

After you run the DBMS_LOGMNR.START_LOGMNR procedure, you can query the V$LOGMNR_CONTENTS view to obtain information about each entry in the log files that you chose to analyze. For example, you could use a command like the following to see who made changes to a particular table:

```
SELECT username, sql_redo
  FROM v$logmnr_contents
 WHERE sql_redo LIKE '%EMP%';
```

The following views contain additional information that may be of interest when you are using the LogMiner:

- **V$LOGMNR_DICTIONARY**   Contains information about the dictionary file

- **V$LOGMNR_LOGS**   Contains information about the log files to be analyzed

- **V$LOGMNR_PARAMETERS**   Contains information about the parameters used with the DBMS_LOGMNR.START_LOGMNR procedure

Using the LogMiner to View Contents of Redo Log Files

You can run LogMiner on one instance of a database while analyzing redo logs from a different instance, as long as both databases are running on the same hardware platform and the log files are from Oracle8.0 or later. To do this, you must specify a dictionary file that was created on the same database as the log files you want to analyze and created with the same database character set.

# Tips Review

Managing an ORDBMS becomes easier as Oracle continues to provide new features. Downtime is minimized when indexes are created online and while unused storage can easily be deallocated using the DROP clause of the ALTER TABLE statement. Locally managed tablespaces manage space more efficiently, minimizing the need for tablespace maintenance. The TO_LOB function provides a way to convert columns from the obsolete data type LONG to LOB. The LogMiner is a new tool that allows the DBA to use the information inside log files to troubleshoot, tune, and plan for future growth.

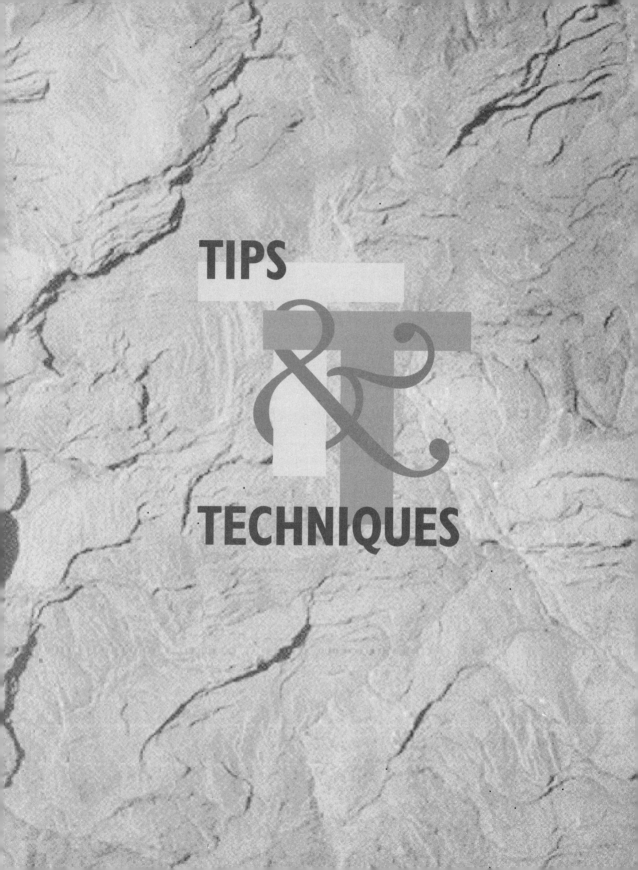

# TIPS & TECHNIQUES

# CHAPTER
## 5

Performance

Performance is a key factor in any successful database implementation. Because it is inexpensive to store large quantities of data, many organizations are choosing to maintain large volumes of data that can be used to make better business decisions. The combination of large volumes of data and the complexity of the queries needed to turn the data into useful information can slow a system down to a crawl. Oracle8i introduces features that improve performance when complex queries are being run against large volumes of data. In this chapter, several of these features will be described in detail along with techniques for using them, as follows:

- Generating statistics with the DBMS_STATS package

- Improving performance of statistics generation, using parallel execution

- Increasing performance on partitioned objects by specifying the granularity of statistics

- Backing up and recovering statistics

- Tuning with sets of statistics

- Performing production tuning studies in a test database

- Automating statistics gathering

- Preserving execution plans, using plan stability

- Automatically creating stored outlines

- Using stored outlines

- Managing stored outlines

- Moving the outline tables

- Migrating to the cost-based optimizer with stored outlines

- Preserving execution plans when upgrading the ORDBMS

- Simulating production statistics in a test environment

- Improving performance with function-based indexes

- Using single-table hash clusters for fast row access

# The DBMS_STATS Package

The DBMS_STATS package contains procedures that allow you to generate and manage statistics for use with the cost-based optimizer. Statistics can also be generated using the ANALYZE command. However, the DBMS_STATS package provides more functionality and is recommended over the ANALYZE command for generating statistics for cost-based optimization, for three reasons. First, the ANALYZE command cannot run in parallel. Second, the method it uses for calculating statistics for partitioned tables is inefficient and can be inaccurate. Finally, ANALYZE cannot replace or delete statistics previously generated by the DBMS_STATS package. The ANALYZE command should still be used for gathering statistics that are not used by the cost-based optimizer, such as the number of chained rows, average free space, or number of unused data blocks.

Following are examples of what you can do with the DBMS_STATS package:

- Generate table statistics in parallel

- Specify the granularity of statistics to be collected for partitioned tables

- Back up and restore statistics

- Generate one or more sets of statistics and store them in a schema rather than in the dictionary

- Copy statistics from one database to another, allowing you to experiment with tuning in different environments

The DBMS_STATS package contains procedures to gather, view, drop, back up, and recover statistics for tables, indexes, schemas, and the entire database. This section will focus primarily on those procedures used to gather statistics and to backup and recover statistics.

## Generating Statistics with the DBMS_STATS Package

If you use the cost-based optimizer, you need to regularly generate statistics for all tables, clusters, and indexes in the database. The DBMS_STATS package contains the following procedures for gathering statistics (1) for individual tables and indexes, (2) for all objects in a particular schema, and (3) for all objects in a database:

**GATHER_TABLE_STATS** for tables
**GATHER_INDEX_STATS** for indexes
**GATHER_SCHEMA_STATS** for all object in a particular schema
**GATHER_DATABASE_STATS** for all objects in a database

The GATHER_SCHEMA_STATS procedure will be used to demonstrate most of the techniques in this section. The syntax is as follows:

```
PROCEDURE GATHER_SCHEMA_STATS
  (ownname VARCHAR2,
```

```
   estimate_percent NUMBER DEFAULT NULL,
   block_sample BOOLEAN DEFAULT FALSE,
   method_opt VARCHAR2 DEFAULT 'FOR ALL COLUMNS SIZE 1',
   degree NUMBER DEFAULT NULL,
   granularity VARCHAR2 DEFAULT 'DEFAULT',
   cascade BOOLEAN DEFAULT FALSE,
   stattab VARCHAR2 DEFAULT NULL,
   statid VARCHAR2 DEFAULT NULL,
   options VARCHAR2 DEFAULT 'GATHER',
   objlist OUT OBJECTTAB,
   statown VARCHAR2 DEFAULT NULL
);
```

Table 5-1 provides a detailed description of each of the parameters that can be used with the GATHER_SCHEMA_STATS procedure. Information about the other statistics-gathering procedures can be found in the Oracle8i Supplied Packages and Reference Manual and the Oracle8i Tuning Manual.

| PARAMETER | DESCRIPTION |
|---|---|
| ownname | The name of the schema to analyze (NULL means the current user's schema). |
| estimate_percent | The percentage of rows to estimate (NULL means compute). The valid range is 0.000001 to 100. |
| block_sample | Indicates whether to use random block sampling instead of the default random row sampling. Random block sampling is more efficient, but if the data is not randomly distributed on disk, then the sample values may be somewhat correlated, which may lead to inaccurate statistics. This parameter is used only when estimating statistics. |
| method_opt | Indicates the method options of the following format (the phrase 'SIZE 1' is required to ensure gathering of statistics in parallel and for use with the hidden option):<br>FOR ALL [INDEXED \| HIDDEN] COLUMNS [SIZE integer].<br>This value is passed to all of the individual tables. |
| degree | The degree of parallelism (NULL means use the table default degree of parallelism). |
| granularity | The granularity of the statistics to collect. This applies only to partitioned tables.<br>**PARTITION**   Gather partition-level statistics.<br>**GLOBAL**   Gather global statistics.<br>**ALL**   Gather all statistics.<br>**SUBPARTITION**   Gather subpartition-level statistics.<br>**DEFAULT**   Gather partition and global statistics. |

**TABLE 5-1.**   *Descriptions of GATHER_SCHEMA_STATS Parameters*

| PARAMETER | DESCRIPTION |
|---|---|
| cascade | Indicates whether to gather statistics on the indexes. Index statistics gathering will not be parallelized. Using this option is equivalent to running the GATHER_INDEX_STATS procedure on each of the indexes in the schema. |
| stattab | The name of a user's statistics table into which Oracle should back up the original statistics before collecting new statistics. |
| tatid | The id to be assigned to the statistics being backed up in the user's statistics tables. |
| options | Used with automated statistics gathering.<br>**GATHER**   Gather statistics for all objects in the schema.<br>**GATHER STALE**   Gather statistics for objects that have stale statistics and return a list of the objects.<br>**GATHER EMPTY**   Gather statistics for objects that don't have statistics and return a list of the objects.<br>**LIST STALE**   Return a list of stale objects.<br>**LIST EMPTY**   Return a list of objects that don't have statistics. |
| objlist | List of objects found to be stale or empty. Used with automated statistics gathering. |
| statown | Schema that owns the stattab table. Specify this if the table is located in a different schema than that identified by the ownname parameter. |

**TABLE 5-1.**   *Descriptions of GATHER_SCHEMA_STATS Parameters* (continued)

**NOTE**
*When creating or rebuilding an index, consider including COMPUTE STATISTICS in the index attributes clause as an efficient way to generate statistics.*

## Improving Performance of Statistics Generation Using Parallel Execution

The statistics-gathering procedures within the DBMS_STATS package automatically use parallel processing; however, there are some parameters that you can set to control the degree of parallelism. In the following PL/SQL example, statistics are gathered and stored in the data dictionary for the schema SCOTT. The method_opt parameter is not specified, so the default value of 'FOR ALL COLUMNS SIZE 1' is used, ensuring that the statistics will be gathered in parallel. The degree of parallelism is specified as 4. If the degree parameter was not specified, the degree of parallelism defined for the table would be used. Statistics will be gathered for indexes because the cascade parameter was set to true; index statistics gathering is never parallelized.

```
BEGIN
   DBMS_STATS.GATHER_SCHEMA_STATS(ownname => 'SCOTT',
                                  degree => 4,
                                  cascade => TRUE
                                  );
END;
```

## Increasing Performance of Partitioned Objects by Specifying the Granularity of Statistics

Partitioned database objects can have statistics generated for the entire object or for individual partitions or subpartitions. It is important to generate statistics at all levels. If a query accesses more than one partition, the global statistics will be used. If it accesses a single partition, the statistics for that partition will be used. You can specify the granularity of statistics to collect for partitioned tables with the granularity parameter. In the following example, the granularity is set to ALL, causing all subpartition, partition, and global statistics to be gathered:

```
BEGIN
   DBMS_STATS.GATHER_SCHEMA_STATS(ownname => 'SCOTT',
                                  granularity => 'ALL'
                                  );
END;
```

The following example uses the GATHER_TABLE_STATS procedure to gather statistics for the sales1 partition in the sales table:

```
BEGIN
   DBMS_STATS.GATHER_TABLE_STATS(ownname => 'SCOTT',
                                 tabname => 'SALES',
                                 partname => 'SALES1',
                                 granularity => 'PARTITION'
                                 );
END;
```

## Backing Up and Recovering Statistics

Statistics stored in the dictionary should be backed up before new statistics are gathered. This can be achieved by creating a table in a schema to store the statistics and exporting the statistics into the table. The statistics can later be recovered by importing them from the schema table back into the dictionary. The following example shows how to create the table and export the statistics for the schema SCOTT:

```
BEGIN
  DBMS_STATS.CREATE_STAT_TABLE('SCOTT', 'MYSTATS');
  DBMS_STATS.EXPORT_SCHEMA_STATS(ownname => 'SCOTT',
                                 stattab => 'MYSTATS'
                                 );
END;
```

The statistics can later be recovered, as shown in the following example:

```
BEGIN
  DBMS_STATS.IMPORT_SCHEMA_STATS(ownname => 'SCOTT',
                                 stattab => 'MYSTATS'
                                 );
END;
```

## Tuning with Sets of Statistics

Generating sets of statistics allows you to tune queries by experimenting with different sets of statistics. For example, suppose you take over administering a database, and you realize that statistics are not being gathered on a regular basis, yet the cost-based analyzer is being used. You know that you should begin gathering statistics on a regular basis, but you are concerned that you may not select the optimal sample size and that the new statistics might cause the optimizer to generate poor plans. To solve this problem, you can use the DBMS_STATS package to store the existing statistics in a table, before generating new statistics. If the queries perform worse than they did originally, you can restore the original statistics. The following example shows how to do this:

```
DECLARE
  t_objlist DBMS_STATS.OBJECTTAB;
BEGIN
  DBMS_STATS.CREATE_STAT_TABLE('TUNING', 'SCOTT_STATS');
  DBMS_STATS.GATHER_SCHEMA_STATS(ownname =>'SCOTT',
                                 stattab => 'SCOTT_STATS',
                                 statid => 'SCOTT1',
                                 statown => 'TUNING',
                                 objlist => t_objlist
                                 );
END;
```

In the above example, a table is created to hold the original statistics for the SCOTT schema in a schema called TUNING. Creating a separate schema for storing statistics makes it easier to keep your statistics organized, particularly if you are generating several sets of statistics for several different schemas. The GATHER_SCHEMA_STATS procedure uses the stattab and statown parameters to specify that the current statistics be stored in the scott_stats table located in the TUNING schema. The optional statid parameter is used to identify this particular set of statistics. This is only necessary if you plan to store several sets of statistics in the same table. For instance, you may want to estimate statistics with several different sample sizes. If you want to save several sets of statistics, you could also create a separate table for each set of statistics. The objlist parameter must be passed to the procedure since it is an OUT parameter. It will not be populated by the GATHER_SCHEMA_STATS procedure when used in this context. It will be populated only when used in conjunction with the options parameter during use of the automatic statistics-gathering feature described later in this section.

The following example shows how you can delete statistics from the dictionary and restore the previously saved statistics:

```
BEGIN
  DBMS_STATS.DELETE_SCHEMA_STATS('SCOTT');
  DBMS_STATS.IMPORT_SCHEMA_STATS('SCOTT', 'MYSTATS',
                                 'ORIG_STATS', 'SCOTT'
                                 );
END;
```

**NOTE**

*Although you can have many copies of statistics saved, the only set that affects the optimizer is what is stored in the dictionary.*

## Performing Production Tuning Studies in a Test Database

By generating statistics in your production environment and copying them to a test environment, you can perform tuning studies to determine how changes to the database will affect performance without requiring the same amount of data to be stored in the test database as is in the production database. This can easily be accomplished by exporting the statistics from the dictionary to a schema table and copying the schema table into a schema on the test database, using utilities like export and import or by using a database link. The following example shows how to use the EXPORT_SCHEMA_STATS procedure:

```
BEGIN
  DBMS_STATS.EXPORT_SCHEMA_STATS(ownname => 'SCOTT',
                                 stattab => 'MYSTATS',
                                 statown => 'MYSCHEMA'
                                 );
END ;
```

## Automating Statistics Gathering

Oracle can automatically monitor tables for DML activity and can determine the approximate number of INSERTS, UPDATES, and DELETES that occurred in the table since the last time statistics were gathered. The GATHER_SCHEMA_STATS or GATHER_DATABASE_STATS procedure of the DBMS_STATS package can then be run periodically, using a script or a job-scheduling tool, to gather statistics for only those tables that have experienced enough DML to make their statistics stale. This can be significantly faster than gathering statistics for all tables in the schema, and it is especially well suited for databases or schemas that contain a large number of tables that are static or that seldom change.

You can designate a table to be monitored by specifying the MONITORING keyword in the CREATE TABLE or ALTER TABLE statement. Monitoring can subsequently be disabled by using the ALTER TABLE statement and specifying NOMONITORING. The following example shows how to create a table with monitoring enabled and how to disable monitoring:

```
CREATE TABLE dept
   (deptno NUMBER(2),
    dname VARCHAR2(10),
    loc VARCHAR2(9)
   )
   TABLESPACE users
   STORAGE (INITIAL 2M NEXT 2M)
   MONITORING;

ALTER TABLE dept NOMONITORING;
```

The options available for use with automated statistics gathering are GATHER, GATHER STALE, GATHER EMPTY, LIST STALE, and LIST EMPTY. These options are described in Table 5-1. The following example shows how to obtain and display a list of objects that have no statistics:

```
DECLARE
  t_objlist DBMS_STATS.OBJECTTAB;
BEGIN
  DBMS_STATS.GATHER_SCHEMA_STATS (ownname => 'SCOTT',
                                  options => 'LIST EMPTY',
                                  objlist => t_objlist
                                  );
  FOR i_objlist IN t_objlist.FIRST .. t_objlist.LAST
  LOOP
     DBMS_OUTPUT.PUT_LINE(t_objlist(i_objlist).objname||' '||
```

```
                            t_objlist(i_objlist).objtype
                      );

  END LOOP;
END;
```

In the preceding example, t_objlist is declared with the type DBMS_STATS. OBJECTTAB. DBMS_STATS.OBJECTTAB is a PL/SQL table of type OBJECTELEM, which is defined as follows:

```
TYPE objectelem IS RECORD(
  ownname VARCHAR2(32),       -- Owner
  objtype VARCHAR2(6),        -- 'TABLE' or 'INDEX'
  objname VARCHAR2(32),       -- Name of table or index
  partname VARCHAR2(32),      -- Name of partition
  subpartname VARCHAR2(23),   -- Name of subpartition
  confidence NUMBER);         -- Not used
```

# Plan Stability

Upgrading the database, migrating from the rule-based optimizer to the cost-based optimizer, changing parameters that affect the sizes of memory structures, or generating new statistics can all affect the performance of your applications by changing the way the optimizer generates execution plans for SQL statements. Plan stability can be used to preserve execution plans prior to making any database changes. After the changes are made, if some SQL statements don't perform as well as they used to, you can instruct the database to use the plans that were captured prior to the change.

## Preserving Execution Plans Using Plan Stability

Plan stability works by creating stored outlines to hold SQL statements along with a corresponding set of hints. The SQL statements are stored in the OL$ table and the hints are stored in the OL$HINTS table; both tables are owned by the OUTLN schema. When the database is instructed to use stored outlines, the optimizer checks to see if a stored outline exists for each SQL statement executed. If it does, then the optimizer uses the hints in the stored outline to generate an execution plan equivalent to the execution plan that would have been generated prior to any changes. The USER_OUTLINES view contains information about stored outlines including the SQL text. The USER_OUTLINE_HINTS view contains the corresponding hints, which are automatically generated by Oracle at the time the outline is created.

## Automatically Creating Stored Outlines

Oracle can automatically capture stored outlines for all queries executed during a session or for all queries executed within the system. You can use this feature to create stored outlines for all SQL statements in a particular application by instructing Oracle to create stored outlines and then running the application. Outline management can be simplified by defining categories and assigning outlines to them. For example, if you have several applications accessing a database, you can define a category name for each application and assign each application's stored outlines to its own category.

Automatic outline creation is enabled by setting the CREATE_STORED_ OUTLINES parameter either to TRUE or to a category name. This can be done using either the ALTER SESSION statement or the ALTER SYSTEM statement. This parameter cannot be set in the init.ora file. If the CREATE_STORED_OUTLINES parameter is set to TRUE, outlines will be stored in the DEFAULT category. All outlines created will be given a unique system-generated name. If an outline already exists for a particular query, the outline won't be created. Oracle will continue creating stored outlines for all SQL statements executed until the CREATE_STORED_OUTLINES parameter is set to FALSE. You can change the category to which outlines get assigned by setting the CREATE_STORED_OUTLINES parameter to a different category name. All subsequently created outlines will be assigned to the new category until the CREATE_STORED_OUTLINES parameter is set to FALSE. Outlines can be created for any SELECT, INSERT, UPDATE, or DELETE statement.

## Using Stored Outlines

In order for Oracle to use stored outlines, you must set the parameter USE_ STORED_OUTLINES to TRUE or to a category name, using either the ALTER SYSTEM or the ALTER SESSION statement. If USE_STORED_OUTLINES is set to TRUE, Oracle will try to match SQL statements to outlines in the DEFAULT category. If USE_STORED_OUTLINES is set to a category name, Oracle will try to match SQL statements to outlines in that category. If no outline is found in the specified category, Oracle will search the DEFAULT category for a matching outline.

The SQL text of a particular query must exactly match the SQL text in an outline before Oracle will use the outline. Any difference is considered a mismatch, including changes in spacing, carriage return variations, embedded hints, or differences in comment text. These are the same rules that the parser uses when checking to see if a statement is already in the shared pool.

Once you activate the USE_STORED_OUTLINES parameter, Oracle will use the specified outlines until you reset the USE_STORED_OUTLINES parameter to a different category or until you set USE_STORED_OUTLINES to FALSE. The cost-based optimizer will automatically be used when USE_STORED_OUTLINES is activated so that it can use the hints stored with the outlines.

## Managing Stored Outlines

Outlines can be managed individually using the CREATE OUTLINE, ALTER OUTLINE, and DROP OUTLINE statements. Outlines can be managed by category

Managing Stored Outlines

with the use of the OUTLN_PKG package. You will need the following privileges to manage outlines:

- CREATE ANY OUTLINE
- ALTER ANY OUTLINE
- DROP ANY OUTLINE

### Creating Stored Outlines for Individual SQL Statements

You can create a stored outline for an individual SQL statement by using the CREATE OUTLINE statement. Unlike enabling outline creation at the system or session level, when you create a stored outline for an individual SQL statement, you can give it a name of your choice. You can also generate more than one outline for a particular statement as long as you store each outline in a different category. The following example shows the syntax for the CREATE OUTLINE statement:

```
CREATE OR REPLACE OUTLINE emp_dept FOR CATEGORY hr_app
  ON SELECT e.last_name, e.first_name, d.name
      FROM employee e, department d
     WHERE e.department_id = d.department_id;
```

### Altering Stored Outlines

You can use the ALTER OUTLINE statement to rename an outline, to reassign it to a different category, or to rebuild an outline under a new system configuration. The following examples demonstrate the use of the ALTER OUTLINE statement:

```
ALTER OUTLINE emp_dept RENAME TO hr_emp_dept;

ALTER OUTLINE hr_emp_dept CHANGE CATEGORY TO human_resources;

ALTER OUTLINE hr_emp_dept REBUILD;
```

### Dropping Stored Outlines

You can drop a stored outline with the DROP OUTLINE statement. After a stored outline is dropped, if the SQL statement is executed again, the optimizer will generate a new execution plan. The following example shows the syntax of the DROP OUTLINE statement:

```
DROP OUTLINE hr_emp_dept;
```

### Using the OUTLN_PKG Package to Manage Stored Outlines

The OUTLN_PKG package contains several procedures to help you manage stored outlines. You can use this package to remove unused outlines, and to remove or reorganize outlines by category.

The DROP_UNUSED procedure can be executed to drop stored outlines that have never been used, as shown in the following example:

```
OUTLN_PKG.DROP_UNUSED;
```

The DROP_BY_CAT procedure is used to drop all stored outlines for a specified category. When you call the procedure, pass it the name of the category that you want to drop, as shown in the following example:

```
OUTLN_PKG.DROP_BY_CAT('CATEGORY_NAME');
```

The UPDATE_BY_CAT procedure is used to reassign stored outlines from one category to another. This procedure is useful to merge outlines from one category into another. For example, if you have a category that contains outlines that you are testing, and you want to incorporate them into a production category. When you call the procedure, pass it the name of the category you want to reassign, followed by the new category name, as shown in the following example:

```
OUTLN_PKG.UPDATE_BY_CAT('OLD_CATEGORY', 'NEW_CATEGORY');
```

**NOTE**
*You must have EXECUTE ANY PROCEDURE privilege or be explicitly granted EXECUTE on the OUTLN_PKG package or individual procedures in order to use the OUTLN_PKG to manage stored outlines.*

## Moving the Outline Tables

The outline and hint data are stored in the OL$ and OL$HINTS tables, which are stored in the System tablespace and owned by the schema OUTLN. The USER_OUTLINES and USER_OUTLINE_HINTS views are based on data from these tables. If you plan to generate more than a few stored outlines, you should move these tables to a different tablespace, so that the System tablespace doesn't run out of space or become fragmented. This can be accomplished by using the export/import utilities or by issuing commands similar to the following:

```
CREATE TABLE new_ol$
  TABLESPACE outline
  AS SELECT * FROM ol$;

DROP TABLE OL$;

RENAME TABLE new_ol$ TO ol$;
```

## Migrating to the Cost-Based Optimizer with Stored Outlines

You should consider migrating your applications from the rule-based optimizer to the cost-based optimizer because only the latter supports all the new enhancements, such as hash joins, improved star query processing, and histograms. Even if you aren't interested in the new features, you should consider migrating to the cost-based optimizer because Oracle has plans to stop supporting the rule-based optimizer at some point in the future. If you are concerned that some SQL statements may not perform as well under the cost-based optimizer, you can use stored outlines to preserve the current level of performance. Generate stored outlines for all SQL statements using the rule-based optimizer, then switch to the cost-based optimizer. If you see degradation in performance of any of your SQL statements, you can use the stored outlines for the problem statements.

The procedure for creating and using stored outlines when migrating to the cost-based optimizer is described in the following steps:

1. Select a category in which the outlines should be stored and tell Oracle to start creating stored outlines. The following statement will cause stored outlines to be generated and stored in the APP1 category:

```
ALTER SESSION SET CREATE_STORED_OUTLINES = app1;
```

2. Run the application to capture stored outlines for all SQL statements.

3. Stop generating stored outlines. The following statement will suspend outline generation:

```
ALTER SESSION SET CREATE_STORED_OUTLINES = FALSE;
```

4. Gather statistics using the DBMS_STATS package. Refer to the earlier section, "Improving Performance of Statistics Generation Using Parallel Execution" on generating statistics using the DBMS_STATS package for details.

5. Set the OPTIMIZER_MODE parameter to CHOOSE.

6. Run the application and identify any problem statements.

7. Locate the stored outline for each problem statement and put these statements in a separate category. The following statement shows how to change the category of a stored outline:

```
ALTER OUTLINE outline_name CHANGE CATEGORY TO app1problems;
```

8. Tell Oracle to use the stored outlines for the problem statements by setting the USE_STORED_OUTLINES, as shown in the following statement:

```
ALTER SESSION SET USE_STORED_OUTLINES = app1problems;
```

**NOTE**
*After you move to the cost-based optimizer, if you find a problem query for which you don't have a stored outline, you can always alter your session to use the rule-based optimizer and capture the outline.*

## Preserving Execution Plans When Upgrading the ORDBMS

When you upgrade to a newer version of Oracle and you are using cost-based optimization, some SQL statements may have their execution plans changed owing to changes in the optimizer. In most cases, the changes will improve performance, but if you don't want to take the risk of a change in an application's behavior, be sure to generate stored outlines before upgrading. You can do this by using the procedure described in the previous section, eliminating the step for gathering statistics.

## Simulating Production Statistics in a Test Environment

You can simulate your production system in a test environment by migrating statistics from the production system to the test system. This allows you to conduct tests such as determining the effects of an upgrade or performing tuning experiments without having to fully populate the tables with data. In conjunction with this, you can move stored outlines by category from the production system to the test system, using the query-based Export option.

The following example shows how to export one category of stored outlines from the OL$ and OL$HINTS tables, using the query-based Export option. The syntax for using the query parameter will depend on the operating system. In Windows NT, the syntax requires the string to be enclosed by three sets of double quotes: exp outln/outln_passwd file=expdat.dmp tables='OL$', 'OL$HINTS' query="""WHERE CATEGORY = 'APP1'""" while in UNIX, the syntax requires that reserved characters like single quotes, double quotes and dollar signs be escaped: exp outln/outln file=expdat.dmp tables=OL\$, OL\$HINTS query=\"WHERE CATEGORY = \'APP1\'\".

# Other Features That Improve Performance

Oracle8i provides two new features that improve performance by speeding up row access. Function-based indexes provide an additional way to create indexes that can

Simulate Production Stats in a Test Environment

be used to provide a fast access path to data. Single-table hash clusters provide fast row access by minimizing the number of reads that must occur before a row is retrieved.

# Improving Performance with Function-Based Indexes

A *function-based index* is an index on an expression, such as an arithmetic expression, or an expression containing a PL/SQL function, a package function, a C callout, or a SQL single row function. Function-based indexes work by precomputing the value from the function and storing it in the index. You can use a function-based index wherever you can use an index on a column, except for columns with LOBs or REFs.

Once you've created a function-based index, you can use the function in a query and the cost-based optimizer will locate and use the index. You can use this feature to efficiently perform case-insensitive searches and linguistic sorts, to query on equations, and to extend the SQL language by creating your own application-specific functions and querying on them.

## Examples Using SQL Functions

```
CREATE INDEX cust_name ON customer (UPPER(name));

SELECT cust_id
  FROM customer
 WHERE name = 'HOOPS';
```

The preceding example uses a SQL function to support a case-insensitive query.

```
CREATE INDEX mx_name on mx_employee
  (NLSSORT(last_name, 'NLS_SORT = Xspanish'));
SELECT *
  FROM mx_employee
ORDER BY last_name;
```

The foregoing example uses a SQL function to support linguistic sorts. Assume you have a separate employee table that contains data for all employees who work in your Mexican manufacturing plant. In Mexican Spanish, the double characters *ch* are treated as a single letter whose sort sequence is between c and d, so that the name Chevez, for example, should appear after the name Cortez. In order for the select statement to work properly, NLS_SORT must be set to MEXICAN SPANISH for the session.

## Example Using an Arithmetic Expression

```
CREATE INDEX total_comp ON employee (salary + commission);

SELECT COUNT(*)
  FROM employee
 WHERE salary + commission > 100000;
```

## Examples Using PL/SQL Functions

For the following example, assume that there are two additional columns in DEMO's product table: list-price NUMBER and actual-cost NUMBER.

```
CREATE OR REPLACE FUNCTION get_markup
   (list_price NUMBER,
    actual_cost NUMBER
    )
RETURN NUMBER DETERMINISTIC
IS
BEGIN
  RETURN (list_price-actual_cost)/actual_cost;
END;

CREATE INDEX markup on PRODUCT (get_markup(list_price, actual_cost));

SELECT description
  FROM product
 WHERE get_markup(list_price, actual_cost) > .50;
```

The keyword DETERMINISTIC is required in the GET_MARKUP function just defined. Functions used in function-based indexes must be DETERMINISTIC, which means that when given the same inputs the function will always return the exact same result. Oracle can't tell if the function's behavior really is deterministic, so if you declare a function to be deterministic and it includes a call to functions that are not deterministic, such as SYSDATE or USER, the results of your queries will be unpredictable.

Function-based indexes cannot be built using PL/SQL expressions that return a VARCHAR2 or RAW datatype because of the length restrictions on indexes. You can get around this limitation, by using the SUBSTR function as long as you know the maximum length of the string that the function will return. In the following example, assume that the function string_function returns a VARCHAR2:

```
CREATE INDEX string_idx ON tab_name
(SUBSTR(string_function(column_arg), 1,10));

  SELECT *
    FROM tab_name
   WHERE SUBSTR(string_function(column_arg),1,10) = 'SOMETHING';
```

In the preceding example, notice that the query must also use the SUBSTR function, complicating the where clause. You can hide the SUBSTR function call by creating a view, as the following shows:

```
CREATE OR REPLACE VIEW tab_view
   AS SELECT col1, col2, ...,
             SUBSTR(string_function(column_arg),1,10) ret_string
      FROM tab_name;
```

The view can now be queried as follows:

```
SELECT *
  FROM tab_view
 WHERE ret_string = 'SOMETHING';
```

## What You Need to Know About Function-Based Indexes

■ The instance must use the cost-based optimizer. Therefore, you must gather statistics for your function-based indexes and their corresponding tables using ANALYZE or the DBMS_STATS package. The rule-based optimizer doesn't recognize function-based indexes.

■ You must have the QUERY REWRITE system privilege to create function-based indexes on tables in your own schema. You must have the GLOBAL QUERY REWRITE system privilege to create function-based indexes on tables in other schemas.

■ The parameter QUERY_REWRITE_ENABLED must be set to TRUE. This can be done at the session level with the ALTER SESSION statement, at the system level with the ALTER SYSTEM statement, or in the init.ora file. This parameter allows the optimizer to rewrite the query so that it can use the index.

■ Users must have EXECUTE privilege on the function used in the index.

■ The index can use only functions that are repeatable. This means that the functions cannot include calls to functions such as SYSDATE or USER or calls to the DBMS_RAND package that generates random numbers.

■ The RETURN clause of the function must use the DETERMINISTIC keyword.

■ A function-based index cannot be built on LOB, REF, nested table, or varray columns.

■ A function-based index cannot use an aggregate function, such as SUM(). Only single-line SQL functions may be used.

■ If you make changes to the function on which an index is based, the index will be disabled. You will have to use the ALTER INDEX statement to ENABLE it again.

**NOTE**
*Indexes created on columns in descending order using DESC are now considered function-based indexes. You do not need the QUERY REWRITE or GLOBAL QUERY REWRITE system privileges to create descending indexes, but you must gather statistics for the index and the corresponding table before the cost-based optimizer will recognize them.*

# Using Single-Table Hash Clusters for Fast Row Access

In some cases, you can achieve faster row access with a single-table hash cluster than with an indexed table. With a single-table hash cluster, the cluster key is hashed and the corresponding row is retrieved with a single read. With an indexed table, the key value must be found in the index, which may take more than one read, then the row is read. However, hashing is useful only in some situations. In particular, you may want to consider using a single-table hash cluster if the table stored in the single-table hash cluster is static and most of the queries against the table are equality queries using the cluster key.

A single table can also be stored in an ordinary hash cluster, but single-table hash clusters are more efficient because, if there is a one-to-one mapping between hash keys and data rows in a single-hash cluster, Oracle can locate a row without scanning all rows in the data block. In an ordinary hash cluster, Oracle scans all the rows in a given block, even if there is only one row with the matching cluster key.

Before creating a single-table hash cluster, you must choose a key to be used as the cluster key from the table that will be loaded into the cluster. The object is to select a column or columns that are most often used in the WHERE clause of equality queries. For best results, this column or columns should uniquely identify a row. Oracle preallocates space for each hash key value when the single-table hash cluster is created; if the hash cluster key is not unique, there will be more than one row per hash value, which will cause chaining. Oracle must then scan all rows in the block to determine which rows match the cluster key.

Suppose that you have a lookup table called item, which has the columns item_no and description, and that the table is mostly queried for the description of a particular item based on item_no—for example,

```
SELECT description
  FROM item
 WHERE item_no = 5821;
```

In this case, the obvious choice for the cluster key is item_no. This type of static lookup table is an excellent choice for a single-table hash cluster. If your business changes from time to time and you find you need to insert a lot of new rows, hashing is not a good choice.

The next consideration is to determine the size of the single-table hash cluster. The object of sizing is to determine how large each row will be and how many rows you will need, then set the SIZE and HASHKEYS accordingly. Oracle guarantees that the initial allocation of space is sufficient to store the hash table according to these settings. Assume the item table has 10,000 rows, each of size 256 bytes, then you might create the single-table hash cluster as follows:

```
CREATE CLUSTER store_item (item_no NUMBER)
  SIZE 256 SINGLE TABLE HASHKEYS 10000
  PCTUSED 80
  PCTFREE 5
  TABLESPACE users
  STORAGE (INITIAL 1M NEXT 1M PCTINCREASE 0);
```

Oracle rounds the HASHKEYS value up to the nearest prime number, so in the preceding example the actual value for HASHKEYS will be 10007. Oracle allocates space for a single-table hash cluster based on either SIZE*HASHKEYS or based on the STORAGE parameters, whichever is larger.

Once the cluster has been created, you are ready to add the table:

```
CREATE TABLE item
  (item_no NUMBER,
   description VARCHAR2(200)
  )
  CLUSTER store_item (item_no);
```

In the preceding example, it is not necessary to specify the tablespace or storage parameters because it will use whatever was defined for the cluster.

**NOTE**
*Only one table can be present in a single-table hash cluster at a time; however, you can drop the table and create a different table in the same cluster.*

# Tips Review

Cost-based optimization provides more functionality than rule-based optimization and should be used for all new applications. In general, cost-based optimization chooses the best execution and eliminates the need for tuning individual SQL statements. To take full advantage of the cost-based optimizer's functionality, you must generate statistics for all objects in the database. The DBMS_STATS package allows you to externally gather and manipulate statistics. You can generate statistics using parallel execution, specify the granularity of the statistics to be gathered, back up and recover statistics, and analyze performance based on different sample sizes. In the rare event that the cost-based optimizer does not choose the best execution plan, you can use the plan stability feature to preserve execution plans.

Consider using function-based indexes to support case-insensitive searches, linguistic sorts, or equations. Function-based indexes speed access to rows that can be retrieved based on a value returned by a function or expression.

Use single-table hash clusters for static tables in which most of the queries are equality queries that use the cluster key. Rows are retrieved with just one read, whereas indexed tables require a minimum of two reads.

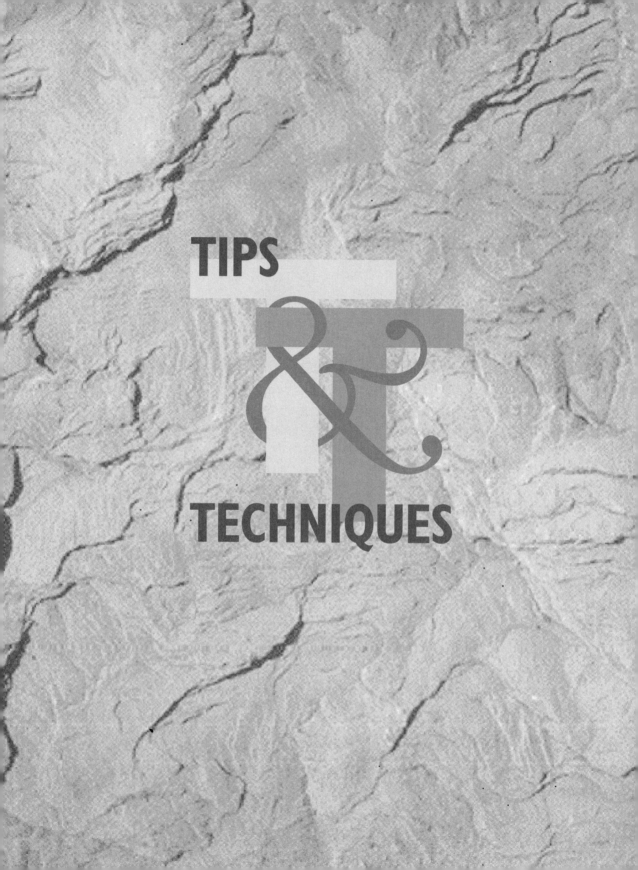

TIPS
&
TECHNIQUES

# CHAPTER
## 6

## Data Warehousing

A *data warehouse* is a repository for corporate or organizational data. The data warehouse usually contains historical data and is populated at regular intervals with data from one or more online transaction processing (OLTP) systems. Data warehouses are typically used in decision support systems, in which the data is analyzed for making strategic business decisions. The analyses performed typically entail the summarizing of large amounts of data, which can compromise a system's resources, taking minutes or even hours to process. OLTP systems, on the other hand, require small, well-defined transactions that must be processed in real-time. Because of the conflicting nature of these two types of systems, they cannot successfully share the same database or database design.

Data warehouses are normally built through use of a dimensional data model, commonly known as a *star schema*. A star schema contains two types of tables: fact tables and dimension tables. *Fact tables* are generally very large tables that contain the quantitative data (facts) about a business. *Dimension tables* are usually much smaller and contain descriptive data about the business. Many of the examples in this chapter will be based on a data warehouse for a chain of department stores designed with the use of a star schema. The fact table is the sales table. The dimension tables are product, store, promotion, and time. At the end of every day, a summary of products sold at each store under a particular promotion (coupon, display, ad, or none) is transferred to the data warehouse. The table definitions are as follows:

```
CREATE TABLE store (
  store_id VARCHAR2(12) CONSTRAINT store_pk PRIMARY KEY,
  store_name VARCHAR2(15),
  city  VARCHAR2(25),
  state VARCHAR2(2),
  region VARCHAR2(2),
  zip VARCHAR2(5));

CREATE TABLE product (
  prod_id VARCHAR2(12) CONSTRAINT prod_pk PRIMARY KEY,
  prod_desc VARCHAR2(15),
  upc NUMBER,
  brand VARCHAR2(12),
  category VARCHAR2(12),
  department VARCHAR2(12));

CREATE TABLE promotion (
  promo_id varchar2(12) CONSTRAINT promo_pk PRIMARY KEY,
  promo_name varchar2(15),
  promo_type varchar2(12));

CREATE TABLE time (
  time_id DATE CONSTRAINT time_pk PRIMARY KEY,
```

```
  month NUMBER,
  quarter NUMBER,
  year NUMBER,
  season VARCHAR2(12));

CREATE TABLE sales (
  CONSTRAINT sales_pk PRIMARY KEY
  (time_id, store_id, prod_id, promo_id),
  time_id DATE NOT NULL CONSTRAINT time_fk
    REFERENCES time(time_id),
  store_id VARCHAR2(12) NOT NULL CONSTRAINT store_fk
    REFERENCES store(store_id),
  prod_id VARCHAR2(12)  NOT NULL CONSTRAINT prod_fk
    REFERENCES product(prod_id),
  promo_id VARCHAR2(12) NOT NULL CONSTRAINT promo_fk
    REFERENCES promotion(promo_id),
  units NUMBER,
  dollars NUMBER,
  cost NUMBER);
```

A data warehouse must provide mechanisms for maintaining large tables, ensuring the consistency of the data, providing good performance for queries that require expensive joins and aggregations, and loading large amounts of data into the warehouse within a short period of time. Oracle8i provides several features that support these requirements. This chapter will discuss the following topics:

- Using range partitioning

- Using hash partitioning

- Using composite partitioning

- Accessing individual partitions and subpartitions

- Using partitioned indexes

- Data dictionary views that describe partitions

- Maintaining partitions

- Using transportable tablespaces to copy a set of tablespaces to another database

- Using transportable tablespaces to move a set of tablespaces to another database

- Using transportable tablespaces to share a read-only tablespace between multiple databases

■ Using transportable tablespaces and partitioning to populate the data warehouse

■ Optimizing star queries

■ Using dimensions to define relationships within the data warehouse

■ Validating dimensions

■ Viewing dimensions

■ Deciding which materialized views to create

■ Using materialized views to store precalculated summaries and joins

■ Choosing a refresh mode for materialized views

■ Choosing a refresh option for materialized views

■ Choosing a build method for materialized views

■ Sizing materialized views

■ Creating materialized views

■ Enabling query rewrite on materialized views

■ Using the DBMS_MVIEW package to refresh materialized views

■ Determining whether a materialized view is being used

■ Setting parameters for summary management

■ Managing Constraints in the Data Warehouse

■ Altering the state of a constraint to facilitate data loads

# Using Partitioning to Manage Large Tables

*Partitioning* is a method of physically dividing large tables and indexes into smaller, more manageable pieces called partitions. A partitioned object is logically the same as an object that is not partitioned. Physically each partition is stored in its own segment.

Partitioning improves the availability and manageability of large tables, making it possible for you to perform administrative tasks such as adding, dropping, or reorganizing a partition without affecting the data in other partitions. Storing each partition in its own tablespace simplifies tasks such as backup, recovery, and I/O balancing. Data can be loaded into one partition while users are accessing other partitions. SQL statements can be optimized to eliminate unnecessary partitions, reducing the amount of data scanned and dramatically improving performance.

Three types of partitioning are supported:

- **Range partitioning**  This was first introduced in release 8.0. Range partitioning works well when the data can be divided on the basis of ranges of column values—in particular, for historical data.

- **Hash partitioning**  New in release 8.1, hash partitioning evenly distributes data among partitions through use of a hashing function. It is intended for data in which there is no appropriate range on which to partition the data.

- **Composite partitioning**  This is a combination of range and hash partitioning. It uses range partitioning to distribute data according to range boundaries, then it further divides the data into subpartitions within each range by use of hash partitioning.

All types of partitioning support three techniques that optimize performance for retrieving data from partitioned tables and for managing these tables:

- **Equipartitioning**  Two tables or indexes are *equipartitioned* if they are partitioned in exactly the same manner. Equipartitioning a table and its indexes promotes partition independence, which means that maintenance operations can be performed on a single partition without its impacting any of the other partitions. A table that is partitioned through use of the composite method is considered to be equipartitioned to another table or index if it is equipartitioned on at least one partitioning method.

- **Partition-wise joining**  A *partition-wise join* is a join that has been broken down into smaller joins between pairs of partitions, which can then be performed either sequentially or in parallel. Performance can be improved in either case. In order to use partitionwise joining, all tables to be joined must be equipartitioned on the same column.

■ **Partition pruning**   The cost-based optimizer can analyze FROM and WHERE clauses in SQL statements and, depending on the selection criteria specified, can eliminate unnecessary partitions. This optimization process is known as *partition pruning*. For example, if the employee table were partitioned so that each department's employees were stored in a separate partition, a query to select data about employees in department 100 would access only the one partition containing department 100. Partition pruning of range partitioned tables can occur only if the SQL SELECT statement contains range, equality, or inlist predicates on the range partitioning columns. For hash partitioned tables, partition pruning can occur only if the SELECT statement contains equality or inlist predicates on the hash partitioning columns. If the index and table are partitioned on different columns, partition pruning can eliminate index partitions even when it cannot eliminate the underlying table's partitions. This type of index is called a *global index* and will be described later in the chapter.

# Using Range Partitioning

Range partitioning distributes data among partitions on the basis of ranges of column values. These columns are called the *partitioning columns*. The values in the partitioning columns of a particular row are called the *partitioning key*. The following example demonstrates how you may partition a table on a date range:

```
CREATE TABLE sales (
  time_id DATE NOT NULL,
  store_id VARCHAR2(12) NOT NULL,
  prod_id VARCHAR2(12) NOT NULL,
  promo_id VARCHAR2(12) NOT NULL,
  units NUMBER,
  dollars NUMBER,
  cost NUMBER
)
  STORAGE (INITIAL 100M NEXT 100M PCTINCREASE 0)
  PARTITION BY RANGE (time_id)
  (PARTITION s1998_qtr1
    VALUES LESS THAN (TO_DATE('01-APR-1998', 'DD-MON-YYYY'))
    TABLESPACE salesdat1,
  PARTITION s1998_qtr2
    VALUES LESS THAN (TO_DATE('01-JUL-1998', 'DD-MON-YYYY'))
    TABLESPACE salesdat2,
  PARTITION s1998_qtr3
```

```
    VALUES LESS THAN (TO_DATE('01-OCT-1998', 'DD-MON-YYYY'))
    TABLESPACE salesdat3,
 PARTITION s1998_qtr4
    VALUES LESS THAN (TO_DATE('01-JAN-1999', 'DD-MON-YYYY'))
    TABLESPACE salesdat4 STORAGE
      (INITIAL 200M NEXT 200M PCTINCREASE0)
);
```

In the foregoing example, the sales table is divided into four partitions, using time_id as the partitioning column. If the database's NLS date format does not include the century along with the year, you must specify the partition bounds, using the TO_DATE() format mask, as shown. The partitions for the first three quarters each have an initial extent of 100MB, which are inherited from the table-level STORAGE clause. Since more sales are expected during the fourth quarter, the fourth quarter's partition has been explicitly assigned an initial extent of 200MB, overriding the table-level STORAGE attribute. Each partition was given a name to indicate its contents. If no partition name were given, Oracle would assign a partition name of the form SYS_P*nnn*. However, because the contents of a partition can be accessed directly by name, it makes sense to give each partition a meaningful name. The syntax for accessing individual partitions will be given later, in the section entitled "Accessing Individual Partitions and Subpartitions."

The range partitioning method defines only the upper bound of each partition, not the lower bound. If you were to load sales data for both 1997 and 1998 into a sales table as partitioned in the foregoing, all of the data for 1997 and the first quarter of 1998 would be loaded into the first partition. If you were to try to load sales data for 1999, you would get an error, and the data would not load because it exceeds the upper bound for all partitions.

## Using Hash Partitioning

Hash partitioning evenly distributes data among partitions by applying a hashing algorithm to a partitioning key and mapping data to partitions based on the result. For example, consider the product table in which most queries will probably involve the product id. If the product id is an arbitrary number, the distribution may be skewed. For example, there may be one thousand products with IDs between 1 and 1000, but only two products with IDs between 1001 and 2000. In this case, hash partitioning makes more sense than trying to partition the table by a range of values. The following example shows how you might partition the product table:

```
CREATE TABLE product (
  prod_id VARCHAR2(12) NOT NULL,
  prod_desc VARCHAR2(12),
  upc NUMBER,
  brand VARCHAR2(12),
```

```
  category VARCHAR2(12),
  department VARCHAR2(12),
  CONSTRAINT product_pk PRIMARY KEY (prod_id)
)
  STORAGE (INITIAL 100M NEXT 100M)
  PARTITION BY HASH(prod_id)
  PARTITIONS 4 STORE IN (proddat1, proddat2, proddat3, proddat4);
```

In the preceding example, the table is divided into four partitions, each with an initial extent of 100MB. To ensure equal distribution of data, the number of partitions must be a power of 2 (that is, 2, 4, 8, 16, and so on). Since the partitions are not explicitly named, Oracle will assign partition names of the form SYS_P*nnn*. The STORE IN clause will store the partitions in the tablespaces specified.

As for range partitions, you can assign a name to each hash partition. However, TABLESPACE is the only physical (storage) attribute you can specify for an individual hash partition. All other attributes are inherited from the table-level defaults. The following example demonstrates an alternative way of partitioning the product table:

```
CREATE TABLE product (
  prod_id     NOT NULL NUMBER,
  prod_desc   VARCHAR2(30)
  ...)
  STORAGE (INITIAL 100M NEXT 100M)
  PARTITION BY HASH(prod_id)
  (PARTITION prod1 TABLESPACE proddat1,
  PARTITION prod2 TABLESPACE proddat2);
```

## Using Composite Partitioning

*Composite partitioning* first uses range partitioning to distribute data among partitions on the basis of ranges of column values; the data in each partition is then subpartitioned through use of hash partitioning. Composite partitioning is useful for facilitating full partition-wise joins. For example, the sales table contains historical data, and many of the queries and maintenance operations will benefit from range partitioning. However, if the sales table is only partitioned by range and many queries also involve joining the sales table with the product table that is hash partitioned, you could use the composite method to enable a full partition-wise join between the two tables. In the previous example, the product table was hash partitioned into four partitions; therefore, to enable partition-wise joins between the product and sales table, you must see that the sales table has four hash subpartitions for each range partition. When a partition-wise join is executed in parallel, the degree of parallelism is limited by the number of partitions; therefore, the maximum degree of parallelism that could be used for a join between the sales and product table is four. The following example partitions the sales table by time_id, then by prod_id:

```
CREATE TABLE sales (
  time_id DATE NOT NULL,
  store_id VARCHAR2(12) NOT NULL,
  prod_id VARCHAR2(12)  NOT NULL,
  promo_id VARCHAR2(12) NOT NULL,
  ...)
  STORAGE (INITIAL 100M NEXT 100M)
  PARTITION BY RANGE(time_id)
  SUBPARTITION BY HASH(prod_id)
  SUBPARTITIONS 4 STORE IN
     (salesdat1, salesdat2, salesdat3, salesdat4)
  (PARTITION s1998_qtr1
    VALUES LESS THAN (TO_DATE('01-APR-1998', 'DD-MON-YYYY')),
   PARTITION s1998_qtr2
    VALUES LESS THAN (TO_DATE('01-JUL-1998', 'DD-MON-YYYY')),
   PARTITION s1998_qtr3
    VALUES LESS THAN (TO_DATE('01-OCT-1998', 'DD-MON-YYYY')),
   PARTITION s1998_qtr4
    VALUES LESS THAN (TO_DATE('01-JAN-1999', 'DD-MON-YYYY'))
  );
```

In the preceding example, there are sixteen subpartitions in total (four for each partition). The subpartitions of each partition are assigned to the four tablespaces specified at the table level. The storage attributes specified for the base table will be used for each subpartition, giving each subpartition an initial extent of 100MB. The subpartitions are not named, so the system will generate names for them, using the format SYS_SUBP*nnn.*

An alternate approach is to explicitly assign a name to one or more of the hash partitions. You can then specify the tablespace in which each subpartition is stored. Any subpartition without an explicit name is assigned a system-generated name. Any subpartition not given an explicit tablespace assignment is placed in a tablespace according to the same algorithm that was used for hash partitioning. This behavior is illustrated by the following example:

```
CREATE TABLE employee
  (employee_id   number not null,
   last_name     varchar2(15),
   first_name    varchar2(15),
   department_id number
  )
  PARTITION BY RANGE (department_id)
  SUBPARTITION BY HASH (employee_id)
  SUBPARTITIONS 4 STORE IN (empdat1, empdat2, empdat3, empdat4)
```

**Use Composite Partitioning**

```
(PARTITION emp_1000 VALUES LESS THAN (1000),
 PARTITION emp_2000 VALUES LESS THAN (2000),
 PARTITION emp_3000 VALUES LESS THAN (3000)
   STORE IN (empdat5, empdat6),
 PARTITION emp_max VALUES LESS THAN (MAXVALUE)
   (SUBPARTITION emp_max1 TABLESPACE empdat7,
    SUBPARTITION emp_max2 TABLESPACE empdat7,
    SUBPARTITION emp_max3 TABLESPACE empdat8,
    SUBPARTITION emp4_max4 TABLESPACE empdat8)
);
```

In the foregoing example, the employee table is partitioned into a total of sixteen subpartitions (four partitions times four subpartitions). The subpartitions for partitions emp1 and emp2 will have system-assigned names and will be stored in the Empdat1, Empdat2, Empdat3, and Empdat4 tablespaces. The subpartitions for the emp_3000 partition will have system-assigned names and will be stored in the empdat5 and empdat6 tablespaces in a round-robin fashion, with two partitions per tablespace. The subpartitions for emp_max have user-specified names and will be stored in the tablespaces specified. In the preceding example, MAXVALUE is used to indicate an infinite upper bound for the emp_max partition.

**NOTE**

*When Oracle assigns rows to partitions, it sorts nulls greater than all other values except MAXVALUE. If a table is partitioned on a nullable column, then the highest partition should have a partition bound of MAXVALUE for that column; otherwise any rows that contain nulls will map above the highest partition and the insert will fail.*

## Accessing Individual Partitions and Subpartitions

You can select data from a partitioned table just as you would any other table. You can also select from individual partitions or subpartitions. If you do this for a range partition, it effectively replaces use of an equivalent WHERE clause. Although you can select from hash partitions and hash subpartitions, it isn't meaningful because the contents of each partition are determined solely by the hashing algorithm. The following example shows you how to access an individual partition:

```
SELECT * FROM employee PARTITION(emp_1000);
```

Assuming the employee table is range or composite partitioned on the basis of department_id, the preceding SELECT statement is equivalent to the following statement:

```
SELECT * FROM employee WHERE department_id < 1000;
```

## Using Partitioned Indexes

Just as tables can be partitioned to improve their availability and maintainability, as well as to enhance query performance, indexes on partitioned tables can also be partitioned. Oracle8i supports two types of index partitioning:

■ A local index is equipartitioned with its underlying table. That is, the index has the same number of partitions and partition keys as the base table.

■ A global index may or may not be partitioned. If it is partitioned, it should not be equipartitioned with the base table.

### Using Local Indexes

A local index automatically inherits the partitioning scheme defined on the underlying table. The local index is partitioned on the same partition key columns as the underlying table and has the same number of partitions as the underlying table. Oracle automatically maintains local index partitions when partitions in the underlying table are changed. In some cases, however, when the underlying table changes, some or all of the local index partitions will need to be rebuilt, as is described in the section "Maintaining Partitions." By definition, local indexes are equipartitioned with the underlying table.

The easiest way to create a local index is simply to add the keyword LOCAL to the CREATE INDEX command:

```
CREATE INDEX prod_idx ON product(prod_id) LOCAL;
```

Unfortunately, using this syntax has all the disadvantages of defining any index without an explicit storage clause. Since no tablespace is specified, each index partition will be stored in the same tablespace as the corresponding table partition. Furthermore, each partition will be created through use of the tablespace default storage parameters. The next example specifies partition-level tablespaces and storage attributes for the local index:

```
CREATE INDEX prod_idx ON product(prod_id) LOCAL
  STORE IN (prodidx1, prodidx2, prodidx3, prodidx4)
  STORAGE (INITIAL 100M NEXT 100M PCTINCREASE 0);
```

As long as no partition names are specified, Oracle will automatically create the same number of partitions as the underlying table. If you choose to explicitly name each partition and store it in a specific tablespace, you must be sure to specify the same number of partitions as are in the base table. The following example shows a local index being created with four partitions; therefore, the base table must also have four partitions:

```
CREATE INDEX prod_idx on product(prod_id) LOCAL
  (PARTITION pidx1 TABLESPACE prodidx1,
  PARTITION pidx2 TABLESPACE prodidx2,
  PARTITION pidx3 TABLESPACE prodidx3,
  PARTITION pidx4 TABLESPACE prodidx4
  );
```

An index that is used to enforce a primary key constraint can be local only if the partitioning key columns are a subset of the index key columns. For example, because the sales table is partitioned by range on time_id, and the primary key for the sales table is made up of time_id, store_id, prod_id, and promo_id, the primary key can be created through use of a local index, as follows:

```
ALTER TABLE sales ADD CONSTRAINT sales_pk   PRIMARY KEY (time_id,
store_id, prod_id, promo_id)
  USING INDEX LOCAL
  STORE IN (salesidx1, salesidx2, salesidx3, salesidx4)
  STORAGE (INITIAL 10M NEXT 10M);
```

In the preceding example, if the primary key did not include time_id, the index would have to be created as a global index.

## Using Global Indexes

Global indexes are sometimes used to improve performance, but generally they are used to enforce uniqueness on columns other than the partitioning columns. Local indexes do not support uniqueness across all partitions on columns that are not partitioning columns. Unlike a local index, which must be equipartitioned with its underlying table, a global index spans the entire partitioned table and may optionally be partitioned. If it is partitioned, it should not be partitioned in the same way as the underlying table. A global index can be partitioned only through use of the range method, and the highest partition must have a partition bound of MAXVALUE to ensure that all rows in the underlying table can be represented in the index.

The following example shows how you could create a partitioned global index on the employee table to enforce uniqueness on the employee_id column:

```
CREATE UNIQUE INDEX emp_idx ON employee (employee_id) GLOBAL
  PARTITION BY RANGE (employee_id)
```

```
(PARTITION emp_idx1 VALUES LESS THAN (2000) TABLESPACE empidx1,
 PARTITION emp_idx2 VALUES LESS THAN (MAXVALUE) TABLESPACE empidx2
);
```

Global indexes can be difficult to maintain. If you create a global index, you are responsible for its partitioning. You must continue to maintain the partitioning whenever the data in the underlying table partition changes as a result of a partition being split, moved, truncated, added, or dropped. You should avoid using global indexes for tables that are partitioned by date if the tables must periodically be purged of rows older than a given date. If you drop the partition containing the oldest data and add a new partition, you will have to rebuild the index. The operations for maintaining global indexes are described later in the chapter.

## Data Dictionary Views that Describe Partitions

The Data Dictionary views shown in Table 6-1 will be helpful when you are working with partitioned tables. Equivalent ALL_ and USER_ views are also available.

## Maintaining Partitions

It is sometimes necessary to perform maintenance operations on partitions. For example, you might need to drop the oldest partition of a historically partitioned table and to add a new partition. The following sections describe all of the operations that can be performed on partitions.

### Guidelines for Maintaining Partitioned Tables and Indexes

Unless otherwise specified, all operations described in this section apply to any partitioned table, regardless of the partition type. Whenever a maintenance operation is performed on a table that affects its partitioning, Oracle will automatically adjust the partitioning of each local index. However, in most cases, it will be necessary to rebuild one or more of the partitions. Oracle will not make any adjustments to the partitions of corresponding global indexes when a change is made to the partitioning of the underlying table; therefore, in most cases, it will be necessary to rebuild one or more partitions of a partitioned global index. If the global index is not partitioned, the entire index will need to be rebuilt. You can determine which partitions need to be rebuilt by querying the user_ind_partitions view for partitioned indexes or by querying the user_indexes view for nonpartitioned indexes, as follows:

```
SELECT index_name, partition_name
  FROM user_ind_partitions
 WHERE status = 'UNUSABLE';
```

Maintaining Partitions

| View Name | Description |
|---|---|
| DBA_PART_TABLES | Object-level partitioning information for partitioned tables |
| DBA_TAB_PARTITIONS | For each table partition, the partition-level partitioning information, the storage parameters for the partition, and partition statistics |
| DBA_PART_KEY_COLUMNS | Partitioning key columns for all partitioned objects |
| DBA_PART_COL_STATISTICS | Column statistics and histogram information for all table partitions |
| DBA_PART_HISTOGRAMS | Histogram data (end-points per histogram) for histograms on all table partitions |
| DBA_TAB_SUBPARTITIONS | For each table subpartition, its name, name of the table and partition to which it belongs, and its storage attributes |
| DBA_SUBPART_KEY_COLUMNS | Subpartitioning key columns for tables (and local indexes) partitioned using the composite method |
| DBA_SUBPART_COL_STATISTICS | Subpartitioning column statistics for tables (and local indexes) partitioned using the composite method |
| DBA_SUBPART_HISTOGRAMS | Actual histogram data (endpoints per histogram) for histograms on table subpartitions |
| DBA_PART_INDEXES | Histogram data (endpoints per histogram) for histograms on all table partitions |
| DBA_IND_PARTITIONS | For each index partition, the partition-level partitioning information, the storage parameters for the partition, and partition statistics |
| DBA_IND_SUBPARTITIONS | For each index subpartition, the partition-level partitioning information, the storage parameters for the subpartition, and partition statistics |

**TABLE 6-1.** *Data Dictionary Views for Partitions*

```
SELECT index_name
FROM user_indexes
WHERE status = 'UNUSUABLE';
```

Unusable index partitions can be rebuilt as follows:

```
ALTER INDEX prod_idx REBUILD PARTITION p1;
```

Unusable nonpartitioned indexes can be rebuilt as follows:

```
ALTER INDEX prod_idx REBUILD;
```

Alternatively, you could drop the entire index and recreate it.

> **NOTE**
> *You can determine if a partitioned index is local or global by selecting the locality column in the USER_PART_INDEXES view.*

## Adding a Range Partition

A partition can be added to accommodate new data. For example, the sales table will require a new partition to hold each new quarter's data. You can add a new partition after the highest partition as long as the partition bound is not MAXVALUE. A matching partition will be added to any local indexes. The local index partition will be created with the default physical attributes of the index. It will be given the same name as the new table partition if possible; otherwise it will be given a system-assigned name. The following example adds a partition to the sales table:

```
ALTER TABLE sales
  ADD PARTITION s1999_qtr
  VALUES LESS THAN (TO_DATE('01-APR-1999', 'DD-MON-YYYY'))
  TABLESPACE salesdat5;
```

If the partition bound is MAXVALUE or if you want to add a partition to the beginning or middle of the table, you must add the partition by splitting the affected partition, as shown later in this section.

## Adding a Hash Partition

A hash partition can be added to redistribute existing data or to make room for new data. When you add a hash partition, the data will automatically be redistributed to include the new partition; however, if the number of partitions is not a power of 2, the data will be unevenly distributed. The following example adds a partition to the product table:

```
ALTER TABLE product
  ADD PARTITION prod3
  TABLESPACE proddat3;
```

## Adding a Composite Partition

A partition may be added to a composite partitioned table in order to accommodate new data or to redistribute data. You can add a new partition to a composite

Maintaining Partitions

partitioned table after the highest partition as long as the partition bound is not MAXVALUE. (If the partition bound is MAXVALUE, you must add the partition by splitting the highest partition.) A matching partition will be added to any local indexes. The following example adds a partition to the sales table:

```
ALTER TABLE sales
  ADD PARTITION s1999_qtr1
  VALUES LESS THAN (TO_DATE('01-APR-1999', 'DD-MON-YYYY'))
  TABLESPACE salesdat5;
```

When a new partition is added, all of the subpartitions are also added. Subpartition names and tablespaces can optionally be specified.

## Moving Partitions

A partition can be moved from one tablespace to another. Moving a partition creates a new segment and drops the old segment; consequently, the MOVE command can be used to defragment a partition. If you specify a target tablespace, the partition is moved from the original tablespace to the target. If no new tablespace is specified, the partition is rebuilt in the current tablespace. The method for moving partitions is the same for all types of partitioned tables. The following example shows you how to move a partition:

```
ALTER TABLE product MOVE PARTITION prod1 TABLESPACE newproddat1;
```

## Dropping Partitions

When you drop a partition, all of the data within the partition is removed. The corresponding index partition is dropped from any local indexes. If the partition contains data, you must disable all referential integrity constraints on the table before you can drop the partition. You cannot drop the last partition in a table. Partitions can be dropped from range or composite partitioned tables but not hash partitioned tables. The following example shows you how to drop a partition from a table:

```
ALTER TABLE employee DROP PARTITION emp_2000;
```

You cannot explicitly drop a local index partition, but you can drop a global index partition. If the global index partition is empty, you can just drop it; if it contains data, you will have to rebuild at least some of the remaining partitions. The following example shows how you can drop a partition from a global index:

```
ALTER INDEX emp_idx DROP PARTITION emp_idx1;
```

## Coalescing Partitions

Coalescing is a way of eliminating a partition and redistributing its contents across all remaining partitions. Only hash partitions can be coalesced. The hash function determines the partition to be eliminated. If the number of partitions remaining is no longer a power of 2, the data will no longer be evenly distributed among the remaining partitions. When a hash partition is coalesced, the corresponding local index partitions will also be coalesced.

```
ALTER TABLE product COALESCE PARTITION;
```

## Truncating Partitions

Truncating a partition removes all of the rows from the partition. If the partition contains data, you must disable all referential integrity constraints on the table before you can truncate the partition. Oracle will automatically truncate the corresponding local index partition. You can de-allocate the space previously allocated to the table partition with the DROP STORAGE clause, or you can retain the space with the REUSE STORAGE clause. In the following example, a partition is truncated and the space is retained:

```
ALTER TABLE sales TRUNCATE PARTITION s1998_qtr1 REUSE STORAGE;
```

## Splitting Partitions

Data can be redistributed in a range or a composite partitioned table by splitting one or more partitions. Local indexes will automatically be split. Oracle will assign system-generated names to the new index partitions. You can query the USER_IND_PARTITIONS view to determine the names, then rename them if you wish. Assume the employee table was range partitioned on department_no. In the following example, the employee table is split such that all employee records stored in the emp_max partition and having a department number less than 4000 will go in the new emp_max partition, while all employee records stored in the emp_4000 partition and having a department number 4000 or greater will go in the new emp_max partition.

```
ALTER TABLE employee
  SPLIT PARTITION emp_max AT (4000)
  INTO (PARTITION emp_4000, PARTITION emp_max);
```

## Merging Partitions

You can merge the contents of two adjacent partitions into a new partition. The new partition's upper bound will be the higher of the two partitions being merged. Any attributes not specified, such as tablespace, will take on the table-level defaults. If you don't specify a new partition name, Oracle will assign one. If the new partition contains subpartitions, Oracle will assign names to the subpartitions. Only partitions

Maintaining Partitions

of range and composite partitioned tables can be merged. The following statement merges two adjacent partitions of the employee table:

```
ALTER TABLE employee MERGE PARTITIONS emp_3000, emp_4000
  INTO PARTITION emp_4000
```

## Exchanging Partitions

Exchanging partitions is typically used to convert multiple tables comprising a partitioned view into one partitioned table or to roll data into a historical table. Assume the sales table contains only data from January 1, 1998 to September 30, 1998 and is partitioned by date into three quarters. Assume also that there is a table containing only fourth-quarter sales data. The fourth-quarter sales data can be rapidly inserted into the sales tables by the addition of a new partition to the sales table and exchanging the contents of the new partition with the contents of the table as shown in the following example:

```
ALTER TABLE sales
  ADD PARTITION s1998_qtr4
  VALUES LESS THAN (TO_DATE('01-JAN-1999', 'DD-MON-YYYY'))
  TABLESPACE salesdat4 STORAGE (INITIAL 2K);
ALTER TABLE sales
  EXCHANGE PARTITION s1998_qtr4 WITH TABLE sales_qtr4
  INCLUDING INDEXES WITH VALIDATION;
```

In the foregoing example, a partition with a small initial extent is added to the sales table. After the new partition is exchanged with the sales_qtr4 table, the table will be empty and have the initial extent size of the newly added partition. If the sales_qtr4 table was indexed exactly the same as the sales table, the INCLUDING INDEXES clause can be used to also exchange the sales_qtr4 indexes with the corresponding index partitions. The WITH VALIDATION clause causes Oracle to return an error if any of the rows in the exchanged table do not map into the partitions or subpartitions being exchanged. Exchanging partitions is valid only for a range partitioned table.

## Renaming Partitions

You can rename partitions and subpartitions in partitioned tables and indexes. The new name must be unique for all partitions and subpartitions within the same table or index. The following statement shows how to rename a partition that was created with a system-generated name:

```
ALTER TABLE product RENAME PARTITION sys_p100 TO prod_part1;
```

# Using Transportable Tablespaces to Move Data Between Databases

The transportable tablespace feature allows you to move or copy one or more tablespaces from one database to another. You can use transportable tablespaces to implement any of the following tasks:

- Feed data into a data warehouse or data mart
- Archive old or historical data
- Share data between multiple databases

Transportable tablespaces are subject to the following limitations:

- The source and target database must be on the same hardware platform. For example, you can transport a tablespace from one Sun Solaris machine to another but not from a Sun Solaris to a database running under AIX.
- The source and target database must have the same database block size and must use the same character set.
- A tablespace cannot be transported to a target database if a tablespace with the same name already exists on the target database.
- Transportable tablespaces do not support any of the following:
    - Snapshot/replication
    - Function-based indexes
    - Scoped REFs
    - Domain indexes
    - 8.0-compatible advanced queues with multiple recipients

## Using Transportable Tablespaces to Copy a Set of Tablespaces

The basic procedure for copying a set of tablespaces involves making the tablespaces read-only, copying the corresponding datafiles, then using export/ import to export the metadata from the data dictionary and import it into the target database. The following steps outline the procedure for copying a set of tablespaces from a source database to a target database.

## Step 1: Select a Self-Contained Set of Tablespaces

A self-contained set of tablespaces does not contain any references that point outside of the set. Any of the following situations would violate this rule:

- The set of tablespaces contains an index for a table that is not included in the set.

- A partitioned table is not fully contained in the set of tablespaces. However, you could transport a subset of a partitioned table by exchanging the partitions to be transported into tables.

- A table inside the set of tablespaces contains a LOB column that points to a LOB outside of the set of tablespaces.

- A referential integrity constraint on a table refers to a parent table that is not in the set of tablespaces. However, if you do not need to maintain the relationship, you can choose not to include referential integrity constraints when you export the tablespaces.

You can determine whether a set of tablespaces is self-contained by executing the built-in PL/SQL procedure DBMS_TTS.TRANSPORT_SET_CHECK, then querying the TRANSPORT_SET_VIOLATIONS view. If there are no violations, the view will be empty.

The TRANSPORT_SET_CHECK procedure takes two parameters: a comma-separated list of the tablespaces that comprise the set, and a BOOLEAN indicating whether referential integrity constraints should be checked. The following example demonstrates this process:

```
EXECUTE DBMS_TTS.TRANSPORT_SET_CHECK('SALESDAT, SALESIDX', TRUE);
SELECT * FROM transport_set_violations;
```

**NOTE**
*Object references, such as REFs, are not checked by the TRANSPORT_SET_CHECK routine. If a tablespace that contains dangling REFs is transported to another database, no violations will be reported by the TRANSPORT_SET_CHECK command; however, errors will occur if a query subsequently follows the dangling REF.*

## Step 2: Generate a Transportable Tablespace Set

Make the tablespaces in the set read-only (if they aren't already). Then use the export utility to export the metadata from the data dictionary. The following example demonstrates this process:

```
ALTER TABLESPACE salesdat READ ONLY;
ALTER TABLESPACE salesidx READ ONLY;

exp TRANSPORT_TABLESPACE=y TABLESPACES=salesdat, salesidx FILE=sales.dmp
```

Exporting tablespaces exports *only* the data dictionary for the tablespace contents. It does not export the actual data in the tablespaces.

When prompted for a username, enter SYS AS SYSDBA. Only the SYS user can transport a tablespace because the stored procedures required to transport a tablespace are owned by SYS.

**NOTE**
*The syntax for connecting "SYS AS SYSDBA" can vary depending on the operating system.*

In the preceding example, any existing constraints, grants, and triggers are exported. If you do not want to export any of these, you can specify the appropriate parameter with the value of 'n' (that is, CONSTRAINTS=n, GRANTS=n, TRIGGERS=n).

**NOTE**
*If you export triggers, they will be exported without a validity check. Any invalid triggers will cause compilation errors during the import.*

## Step 3: Transport the Tablespace Set

This step simply involves copying the datafiles to a location in which they can be accessed by the target database. You can use any command available to the operating system, including but not limited to a copying utility and ftp.

## Step 4: Plug in the Tablespace Set

This step involves using the import utility, then optionally placing the transported tablespaces in read/write mode. Create a file containing the following:

```
TRANSPORT_TABLESPACE=y
DATAFILES=('/target/salesdat.dbf', '/target/salesidx.dbf')
FILE=sales.dmp
LOG=trans_sales.log
```

Transportable Tablespaces
to Copy a Set of Tablespaces

Run import with the parfile parameter:

```
imp parfile=filename
```

When prompted for a username, enter SYS AS SYSDBA.

 **NOTE**
*There must be a corresponding user ID in the target*
*database for all of the owners of objects in the*
*transported tablespaces; otherwise, the import will fail.*

The only parameters that are required with the import command are
TRANSPORT_TABLESPACE and DATAFILES. Table 6-2 describes optional
parameters that you could use with import.

After the import completes, check the log file to make sure that no errors
occurred. If the import completes successfully, you can put the tablespace in
read/write mode, as shown:

```
ALTER TABLESPACE salesdat READ WRITE;
ALTER TABLESPACE salesidx READ WRITE;
```

 # Using Transportable Tablespaces to Move a Set of Tablespaces

The procedure for moving one or more tablespaces from one database to another is
similar to the procedure for copying a tablespace. Assuming that both databases can
access the file system on which the datafiles for the tablespaces reside, it is not

| Parameter | Description |
| --- | --- |
| TABLESPACES | List of tablespaces to be imported. |
| TTS_OWNERS | List of users who own the data in the transportable tablespace set. |
| FROMUSER | The owner of the objects in the source database. This parameter can be used with TOUSER to change ownership of objects when they are imported into the target database. |
| TOUSER | The owner of the objects in the target database. This parameter can be used with FROMUSER to change ownership of objects when they are imported into the target database. |

**TABLE 6-2.** *Optional Parameters to Use with Import*

necessary for you to copy the datafiles. Once you've verified that the transport completed successfully, simply drop the tablespace from the source database as follows:

```
ALTER TABLESPACE salesdat OFFLINE;
DROP TABLESPACE salesdat INCLUDING CONTENTS;
```

## Using Transportable Tablespaces to Share a Read-Only Tablespace Between Multiple Databases

You can share a read-only tablespace between multiple databases as follows:

- Select a source database that owns the tablespace.

- Generate a transportable tablespace set from the source database (see Steps 1 and 2 earlier).

- Plug the tablespace set into each of the target databases (see Step 4 earlier).

**CAUTION**
*Do not take the tablespace out of read-only mode in any of the databases because it could corrupt the tablespace. If at a later time you drop the transported tablespace in all but one of the databases, you can put it in read/write mode.*

## Using Transportable Tablespaces and Partitioning to Populate the Data Warehouse

The combination of partitioning and transportable tablespaces makes it faster and easier for you to populate a data warehouse than is possible with traditional export and refresh scenarios. For example, consider the sales table that contains historical data and is partitioned by range, with one partition for each quarter. Assume that the data warehouse is populated once every quarter from an OLTP system. A table could be created in the OLTP database or a staging database that would contain summarized data from the OLTP system's sales transaction table for the most recent quarter. The tablespace containing the summary table could then be transported to the data warehouse. Once it is in the data warehouse, a new partition can be created in the sales table, and the new data can be brought into the sales table by exchanging partitions.

# Using a Star Schema

As mentioned earlier, a star schema is a database design that is often used to implement data warehouses. A star schema contains two types of tables: fact tables and dimension tables. Fact tables are tables that contain the quantitative data (facts) about a business. Fact tables tend to be quite large (nowadays they are measured in millions of records and gigabytes or terabytes of data), depending on the volume of business and amount of detailed and/or historical data that must be stored. Dimension tables are usually much smaller and contain descriptive data about the business.

Each fact table and each dimension table must have a primary key. The primary key for the fact table usually consists of a combination of foreign keys from the dimension tables. The fact table usually has one or more concatenated indexes composed of some combination of the foreign keys that make up the primary key. A query that joins a number of dimension tables to a fact table is called a star query. A star query uses a star join, which joins the foreign keys of the dimension tables to the primary key of the fact table. Figure 6-1 shows what the star schema is for the sales fact table, with dimension tables product, promotion, store, and time.

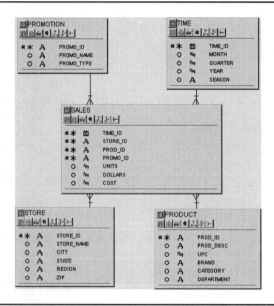

**FIGURE 6-1.** *Star schema for the department store model*

## Optimizing Star Queries

To optimize the execution of star queries, you must use the cost-based optimizer, which requires that you gather statistics regularly on each of the tables in the star schema, using the ANALYZE command or the DBMS_STATS package (described in Chapter 5). Each dimension table must have a primary key constraint on its key column(s), and the fact table must have either a primary key constraint or an index that is a concatenation of the foreign keys from the dimension tables.

Consider the following example of a star query that selects the total sales on sweaters sold in New York in the third quarter:

```
SELECT SUM(s.dollars) total_sales
  FROM sales s, time t, product p,  stores st
 WHERE st.state = 'NY'
   AND p.category = 'SWEATERS'
   AND t.quarter = 3
/* Join the fact table (sales) to the dimension tables */
   AND st.store_id = s.store_id
   AND p.prod_id = s.prod_id
   AND t.time_id = s.time_id;
```

To optimize this particular star query, the optimizer needs to find primary key constraints on the dimension tables—store_id in the store table, prod_id in the product table, and time_id in the timetable. In addition, the sales (fact) table must have either a primary key constraint or a concatenated index on the columns store_id, prod_id, and time_id.

You may want to put additional indexes on the sales table to support queries that don't include all of the possible dimensions. For example, if you were interested in just the total sales from all stores in New York during the third quarter, you might want to create a concatenated index consisting solely of the columns store_id and time_id.

If you have created the indexes or constraints as just outlined, the optimizer should choose an efficient star query as its execution plan. If you find that you need to improve the plan, you can use the following hints:

```
/*+ STAR */
/*+ ORDERED USE_NL(sales) INDEX(sales sales_index) */
```

The STAR hint tells Oracle to use a star query plan, if possible. A star plan puts the largest table in the query (the fact table) last in the join order and joins it with a NESTED LOOPS join on the fact table's concatenated index. The star hint can be applied only when there are at least three tables specified in the query and when the fact table's concatenated index has at least three columns.

The USE_NL hint tells Oracle to perform a NESTED LOOPS join, using the specified table as the driving table in the join.

# Summary Management

A data warehouse is typically populated with large amounts of detailed data that is usually stored in one or more fact tables. The detailed data is used to perform analyses that often involve summarizing the data across dimensions, such as time, product, and store. For example, an analyst might want to compare sales revenue generated from women's clothing sold in the Northeast to sales revenue generated from women's clothing sold in the Southeast. Queries that perform these kinds of aggregations (summaries) can be very expensive in terms of time and resources.

Oracle8i's summary management includes capabilities that address two serious problems in managing a data warehouse. The first is how to get data out of the warehouse, in terms of complex queries, involving aggregations and summaries, potentially across many tables and millions of rows. The second is how to keep the data in the warehouse updated in a timely manner in a 24 × 7 world.

On the output side, summary management can dramatically improve query performance by precalculating aggregations and performing joins and storing the result set in a schema object called a *materialized view.* If the same (or similar) queries are repeatedly executed by many different users, you can consult the result set stored in the materialized view rather than performing the calculations and joins for each query. The optimizer uses the query rewrite component of summary management to determine if there are any materialized views that satisfy a particular query and automatically rewrites the query to use the materialized view. A dimension, a new database object provided in Oracle 8i, provides critical input to the optimizer's query rewrite component in determining whether a materialized view can be used to satisfy a particular query.

On the input side, summary management provides options for refreshing materialized views when the data in the underlying detail tables is updated. These options may involve creating and utilizing a materialized view log, another new object that can help with "changed data propagation" by only refreshing changed or new rows in the warehouse rather than by recreating the materialized view. Oracle8i also includes functions to determine which materialized views should be created, to estimate the size of materialized views, and to report on utilization of existing materialized views.

Although this discussion concentrates on the use of summary management techniques in a star schema in a data warehouse, where data is stored in a denormalized star schema design, it is also applicable to normalized database designs traditionally found in OLTP systems or operational data stores (ODS) or in more complex data warehouse designs.

# Using Dimensions to Define Relationships within the Data Warehouse

In order to manage summaries automatically through use of materialized views, you should create dimensions that define the functional dependencies and hierarchical relationships that exist within, and among, each of the tables. The optimizer uses the dimensions along with materialized views to perform query rewrite. Dimensions are not always necessary for query rewrite, but some queries cannot be rewritten without them. Dimensions are particularly useful for rewriting queries that contain a reference to a column that is not stored in a materialized view but that can be obtained by joining the materialized view back to the appropriate dimension table. Dimensions are also important when a query requests an aggregate at a higher level in a hierarchy than what exists in the materialized view. In addition to playing an important role in query rewrite, dimensions are required by the summary advisor to make recommendations about which materialized views to create or drop. The following examples show how you might define dimensions for the dimension tables in the department store's data warehouse:

```
CREATE DIMENSION product_dim
  LEVEL item IS product.prod_id
  LEVEL category IS product.category
  LEVEL department IS product.department
  LEVEL brand IS product.brand
  HIERARCHY merchandise (
    item CHILD OF
    category CHILD OF
    department)
  HIERARCHY brand (
    item CHILD OF
    brand)
  ATTRIBUTE item DETERMINES upc
  ATTRIBUTE item DETERMINES prod_desc;
```

In the preceding example, the product_dim dimension has multiple hierarchies. Items can roll up to categories, and categories can roll up to departments. In addition, items can roll up to brands. The DETERMINES clause tells the optimizer to join back to the product table to get prod_desc when a query requests prod_desc, and there is a materialized view containing prod_id instead of prod_desc that satisfies the query. Consequently, the relationship between a hierarchy and its dependent attributes must be one-to-one. For example, in the product_dim dimension, for each item there is one upc and for each upc there is one item.

```
CREATE DIMENSION time_dim
  LEVEL day IS time.time_id
```

```
LEVEL month IS time.month
LEVEL quarter IS time.quarter
LEVEL year IS time.year
LEVEL season IS time.season
HIERARCHY calendar (
  day CHILD OF
  month CHILD OF
  quarter CHILD OF
  year)
HIERARCHY season (
  day CHILD OF
  season);
```

In the preceding example, the time dimension also has multiple hierarchies, calendar and season. The hierarchies can be used by query rewrite to determine if a query can be satisfied with a materialized view that has a finer granularity. For example, if sales are summarized by month in a materialized view, the view can be used to satisfy a query that summarizes sales by year.

When all of the levels in a dimension are defined on columns from the same table, as in the preceding examples, it is called a *denormalized dimension.* In a dimensional data model, it is common to denormalize tables in order to improve performance. The following geography dimension is built from the denormalized store table:

```
CREATE DIMENSION geography_dim
  LEVEL store IS store.store_id
  LEVEL zip IS store.zip
  LEVEL city_state IS (store.city, store.state)
  LEVEL region IS store.region
  HIERARCHY location (
    Store CHILD OF
    zip CHILD OF
    city_state CHILD OF
    region)
    ATTRIBUTE store DETERMINES store_name;
```

When the levels in a dimension are defined on columns from different tables, it is called a *normalized dimension.* Consider a normalized data model in which the store table contains only the zip, and an additional table zipcode is created with the columns zip, city, state, and region. Using this normalized model, the geography dimension could be rewritten as follows:

```
CREATE DIMENSION geography_dim
  LEVEL store IS store.store_id
```

```
LEVEL zip IS zipcode..zip
LEVEL city_state IS (zipcode.city, zipcode.state)
LEVEL region IS zipcode.region
HIERARCHY location (
  store CHILD OF
  zip CHILD OF
  city_state CHILD OF
  region
    JOIN KEY store.zip REFERENCES zip);
```

Dimensions must have hierarchical integrity, meaning that each child can only have one parent. For example, in the geography_dim dimension, each store belongs to one zip code, each zip code belongs to one city, and each city belongs to one state. The columns of each hierarchy level cannot be null, which should be enforced by use of NOT NULL constraints on the underlying table. In a normalized dimension, the joins between the tables must guarantee that each child row joins with one and only one parent row. This condition is enforceable by the addition of foreign key and not NULL constraints on the child join key(s) and by the placement of a primary key constraint on the parent join key(s). The columns in a hierarchy level cannot occur in more than one dimension. For example, you couldn't create a geographical dimension using the columns from the normalized store and zipcode tables and then create another geographical dimension using the fields from the zipcode table.

## Validating Dimensions

It is important that the relationships defined in the dimension be correct, otherwise rewritten queries could return incorrect results. Each time new data is loaded into the data warehouse, dimensional integrity should be validated before the materialized views are refreshed. This can be done through use of the DBMS_OLAP.VALIDATE_DIMENSION procedure. The first argument to the procedure is the dimension name. The second argument is the owner of the dimension. The third argument should be specified as FALSE to indicate that all rows for the tables of the dimension should be validated or as TRUE to validate just the new rows. The final argument should be specified as TRUE to verify that all columns that are defined as levels in the hierarchy are nonnull. Alternatively, this argument can be set to FALSE if nonnullness is guaranteed by NOT NULL constraints. The following example shows you how to call this procedure:

```
EXECUTE DBMS_OLAP.VALIDATE_DIMENSION('GEOGRAPHY_DIM', 'MYSCHEMA', FALSE, TRUE);
```

If any exceptions are found, the owner, table name, dimension name, relationship, and the ROWID are inserted into the MVIEW$_EXCEPTIONS table, which is automatically created in the user's schema when the procedure is called. This data can then be used to obtain the invalid rows. For example, the geography_dim dimension is based on the store table, so invalid records can be obtained from the store table as follows:

```
SELECT *
  FROM store
 WHERE ROWID IN (SELECT bad_rowid
                   FROM mview$_exceptions
                );
```

 ## Viewing Dimensions

The DEMO_DIM package provides two procedures for displaying the dimensions that have been defined. The DEMO_DIM.PRINT_DIM can be used to display a specific dimension, and the DEMO_DIM.PRINT_ALLDIMS can be used to display all dimensions. Before executing either of these procedures, you must run the ORACLE_HOME/rdbms/demo/summgmt/smdim.sql script to create the DEMO_DIM package. The following example shows how you may call the DEMO_DIM.PRINT_DEM procedure to display the geography_dim dimension:

```
EXECUTE DEMO_DIM.PRINT_DIM('GEOGRAPHY_DIM');
```

To display all dimensions, call the DEMO_DIM.PRINT_ALLDIMS procedure without any arguments, as shown:

```
EXECUTE DEMO_DIM.PRINT_ALLDIMS();
```

Following is a sample of what the output from these procedures looks like:

```
DIMENSION MYSCHEM.GEOGRAPHY_DIM

LEVEL CITY IS MYSCHEMA.STORE.CITY

LEVEL REGION IS MYSCHEMA.STORE.REGION

LEVEL STATE IS MYSCHEMA.STORE.STATE

LEVEL ZIP IS MYSCHEMA.STORE.ZIP

HIERARCHY LOCATION (

ZIP

CHILD OF CITY
```

```
CHILD OF STATE

CHILD OF REGION

)
```

## Deciding Which Materialized Views to Create

After the data warehouse has been created and populated and statistics have been gathered, you can use the DBMS_OLAP.RECOMMEND_MV procedure to have Oracle make recommendations on which views to create. In order to get good recommendations, you must have created all of your dimensions and put foreign key constraints on your fact tables, linking them to the dimension tables. The following steps show how to execute the DBMS_OLAP.RECOMMEND_MV procedure and obtain a list of recommendations from within SQL*Plus:

■ Connect to SQL*Plus as the schema owner.

■ EXECUTE DBMS_OLAP.RECOMMEND_MV (NULL, 1024000000, NULL, 0);

The first parameter is specified as NULL to obtain recommendations for all fact tables; alternatively, you can specify one or more table names enclosed in quotes and separated by commas. The second parameter is the amount of space in bytes that is available for creating materialized views. The third parameter is a list of materialized views, separated by commas, to be retained. In this case, no materialized views have been created yet, so NULL is used. The last parameter specifies the percentage of existing materialized views that should be retained; again, because none have been created, 0 is specified. The output from this procedure will go into a table in the user's schema called MVIEW$_RECOMMENDATIONS, which is automatically created when the procedure is called.

■ Run the sadvdemo.sql script located in the ORACLE_HOME/rdbms/demo/summgmt directory to create a package that can be used to display the recommendations.

■ SET SERVEROUTPUT ON SIZE 900000. (You should size SERVEROUTPUT to a large number so that all of the recommendations can be displayed.)

■ EXECUTE DEMO_SUMADV.PRETTYPRINT_RECOMMENDATIONS

Following are a few of the recommendations made for the department store example:

```
Recommendation Number = 1

Recommended Action is CREATE new summary:
```

Deciding the Materialized Views to Create

```
SELECT PRODUCT.PROD_ID, PRODUCT.CATEGORY, PRODUCT.DEPARTMENT, PRODUCT.BRAND,

TIME.MONTH, TIME.QUARTER, TIME.YEAR , COUNT(*), SUM(SALES.COST),

COUNT(SALES.COST), SUM(SALES.DOLLARS), COUNT(SALES.DOLLARS),

SUM(SALES.UNITS), COUNT(SALES.UNITS)

FROM MYSCHEMA.SALES, MYSCHEMA.PRODUCT, MYSCHEMA.TIME

WHERE SALES.PROD_ID = PRODUCT.PROD_ID AND SALES.TIME_ID = TIME.TIME_ID

GROUP BY PRODUCT.PROD_ID, PRODUCT.CATEGORY, PRODUCT.DEPARTMENT,

PRODUCT.BRAND, TIME.MONTH, TIME.QUARTER, TIME.YEAR

Storage in bytes is 56400

Percent performance gain is 33.8224347538876

Benefit-to-cost ratio is .000599688559466091

Recommendation Number = 2

Recommended Action is CREATE new summary:

SELECT PRODUCT.PROD_ID, PRODUCT.CATEGORY, PRODUCT.DEPARTMENT, PRODUCT.BRAND,

TIME.SEASON , COUNT(*), SUM(SALES.COST), COUNT(SALES.COST),

SUM(SALES.DOLLARS), COUNT(SALES.DOLLARS), SUM(SALES.UNITS),

COUNT(SALES.UNITS)

FROM MYSCHEMA.SALES, MYSCHEMA.PRODUCT, MYSCHEMA.TIME

WHERE SALES.PROD_ID = PRODUCT.PROD_ID AND SALES.TIME_ID = TIME.TIME_ID

GROUP BY PRODUCT.PROD_ID, PRODUCT.CATEGORY, PRODUCT.DEPARTMENT,

PRODUCT.BRAND, TIME.SEASON
```

In the foregoing listing of recommendations, notice how the time_dimension was used to determine that grouping should be done by month, quarter, year, and also by season.

The DBMS_OLAP.RECOMMEND_MV procedure is a good starting point in determining which materialized views to create, but you'll find that it makes a lot of recommendations. For example, when run in the sample department store's schema, it recommended 29 materialized views. You will want to be somewhat selective when deciding on which materialized views to create because too many materialized views can be a maintenance headache owing to the complexities associated with keeping them refreshed. Instead of creating several different materialized views, with the same GROUP BY clause, you may create one view that includes all of the measures. Select the proper granularity. For example, if you have a materialized view that summarizes data by month, the optimizer can use that view to rewrite queries that summarize the same data by quarter or year.

## Using Materialized Views to Store Precalculated Summaries and Joins

Materialized views improve the performance of queries by precomputing the results of queries and storing them in the materialized view. The existence of materialized views is totally transparent to users; therefore, materialized views can be dropped without affecting the integrity of a user's application. Materialized views can be accessed directly by name; however, this is not recommended because it removes the transparency, and any changes made to the materialized view can directly affect applications. If the optimizer finds an existing materialized view that satisfies a query, it will rewrite the query to use the view instead of accessing the base tables.

To the developer or DBA responsible for creating the materialized view, the procedure to follow for creating the view will be the same whether the view contains aggregations, joins, or both: However, the refresh mode and option you can use for the materialized view are directly dependent on how the view's contents were obtained. In this regard, Oracle differentiates between three types of materialized views:

- The first type, a materialized join view, is based on a query that performs an inner or outer equijoin but contains no aggregations, such as SUM(column_name).

- The second type, a single-table aggregate view, contains aggregations but no joins.

- The third type of materialized view contains both joins and aggregates.

## Choosing a Refresh Mode for Materialized Views

One of the benefits of materialized views is that they can be automatically refreshed whenever any of the underlying tables upon which the materialized view is based are updated. A materialized view can be refreshed whenever a COMMIT is performed on one of the master tables or upon demand through use of one of the procedures in the DBMS_MVIEW package. Use of the ON COMMIT refresh method has the advantage of keeping the materialized view transactionally accurate; however, it is available only for materialized views built from queries containing single table aggregates or joins only. In addition, you need to check the alert log and trace files after each COMMIT to make sure that no errors occurred. If errors are found, you will have to manually refresh the materialized view. The ON DEMAND refresh method can be used for all types of materialized views.

## Choosing a Refresh Option for Materialized Views

You can choose whether a refresh should be complete, fast, forced, or not performed at all. A complete refresh totally refreshes the materialized view from the original query. Any materialized view can be completely refreshed at any time; however, a complete refresh can be very time consuming, since it involves reexecution of the query upon which the materialized view is built. Fast refresh is the preferred refresh method because, as its name implies, it is much faster than a complete refresh. A fast refresh works by incrementally applying changes made to the master tables that have either been recorded in materialized view logs or in direct loader logs. A number of requirements must be satisfied before a materialized view can qualify for fast refresh, depending on whether it contains joins, aggregates, or both. Table 6-3 lists the requirements that need to be met in order for fast refresh to occur, for each type of materialized view.

The default refresh method is FORCE, which attempts to do a fast refresh. If fast refresh is not possible, FORCE does a complete refresh.

## Choosing a Build Method for Materialized Views

Materialized views can be built at the time they are created through use of the BUILD IMMEDIATE clause of the CREATE MATERIALIZED VIEW statement or at a later time if the BUILD DEFERRED clause is specified. You may want to defer building a materialized view if you are concerned about competition for resources at the time of the build. You can use the DBMS_MVIEW.REFRESH procedure to build the materialized view during a slow period.

| Requirement for Fast Refresh | Joins Only | Joins and Aggregates | Single Table Aggregates |
|---|---|---|---|
| Must be based on detail tables only | X | X | X |
| Must be based on a single table | | | X |
| Each table can appear only once in the FROM list | X | X | X |
| Cannot contain nonrepeating expressions, such as SYSDATE and ROWNUM | X | X | X |
| Cannot contain references to RAW or LONG RAW | X | X | X |
| Cannot contain the GROUP BY clause | X | | |
| The SELECT list of the query must include the ROWIDs of all of the detail tables | X | | |
| Expressions can be included in the GROUP BY and SELECT clauses as long as they are the same in each | | X | X |
| Aggregates are allowed but cannot be nested | | X | X |
| If the SELECT clause contains AVG, it must also contain COUNT | | X | X |
| If the SELECT clause contains SUM, it must also contain COUNT | | | X |
| If the SELECT clause contains VARIANCE, it must also contain COUNT and SUM | | X | X |
| If the SELECT clause contains STDDEV, it must also contain COUNT and SUM | | | |
| The join predicates of the WHERE clause can include AND but not OR | X | X | |
| The HAVING and CONNECT BY clauses are not allowed | X | X | X |
| Subqueries, inline views, or set functions such as UNION are not allowed | X | X | X |
| A WHERE clause is not allowed | | | X |
| COUNT(*) must be present | | | X |

**TABLE 6-3.**   *Requirements for Fast Refresh*

| Requirement for Fast Refresh | Joins Only | Joins and Aggregates | Single Table Aggregates |
|---|---|---|---|
| MIN and MAX are not allowed | | | X |
| Unique constraints must exist on the join columns of the inner join table, if an outer join is used | X | | |
| A materialized view log must exist that contains all columns referenced in the materialized view, and it must have been created with the LOG NEW VALUES clause | | | X |
| A materialized view log must exist for each detail table containing ROWID | X | | |
| Any nonaggregate expressions in the SELECT and GROUP BY clauses must be straight columns | | | X |
| DML allowed on detail tables | X | | X |
| Direct path data load allowed | X | X | X |

**TABLE 6-3.**   *Requirements for Fast Refresh* (continued)

## Sizing Materialized Views

Materialized views are stored in tablespaces just like tables and indexes. You can use the DBMS_OLAP.ESTIMATE_SIZE procedure to determine how much space will be required by a materialized view. The following example shows you how to use this procedure:

```
SET SERVEROUTPUT ON
DECLARE
   v_rows NUMBER;
   v_bytes NUMBER;
BEGIN
   DBMS_OLAP.ESTIMATE_SUMMARY_SIZE
     ('SALES_DETAIL',
      'SELECT p.prod_desc, st.store_name, pr.promo_name,
             t.time_id, s.units, s.dollars, s.cost
        FROM product p, store st, promotion pr, time t, sales s
       WHERE s.prod_id = p.prod_id and st.store_id = s.store_id
         AND pr.promo_id = s.promo_id and s.time_id = t.time_id',
      v_rows, v_bytes
     );
```

```
    DBMS_OUTPUT.PUT_LINE(TO_CHAR(v_rows) || ' ' || TO_CHAR(v_bytes));
END;
```

# Creating Materialized Views

A materialized view is essentially a view that is physically stored in the database as a table and one or more system-generated indexes. You must have CREATE TABLE, CREATE INDEX, and CREATE VIEW system privileges in addition to the CREATE MATERIALIZED VIEW and QUERY REWRITE privileges before you can create a materialized view.

## Creating Materialized Join Views

The following example shows you how to create a materialized view that contains only joins with no aggregates:

```
CREATE MATERIALIZED VIEW LOG ON sales
  PCTFREE 5
  TABLESPACE mv_logs
  STORAGE (INITIAL 1M NEXT 1M) WITH ROWID;

CREATE MATERIALIZED VIEW LOG ON product
  PCTFREE 5
  TABLESPACE mv_logs
  STORAGE (INITIAL 20K NEXT 20K) WITH ROWID;

CREATE MATERIALIZED VIEW sales_prod_detail
  BUILD IMMEDIATE
  REFRESH FAST ON COMMIT
AS
  SELECT s.rowid sales_rowid, p.rowid prod_rowid,
         p.prod_desc,  p.brand, p.category, p.department,
         s.units, s.dollars, s.cost
    FROM sales s, product p
  WHERE p.prod_id = s.prod_id;
```

As shown in the foregoing example, a materialized view log must be created for each of the detail tables involved in the query in order for a join-only materialized view to qualify for fast refresh. Only the ROWID of the detail table is necessary. The ROWID for each of the detail tables must also be included in the SELECT clause of the CREATE MATERIALIZED VIEW statement. This is also a requirement for fast refresh on a join-only materialized view, as outlined in Table 6-3. If either of these requirements are not met, it may still be possible for Oracle to perform a fast refresh, depending on what updates actually occurred, as long as the materialized view is created with REFRESH FORCE instead of REFRESH FAST. Refer to Table 6-3 for other requirements for fast refresh.

### Single-Table Aggregate Materialized Views
The following example shows you how to create a single-table aggregate materialized view:

```
CREATE MATERIALIZED VIEW LOG ON sales
  WITH ROWID (store_id, prod_id, units, dollars, cost)
  INCLUDING NEW VALUES;

CREATE MATERIALIZED VIEW sales_summary
  BUILD DEFERRED
  REFRESH FAST ON DEMAND
AS
  SELECT s.store_id, prod_id, COUNT(*), SUM(s.cost),
         COUNT(s.cost), SUM(s.dollars),
         COUNT(s.dollars), SUM(s.units), COUNT(s.units)
    FROM sales s
   GROUP BY s.store_id, s.prod_id;
```

As shown in the preceding example, a materialized view log is created with the INCLUDING NEW VALUES clause containing all of the columns in the materialized view's SELECT clause. This is required to support fast refresh on a single-table aggregate materialized view. Notice that the COUNT and SUM functions were included on all of the fact columns in the sales table. This was done to increase the likelihood that the materialized view will be used for query rewrite. Single-table aggregate materialized views have special requirements involving the presence or absence of certain aggregate functions. Table 6-4 shows these requirements.

| Exists | Required | Optional |
|---|---|---|
| COUNT(expression) | | |
| SUM(expression) | COUNT(expression) | |
| AVG(expression) | COUNT(expression) | SUM(expression) |
| STDDEV(expression) | COUNT(expression) | SUM(expression * expression) |
| VAR(expression) | COUNT(expression) | SUM(expression * expression) |

**TABLE 6-4.** *Requirements for Single-Table Aggregate Materialized Views*

If the aggregate function in the first column exists, then the aggregate function in the second column must also exist. The aggregate function in the third column can optionally exist. A single-table aggregate view must always include COUNT(*).

### Materialized Views with Joins and Aggregates

The following example shows you how to create a materialized view containing both joins and aggregates:

```
CREATE MATERIALIZED VIEW prod_season
  REFRESH FAST ON DEMAND
AS
  SELECT t.season, p.department,
         p.category, count(units) AS unit_count,
         SUM(units) AS unit_sum,
         AVG(units) AS unit_avg,
         COUNT(dollars) AS dollar_count,
         SUM(dollars) AS dollar_sum,
         AVG(dollars) AS dollars_avg,
         STDDEV(units) AS unit_std
    FROM sales s, product p, time t
   WHERE s.prod_id = p.prod_id and s.time_id = p.time_id
   GROUP BY t.season, p.department, p.category;
```

For fast refresh to occur, all of the group-by columns must appear in the SELECT list. The AVG and SUM aggregate functions require the COUNT function. The STDDEV aggregate function requires the COUNT and SUM functions. Note that materialized view logs were not created because they generally are not required for materialized views that contain joins and aggregates. The exception is when the base tables will be updated through use of DML instead of through use of SQL*Loader with the direct load option or some other loader tool that uses the Oracle direct path API. Either of these load methods will create direct loader logs that can be used for fast refresh.

## Enabling Query Rewrite on Materialized Views

In order for a materialized view to be available for query rewrite, it must have been created with the ENABLE QUERY REWRITE clause or altered with the ENABLE QUERY REWRITE clause. Refer to the section. "Setting Parameters for Summary Management" for other initialization parameters that must be set for query rewrite. Query rewrite can be explicitly disabled with the DISABLE QUERY REWRITE clause of the CREATE or ALTER MATERIALIZED VIEW statement. You may want to disable query rewrite before new data is loaded into the data warehouse to prevent users from accessing stale data. Since not all views will be refreshed simultaneously, queries that use multiple materialized views that are in the process of being refreshed may return unpredictable results. You can reenable query rewrite after all materialized views have been refreshed. You need the GRANT REWRITE system privilege to enable materialized views in your own schema for query rewrite. You need the GRANT GLOBAL REWRITE PRIVILEGE to enable materialized views for query rewrite in another schema or if the materialized view references objects in another schema.

## Using the DBMS_MVIEW Package to Refresh Materialized Views

The DBMS_MVIEW package contains three procedures for performing ON DEMAND refresh of materialized views. Some initialization parameters are required for warehouse refresh and must be set before any of these procedures are run. The required parameters can be found in the section "Setting Parameters for Summary Management." To help in the diagnosis of any problems that might occur during the refresh process, each of the procedures generates a log called *refresh log,* which will be located in the directory specified by the UTL_FILE_DIR parameter.

The DBMS_MVIEW.REFRESH procedure is used to refresh one or more specified materialized views. The parameters are described in Table 6-5. Note that this procedure can also be used to refresh snapshots. Some of the parameters listed are specific to snapshot refresh and are not used for warehouse refresh.

The following example shows you how to execute the DBMS_MVIEW.REFRESH procedure:

```
BEGIN
    DBMS_MVIEW.REFRESH('SALES_SUMMARY, PROD_SEASON',
        'F?',   '',  FALSE, TRUE, 0, 0, 0, FALSE);
END;
```

In the preceding example, the sales_summary materialized view is refreshed fast, while the prod_season materialized view is refreshed force. No particular rollback segments is specified. If an error occurs while you are refreshing the sales_summary materialized view, errors will be written to the refresh log, and the process will continue refreshing prod_season.

The DBMS_MVIEW.REFRESH_ALL_MVIEWS procedure is used to refresh all materialized views. Table 6-6 describes the parameters used with this procedure.

The following example shows you how to use DBMS_MVIEW.REFRESH_ALL_MVIEWS and how to display the number of errors returned:

```
SET SERVEROUTPUT ON
DECLARE
    v_failure number;
```

```
BEGIN
    DBMS_MVIEW.REFRESH_ALL_MVIEWS(v_failures, 'A',
                                  'RBS_LARGE', TRUE, FALSE
                                  );
    DBMS_OUTPUT.PUT_LINE(TO_CHAR(v_failure));
END;
```

In the foregoing example, all materialized views are refreshed. The Rbs_large rollback segment is used, and the process will continue refreshing if any errors occur.

| Parameter | In/Out | Description |
|---|---|---|
| List | In | List of materialized views to be refreshed, separated by commas. |
| Method | In | A list of refresh methods to be used, one for each materialized view specified in the list parameter. **'F' (Fast)** Incrementally applies changes. **'?' (Force)** Performs fast refresh, if possible; otherwise it performs a complete refresh through recalculation of the materialized view from its defining query. **'C' (Complete)** For data warehouse refreshes (atomic_refresh=FALSE); this is the same as a force refresh. **'A' (Always)** Unconditionally performs a complete refresh through recalculation of the materialized view from its defining query. |
| Rollback_seg | In | Name of a specific rollback segment to use. |
| Push_deferred_rpc | In | Used with snapshot refresh set to FALSE. |
| Refresh_after_errors | In | Controls how errors are handled when refreshing multiple materialized views. If set to TRUE, it will continue refreshing the remaining materialized views when errors occur. If set to FALSE, it will stop all further refreshes. |
| Purge_option | In | Used with snapshot refresh. Set to 0. |
| Parallelism | In | Used with snapshot refresh. Set to 0. |
| Heap_size | In | Used with snapshot refresh. Set to 0. |
| Atomic_refresh | | Set to FALSE to perform a warehouse refresh such that the refresh of each materialized view is performed as a single transaction. TRUE should be used only with snapshot refresh. |

**TABLE 6-5.** *Parameters Description for DBMS_MVIEW.REFRESH*

DBMS_MVIEW Package to Refresh Materialized Views

| Parameter | In/Out | Description |
|---|---|---|
| Number_of_failures | Out | Returns the number of errors that occurred during processing. |
| Method | In | A single refresh method to be used for all materialized views.<br>**'F' (Fast)**   Incrementally applies changes.<br>**'?' (Force)**   Performs fast refresh, if possible; otherwise it performs a complete refresh by recalculation of the materialized view from its defining query.<br>**'C' (Complete)**   For data warehouse refreshes (atomic_refresh=FALSE); this is the same as a force refresh.<br>**'A' (Always)**   Unconditionally performs a complete refresh by recalculation of the materialized view from its defining query. |
| Rollback_seg | In | Name of a specific rollback segment to use. |
| Refresh_after_errors | In | Controls how errors are handled when refreshing multiple materialized views. If set to TRUE, it will continue the refreshing of the remaining materialized views when errors occur. If set to FALSE, it will stop all further refreshes. |
| Atomic_refresh | In | Set to FALSE to perform a warehouse refresh such that the refresh of each materialized view is performed as a single transaction. TRUE should be used only with snapshot refresh. |

**TABLE 6-6.**   *Parameter Description for DBMS_MVIEW.REFRESH_ALL_MVIEWS*

The DBMS_MVIEW.REFRESH_DEPENDENT procedure is used to refresh materialized views that depend on a specific table. Table 6-7 describes the parameters used with this procedure.

```
SET SERVEROUTPUT ON
DECLARE
   v_failures NUMBER;
BEGIN
   DBMS_MVIEW.REFRESH_DEPENDENT(v_failures, 'STORE, PRODUCT',
                               'CF', 'RBS_LARGE', TRUE, FALSE
                               );
   DBMS_OUTPUT.PUT_LINE(TO_CHAR(v_failures));
END;
```

| Parameter | In/Out | Description |
|---|---|---|
| Number_of_failures | Out | Returns the number of errors that occurred during processing. |
| List | In | List of materialized views to be refreshed, separated by commas. |
| Method | In | A list of refresh methods to be used, one for each materialized view specified in the list parameter:<br>**'F' (Fast)**   Incrementally applies changes.<br>**'?' (Force)**   Performs fast refresh, if possible; otherwise it performs a complete refresh by recalculation of the materialized view from its defining query.<br>**'C' (Complete)**   For data warehouse refreshes (atomic_refresh=FALSE); this is the same as a force refresh.<br>**'A' (Always)**   Unconditionally performs a complete refresh by recalculation of the materialized view from its defining query. |
| Rollback_seg | In | Name of a specific rollback segment to use. |
| Refresh_after_errors | In | Controls how errors are handled when refreshing multiple materialized views. If set to TRUE, it will continue the refreshing of the remaining materialized views when errors occur. If set to FALSE, it will stop all further refreshes. |
| Atomic_refresh | In | Set to FALSE to perform a warehouse refresh so that each refresh is performed as a single transaction. TRUE should be used only with snapshot refresh. |

**TABLE 6-7.**   *Parameter Description for DBMS_MVIEW.REFRESH_DEPENDENT*

In the preceding example, all materialized views that reference the store table are refreshed complete; all materialized views that reference the product table are refreshed fast. The refresh transactions use the Rbs_large rollback segment. Refreshing will continue if any errors occur.

# Determining If a Materialized View Is Being Used

You can find out if a materialized view is being used by examining the execution plan for the query. Alternatively, the Oracle Trace option can be used to collect statistics and advise which materialized views are being used. After Oracle Trace has collected sufficient statistics, you can call the DBMS_OLAP.EVALUATE_ UTILIZATION_W procedure. This procedure will create a table called

MVIEW$EVALUATIONS and populate it with all of the materialized views that have been used along with the frequency and benefit-to-cost ratio.

**NOTE**
*The DBMS_OLAP.EVALUATE_UTILIZATION_W does not require any parameters.*

## Setting Parameters for Summary Management

In order to take full advantage of the features of summary management, you must set certain parameters, either in the init.ora file or by using the ALTER SYSTEM or ALTER SESSION commands. These parameters affect warehouse refresh, query rewrite, and advisor workload.

The refresh process uses job queues to perform the refresh and the UTL_FILE package to generate refresh logs. Table 6-8 describes the parameters used to configure warehouse refresh.

Query rewrite requires the cost-based optimizer and is available only in release 8.1.5 or later. Table 6-9 describes how you may set the parameters required for query rewrite.

In order to use the Oracle Trace option to collect statistics to determine which materialized views to create, you need to set several parameters. Table 6-10 describes the parameters needed for the Oracle Trace option.

## Managing Constraints in the Data Warehouse

Integrity constraints are important if the integrity of data is to be maintained. They also facilitate join operations and are necessary for taking advantage of all of the

| Parameter | Description |
| --- | --- |
| JOB_QUEUE_PROCESSES | Warehouse refresh automatically requests job queues. This parameter should be set to the maximum number of materialized views that will be refreshed concurrently. The range of acceptable values is between 1 and 36. |
| JOB_QUEUE_INTERVAL | Specifies the interval in seconds that the job queue scheduler checks to see if a new job has been submitted to the job queue. |
| UTL_FILE_DIR | The directory where the refresh log is written. If this parameter is not set, no log will be created. |

**TABLE 6-8.** *Parameters Required for Warehouse Refresh*

| Parameter | Description |
|---|---|
| OPTIMIZER_MODE | Query rewrite will not occur unless the cost-based optimizer is used. Therefore, all tables must be analyzed, and OPTIMIZER_MODE must be set to ALL_ROWS, FIRST_ROWS, or CHOOSE. |
| QUERY_REWRITE_ENABLED | Must be set to TRUE. |
| QUERY_REWRITE_INTEGRITY | Valid values are:<br>**ENFORCE**  Rewrites do not occur if the data in the materialized view is inconsistent or if it violates integrity. This is the default value.<br>**NO_ENFORCE**  Rewrites are allowed when you are using relationships that have been declared but that are not enforced by Oracle.<br>**USE_STALE**  Rewrites are allowed when you are using unenforced relationships, and materialized views are eligible for rewrite even if they are inconsistent with the underlying detail data. |
| COMPATIBLE | Must be 8.1 or higher. |

**TABLE 6-9.**  *Parameters Required for Query Rewrite*

features of summary management. In a data warehouse that is built using a star schema, it is important to put primary key constraints on all of the dimension tables. It is also important to put a primary key constraint on each fact table consisting of a combination of foreign keys from the dimension tables. In addition, each fact table should have foreign key constraints referencing each of its corresponding dimension tables. Unfortunately, the overhead associated with maintaining integrity constraints can make it difficult and time consuming for you to perform some tasks in a data warehouse that contains many gigabytes of data. Examples are tasks such as loading large amounts of data, performing batch operations, and importing or exporting one table at a time.

## Altering the State of a Constraint to Facilitate Data Loads

To alleviate some of the problems associated with integrity constraints, Oracle allows you to alter the state of a constraint. An integrity constraint can be in any one of four states: DISABLE NOVALIDATE, ENABLE NOVALIDATE, ENABLE VALIDATE, and DISABLE VALIDATE.

| Parameter | Description |
|---|---|
| ORACLE_TRACE_COLLECTION_NAME | Trace collection filename. The extensions .cdf and .dat will be added. |
| ORACLE_TRACE_COLLECTION_PATH | The directory in which the Oracle Trace collection definition (.cdf) and data collection (.dat) files are located. The default is /otrace/admin/cdf under ORACLE_HOME. |
| ORACLE_TRACE_COLLECTION_SIZE | Maximum size in bytes of the Oracle Trace collection file. When the file reaches the maximum size, collection is disabled. A value of zero means an unlimited size is allowed. |
| ORACLE_TRACE_ENABLE | Set to TRUE to enable Oracle Trace collections. Collection will not begin unless the ORACLE_TRACE_COLLECTION_NAME is set. |
| ORACLE_TRACE_FACILITY_NAME | Name of Oracle Trace product definition file (.fdf file). This should be set to the default value of oracled. |
| ORACLE_TRACE_FACILITY_PATH | The directory in which the Oracle Trace product definition file is located. The default is /otrace/admin/fdf under ORACLE_HOME. |

**TABLE 6-10.** *Parameters Required for Oracle Trace*

■ The DISABLE NOVALIDATE state does not enforce the constraint, allowing invalid data to be entered. This state is useful when you want to load data without the overhead associated with enforcing constraints.

■ The ENABLE NOVALIDATE constraint allows a table to contain invalid data, but it will not allow the entry of new invalid data. This state is used as an intermediate state when you are loading data from OLTP systems in which the data is already known to be valid. The fastest way to move a set of constraints from the DISABLE NOVALIDATE state to the ENABLE VALIDATE state is to first ENABLE NOVALIDATE all of the constraints, then individually ENABLE VALIDATE each constraint. The validation will still be time consuming; however, validating a constraint that is already enabled doesn't require any DML locks during validation, so you can perform DML as soon as the constraints are in the ENABLE NOVALIDATE state. This state can also be used with the RELY clause to avoid constraint enforcement performance overhead. This is generally useful only with materialized views and query rewrite. Query rewrite requires the existence of constraints to determine join information, but it does not require them to be enforced. Refer to the section "Setting Parameters for Summary Management" for information on materialized views and query rewrite.

- The ENABLE VALIDATE constraint state is the default state. It ensures that all new and existing data is in compliance with the constraint. OLTP systems make use of this state to prevent invalid data entry. If a table contains any invalid data, it cannot be brought into the ENABLE VALIDATE state. To determine which rows are invalid, you can use the ALTER TABLE statement with the EXCEPTIONS option in the ENABLE clause to insert the ROWID, table owner, table name, and constraint name of all invalid rows into a specified table. This exception table can be created with the ORACLE_HOME/rdbms/admin/utlexcpt.sql script. The table created by this script is named exceptions. You can create one or more exception tables with different names by copying the script and modifying it.

**NOTE**
*You can't enable a referential integrity constraint unless the referenced unique or primary key constraint is already enabled.*

- The DISABLE VALIDATE state disables the constraint and drops the index on the constraint but keeps the constraint valid. This state is used when you are loading data into a range partitioned table from a nonpartitioned table that contains a distinct range of values in the unique key. The advantage of using this state is that you save space by not having an index. As long as the unique key coincides with the partitioning key of the partitioned table, disabling of the the constraint saves overhead. For more information on loading a partitioned table with data from a nonpartitioned table, refer to the earlier section in this chapter called "Exchanging Partitions."

The following example shows you how to use the ALTER TABLE command to change the state of a constraint to ENABLE VALIDATE and place any exceptions in the exception table:

```
ALTER TABLE sales MODIFY CONSTRAINT fk_constraint
  ENABLE VALIDATE EXCEPTIONS INTO exceptions;
```

The following steps show how you might use the different states when loading data into the data warehouse:

1. Put all of the affected constraints in the DISABLE NOVALIDATE state.

2. Load the data.

3. Put all of the affected constraints in the ENABLE NOVALIDATE state.

4. Put each of the affected constraints individually in the ENABLE VALIDATE state.

# Tips Review

Data warehousing presents a new set of challenges to the DBA. Oracle8i provides a new set of features that address each of the challenges. Large tables are difficult to manage. Range partitioning was introduced in Oracle 8.0, allowing large tables to be broken down into smaller, more manageable tables. Two new methods for partitioning tables, hash partitioning and composite partitioning, are introduced in Oracle8i.

Transportable tablespaces provide an efficient way of populating the data warehouse from other databases. Partitioning and transportable tablespaces can be used together to seamlessly move historical data into the warehouse.

Most data warehouses are built by use of the dimensional data model, commonly referred to as a star schema, which consists of one or more large fact tables and several smaller dimension tables. Queries that join a fact table to dimension tables are called star queries. Oracle8i has the ability to optimize star queries, provided that the appropriate indexes and constraints are defined.

Decision support systems are frequently used to summarize large amounts of detail data for the production of analytical reports. This type of reporting can require a great deal in the way of system resources. Summary management was introduced to solve this problem. Relationships within the data are defined through the use of dimensions, then materialized views are created to store the precalculated results of the queries. The query rewrite facility can then use the dimensions and materialized views to rewrite queries to use the materialized views rather than querying the detail tables.

Constraints are important for maintaining the integrity of data; however, they can also slow down much of the processing that needs to occur in the data warehouse, such as loading data and other kinds of batch processing. Oracle now provides a way to temporarily disable constraints during these operations.

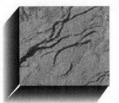

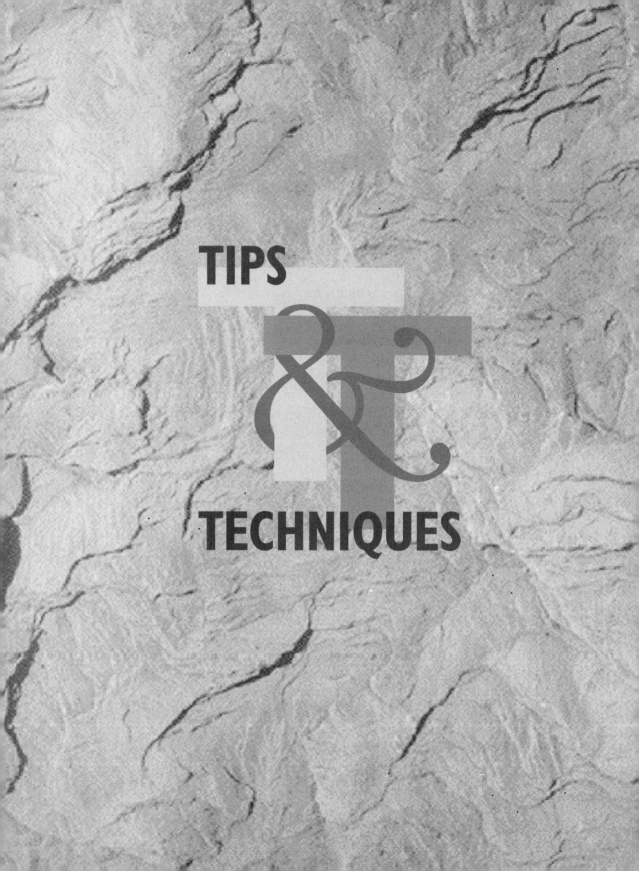

# TIPS
&
# TECHNIQUES

# CHAPTER
## 7

Security

The security features in Oracle8i provide support for broad to fine-grained security enforcement levels and management capabilities. This chapter covers techniques for combining several of these new features to enforce the security rules of your application at the database level.

- Customizing database access restrictions using database event triggers
- Extending the USERENV function with SYS_CONTEXT
- Securing data access by IP address with SYS_CONTEXT
- Exposing USERENV attributes in check constraints with SYS_CONTEXT
- Using DBMS_RLS to provide row-level and application-oriented security
- Providing application-specific security

# Database Event Triggers

Database event triggers fire as the result of the non-DML actions specified in Table 7-1. These triggers can be used alone to enforce security or together with other Oracle8i security features for fine-grained security management.

There are two categories of database events, each having an associated set of attributes:

- **Resource manager** Related to instance startup and shutdown and to server error message events

- **Client** Related to logon and logoff and to DDL operations

The trigger levels, which are listed in the Type column, indicate whether you can define the trigger to fire for each session in the database (ON DATABASE) or you can assign it to a specific schema (ON *schemaname*.SCHEMA). The Transaction column shows whether the trigger starts and runs its own separate transaction (SEPARATE) or whether the transaction runs within the same transaction as the event that fired it (SAME). The BEFORE, AFTER column indicates whether the trigger fires before or after the event.

**CAUTION**
*Transactions indicated in Table 7-1 as SAME should not be used to log error messages into a table, since the error may roll back the insertion of that message into the table.*

| Triggering Event | Description | Category | BEFORE, AFTER | Type | Transaction |
|---|---|---|---|---|---|
| ALTER | When a catalog object is altered | Client | AFTER, BEFORE | Database, schema | SAME |
| CREATE | When a catalog object is created | Client | AFTER, BEFORE | Database, schema | SAME |
| DROP | When a catalog object is dropped | Client | AFTER, BEFORE | Database, schema | SAME |
| LOGOFF | When a client disconnects from the database | Client | BEFORE | Database, schema | SAME |
| LOGON | When a client connects to the database | Client | AFTER | Database, schema | SEPARATE |

**TABLE 7-1.** *List of Database Event Triggers*

| Triggering Event | Description | Category | BEFORE, AFTER | Type | Transaction |
|---|---|---|---|---|---|
| SERVERERROR | When a specified error occurs or when any error occurs if none was specified at trigger creation time | Resource Manager | AFTER | Database, Schema | SEPARATE |
| SHUTDOWN | When an instance is shut down | Resource Manager | BEFORE | Database | SEPARATE |
| STARTUP | When a database is opened | Resource Manager | AFTER | Database | SEPARATE |

**TABLE 7-1.**   *List of Database Event Triggers* (continued)

**NOTE**
*These triggers do not affect users logging on as SYSDBA.*

A sample database event trigger would look like the following:

```
CREATE OR REPLACE TRIGGER log_errors_as
  AFTER SERVERERROR ON DATABASE
BEGIN
  IF IS_SERVERERROR(1017)
  THEN
    -- The user has supplied an invalid username or password
    <do special handling>
  ELSE
    <log error message information into a table>
  END IF;
END;
```

## Customizing Access Restrictions Using Database Event Triggers

When the logon fails, it is often handy to have a more informative error message than the standard one supplied by Oracle. For example, many database environments have scheduled maintenance periods. Even though these periods may be scheduled during off-hours, a user may still attempt to log on during that time. This may be especially true for an application that is available to the Internet 24×7 (twenty-four hours a day seven days a week). During maintenance, the database might be placed in restricted mode (allowing only users with RESTRICTED SESSION privilege to log on). The error message nonprivileged users will receive is not very informative: "ORA-01035: ORACLE only available to users with RESTRICTED SESSION privilege."

The RESTRICTED SESSION privilege does not inhibit those with the privilege from logging on. For example, a DBA might do a startup restrict to perform an export. While the export is proceeding, the SYSTEM user will still be allowed to log on from SQL*Plus.

The following trigger can be used to keep all users out of the database during the export except those who can log on as SYSDBA. In addition, you can supply all of the failed logons with an error message that explains more informatively why they cannot connect to the database. You can disable this trigger when the export or other maintenance is completed and enable it the next time it is needed.

You should not create objects in the SYSTEM account unless specifically instructed to do so by Oracle. This is done mainly to keep a clean and manageable environment. Create a separate account with DBA privileges, and assume it to be SYSTEM_MANAGER. The SYSTEM_MANAGER account will contain objects, such as database event triggers, that can affect the database server at a fundamental level. The SYSTEM_MANAGER account should have its own default tablespace.

**CAUTION**
*Be careful when creating database event triggers since they require careful planning and can have a deleterious effect if not designed properly. Take into account all of the users who will need access to the database system before you create a database event trigger that restricts access. If, for example, access were restricted in the trigger to SYS and SYSTEM (as in the next example) and Oracle Enterprise Manager were being used for proactive monitoring, it would be disabled. This is because the Oracle Enterprise Manager repository owner and the DBSNMP user, both of whom require access to the database to perform monitoring, would no longer be able to connect to the database.*

```
CREATE OR REPLACE TRIGGER after_logon_al
  AFTER LOGON ON DATABASE
BEGIN
  -- Disallow logons with an informative message.
  RAISE_APPLICATION_ERROR (-20002, 'The database is '||
                      ' undergoing maintenance.'||
                      ' It will be back up at around 06:00 EST.'
                      );
END;
```

**NOTE**

*If you choose to use the method that restricts all logons, you may not be able to connect normally via any username, even ones assigned to the DBA role. In this case, dropping the trigger will require your connecting as SYSDBA.*

This concept may be extended by using a restriction (WHEN clause) in the trigger to define users who can log on even when the trigger is enabled. The next example shows this, as well as additional functionality that provides auditing capabilities by storing information about logon attempts in a table. Note that to support the INSERT statement in this example, you will have to create a table named after_logon_audit (with columns date_time DATE, username VARCHAR2(30), ip_address VARCHAR2(15)) in the schema that owns the trigger.

```
CREATE OR REPLACE TRIGGER after_logon_al
  AFTER LOGON ON DATABASE
-- Allow these two users to log on normally
WHEN (USER NOT IN ('SYSTEM', 'SYS'))
BEGIN
  -- Store information about this logon attempt
  INSERT INTO after_logon_audit
    (date_time, username, ip_address)
    VALUES (SYSDATE, USER, SYS_CONTEXT('USERENV', 'IP_ADDRESS'));
  COMMIT;
  -- Disallow logons with an informative message.
  RAISE_APPLICATION_ERROR (-20002, 'The database is '||
                            ' undergoing maintenance.'||
                            ' It will be back up at around 06:00 EST.'
                          );
END;
```

# The Virtual Private Database Feature

Oracle8i provides a virtual private database feature that is used to associate a security policy with a specific table or view. This feature enables you to create a contextual environment for every application that is used against the database. Complex rules can be shared by multiple tables and views and can be combined with the ability to set up the users' environments at logon time. This leads to the strict enforcement of security rules no matter what tool is used. The virtual private database feature has two main capabilities:

- **Fine-grained access control** the ability to assign security policies to views and tables

■ **Application context**   the ability to securely populate and retrieve cached attributes containing information about your application

This section will introduce a number of 8i-specific security concepts by describing several scenarios for enforcing security in a human resources (HR) application. The terms *namespace* and *context* and the *USERENV* function—all central to understanding and using these concepts—are explained here.

## Namespaces

A namespace is an area in which no two objects can have the same name. Standard namespaces include those that prohibit, for example, a table and view from having the same name within the same schema. For most objects there is a one-to-one relationship with a type of namespace. For example, indexes have one namespace while constraints have another. Consequently, an index and a constraint in the same schema can have the same name and, conversely, two indexes in the same schema cannot have the same name.

The namespace that contains tables also contains other types of objects, views, sequences, private synonyms, stand-alone stored procedures, stand-alone functions, packages, and snapshots, which all share the same namespace with tables. The fact that all of these database objects are in the same namespace means, for example, that a table cannot be created that has the same name as a view in the same schema.

## Context

An application context associates a type of namespace called a *context namespace* with an accompanying PL/SQL package that will hold application security attributes. The CREATE CONTEXT command is used to create a context namespace.

## USERENV

The USERENV function returns information about a session's environment. It can be used directly in a SELECT statement by supplying an *option/attribute* specifying the type of information needed. For example, to find out the instance identification number, you use

```
SELECT USERENV('INSTANCE')
  FROM dual;
```

Actually, USERENV simply refers to a special context namespace, the user environment, which is automatically created by Oracle.

**Extending USERENV Function with SYS_CONTEXT**

## Extending the USERENV Function with SYS_CONTEXT

USERENV is not new to Oracle8i, but its capabilities have been expanded. Oracle6 supported four attributes for USERENV, Oracle7 supported five, and Oracle8i supports eight. You can extend the USERENV list of options if you use it within a call to the Oracle8i function *SYS_CONTEXT*. SYS_CONTEXT supplies information based on a specified context namespace and has the following syntax:

```
SYS_CONTEXT('<context namespace>', '<attribute name>');
```

If you use 'USERENV' as the context namespace, you will have available attributes in addition to the standard eight. The instance id can now be found by using the following SELECT statement:

```
SELECT SYS_CONTEXT('USERENV', 'INSTANCE')
  FROM dual;
```

Table 7-2 shows the complete list of USERENV attributes when it is used within the SYS_CONTEXT function.

**NOTE**
*The USERENV attribute ISDBA is not included in Table 7-2 since it does not work when used in a call to SYS_CONTEXT.*

## Securing Data Access by IP Address with SYS_CONTEXT

Some USERENV attributes are especially useful for security purposes. One in particular is the IP_ADDRESS attribute that returns the IP address of a client connected via the TCP protocol. This can be used in a view to limit data access to a group of machines that share part of an IP address. This emulates the behavior of firewalls without your having to program a router. For example,

```
CREATE OR REPLACE VIEW emp_intranet AS
  SELECT *
    FROM emp
    WHERE SYS_CONTEXT('USERENV', 'IP_ADDRESS') LIKE '111.255%';
```

## Exposing USERENV Attributes in Check Constraints with SYS_CONTEXT

Some of the USERENV options cannot be seen from within check constraints. You can access those options by using them as attributes in calls to SYS_CONTEXT.

| Attribute | Returns |
|---|---|
| CLIENT_INFO | Up to 64 characters of user information that can be stored by an application using the DBMS_APPLICATION_INFO built-in. Check your application's documentation to see how this attribute is being used. |
| CURRENT_SCHEMA | The current schema name, which can be changed with ALTER SESSION SET SCHEMA |
| CURRENT_SCHEMAID | The current schema ID |
| CURRENT_USER | The current session username. This is different from SESSION_USER since it may be altered from within a stored procedure (for example, using invoker-rights). |
| CURRENT_USERID | The current session ID |
| ENTRYID | The available audit entry identifier. AUDIT_TRAIL must be set to TRUE in the init.ora file. |
| INSTANCE | The identification number of the current instance |
| IP_ADDRESS | The IP address of the client |
| LANG | The ISO abbreviation for the language for the current session |
| LANGUAGE | The language and territory used by the current session along with the database character set in the form: *language_territory.characterset*. For example, AMERICAN_AMERICA.WE8ISO8859P1. |
| NLS_CALENDAR | The NLS calendar used for dates |
| NLS_CURRENCY | The currency symbol |
| NLS_DATE_FORMAT | The current date format |
| NLS_DATE_LANGUAGE | The language used for days of the week, months, and other components of the date |
| NLS_SORT | An indicator specifying a BINARY or INTEGER collating sequence for the character set |
| NLS_TERRITORY | The territory name that is used to specify some default date and numeric formats. NLS_TERRITORY corresponds to the territory portion of the value returned by LANGUAGE— in this case, AMERICA. |
| SESSION_USER | The name of the current user who is logged on |
| SESSION_USERID | The logged-on user ID |
| SESSIONID | The auditing session identifier |
| TERMINAL | The operating system ID for the current session's terminal |

**TABLE 7-2.**   *List of USERENV Attributes When Used with SYS_CONTEXT*

Expose USERENV Attributes with SYS_CONTEXT

For example, assume that an additional column—ip_address VARCHAR2(15)—has been added to SCOTT'S emp table and that its value is set to the IP address of the machine on the employee's desk. You could restrict the ability to change the value in that column to client applications that are logged on from similar IP addresses. This can be done using essentially the same method as in the previous example but this time applying it to the new emp.ip_address column as a check constraint.

```
ALTER TABLE emp
  ADD (CONSTRAINT emp_ip_address_chk
       CHECK (ip_address LIKE
              SUBSTR(SYS_CONTEXT('USERENV', 'IP_ADDRESS'),1,7)||'%'
             )
      );
```

## Using DBMS_RLS to Provide Row-Level and Application-Oriented Security

It is possible to provide a fine-grained level of security by applying programmatic and dynamic characteristics to your security policy. The means for doing this are provided in the DBMS_RLS built-in package. The DBMS_RLS package, which is available only in the Enterprise Edition of the Oracle database, can enforce security policies such as the following:

- Allowing hospital physicians to see the records of only their own patients, customers to see only their own orders, managers to see only the employees in their own departments.

- Supporting different security policies for different types of SQL statements—for example, allowing users to SELECT all of the records in the emp table but UPDATE those employees only in their own departments.

Enforcement of these rules is accomplished by defining security policies in a package and then assigning that set of policies to a table on view. Each policy dynamically creates a predicate that will be attached to the WHERE clause of any DML and SELECT statement that is performed against that table. The enforcement policy is active regardless of the application the client is using to access the data.

**NOTE**

*If you have previously coded security policies into your triggers for update statements, you may want to consider rebuilding them as policies utilizing DBMS_RLS. Since DBMS_RLS does its check during the time the update set is being created, it eliminates the overhead of retrieving a larger set of rows and checking them one by one with a row-level trigger.*

## The DBMS_RLS Procedures

There are two basic steps in enforcing a policy.

1. Create a package that contains customized security policy code

2. Assign the policy to a table using DBMS_RLS.ADD_POLICY

**NOTE**
*You may assign the same policy to more than one table. You may also create more complex policies that require steps in addition to the ones just listed.*

The DBMS_RLS procedures are fairly straightforward. Table 7-3 shows the DBMS_RLS procedures, descriptions, and parameters. The schema that owns the table or view to which the policy is assigned does not have to be the same schema that owns the function that contains the security policy code.

**CAUTION**
*Issuing any of the procedures in the DBMS_RLS package will commit any uncommitted transactions in the current session.*

| Procedure Name | Description | Parameters |
| --- | --- | --- |
| ADD_POLICY | Assigns a security policy to a table or view. (Note that policy code must reside in a separate package.) | **object_schema:** schema containing the table or view that will receive the assignment of this policy.<br>**object_name:** name of the table or view to which the policy is added.<br>**policy_name:** name of the policy. It must be unique for the same table or view. The policy_name, when assigned to a table or view, represents the set of parameters contained in this procedure (less the enable parameter).<br>**function_schema:** name of the schema that holds the security code function.<br>**policy_function:** name of the package.function that contains the security policy code. |

**TABLE 7-3.**   *List of DBMS_RLS Procedures and Parameters*

| Procedure Name | Description | Parameters |
|---|---|---|
| | | **statement_types:** the type of statement on which this policy will take effect. It can be any or all of SELECT, INSERT, UPDATE, DELETE. Default is all of them. **update_check:** if set to TRUE, causes the policy to be rechecked and reenforced after an INSERT or UPDATE. Default is FALSE. **enable:** if set to TRUE, the policy is enabled when it is assigned. Default is TRUE. |
| DROP_POLICY | Removes the assignment of a security policy from a table or view. | object_schema object_name policy_name |
| ENABLE_POLICY | Enables or disables a policy that has previously been assigned to a table or view via the ADD_POLICY procedure. | object_schema object_name policy_name **enable:** TRUE to enable the policy, FALSE to disable. |
| REFRESH_POLICY | Causes all cached statements associated with the policy to be reparsed, guaranteeing that any changes to the policy will immediately be enforced. It cannot refresh a disabled policy. | object_schema object_name policy_name |

**TABLE 7-3.** *List of DBMS_RLS Procedures and Parameters* (continued)

**NOTE**
*Policies can be seen in the USER_POLICIES view.*

## Creating a Security Policy Package

Building a complex security policy package first requires specifying the policy to be enforced. The following security policy will be enforced against the emp table when all of the steps in this section are completed:

- Only the owner of the security package and SCOTT will have the right to issue SELECT or UPDATE statements directly against emp.

- All others' rights to directly SELECT from or UPDATE the emp table will be done via a view called employees.

- SELECT and UPDATE rights will be determined at run time based on the job level of the employee who is attempting to perform the action.

  - Managers and above can SELECT all employee records but can UPDATE only the records of employees that they directly manage.

  - Other employees can SELECT only the records of other employees in their departments, and they may not UPDATE any employee records.

  - Anyone else logged on to the system (that is, anyone who is not listed as an employee in the emp table) cannot see any employees.

A package that contains a policy for SELECTing from scott.emp will be defined in this first example. This SELECT policy will enforce the rule that users who do not have the rank of manager or above can see only employees in their own department, while managers and above can see all employee records. For this example, you will give the scott.emp table an additional column called oracle_username VARCHAR2(30) NOT NULL. In addition, you will add a view to Scott's schema with the following definition:

```
CREATE OR REPLACE VIEW employees
  AS SELECT *
       FROM emp;
```

Adding the employees view on scott.emp avoids causing an infinite loop for policies that must query the policy table from within the security function. The security function in the example queries the emp table to find the job and department of the currently logged-on user. If this function were assigned to the emp table itself, then the query inside the function would cause another query to occur against emp, which would cause another, and so on.

To enforce the security on the data in the emp table, revoke SELECT rights on the table to all accounts except the one managing security. In this case, assume that the account managing human resources security is called HR_SECURITY_ MANAGER. HR_SECURITY_MANAGER will be the manager of the human resources application, not a database administrator. Do not grant the DBA role to HR_SECURITY_MANAGER. SELECT rights should be granted on the employees view to all who may need to see it.

 **NOTE**
*Remember that to add a NOT NULL column to a table, you first must create the new column as NULLABLE, add values into that column, and then ALTER the table so that the column is NOT NULL.*

The oracle_username column will hold the Oracle logon account name for each employee. Good design and business rules would dictate that this column should also have a unique index on it.

Every policy function must have two parameters:

- **IN VARCHAR2**  Representing the schema that owns the table or view upon which the policy will be applied. In the example it is named i_object_schema.

- **IN VARCHAR2**  Representing the name of the table or view upon which the policy will be applied. In the example it is named i_object_name.

The return type needs to be a VARCHAR2. The return value will be a predicate which will later be added as a filter to the DML or SELECT statement applied to the table named in the second parameter of the policy function. The maximum allowed length of the predicate is 2,000 bytes. For example,

```
FUNCTION select_employees_predicate
    (i_object_schema all_objects.owner%TYPE,
     i_object_name all_objects.object_name%TYPE
    )
    RETURN VARCHAR2;
```

This first example will show the creation of a policy package called hr_table_security by the HR_SECURITY_MANAGER user.

```
CREATE OR REPLACE PACKAGE hr_table_security
AS
  SUBTYPE emp_type IS scott.emp%ROWTYPE;
  SUBTYPE predicate_type IS VARCHAR2(2000);
  cons_disallow_all_reads CONSTANT CHAR(3) := '1=2';
  FUNCTION select_employees_predicate
    (i_object_schema all_objects.owner%TYPE,
     i_object_name all_objects.object_name%TYPE
    )
    RETURN VARCHAR2;
END;
```

The hr_security package contains a constant called cons_disallow_all_reads. This will be used as the predicate for those queries in which the users are not allowed to see any rows—in other words, when an invalid user performs a SELECT against the view employees, such as

```
SELECT *
  FROM employees;
```

the query will be altered in the background to

```
SELECT *
  FROM employees WHERE 1=2;
```

Since the predicate 1=2 will always be false, the query will not return any rows.

If the function returns a string of zero length, no restriction will be placed in the original DML or SELECT statement. This characteristic is used in the function example to allow managers to see all the employees' records because NULL is assigned to the variable v_predicate when the user is a manager. If an unforeseen error occurs when the function is called, a zero-length string will not be returned because a WHEN OTHERS exception handler returns a value that disallows all reads.

Now create the hr_table_security package body.

```
CREATE OR REPLACE PACKAGE BODY hr_table_security
AS
  PROCEDURE get_current_user_information
    (o_emp OUT emp_type)
  IS
  BEGIN
    SELECT *
      INTO o_emp
      FROM scott.emp
     WHERE oracle_username = SYS_CONTEXT('USERENV', 'SESSION_USER');
  EXCEPTION
    WHEN OTHERS
    THEN
      -- If there is an error, return NULL
      --   (i.e. there is no user information).
      NULL;
  END;
  --
  FUNCTION is_at_least_a_manager
    (i_job scott.emp.job%TYPE)
    RETURN BOOLEAN
  IS
  BEGIN
    RETURN i_job IN ('MANAGER', 'PRESIDENT');
  END;
  --
  -- select_employees_predicate allows SELECTs
  --    to return only rows of employees in
  --    the same department as the person logged on
  --    (except managers who can SELECT all
  --     employee records).
  FUNCTION select_employees_predicate
    (i_object_schema all_objects.owner%TYPE,
     i_object_name all_objects.object_name%TYPE
    )
    RETURN VARCHAR2
```

```
   IS
     vr_emp emp_type;
     v_predicate predicate_type := cons_disallow_all_reads;
   BEGIN
     get_current_user_information(vr_emp);
     IF is_at_least_a_manager(vr_emp.job)
     THEN
       -- The user is managerial. Assign a zero length
       --   string so that there will be no restriction.
       v_predicate := NULL;
     ELSIF vr_emp.deptno IS NOT NULL
     THEN
       -- The user is not managerial. Restrict their access to
       --   seeing only employees in their own department.
       v_predicate := 'deptno = '||vr_emp.deptno;
     ELSE
       -- The user is not a valid employee. Make sure that
       --   cons_disallow_all_reads is the value in v_predicate.
       v_predicate := cons_disallow_all_reads;
     END IF;
     RETURN v_predicate;
   EXCEPTION
     WHEN OTHERS
     THEN
       -- If there are any other errors, make sure
       --   the user can't see any records.
       RETURN cons_disallow_all_reads;
   END;
END;
```

## Assign the Policy to the View

In the next step, you are going to assign the policy to the employees' view. You can issue the statement as the HR_SECURITY_MANAGER user.

**NOTE**

*Execute privilege must be granted on DBMS_RLS to HR_SECURITY_MANAGER.*

```
BEGIN
  DBMS_RLS.ADD_POLICY('SCOTT', 'EMPLOYEES', 'SELECT_EMPLOYEES_POLICY',
                      'HR_SECURITY_MANAGER',
                      'hr_table_security.select_employees_predicate',
                      'SELECT'
                     );
END;
```

This statement creates a security policy called select_employees_policy and assigns it to the scott.employees view. It specifies that a predicate will be created dynamically at run time using the hr_table_security.select_employees_predicate function. Lastly, it specifies that the select_employees_policy security policy will be used only when SELECTs are issued against the view.

If a SELECT is now issued against the employees' view, the database users who are managers or the president can see all of the records in emp. Other database users who are also employees can see the other employees in their department, while all other database users have been prohibited from seeing any of the rows in emp.

**CREATING DIFFERENT SECURITY POLICIES FOR SELECT AND UPDATE**    Another security function will now be introduced into the hr_table_security package to provide an UPDATE policy for the emp table. You will need to revoke UPDATE rights on the emp table and grant UPDATE rights on the employees view. Following is the code for the new hr_table_security package and package body, which now includes the update_employees_security function:

```
CREATE OR REPLACE PACKAGE hr_table_security
AS
  SUBTYPE emp_type IS scott.emp%ROWTYPE;
  SUBTYPE predicate_type IS VARCHAR2(2000);
  cons_disallow_all_reads CONSTANT CHAR(3) := '1=2';
  FUNCTION update_employees_predicate
    (i_object_schema all_objects.owner%TYPE,
     i_object_name all_objects.object_name%TYPE
    )
    RETURN VARCHAR2;
  FUNCTION select_employees_predicate
    (i_object_schema all_objects.owner%TYPE,
     i_object_name   all_objects.object_name%TYPE
    )
    RETURN VARCHAR2;
END;
```

Now create the hr_table_security package body, as follows:

```
CREATE OR REPLACE PACKAGE BODY hr_table_security
AS
  PROCEDURE get_current_user_information
    (o_emp OUT emp_type)
  IS
  BEGIN
    SELECT *
      INTO o_emp
      FROM scott.emp
```

```
      WHERE oracle_username = SYS_CONTEXT('USERENV', 'SESSION_USER');
EXCEPTION
  WHEN OTHERS
  THEN
      -- If there is an error, return NULL
      --    (i.e. there is no user information).
      NULL;
END;
FUNCTION is_at_least_a_manager
  (i_job scott.emp.job%TYPE)
  RETURN BOOLEAN
IS
BEGIN
  RETURN i_job IN ('MANAGER', 'PRESIDENT');
END;
--
-- update_employees_predicate enforces the rule
--    that only managers and above can update employees.
FUNCTION update_employees_predicate
  (i_object_schema all_objects.owner%TYPE,
   i_object_name all_objects.object_name%TYPE
  )
  RETURN VARCHAR2
IS
  vr_emp emp_type;
  v_predicate predicate_type := cons_disallow_all_reads;
BEGIN
  get_current_user_information(vr_emp);
  IF is_at_least_a_manager(vr_emp.job)
  THEN
      -- The user is managerial. Allow them to update only
      --    employee records for their own department.
      v_predicate := 'deptno = '||vr_emp.deptno;
  END IF;
  RETURN v_predicate;
EXCEPTION
  WHEN OTHERS
  THEN
      -- If there are any other errors, make sure
      --    the user can't update any records.
      RETURN cons_disallow_all_reads;
END;
--
-- select_employees_predicate allows SELECTs
--    to return only rows of employees in
--    the same department as the person logged on
--    (except managers who can SELECT all
--      employee records).
```

```
FUNCTION select_employees_predicate
  (i_object_schema all_objects.owner%TYPE,
   i_object_name all_objects.object_name%TYPE
  )
  RETURN VARCHAR2
IS
  vr_emp emp_type;
  v_predicate predicate_type := cons_disallow_all_reads;
BEGIN
  get_current_user_information(vr_emp);
  IF is_at_least_a_manager(vr_emp.job)
  THEN
    -- The user is managerial. Assign a zero length
    --   string so that there will be no restriction.
    v_predicate := NULL;
  ELSIF vr_emp.deptno IS NOT NULL
  THEN
    -- The user is not managerial. Restrict their access to
    --   seeing only employees in their own department.
    v_predicate := 'deptno = '||vr_emp.deptno;
  ELSE
    -- The user is not a valid employee. Make sure that
    --   cons_disallow_all_reads is the value in v_predicate.
    v_predicate := cons_disallow_all_reads;
  END IF;
  RETURN v_predicate;
EXCEPTION
  WHEN OTHERS
  THEN
    -- If there are any other errors, make sure
    --   the user can't see any records.
    RETURN cons_disallow_all_reads;
  END;
END;
```

**ADDING THE UPDATE SECURITY POLICY TO THE TABLE**    Now that
the update_employees_predicate function has been added to the hr_table_security
package, the policy needs to be assigned to the employees view. As seen before
with the SELECT policy, the DBMS_RLS.ADD_POLICY procedure will be used to
perform this action, as the following example shows:

```
BEGIN
  DBMS_RLS.ADD_POLICY('SCOTT', 'EMPLOYEES', 'UPDATE_EMPLOYEES_POLICY',
                       'HR_SECURITY_MANAGER',
                       'hr_table_security.update_employees_predicate',
                       'UPDATE'
                       ) ;
END ;
```

Row-Level App-Oriented
Security w/DBMS_RLS

Notice the statement type of UPDATE. This means that the policy will be used only when updating the employees view. Two policies have now been assigned to the employees view. One will be used for UPDATEs and the other for SELECTs.

## Providing Application-Specific Security

An *application context* can be used as a secure cache for storing information—as attributes—that will later be retrieved and used to make access-control decisions. An application context can have its own attributes. USERENV was used earlier as the context namespace with the SYS_CONTEXT function (for example, SYS_CONTEXT('USERENV', 'INSTANCE')). In that case, USERENV was the application context with predefined attributes such as IP_ADDRESS and INSTANCE. Using the CREATE CONTEXT command, an application-specific context namespace can be created, providing a means to set application-specific attributes that can be used throughout the user's session.

An application context represents the name of a context (context namespace) associated with a specific package to populate application context attributes. Once the context and the package have been associated via the CREATE CONTEXT command, you can use SYS_CONTEXT to reference the attribute values in the same way as attributes of the USERENV context are referenced. This is shown in the next two examples, in which MY_CONTEXT and MY_ATTRIBUTE are application context attributes created by the application developer.

```
SELECT SYS_CONTEXT('USERENV', 'LANGUAGE')
   FROM dual;

SELECT SYS_CONTEXT('MY_CONTEXT', 'MY_ATTRIBUTE')
   FROM dual;
```

The application context functions as a cache for repeatedly used application-oriented information. For example, all the information about a user that is contained in the emp table can be cached. A performance benefit can result, since the need to repeatedly SELECT from the emp table to get this information is eliminated. An order entry application provides another example where this may be useful. The user's ID can be cached as an attribute in the application context. It can then be used throughout the session so that the user is restricted to seeing only his or her own orders.

The following six steps will create an application context to supply related security information for the human resources application system using a customized context in conjunction with DBMS_RLS.

1. Plan the policy.

2. Create the context.

3. Create an application security package that defines the attributes for the context.

4. Set up the application security package to have its attributes automatically populated when the user logs on.

5. Create a table policy security package to be used in a policy to secure the emp table. The security function in the package will make use of the attributes in the application context.

6. Assign or refresh the policy to the employees view.

**NOTE**
*It is recommended that you perform these tasks in an account designated specifically to manage the application's security. The HR_SECURITY_MANAGER account referenced in the earlier examples can be used for this. The account should be granted the CREATE ANY CONTEXT privilege.*

## Plan the Policy

Building a complex security policy package first requires specifying the policy to be enforced. The following security policy will be enforced against the emp table when all of the steps are completed. For this example, use the security rules that were defined in the earlier section, "Creating a Security Policy Package."

## Create the Context

Creating an application context is straightforward. Simply create an association between a name for the context and the package that holds the application security function. Building the application context from these two components restricts users to establishing their application contexts solely through the use of the package assigned to that application context. In other words, users cannot bypass the application context by supplanting it with a security package that they designed themselves.

The application context attributes must be populated from within the designated application security package's procedures by calls to the DBMS_SESSION.SET_CONTEXT built-in. This defeats users' attempts to directly change the attribute values. If users do try to call DBMS_SESSION.SET_CONTEXT outside of the application security package, they receive the following error: ORA-01031: insufficient privileges.

In the following example, the HR_SECURITY_MANAGER user is issuing the CREATE_CONTEXT command:

```
CREATE OR REPLACE CONTEXT hr_context
  USING hr_security_manager.hr_application_security;
```

**NOTE**
*Neither the schema nor the package specified in the*
*USING clause need exist at the time the CREATE*
*CONTEXT command is executed.*

### Create an Application Security Package That Defines the Attributes for the Context

The application security package will populate the application context attributes and will later be configured to run at logon time, automatically setting the user's application context. The DBMS_SESSION.SET_CONTEXT built-in will be used in the package to set the attributes.

DBMS_SESSION.SET_CONTEXT procedure has three parameters:

- **Namespace**   The context namespace to use for the application context. (The context must have previously been created via the CREATE CONTEXT command.)

- **Attribute**   The name of the attribute to be set.

- **Value**   The value that will be retrieved when accessing the attribute from SYS_CONTEXT (limited to 256 bytes).

The hr_application_security package can be created as the HR_SECURITY_ MANAGER user. HR_SECURITY_MANAGER must have SELECT privileges on scott.emp. For security reasons, HR_SECURITY_MANAGER should be the only user that has direct SELECT privileges on scott.emp.

```
CREATE OR REPLACE PACKAGE hr_application_security
AS
  PROCEDURE set_hr_context_attributes;
END;
```

Notice that there are no required parameters for the application security procedure.
Now create the package body:

```
CREATE OR REPLACE PACKAGE BODY hr_application_security
AS
  PROCEDURE set_hr_context_attributes
  IS
    vr_emp scott.emp%ROWTYPE;
  BEGIN
    SELECT empno, oracle_username, job, deptno
      INTO vr_emp.empno, vr_emp.oracle_username,
```

```
            vr_emp.job, vr_emp.deptno
      FROM scott.emp
      WHERE oracle_username = SYS_CONTEXT('USERENV', 'SESSION_USER');
      -- populate the application context attributes that will
      --   later be read with the SYS_CONTEXT function.
      DBMS_SESSION.SET_CONTEXT('HR_CONTEXT', 'EMPNO',
                               vr_emp.empno
                              );
      DBMS_SESSION.SET_CONTEXT('HR_CONTEXT', 'ORACLE_USERNAME',
                               vr_emp.oracle_username
                              );
      DBMS_SESSION.SET_CONTEXT('HR_CONTEXT', 'JOB', vr_emp.job);
      DBMS_SESSION.SET_CONTEXT('HR_CONTEXT', 'DEPTNO', vr_emp.deptno);
  EXCEPTION
    WHEN OTHERS
    THEN
      -- Allow the HR_CONTEXT attributes to be NULL. The various table
      -- policies will detect this and disallow access to table.
      NULL;
  END;
END;
```

## Set Up the Application Security Package to Have Its Attributes Automatically Populated When the User Logs On

Although you can set the application context attributes from a call within the application, it may be preferable to set them initially and automatically when the user connects to the database. A database event trigger can be created that will fire for each user connecting to the database. The trigger calls a package that populates the attributes. In this example, the after_logon_al trigger calls the hr_application_security.set_hr_context_attributes procedure, which populates the attributes of the user's HR_CONTEXT application context.

**NOTE**
*The CREATE TRIGGER statement should be run as the SYSTEM_MANAGER user described earlier.*

```
CREATE OR REPLACE TRIGGER after_logon_al
  AFTER LOGON ON DATABASE
BEGIN
  -- Populate the application context attributes
  hr_security_manager.hr_application_security.set_hr_context_attributes;
END;
```

### Create a Table Policy Security Package to Be Used in a Policy to Secure the emp Table

This example is similar to one presented earlier in this chapter under "Creating a Security Policy Package." A table security package will be created that contains the rules for accessing scott.emp. However, there is a crucial difference between the current example and the previous one. In the previous example, a view was created on the emp table, and a policy was attached to the view instead of the table. This was because attaching the policy directly to the table effectively would have caused an infinite loop, since the table had to SELECT from itself to construct its own access policy.

Now there is no need to check the emp table to determine the user's security information since it was cached in the user's human resources application context (HR_CONTEXT) when the user logged on to the database via the database event trigger, that called the hr_application_security.set_hr_context_attributes procedure. It is necessary, though, to use the employees view for a different but related reason.

If a table policy is attached to the emp table and used when the application context attributes are being populated, it will always populate the context attributes with NULLs. This is because the application context attributes start out as NULL. The row-level security will inhibit users' ability to populate the application context attributes while they are in this state. To get around this, the security policy will again be attached to the view. The logon trigger will then SELECT from emp instead of employees and will not have any problems getting data to populate the attributes.

The following example recreates the hr_table_security package, this time using the application context attributes rather than by issuing a SELECT against the emp table. Not only is the code more concise, it is also more efficient. Using the cached application context attributes requires only the initial hit against scott.emp instead of SELECTing the same information from emp each time the employees view is queried.

**NOTE**

*There are, however, situations in which the version of hr_table_security shown earlier is preferable to the version shown next. For example, it may be important in some applications not to use a cached attribute value but rather to use the most up-to-date information to form the correct predicate.*

This package should be created as the application security manager user HR_SECURITY_MANAGER.

```
CREATE OR REPLACE PACKAGE hr_table_security
AS
  cons_disallow_all_reads CONSTANT CHAR(3) := '1=2';
  SUBTYPE predicate_type IS VARCHAR2(2000);
  FUNCTION update_employees_predicate
    (i_object_schema all_objects.owner%TYPE,
     i_object_name all_objects.object_name%TYPE
    )
    RETURN VARCHAR2;
  --
  FUNCTION select_employees_predicate
    (i_object_schema all_objects.owner%TYPE,
     i_object_name all_objects.object_name%TYPE
    )
    RETURN VARCHAR2;
    END;
```

Now create the package body.

```
CREATE OR REPLACE PACKAGE BODY hr_table_security
AS
  FUNCTION is_at_least_a_manager
    (i_job scott.emp.job%TYPE)
    RETURN BOOLEAN
  IS
  BEGIN
    RETURN i_job IN ('MANAGER', 'PRESIDENT');
  END; -- is_at_least_a_manager
  --
  -- update_employees_predicate enforces the rule
  --    that only managers and above can update employees.
  FUNCTION update_employees_predicate
    (i_object_schema all_objects.owner%TYPE,
     i_object_name all_objects.object_name%TYPE
    )
    RETURN VARCHAR2
  IS
    v_predicate predicate_type := cons_disallow_all_reads;
  BEGIN
    IF is_at_least_a_manager(SYS_CONTEXT('HR_CONTEXT','JOB'))
    THEN
      -- The user is managerial. Allow them to update only
      --   employees records for their own department.
      v_predicate := 'deptno = '||SYS_CONTEXT('HR_CONTEXT', 'DEPTNO');
```

```
    END IF;
    RETURN v_predicate;
 EXCEPTION
    WHEN OTHERS
    THEN
       -- If there are any other errors, make sure
       --   the user can't update any records.
       RETURN cons_disallow_all_reads;
 END;
 --
 -- select_employees_predicate allows SELECTs
 --   to return only rows of employees in
 --   the same department as the person logged on
 --   (except managers who can SELECT all
 --    employee records).
 FUNCTION select_employees_predicate
    (i_object_schema all_objects.owner%TYPE,
     i_object_name all_objects.object_name%TYPE
    )
    RETURN VARCHAR2
 IS
    v_predicate predicate_type := cons_disallow_all_reads;
 BEGIN
    IF is_at_least_a_manager(SYS_CONTEXT('HR_CONTEXT','JOB'))
    THEN
       -- The user is managerial. Assign a zero length
       --   string so that there will be no restriction.
       v_predicate := NULL;
    ELSIF SYS_CONTEXT('HR_CONTEXT', 'DEPTNO') IS NOT NULL
    THEN
       -- The user is not managerial. Restrict their access to
       --   seeing only employees in their own department.
       v_predicate := 'deptno = '||
         SYS_CONTEXT('HR_CONTEXT', 'DEPTNO');
    ELSE
       -- The user is not a valid employee. Make sure that
       --   cons_disallow_all_reads is the value in v_predicate.
       v_predicate := cons_disallow_all_reads;
    END IF;
    RETURN v_predicate;
 EXCEPTION
    WHEN OTHERS
    THEN
       -- If there are any other errors, make sure
       --   the user can't see any records.
       RETURN cons_disallow_all_reads;
 END;
END;
```

### Assign or Refresh the Policy to the Employees View

The final step is to assign the SELECT and UPDATE policies to scott.employees. This can be done with DBMS_RLS.ADD_POLICY. If the policies are already assigned, then they should be refreshed with DBMS_RLS.REFRESH_POLICY to ensure that the most recent version of the security package will be used by all users.

```
BEGIN
   DBMS_RLS.REFRESH_POLICY('SCOTT', 'EMPLOYEES', 'UPDATE_EMPLOYEES_POLICY');
   DBMS_RLS.REFRESH_POLICY('SCOTT', 'EMPLOYEES', 'SELECT_EMPLOYEES_POLICY');
END ;
```

Alternatively, the policy assignments can be recreated by dropping the policies and then recreating them, as follows:

```
BEGIN
   DBMS_RLS.DROP_POLICY('SCOTT', 'EMPLOYEES', 'UPDATE_EMPLOYEES_POLICY');
   DBMS_RLS.ADD_POLICY('SCOTT', 'EMPLOYEES', 'UPDATE_EMPLOYEES_POLICY',
                       'HR_SECURITY_MANAGER',
                       'hr_table_security.update_employees_predicate',
                       'UPDATE'
                       );
   DBMS_RLS.DROP_POLICY('SCOTT', 'EMPLOYEES', 'SELECT_EMPLOYEES_POLICY');
   DBMS_RLS.ADD_POLICY('SCOTT', 'EMPLOYEES', 'SELECT_EMPLOYEES_POLICY',
                       'HR_SECURITY_MANAGER',
                       'hr_table_security.select_employees_predicate',
                       'SELECT'
                       );
END;
```

# Tips Review

Oracle8i provides new features that expand database security management abilities. The virtual private database feature and database event triggers are the ones that have been explored in this chapter. Fine-grained access control is prepared by using the DBMS_RLS built-in to associate a security policy with a table or view. Code within the security policy prepares a predicate that is then added to the original DML or SELECT statements to restrict access to the data if necessary.

Application context attributes can be populated by custom code and used from within an application to participate in fine-grained access control. SYS_CONTEXT is used to retrieve information from the attributes, while database event triggers can be used to automatically populate the attributes at logon time.

# PART
# III

## Application
## Development

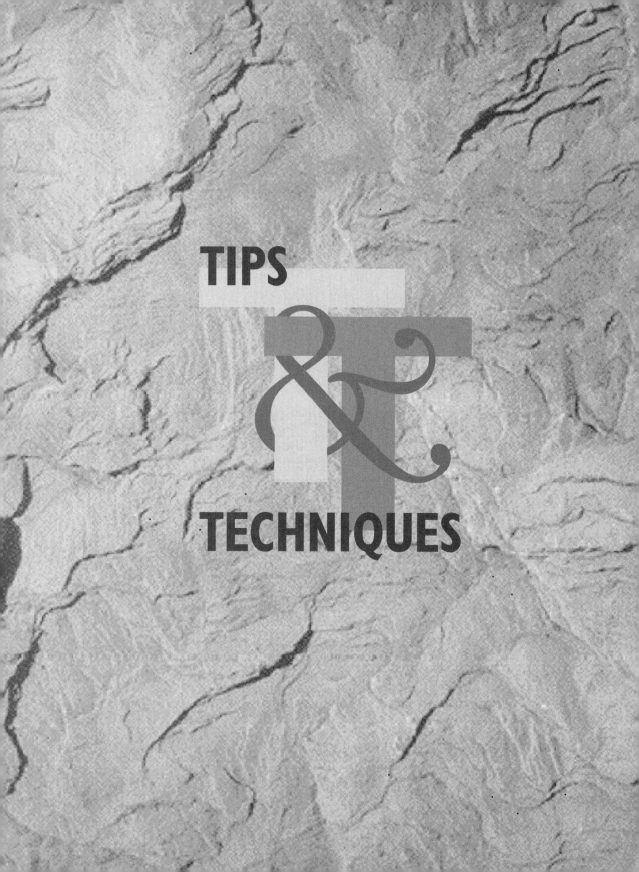

TIPS
&
TECHNIQUES

# CHAPTER

# 8

## PL/SQL

From the perspective of a developer or a DBA, PL/SQL in Oracle8i has been enhanced in three ways.

First, there are new coding techniques. They include a simplified method for embedding dynamic SQL statements in PL/SQL. With dynamic SQL, data definition, data control, and session control statements can be issued within PL/SQL routines. Invoker-rights routines have been introduced that allow routines to be run with the privileges of the user, not the privileges of the creator of the routine. Routines now can be declared to be autonomous and have their transactions complete with COMMIT and ROLLBACK statements that do not influence the transaction status of the calling routine. These are referred to as autonomous transactions. Also, temporary tables have been introduced that constitute temporary-records work areas, the contents of which come and go with either a user's session or a user's transaction.

Second, new coding alternatives can be used with Oracle's collection data types that can boost the performance of nested tables, varrays, and indexed-by binary-integer tables. Collections can be bulk bound to improve performance when collections are passed between the PL/SQL and SQL engines. The NOCOPY parameter flag can improve performance when collections are passed between PL/SQL routines.

Third, two new PL/SQL built-in packages help track and gauge the run-time performance of PL/SQL routines. DBMS_PROFILER tracks named PL/SQL routines and reports on their execution times and the number of times they are called on a line-by-line basis. DBMS_TRACE can be used as a debugging tool that tracks the exceptions generated and the routine calls of application code at run time.

The following nine Tips & Techniques—each of which includes coding examples—presented in this chapter are designed to give an overview of the feature.

- Issuing native dynamic SQL in PL/SQL

- Using invoker-rights to share code and address multiple schema

- Creating autonomous transactions to audit and track activity

- Using temporary tables to maintain user state, to boost subquery processing, and to enhance distributive processing

- Bulk binding collections to improve performance

- Bulk binding in native dynamic SQL

- Using NOCOPY to enhance performance when passing collectors with and without bulk binding

- Monitoring the execution times of named routines with DBMS_PROFILER

- Monitoring run-time PL/SQL calls and exceptions with DBMS_TRACE

# New Coding Techniques with Dynamic SQL, Invoker-Rights, Autonomous Transactions, and Temporary Tables

The new coding techniques include a simplified method for embedding dynamic SQL statements in PL/SQL and handling data definition, data control, and session control statements issued within PL/SQL routines. Invoker-rights routines allow routines to be run with the privileges of the user, not the privileges of the creator of the routine. Autonomous transactions are routines that have their transactions complete with COMMIT and ROLLBACK statements that do not influence the transaction status of the calling routine. Temporary tables constitute temporary work areas, the row contents of which are determined by either a user's session or a user's transaction. These new coding techniques are the subjects of this section.

## Issuing Native Dynamic SQL in PL/SQL

PL/SQL programs contain SQL statements selecting, updating, inserting, and deleting from tables. SQL statements within PL/SQL can be divided into two types: static and dynamic. Static SQL statements are fully specified at compile-time except perhaps for bind variables, which may be passed to the SQL statement. The table names and column names are known at compile-time, though the value a column may take as specified in a WHERE clause may be only a bind variable. Static SQL statements do not change between executions. Examples of dynamic SQL statements are those in which the table names and/or column names are not known at compile-time. The table or column names will be passed to the statement at run time. More generally, dynamic SQL allows any schema-object name to be passed at PL/SQL run time to a Data Manipulation Language (DML) or SELECT statement. In addition, it allows issuing from within PL/SQL of Data Definition Language (DDL) such as CREATE TABLE or CREATE INDEX, Data Control Language (DCL) such as GRANT, Session Control Language (SCL) such as ALTER SESSION, and PL/SQL anonymous blocks such as BEGIN . . . END PL/SQL statements. Dynamic SQL statements are essentially character strings stored in PL/SQL blocks.

When the full text of a SQL statement is known at compile-time, static SQL should be used. It has the benefits of validating the existence of objects referenced and of validating privileges and access to the objects. In general, static SQL will perform better than dynamic SQL. When the full text is not known, dynamic SQL is available. In addition, DDL, DCL, and SCL statements can be executed in dynamic SQL. These are not available in narrowly defined static SQL that covers only DML and SELECT statements. Dynamic WHERE, ORDER BY, GROUP BY, or HAVING clauses can be passed at run time with dynamic SQL, thus allowing users to modify search, sort, or aggregating criteria. Objects that do not exist at compile-time can be supplied at run time—for example, a table name. Objects that change can be referenced at run time—for example, a column name—with dynamic SQL.

With Oracle8i, Oracle has simplified the using of dynamic SQL and enhanced its performance over the earlier DBMS_SQL built-in package implementation. DBMS_SQL is still available with Oracle8i. The new implementation is referred to as *native dynamic SQL.* Less code and less complex coding is required to use the new native dynamic SQL implementation. Moreover, it is more intuitive, so that users need rely only on knowledge of SQL. DBMS_SQL is implemented by use of a procedural API that requires procedure calls and data to be copied repeatedly from PL/SQL memory areas into the memory managed by the DBMS_SQL package. Native dynamic SQL is integrated into the PL/SQL engine; PL/SQL has "native" support for SQL. The SQL statement and bind variables are prepared, and then the statement is executed in one step. On the negative side, the SQL statement is re-parsed every time it is reused in native dynamic SQL, whereas the parse phase of the SQL statement in a DBMS_SQL procedure is done only once. Overall performance of native dynamic SQL may be 50 percent to 300 percent faster than DBMS_SQL.

**NOTE**

*To use the native dynamic SQL features of Oracle8i, make sure the COMPATIBLE init.ora parameter is set to a value of 8.1.0 or higher.*

The trade-offs between the two implementations may override issues of performance and ease of use. DBMS_SQL supports SQL statements greater than 32K, whereas native dynamic SQL has a limit of 32K. DBMS_SQL is supported for client-side programming, whereas native dynamic SQL is not. On the other side of the trade-off, the DBMS_SQL package does not support user-defined types, whereas native dynamic SQL supports all types supported by static SQL in PL/SQL, including user-defined objects, collections, and REF CURSORs. Native dynamic SQL supports fetching into records, whereas DBMS_SQL does not. For a more detailed discussion of these differences, see the Oracle8i Application Developer's Guide—Fundamentals.

There are essentially two coding components to native dynamic SQL. First, to parse and execute a dynamic SQL statement, you should use EXECUTE IMMEDIATE. Its full general syntax is

```
EXECUTE IMMEDIATE dynamic_string
  [INTO {define_variable [, defined_variable] … | record}]
  [USING [IN | OUT | IN OUT] bind_argument
    [,[IN | OUT | IN OUT] bind_argument] … ];
```

Only an EXECUTE IMMEDIATE and the dynamic string containing the SQL statement are required. For non-multirow queries, all you need is EXECUTE IMMEDIATE. Second, to use multirow queries, OPEN-FOR, FETCH, and CLOSE statements are required. Their full syntax is

```
OPEN {cursor_variable | :host_cursor_variable}
  FOR dynamic_string
    [USING bind_argument[, bind_argument]...];
...
FETCH {cursor_variable | :host_cursor_variable}
   INTO {define_variable[, define_variable]... | record};
... process rows
CLOSE {cursor_variable | :host_cursor_variable};
```

The host-cursor variable in the OPEN and CLOSE statements refers to a host language environment that supports SQL, such as C support through the Oracle Call Interface API. Host languages are beyond the scope of this chapter and will not be covered. The USING clauses are discussed in the following pages when they appear in code samples; they essentially map declared variables to bind variables. The INTO clauses allow either single row or multiple rows of fetched records to be placed in user-defined variables or records.

The OPEN and CLOSE statements use a weakly typed cursor variable—that is, one without a RETURN clause type-casting the data types of the fetched fields. Declaring a cursor variable, which the foregoing assumes has occurred, opens an unnamed work area in memory, to which the cursor variable points, and into which the multirow query information is placed. In fact, the syntax for OPEN, FETCH, and CLOSE exactly matches that of cursor variables, except that the cursor variable is weakly typed. The example code to follow will clarify cursor variable usage. The records are then fetched into user-defined variables or a record of a set of variables with the FETCH statement.

As a first example of the use of native dynamic SQL, look at the following procedure, which creates a clone of a table with an EXECUTE IMMEDIATE statement.

 **NOTE**
*Throughout Chapter 8, DBMS_OUTPUT.PUT_LINE commands have been introduced into the routines for debugging purposes, as well as for other purposes. To use these DBMS_OUTPUT.PUT_LINEs, when running the routines from the SQL*Plus command prompt, first SET SERVEROUTPUT ON at the SQL*Plus prompt.*

```
CREATE OR REPLACE PROCEDURE clone_table
  (i_table_name IN VARCHAR2)
AS
```

```
   -- variable to hold dynamic SQL statement
   v_sql_stmt VARCHAR2(2000);
   -- variable to hold new clone table name
   v_new_tab_name VARCHAR2(30);
BEGIN
   -- table names can only be 30 characters
   -- and so to append 'tmp' use SUBSTR function
   v_new_tab_name := SUBSTR(i_table_name,1,27)||'tmp';
   -- debugging code that requires SET SERVEROUTPUT ON
   -- from sql*plus command prompt
   DBMS_OUTPUT.PUT_LINE(v_new_tab_name);
   -- create the dynamic SQL string
   v_sql_stmt := 'CREATE TABLE '||v_new_tab_name||
                  ' AS SELECT * FROM '||i_table_name;
   -- more debugging
   DBMS_OUTPUT.PUT_LINE(v_sql_stmt);
   -- execute the dynamic SQL
   EXECUTE IMMEDIATE v_sql_stmt;
END;
```

Passing the name of an existing table into this procedure reproduces the table with the appended string tmp, potentially truncating the table name if it is longer than 27 characters. A more sophisticated version of this procedure would validate that the table name passed represents an existing table and that it has not already been cloned.

**NOTE**

*Users who execute clone_table must have the system privilege of creating tables explicitly granted to them. Assigning the role of resource is not sufficient to create a table through a procedure.*

For a test of this procedure and ones to follow, rows can be created and inserted into a test table, using native dynamic SQL. The test table created is called test_tab.

```
CREATE OR REPLACE PROCEDURE create_test_tab
AS
   v_sql_stmt VARCHAR2(2000);
   -- a counter variable for inserted data
   v_cnt NUMBER;
BEGIN
   -- dynamic SQL statement
   v_sql_stmt := 'CREATE TABLE test_tab(
                   x NUMBER,
                   y NUMBER,
                   a VARCHAR2(20))';
```

```
  -- execute dynamic SQL statement creating table
  EXECUTE IMMEDIATE v_sql_stmt;
  -- load five records into test_tab
  -- using counter v_cnt and for-loop
  FOR v_cnt IN 1..5
  LOOP
    v_sql_stmt := 'INSERT INTO test_tab
                   VALUES(:1, :2, :3)';
    EXECUTE IMMEDIATE v_sql_stmt
      USING v_cnt, v_cnt + 1.0, 'a'||TO_CHAR(v_cnt);
  END LOOP;
  COMMIT;
END;
```

The INSERT statement must be written as a dynamic SQL statement, since the test_tab table does not exist in the schema at compile-time, and so compilation of static SQL would fail. In the INSERT statement, placeholders :1, :2, and :3 are used instead of user-declared variables. The USING clause of the EXECUTE IMMEDIATE statement maps the user-declared variable v_cnt and expressions, using this variable to the placeholders. The placeholders are acting as bind variables, and the USING clause binds the declared variables to them. Without the bind variables (that is, using user-declared variables in the INSERT statement and avoiding the USING clause), a new implicit cursor would be opened on each loop iteration with different values for the declared variables. With bind variables, only one cursor is opened and then reused. Performance is enhanced as the repeated SQL statements—here the INSERT—reuse the cursor.

Once the procedures clone_table and create_test_tab have been created, they can be executed at the SQL*Plus prompt.

```
EXECUTE create_test_tab;
EXECUTE clone_tab('test_tab');
```

The tables test_tab and test_tabtmp will be created with identical contents.

Two points of possible confusion and error can now be clarified. First, the USING clause does not support passing an explicit or literal NULL. This would generate a *PLS-00457: in the USING clause, expressions have to be of SQL types* error at compile-time. The work-around is to pass a variable whose value is NULL.

```
v_char := NULL;
v_sql_stmt := 'INSERT INTO test_tab
               VALUES(:1, :2, :3)';
EXECUTE IMMEDIATE v_sql_stmt
  USING v_cnt, v_cnt + 1.0, v_char;
```

Passing the NULL value via a user-declared variable accomplishes the task.

Second, the names of existing schema objects cannot be passed as bind variables in the USING clause. So coding the clause USING i_table_name with the EXECUTE IMMEDIATE statement and binding it to a SELECT * FROM :1 clause in the CREATE TABLE statement of clone_table would generate an *ORA-00903: invalid table name* error at run time. The following is the correct coding method; it does not use a bind variable or a USING clause.

```
v_sql_stmt := 'CREATE TABLE '||v_new_tab_name||
                 ' AS SELECT * FROM '||i_table_name;
EXECUTE IMMEDIATE v_sql_stmt;
```

The parameter—i_table_name—must be in the dynamic SQL string as the code is written here and as it was written in clone_table.

To make a final point about bind variables and placeholders, let us suppose in test_tab—the test table—both number columns were loaded with the same value, the value of v_cnt. The code from create_test_tab might be modified as shown in the following, binding v_cnt to :1 twice or binding it to :1 and :2.

```
v_sql_stmt := 'INSERT INTO test_tab
                 VALUES(:1, :1, :3)';
EXECUTE IMMEDIATE v_sql_stmt
  USING v_cnt, v_cnt, 'a'||TO_CHAR(v_cnt);

v_sql_stmt := 'INSERT INTO test_tab
                 VALUES(:1, :2, :3)';
EXECUTE IMMEDIATE v_sql_stmt
  USING v_cnt, v_cnt, 'a'||TO_CHAR(v_cnt);
```

To demonstrate a multirecord query, consider that the following code selects against the test_tab table when the user supplies a WHERE clause and prints the selected records to the screen. This procedure requires the user to enter the command SET SERVEROUTPUT ON from the SQL*Plus prompt to have the DBMS_OUTPUT command print to the screen. To fetch the multirecord result set, you must declare a weakly typed cursor variable.

```
CREATE OR REPLACE PROCEDURE print_test_tab
  (i_where_clause IN VARCHAR2 DEFAULT NULL)
  -- if no where clause is passed it defaults to NULL
AS
  -- declare a weakly type cursor
  TYPE generic_cv IS REF CURSOR;
  -- create a cursor variable from cursor
  cv_gen generic_cv;
  -- create a record variable from the test_tab
  -- for the fetch into
```

```
   rec_test_tab test_tab%ROWTYPE;
   -- create a variable for the where clause
   v_where VARCHAR2(2000);
   -- variable to hold dynamic SQL statement
   v_sql_stmt VARCHAR2(2000);
BEGIN
   -- if no where clause is passed it defaults to NULL
   -- and all records are shown
   IF i_where_clause IS NULL
   THEN
      v_where := NULL;
   ELSE
      v_where := 'WHERE '||TRIM(i_where_clause);
   END IF;
   v_sql_stmt := 'SELECT * FROM test_tab '||v_where;
   -- debugging line
   DBMS_OUTPUT.PUT_LINE(v_sql_stmt);
   OPEN cv_gen FOR v_sql_stmt;
   LOOP
      FETCH cv_gen INTO rec_test_tab;
         EXIT WHEN cv_gen%NOTFOUND;
      -- debugging line showing fetch
      DBMS_OUTPUT.PUT_LINE(rec_test_tab.x||
         ' '||rec_test_tab.y||' '||rec_test_tab.a);
   END LOOP;
   CLOSE cv_gen;
EXCEPTION
   WHEN OTHERS
   THEN
      IF cv_gen%ISOPEN
      THEN
         CLOSE cv_gen;
      END IF;
END;
```

The only tricky part in building the WHERE clause is in the use of single quotes. Since the clause is constructed from a parameter, and the parameter is a string of type VARCHAR2, the entire string must be enclosed in single quotes. The following works when the column being used is a number:

```
SQL> EXECUTE print_test_tab('x < 3')
SELECT * FROM test_tab WHERE x < 3
1 2 a1
2 3 a2
```

The WHERE-clause string is passed to the select statement correctly for a numeric value as the unquoted string x < 3. However, when the WHERE clause must include a character string—for example, to test against the value of the VARCHAR2 column 'a' in this case—the use of two single quotes on both sides of the string within the parameter ensures that the string value will include a single quote:

```
SQL> EXECUTE print_test_tab('x < 5 AND a LIKE ''%1''')
SELECT * FROM test_tab WHERE x < 5 AND a LIKE '%1'
1 2 a1
```

The double single quotes around %1 are needed so that single quotes appear around the string in the WHERE clause of the select statement.

**NOTE**
*The function TRIM() in the print_test_tab procedure is a new PL/SQL function that trims left-hand-side, right-hand-side, or both characters from a passed argument. In the manner just discussed, it trims blanks or white spaces from both sides. (See the Oracle8i SQL Reference for the full syntax.)*

To demonstrate the usefulness of the native dynamic SQL let us now present three procedures.

The first procedure changes a user's password. The SQL*Plus PASSWORD command allows SQL*Plus users to change their passwords. Passwords can also be changed by privileged users with Oracle Enterprise Manager (OEM). Oracle recommends not using the ALTER USER command as is done in the forthcoming example since it does not fully support the password verification functionality introduced with Oracle8. Oracle recommends using the PASSWORD command with SQL*Plus or OEM. Unfortunately, application users often do not have access to SQL*Plus or OEM, and the change_pwd procedure can be used as a template to build a change-password procedure called from Oracle Forms or another GUI application tool. As this Tip explains, change_pwd would be executed by any user assigned the role of DBA or with the ALTER ANY USER privilege. Alternatively, it could be created in every user's schema. But when combined with invoker-rights, as shown in the next Tip, "Using Invoker-Rights to Share Code and Address Multiple Schemas," it can be used as a template procedure to which all users are given access and with which any users could change their password.

The second procedure is used to remove duplicate records from a table. This procedure is handy for cleaning up redundant records in a table, so that, for example, a primary key may be created on a column or group of columns.

The third procedure is used to remove all objects from a user's schema of a particular type. This procedure is also a handy cleaning-up routine and provides another example of a multirow select.

The procedure change_pwd is passed a new password and then alters the executing user's password after veriffication of the new password. To use change_pwd interactively, the user must first enter the command SET SERVEROUTPUT ON at the SQL*Plus prompt.

```
CREATE OR REPLACE PROCEDURE change_pwd
  (i_new_pwd IN VARCHAR2 DEFAULT NULL)
AS
  v_sql_stmt VARCHAR2(2000);
BEGIN
  IF i_new_pwd IS NULL
  THEN
    DBMS_OUTPUT.PUT_LINE('A password is required.');
    DBMS_OUTPUT.PUT_LINE(
      'Usage: EXECUTE change_pwd(''new_password'')');
  ELSE
    v_sql_stmt := 'ALTER USER '||USER||
                  ' IDENTIFIED BY '||i_new_pwd;
    -- debugging line
    DBMS_OUTPUT.PUT_LINE(v_sql_stmt);
    EXECUTE IMMEDIATE v_sql_stmt;
    DBMS_OUTPUT.PUT_LINE(USER||
      '''s password has been changed.');
  END IF;
EXCEPTION
 WHEN OTHERS
 THEN
  DBMS_OUTPUT.PUT_LINE(
    'Try again password not changed.');
  DBMS_OUTPUT.PUT_LINE(
    'Usage: EXECUTE change_pwd(''new_password'')');
END;
```

Executing change_pwd and trying to pass NULL or a null string moves execution into the IF-THEN block. The message generated is

```
A password is required.
Usage: EXECUTE change_pwd('new_password')
```

Note that the new password must be passed as a single quoted string.

As a second example of native dynamic SQL, let us consider the remove_dups procedure, which is designed to take a table name and condition that defines a unique record in the table and then remove the duplicate records based on the condition. If no condition is passed, the procedure does nothing but return a row count of zero. If a valid condition is passed, the duplicate records are removed from the table and a row count of the number removed is returned to the SQL*Plus screen. Again, the DBMS_OUTPUT commands require that the command SET SERVEROUTPUT ON be run at the command prompt.

```
CREATE OR REPLACE PROCEDURE remove_dups
   (i_table_name IN VARCHAR2,
    i_condition IN VARCHAR2 DEFAULT NULL
   )
AS
   v_where_clause VARCHAR2(2000) := ' WHERE '||i_condition;
   v_sql_stmt VARCHAR2(4000);
   v_row_cnt NUMBER := 0;
BEGIN
   -- two debug lines
   DBMS_OUTPUT.PUT_LINE(i_condition);
   DBMS_OUTPUT.PUT_LINE(v_where_clause);
   IF i_condition IS NOT NULL
   THEN
      v_sql_stmt := 'DELETE FROM '||i_table_name||' tab_dups
                     WHERE ROWID NOT IN
                        (SELECT MAX(ROWID)
                         FROM '||i_table_name||' tab_max
                         '||v_where_clause||')';
      -- debug line
      DBMS_OUTPUT.PUT_LINE(v_sql_stmt);
      EXECUTE IMMEDIATE v_sql_stmt;
      COMMIT;
      -- capture number of records removed
      -- from the implicit cursor attribute %ROWCOUNT
      v_row_cnt := SQL%ROWCOUNT;
      -- print to screen number of records removed
      DBMS_OUTPUT.PUT_LINE(
         'Number of records deleted: '||v_row_cnt);
   ELSE
      -- print zero as the number of records removed
      DBMS_OUTPUT.PUT_LINE('No where clause, nothing done.');
      DBMS_OUTPUT.PUT_LINE(v_row_cnt);
   END IF;
END;
```

The heart of this procedure is in the v_sql_stmt, in which the table is joined to itself in a correlated subquery based on the duplicate-record criteria. Only one record with each unique combination will be retained (the one with the highest ROWID); all others are deleted. An example will clarify the logic of the procedure.

The procedure create_test_tab created a table test_tab that can be used to demonstrate remove_dups. First, load some duplicate records into test_tab from SQL*Plus.

```
INSERT INTO test_tab(x, y, a) VALUES(1, 2, 'a1');
INSERT INTO test_tab(x, y, a) VALUES(1, 3, 'a1');
INSERT INTO test_tab(x, y, a) VALUES(1, 4, 'a1');
INSERT INTO test_tab(x, y, a) VALUES(2, 5, 'a2');
INSERT INTO test_tab(x, y, a) VALUES(2, 6, 'a2');
COMMIT;
```

Suppose that columns 'x' and 'a' of test_tab comprise a unique record and that duplicates are to be removed on the values found on these two columns. Column 'x' is defined as a data type number and 'a' is defined as VARCHAR2(20). From SQL*Plus the criteria passed to the remove_dups function as the condition would be the single-quoted string 'tab_dups.x = tab_max.x AND tab_dups.a = tab_max.a') along with a single quoted table name, 'test_tab'.

```
EXECUTE remove_dups('test_tab','tab_dups.x = tab_max.x AND
tab_dups.a = tab_max.a')
```

The DELETE statement resolves itself to the following with these parameters passed:

```
DELETE FROM test_tab outer
 WHERE ROWID NOT IN
       (SELECT MAX(ROWID)
          FROM test_tab inner
         WHERE tab_dups.x = tab_max.x
           AND tab_dups.a = tab_max.a
       );
```

The DELETE statement preserves one record from each group of records that meet the criteria expressed in the WHERE clause of the subquery.

It is worth noting that in remove_dups, attributes of the implicit cursor opened with the DELETE statement can be referred to when the statement is run as dynamic SQL through the EXECUTE IMMEDIATE statement. From the point of view of cursor attributes, dynamic SQL statements behave like any SQL statement.

```
EXECUTE IMMEDIATE v_sql_stmt;
-- capture number of records removed
-- from the implicit cursor attribute %ROWCOUNT
v_row_cnt := SQL%ROWCOUNT;
-- print to screen number of records removed
DBMS_OUTPUT.PUT_LINE(
  'Number of records deleted: '||v_row_cnt);
```

The cursor attribute %ROWCOUNT is captured in the v_row_cnt. The other three cursor attributes, %FOUND, %ISOPEN, and %NOTFOUND, are also available.

The third procedure, drop_objs, is designed to accept an object name and an object type and to remove from a user's schema all objects matching the type and name. Since wildcard values may be passed for type, name, or both, a multirow query is used.

```
CREATE OR REPLACE PROCEDURE drop_objs
  (i_obj_name IN VARCHAR2,
   i_obj_type IN VARCHAR2
  )
AS
  -- declare a weakly typed cursor
  TYPE generic_cv IS REF CURSOR;
  -- create a cursor variable from cursor
  cv_userobjs generic_cv;
  -- create a record based on user_objects table
  -- to fetch into
  rec_userobjs user_objects%ROWTYPE;
  -- two variables to hold dynamic SQL statements
  v_sql_stmt VARCHAR2(2000);
  v_sql_stmt2 VARCHAR2(2000);
BEGIN
  -- the first dynamic SQL statement returns records
  -- matching object name and object type passed,
  -- object type is passed as a bind variable
  -- for performance
  v_sql_stmt :=
    'SELECT object_name, object_type
       FROM user_objects
      WHERE object_name LIKE UPPER('''||i_obj_name||''')
        AND object_type LIKE UPPER(:ot)';
  -- debugging line
  DBMS_OUTPUT.PUT_LINE(v_sql_stmt);
  -- open the cursor binding object type to :ot,
  -- fetch the records, and execute the second dynamic
  -- SQL statement dropping the objects
  OPEN cv_userobjs FOR v_sql_stmt USING i_obj_type;
  LOOP
  FETCH cv_userobjs
    INTO rec_userobjs.object_name, rec_userobjs.object_type;
      EXIT WHEN cv_userobjs%NOTFOUND;
    v_sql_stmt2 := 'DROP '||rec_userobjs.object_type||
                     ' '||rec_userobjs.object_name;
    -- second debugging line
    DBMS_OUTPUT.PUT_LINE(v_sql_stmt2);
    EXECUTE IMMEDIATE v_sql_stmt2;
  END LOOP;
  CLOSE cv_userobjs;
END;
```

For example, any object that had tmp in its name can now be dropped with
EXECUTE drop_objs('%tmp%', '%') from SQL*Plus.

## Using Invoker-Rights to Share Code and Address Multiple Schemas

The default behavior of stored procedures, functions, packages, and SQL types is to
resolve object references at compile-time in the schema of the creator or definer
and to execute the code with the privileges of the definer. These are referred to as
*definer-rights routines* and are bound to the schema of the definer. Routines that
are not bound to the schema of the definer are called *invoker-rights routines.*
Invoker-rights routines are new with Oracle8i. They execute with the privileges of
the invoker or current user of the routine. An invoker-rights routine can be created
in one schema and then run in another without recompiling the routine in the
second schema. The code can be shared and, as with any centralized code, it is
easier to maintain. Furthermore, when an invoker-rights routine calls a definer-rights
routine, both the schema of the invoker and, in part, that of the definer will be
addressable by the invoker. In invoking a definer-rights routine from an invoker-
rights routine, the user transitions from the invoker to the definer, and both schemas
are addressable. The latter is particularly useful in auditing, where the definer's
schema is also the auditing schema. Also, applications that have multiple similar
schemas storing similar data will find invoker-rights routines particularly useful
because then routines can be centralized.

The AUTHID clause in the syntax for creating routines states how references to
database objects are to be resolved. AUTHID CURRENT_USER defines an invoker-
rights routine, where external references are to be resolved through the privileges
and schema of the invoker. AUTHID DEFINER, the default, is used for definer-rights
routines. The AUTHID specification for a package covers all routines defined within
the package. The syntax is as follows:

```
CREATE [OR REPLACE] FUNCTION [schema_name.]function_name
  [(parameter_list)]
  RETURN datatype
  [AUTHID {CURRENT_USER | DEFINER}] {IS | AS}

CREATE [OR REPLACE] PROCEDURE [schema_name.]procedure_name
  [(parameter_list)]
  [AUTHID {CURRENT_USER | DEFINER}] {IS | AS}

CREATE [OR REPLACE] PACKAGE [schema_name.]package_name
  [AUTHID {CURRENT_USER | DEFINER}] {IS | AS}

CREATE [OR REPLACE] TYPE [schema_name.]object_type_name
  [AUTHID {CURRENT_USER | DEFINER}] {IS | AS} OBJECT
```

Notice that triggers are not on this list. Triggers are always definer-rights routines, but they can call invoker-rights routines that will then be resolved with the privileges and schema references of the trigger owner.

External reference resolution as invoker covers only certain types of processing. All other types of processing are resolved to the privileges and schema of the definer. Five types of statements are possible invoker-rights statements.

1. DML and SELECT statements: SELECT, INSERT, UPDATE, and DELETE

2. Cursor control statements: OPEN and OPEN-FOR

3. Native dynamic SQL statements: EXECUTE IMMEDIATE and OPEN-FOR-USING

4. Transaction control statements: LOCK TABLE

5. SQL parsing statements: DBMS_SQL.PARSE()

### Triggers, Rights, and USERs

Selecting the pseudocolumn USER from within an invoker-rights routine will return the name of the logged-in user. A trigger that then called an invoker-rights routine that in turn referenced the pseudo column USER would return the name of the logged-in user. Similarly, referencing SYS_CONTEXT('USERENV', 'SESSION_USER') in an invoker-rights routine will return the logged-in user. SYS_CONTEXT is described in Chapter 7. Differences can arise when referencing SYS_CONTEXT('USERENV', 'CURRENT_USER'), which returns the current session-user name, within an invoker-rights routine. Here the schema name in which the routine is run will be returned, and this may differ from the logged-in user. An example may clarify. Suppose an invoker-rights routine is created that references all three variables under discussion in user X's schema. User X grants execute privileges on the routine to user Y. User Y in turn calls the routine from, say, a row-level insert trigger on some table in their schema. In addition, user Y grants insert privileges on the table to user Z. When either user X or user Y calls the invoker-rights routine, all three variables return their respective username. When user Z implicitly calls the invoker-rights routine with an insert into the table, the variables USER and SYS_CONTEXT('USERENV', 'SESSION_USER') both return Z or the logged-in user, but SYS_CONTEXT('USERENV', 'CURRENT_USER') will return Y as the schema in which the invoker-rights routine was run. Similar remarks hold for SYS_CONTEXT('USERENV', 'SESSION_USERID') and SYS_CONTEXT('USERENV', 'CURRENT_USERID').

Procedures, functions, and packages are not on this list. The implication is that an invoker-rights routine that calls another non-invoker-rights routine will run that routine with the privileges and object resolution of the definer. The schemas of both invoker and definer will be addressable. The following example illustrates this point.

First, the procedure change_pwd from the previous Tip will be transformed to an invoker-rights routine. The schema of user SYSTEM_MANAGER from Chapter 7 will own the code, and the user DEMO will execute the code.

```
CREATE OR REPLACE PROCEDURE change_pwd
  (i_new_pwd IN VARCHAR2 DEFAULT NULL)
  -- invoker rights flag
  AUTHID CURRENT_USER
AS
  v_sql_stmt VARCHAR2(2000);
BEGIN
  IF i_new_pwd IS NULL
  THEN
    DBMS_OUTPUT.PUT_LINE(A password is required.');
    DBMS_OUTPUT.PUT_LINE(
      'Usage: execute change_pwd(''new_password'')');
  ELSE
    v_sql_stmt := 'ALTER USER '||USER||
                   ' IDENTIFIED BY '||i_new_pwd;
    -- debugging line
    DBMS_OUTPUT.PUT_LINE(v_sql_stmt);
    EXECUTE IMMEDIATE v_sql_stmt;
    DBMS_OUTPUT.PUT_LINE(
      USER||'''s password has been changed.');
  END IF;
EXCEPTION
  WHEN OTHERS
  THEN
    DBMS_OUTPUT.PUT_LINE(
      'Try again password not changed.');
    DBMS_OUTPUT.PUT_LINE(
      'Usage: execute change_pwd(''new_password'')');
END;
```

One change converted the foregoing procedure to an invoker-rights procedure, the addition of AUTHID CURRENT_USER to the CREATE header. After creating change_pwd in the schema of SYSTEM_MANAGER, a user granted SYSDBA, grants DEMO the privilege to execute it with the following command issued by SYSTEM_MANAGER in SQL*Plus.

```
GRANT EXECUTE ON change_pwd TO demo;
```

Invoker-Rights Share Code and Address Multi Schemas

Demo can now execute change_pwd in its schema with the following command, say, changing the password of DEMO to bob.

```
EXECUTE system_manager.change_pwd('bob')
```

If DEMO has access to an alias for system_manager.change_pwd (either a PUBLIC synonym or a synonym in the demo schema), then change_pwd can be run without references to its owner

```
SQL> CREATE SYNONYM change_pwd
  FOR system_manager.change_pwd;
SQL> EXECUTE change_pwd('bob')
```

Without creating change_pwd as an invoker-rights procedure, DEMO could execute the procedure. DEMO has been granted the execute privilege, but an *ORA-01031: insufficient privileges* exception would be raised on attempting to execute the ALTER USER statement within change_pwd. Without invoker rights, DEMO is effectively attempting to alter the password of SYSTEM_MANAGER, but DEMO has not been granted the role of DBA nor the privilege to ALTER ANY USER.

 **CAUTION**
*SQL\*Plus has a new command PASSWORD that allows SQL\*Plus users to change their passwords. Passwords can also be changed with Oracle Enterprise Manager (OEM). Oracle recommends not using the ALTER USER command since it does not fully support the password verification functionality introduced with Oracle8. Oracle recommends using SQL\*Plus or OEM. Unfortunately, application users often do not have access to SQL\*Plus or OEM for security and deployment reasons. In such cases, the change-password procedure can be used as a template to build a change-password procedure called from Oracle Forms or another GUI application tool.*

To exemplify an invoker-rights routine calling a definer-rights routine and addressing the schema of the definer, an audit log insert can be added to the change_pwd procedure. The SYS_CONTEXT function—described in Chapter 7—will be used to return the logged-on user or SESSION_USER, the TERMINAL of the user, and the IP_ADDRESS of the user making the password change. To reproduce the example, first create the table audit_pwd_change in the schema of SYSTEM_MANAGER.

```
CREATE TABLE audit_pwd_change
 (user_name VARCHAR2(30),
  terminal VARCHAR2(45),
  ip_address VARCHAR2(15),
  change_date DATE
 );
```

Second, create the procedure insert_audit_pwd_change also in the schema of SYSTEM_MANAGER.

```
CREATE OR REPLACE PROCEDURE insert_audit_pwd_change
  (i_name_user IN VARCHAR2,
   i_terminal IN VARCHAR2,
   i_ip_address IN VARCHAR2,
   i_date_change IN DATE
  )
  -- explicitly defined as a definer-rights procedure
  AUTHID DEFINER
AS
BEGIN
  INSERT INTO audit_pwd_change(user_name, terminal,
                               ip_address, change_date)
    VALUES(i_name_user, i_terminal,
           i_ip_address, i_date_change);
  COMMIT;
END;
```

Note that insert_audit_pwd_change has been explicitly declared to be a definer-rights procedure. The declaration is unnecessary since it is the default.

Third, modify the change_pwd procedure to call insert_audit_pwd_change. The following code slice shows where the addition would be made.

```
...
   EXECUTE IMMEDIATE v_sql_stmt;
   DBMS_OUTPUT.PUT_LINE(
     USER||'''s password has been changed.');
   insert_audit_pwd_change(
     SYS_CONTEXT('USERENV', 'SESSION_USER'),
     SYS_CONTEXT('USERENV', 'TERMINAL'),
     SYS_CONTEXT('USERENV', 'IP_ADDRESS'),
     SYSDATE);
  END IF;
EXCEPTION
...
```

DEMO on running change_pwd will now not only change its password but also insert a record into the audit log table audit_pwd_change in the schema of

SYSTEM_MANAGER. Demo will be addressing both schemas with its call to change_pwd.

Invoker-rights routines are useful in applications that contain multiple and similar schemas. If the schemas are not similar, a problem of schema resolution can arise at compile-time. If in the schema of the definer or creator of the invoker-rights routine, the schema objects referenced do not exist, the PL/SQL compiler will raise an error. For example, in the case in which the test_tab table does not exist, but is referenced by the following function code, the error *PLS-00201: identifier 'TEST_TAB' must be declared* occurs. The table test_tab was defined in the previous Tip with two NUMBER fields, 'x' and 'y', and one VARCHAR2(20) field, 'a'.

```
CREATE OR REPLACE FUNCTION sum_test_tab
  (i_a IN VARCHAR2)
  RETURN NUMBER
  AUTHID CURRENT_USER
AS
  v_sum NUMBER;
BEGIN
  -- returns the sum of the x and y fields for values of the 'a' field
  SELECT SUM(x + y)
    INTO v_sum
    FROM test_tab
   WHERE a LIKE LOWER(i_a);
  RETURN v_sum;
END;
```

To accommodate the PL/SQL compiler, template objects must be created in the schema of the definer. In the case of sum_test_tab, the table test_tab must be created in the schema of SYSTEM_MANAGER where the function is to be compiled.

Views display the same behavior as database triggers described earlier. The view owner constitutes the invoker and any invoker-rights routine called within a view are resolved in the schema of the view owner. For example, after SYSTEM_MANAGER has granted DEMO execute privileges on the sum_test_tab function and DEMO has created a synonym for system_manager.sum_test_tab as sum_test_tab, DEMO can create a view that uses the sum_test_tab function.

```
CREATE VIEW vw_sum_test_tab_a1
AS
 SELECT sum_test_tab('a1') vw_sum_test_tab_a1
   FROM dual;
```

DEMO selecting from its view vw_sum_test_tab_a1 will return values from the version of the test_tab table in its schema. If the SELECT statement in the view creation statement is not given a column alias, an *ORA-00998: must name this expression with a column alias* error is raised.

## Creating Autonomous Transactions to Audit and Track

Database triggers, functions, procedures, methods of a SQL object type, and nonnested top-level anonymous blocks are declared to be autonomous transactions with the compiler directive PRAGMA AUTONOMOUS_TRANSACTION. Packaged functions and packaged procedures can also be individually declared autonomous, but the entire package cannot be declared autonomous. Unlike nonautonomous database triggers, all autonomous routines, including database triggers, permit COMMIT, ROLLBACK, ROLLBACK TO, SAVEPOINT, and SET TRANSACTION transaction-control statements. What Oracle calls an "autonomous transaction" would be better called an "autonomous routine," but care must be taken with the commit and rollback behavior of these autonomous entities, which focuses attention on their transaction characteristics.

A *transaction* is a group of SQL statements that work together inserting, updating, or deleting data. A COMMIT or a ROLLBACK statement defines the end of a transaction. *Autonomous transactions* are routines started by another main routine, but their COMMIT, ROLLBACK, or SAVEPOINT behavior has no effect on the status of SQL statements—committed, rolled back, or save-pointed—occurring in the main routine. Autonomous transactions operate completely independent of the processing or transaction control statements within the main routine. For example, rolling back to a SAVEPOINT in a main routine with an intervening call to an autonomous transaction does not roll back the autonomous transaction. There is an important exception to the rule of independent behavior: pending transactions in an autonomous transaction or routine must be resolved through a COMMIT or ROLLBACK statement before processing is continued by the main routine. Failure to resolve pending autonomous transactions can result in the rolling back of both the autonomous and main routines.

In contrast to autonomous transactions or autonomous routines, there is a nested routine that is called as a procedure from within another procedure. The commit or rollback behavior of the nested procedure would commit or roll back uncommitted SQL statements in the main procedure.

Just as the locking and transaction control behavior of an autonomous transaction is independent of the main routine, they are also independent of each other when one autonomous transaction calls another. Transaction or routine dependencies occur with autonomous transactions only when they call nonautonomous routines, then the commit or rollback behavior within the called nonautonomous routine commits or rolls back the autonomous calling transaction or routine.

**NOTE**
*When calculating the number of concurrent transactions in a database instance, you must include autonomous transactions. The init.ora parameter TRANSACTIONS sets the maximum number of concurrent transactions. It, along with the init.ora parameter SESSIONS, is determined automatically at instance startup by the init.ora parameter PROCESSES, if neither SESSIONS nor TRANSACTIONS is set explicitly. The relationships are SESSIONS equals (1.1\*PROCESSES + 5) and TRANSACTIONS equals (1.1\*SESSIONS). If the SESSIONS and TRANSACTIONS parameters are not set explicitly, then the value of PROCESSES may need adjusting for autonomous transactions.*

Autonomous transactions or routines are useful for auditing sensitive database records, where an audit log of any processing touching a table is needed regardless of the success of the main transaction. In the tracking and debugging of batch processing procedures, autonomous routines can be devised that log the stages of processing, keeping a timing record for different stages and in the case of failure marking the point of failure.

All pending transactions in an autonomous routine must be resolved with either a COMMIT or a ROLLBACK before you return to the main calling routine. Failure to resolve pending autonomous transactions will result in exceptions being raised and transactions rolled back in both the main and autonomous routines. Changes made by autonomous routines are visible to other routines after the autonomous routine issues a COMMIT statement. In the case of the main routine, the changes are visible on resumption with the default isolation level of READ COMMITTED. To hide autonomous routine changes from the calling main routine on resumption, you can set the isolation level to a serial read.

```
SET TRANSACTION ISOLATION LEVEL SERIALIZABLE;
```

The foregoing SET command in the main routine will hide the changes made by autonomous transactions from code executed in the main routine.

 **CAUTION**
*Care should be taken in designing applications that use autonomous transactions to avoid possible deadlocks. The main and autonomous routines have their own locking mechanisms, but database records held by the main routine and requested by a called autonomous routine can lead to deadlocks as the autonomous routine cannot complete and exit waiting for the resources held by the main routine.*

As an example of an autonomous database trigger, consider that the following audit_test_tab_trg trigger it inserts into the audit_test_tab table a record whenever there is an INSERT, UPDATE, or DELETE statement issued against the test_tab table. The record contains the username, terminal of origin, the old and new values, and the date of the attempted DML action. These records will be inserted into audit_test_tab regardless of the success or failure of the DML statements issued against test_tab. Such a trigger would be useful whenever activity around sensitive data needs to be tracked. Test_tab has the same description as presented in all Tips.

```
SQL> DESC test_tab
 Name      Null?    Type
 --------  -------  -------------
 X                  NUMBER
 Y                  NUMBER
 A                  VARCHAR2(20)
```

The structure of audit_test_tab is given in the following CREATE TABLE statement.

```
CREATE TABLE audit_test_tab
  (audit_id NUMBER,
   user_name VARCHAR2(30)
     CONSTRAINT user_name_nn NOT NULL,
   terminal VARCHAR2(60),
   action VARCHAR2(6)
     CONSTRAINT action_ck CHECK
       (action IN ('INSERT', 'UPDATE', 'DELETE')),
   x_old NUMBER,
   x_new NUMBER,
   y_old NUMBER,
   y_new NUMBER,
   a_new VARCHAR2(20),
   a_old VARCHAR2(20),
   audit_date DATE
     CONSTRAINT audit_date_nn NOT NULL
  );
```

A primary key on the audit_id field is created, and a sequence audit_id_seq is created to populate the field.

```
ALTER TABLE audit_test_tab
  ADD CONSTRAINT audit_test_tab_pk
  PRIMARY KEY(audit_id)
  USING INDEX TABLESPACE indx;

CREATE SEQUENCE audit_id_seq;
```

Autonomous Transactions to Audit and Track

The trigger itself is created with the compiler directive PRAGMA AUTONOMOUS_ TRANSACTION.

```
CREATE OR REPLACE TRIGGER audit_test_tab_trg
  BEFORE INSERT OR DELETE OR UPDATE
    ON test_tab FOR EACH ROW
DECLARE
  PRAGMA AUTONOMOUS_TRANSACTION;
  -- a variable to hold DML action insert,
  -- update or delete flag
  v_action VARCHAR2(6);
BEGIN
  IF INSERTING
  THEN
    v_action := 'INSERT';
  ELSIF UPDATING THEN
    v_action := 'UPDATE';
  ELSE
    v_action := 'DELETE';
  END IF;
  INSERT INTO audit_test_tab
    VALUES(audit_id_seq.NEXTVAL, USER,
           SYS_CONTEXT('USERENV', 'TERMINAL'),
           v_action, :old.x, :new.x,
           :old.y, :new.y,
           :old.a, :new.a, SYSDATE
          );
  -- a commit is necessary so pending transactions
  -- do not raise an exception message
  COMMIT;
END;
```

The use of the COMMIT statement before the trigger's END statement is necessary to resolve pending transactions before control is returned to the calling routine. The database engine is implicitly calling the trigger during DML processing. If pending transactions are not resolved, an *ORA-06519: active autonomous transaction detected and rolled-back* exception will be raised, and the trigger and DML statement originating the trigger will fail.

A second example creates a set of autonomous procedures in a package called batch_job_track, which is designed to track times within batch PL/SQL routines. The procedure batch_log_insert takes a user-defined batch name as input and creates a record in the batch_log table to track the named batch job. The record created consists of a log_id as primary key, batch_name holding the name passed, batch_date, and user_name. Batch_log_insert would be called once at the beginning of a PL/SQL job. The second procedure batch_detail_insert would be called at the beginning and end of DML or other statements within the PL/SQL job to capture running times between statements. Batch_detail_insert inserts a record into the batch_log_detail table that is a child table to the batch_log table. The record inserted by batch_detail_insert consists of a log_id as a foreign key referencing the log_id from the parent table, a log_detail_id tracking the current detail, and a time_in_sec holding the time in seconds since midnight. The primary key of batch_log_detail is a combination key consisting of log_id and log_detail_id. A third included procedure called batch_log_rep analyzes the times recorded in batch_log_detail and reports the times between processing statements. The procedure batch_time_rep is overloaded and can be called with or without passing in a log_id. Without a log_id, batch_time_rep can be called at the end of the PL/SQL batch job to generate a report on the job. It then relies on the value of a package global variable to define the log_id value. With a log_id passed in, batch_log_rep can be called any time to generate a report on times between processing statements in a batch-job run. A batch-job run can be identified by its log_id and batch_name stored in the batch_log table.

First, the code creates the two tables for logging batch jobs and defines the relationship between them.

```
CREATE TABLE batch_log
  (log_id NUMBER,
   batch_name VARCHAR2(30),
   batch_date DATE,
   user_name VARCHAR2(30)
  );

CREATE TABLE batch_log_detail
  (log_id NUMBER,
   log_detail_id NUMBER,
   time_in_sec NUMBER
  );

ALTER TABLE batch_log
  ADD CONSTRAINT batch_log_pk
  PRIMARY KEY(log_id)
  USING INDEX TABLESPACE indx;

ALTER TABLE batch_log_detail
  ADD CONSTRAINT batch_log_detail_pk
  PRIMARY KEY(log_id, log_detail_id)
  USING INDEX TABLESPACE indx;

ALTER TABLE batch_log_detail
  ADD CONSTRAINT batch_detail_to_batch_fk
  FOREIGN KEY(log_id) REFERENCES batch_log(log_id);
```

A sequence is created to insert the log_id primary key on the batch_log table. Log_detail_id starts its numbering anew and sequentially with each batch job and is handled internally in the procedure batch_detail_insert.

```
CREATE SEQUENCE log_id_seq;
```

The package specification and body is in the following code.

```
CREATE OR REPLACE PACKAGE batch_jobs_track
AS
  -- declare a weakly type cursor
  TYPE generic_cv IS REF CURSOR;
  PROCEDURE batch_log_insert
    (i_batch_name IN VARCHAR2);
  --
  PROCEDURE batch_detail_insert;
  -- batch_time_rep can be executed alone with a log_id passed
  -- or can be executed without a parameter passed and
  -- implicitly when the global variable v_log_id is set
  PROCEDURE batch_time_rep
    (i_log_id IN batch_log_detail.log_id%TYPE DEFAULT NULL);
  -- declare a package global variable to hold the log_id,
  -- the log_id is first created in batch_log_insert,
  -- retrieved into the global variable
  -- in batch_detail_insert
  -- and accessed again in batch_time_rep
  v_log_id NUMBER := 0;
END;

CREATE OR REPLACE PACKAGE BODY batch_jobs_track
AS
  PROCEDURE batch_log_insert
    (i_batch_name IN VARCHAR2)
  IS
    -- compiler directive to create procedure
    -- as autonomous
    PRAGMA AUTONOMOUS_TRANSACTION;
  BEGIN
    INSERT INTO batch_log
      VALUES(log_id_seq.NEXTVAL, i_batch_name,
             SYSDATE, USER);
    COMMIT;
  END;
  --
  PROCEDURE batch_detail_insert
  IS
    PRAGMA AUTONOMOUS_TRANSACTION;
```

```
  -- declare a variable to hold
  -- the MAX plus one log_detail_id
  v_log_detail_id NUMBER;
BEGIN
  -- retrieve the current value of batch_log's PK
  -- into global variable
  SELECT MAX(log_id)
    INTO v_log_id
    FROM batch_log;
  -- if this is the first record to be inserted into
  -- batch_log_detail for this batch run,
  -- then a select of the maximum log_detail_id for
  -- this log_id would return a NULL
  -- in this case and set the returned value to 1
  -- in the following select
  SELECT NVL(MAX(log_detail_id),0) + 1
    INTO v_log_detail_id
    FROM batch_log_detail
   WHERE log_id = v_log_id;
  -- insert the new record with time
  INSERT INTO batch_log_detail
    VALUES(v_log_id, v_log_detail_id,
           TO_CHAR(SYSDATE, 'SSSSS'));
  COMMIT;
END;
--
PROCEDURE batch_time_rep
  (i_log_id IN batch_log_detail.log_id%TYPE DEFAULT NULL)
IS
  TYPE time_comparison_rec IS RECORD
    (lower_time batch_log_detail.time_in_sec%TYPE,
     higher_time batch_log_detail.time_in_sec%TYPE,
     log_detail_id batch_log_detail.log_detail_id%TYPE
    );
  rec_time_comparison time_comparison_rec;
  -- part of the select statement that selects the times
  -- from batch_log_detail and remains constant
  cons_stmt_body VARCHAR2(1000) :=
    'SELECT a.time_in_sec lower_time,
            b.time_in_sec higher_time,
            a.log_detail_id
       FROM batch_log_detail a, batch_log_detail b
      WHERE a.log_id = b.log_id (+)
        AND a.log_detail_id = b.log_detail_id - 1';
  -- a second constant piece of the select that
  -- is later concatenated to the above
  v_stmt_tail VARCHAR2(2000) := ' ORDER BY a.log_detail_id';
  cv_time_comparison generic_cv;
```

```
BEGIN
   -- create the report title
   DBMS_OUTPUT.PUT_LINE(
      '..... Batch Time In Seconds Within Steps.....');
   DBMS_OUTPUT.PUT_LINE(
      'Time In Step .......... Seconds');
   IF i_log_id IS NOT NULL
   THEN
      -- if a specific log_id was passed into the procedure
      -- use it to fill out select statement
      v_stmt_tail := '  AND a.log_id = '||i_log_id||v_stmt_tail;
   ELSE
      -- alternatively use the package global variable
      -- v_log_id as assigned a value in
      -- batch_detail_insert for select statement
      v_stmt_tail := '  AND a.log_id = '||v_log_id||v_stmt_tail;
   END IF;
   OPEN cv_time_comparison FOR cons_stmt_body||v_stmt_tail;
   LOOP
      FETCH cv_time_comparison INTO rec_time_comparison;
      EXIT WHEN cv_time_comparison%NOTFOUND;
      -- while in loop print time differential between steps
      IF rec_time_comparison.higher_time IS NOT NULL
      THEN
         DBMS_OUTPUT.PUT_LINE
            ('In Step '||
            TO_CHAR(rec_time_comparison.log_detail_id)||
            '.................'||
            TO_CHAR(rec_time_comparison.higher_time -
                    rec_time_comparison.lower_time
                   )
            );
      END IF;
   END LOOP;
   CLOSE cv_time_comparison;
EXCEPTION
   WHEN OTHERS
   THEN
      IF cv_time_comparison%ISOPEN
      THEN
         CLOSE cv_time_comparison;
      END IF;
   END;
END;
```

As an example of their usage, consider the procedures in the batch_jobs_track package, which can be integrated into a procedure time_batch. The procedure compares loading the test_tab table with a FOR-IN-LOOP to loading the table with a FOR-IN-LOOP with a RETURNING-INTO statement. Does the addition of the RETURNING-INTO clause add significantly to the performance time? Index-by binary-integer table types are created based on the structure of the test_tab table. Variables declared to be index-by binary-integer types are loaded with 50,000 records and then inserted into the test_tab table twice—once with and once without a RETURNING-INTO. When the RETURNING-INTO clause is used it loads another set of index-by binary-integer variables.

```
CREATE OR REPLACE PROCEDURE time_batch
AS
  -- create two index-by binary-integer tables data types
  -- with an eye to the structure of the test_tab table
  TYPE num_ibt IS TABLE OF NUMBER(5)
    INDEX BY BINARY_INTEGER;
  TYPE descr_ibt IS TABLE OF VARCHAR2(20)
    INDEX BY BINARY_INTEGER;
  -- declare six index-by binary-integer variables
  -- based on the above created data types
  ibt_x_nums  num_ibt;
  ibt_y_nums num_ibt;
  ibt_a_descrs descr_ibt;
  ibt_x_nums2  num_ibt;
  ibt_y_nums2 num_ibt;
  ibt_a_descrs2 descr_ibt;
BEGIN
  -- create record in batch_log parent table
  -- for new batch job called "batch test"
  batch_jobs_track.batch_log_insert('batch_test');
  -- create first record in batch_log_detail
  -- child table capturing start time
  -- for the following processing statement
  batch_jobs_track.batch_detail_insert;
  -- load a set of index-by binary integer variables
  -- with 50000 values
  -- in preparation to load the test_tab table
  FOR j IN 1..50000
  LOOP
    ibt_x_nums(j) := j;
    ibt_y_nums(j) := j+1;
    ibt_a_descrs(j) := 'Test No. ' || TO_CHAR(j);
  END LOOP;
  -- capture stop time for previous processing group
  -- and start time for next processing group
  batch_jobs_track.batch_detail_insert;
  -- load the table with a for-in-loop
```

```
-- without a returning clause
FOR i IN 1..50000
LOOP
  INSERT INTO test_tab
    VALUES (ibt_x_nums(i), ibt_y_nums(i),
            ibt_a_descrs(i));
END LOOP;
COMMIT;
-- capture stop time for previous work
-- and start time for next processing group
batch_jobs_track.batch_detail_insert;
-- load the table with a for-in-loop statement
-- with a returning clause
FOR i IN 1..50000
LOOP
  INSERT INTO test_tab
    VALUES (ibt_x_nums(i), ibt_y_nums(i),
            ibt_a_descrs(i))
    RETURNING x, y, a
      INTO ibt_x_nums2(i), ibt_y_nums2(i),
           ibt_a_descrs2(i);
END LOOP;
COMMIT;
-- capture end processing time for group
batch_jobs_track.batch_detail_insert;
-- debugging line showing returned values
DBMS_OUTPUT.PUT_LINE(
  'x at ten: '||ibt_x_nums2(10)||' y at ten: '||
  ibt_y_nums2(10)||' a at ten: '||ibt_a_descrs2(10));
-- run report on batch job
batch_jobs_track.batch_time_rep;
END;
```

The following example report generated by batch_time_rep shows that a
FOR-IN-LOOP with a RETURNING clause—Step 3—added 20 percent more
processing time than a FOR-IN-LOOP without a RETURNING clause—Step 2.

```
.....Batch Time In Seconds Within Step.....
Time In Step ........... Seconds
In Step 1............... 2
In Step 2...............40
In Step 3...............48
```

The distinguishing features of the code in batch_jobs_track are (1) that it records
times to a database table and (2) that, more importantly, the times written to the
database will remain, even if the main routine—time_batch—fails and its transactions
are rolled back. Autonomous transaction code, like that in the procedures in the

package batch_jobs_track, show the processing times of different code sections, suggest areas within batch jobs to tune, and can also be used to locate points of failure. The record written prior to failure will persist and point to the next piece of processing as the weak point.

## Using Temporary Tables to Maintain User State, to Boost Subquery Processing, and to Enhance Distributive Processing

Oracle8i introduces temporary tables that can be created to hold records that are private to a particular user, so called *session-private data*. This data will persist for a period defined either for a transaction within a user session or for the entire session. The structure of a temporary table is permanent; only its contents are temporary. Users cannot view another user's records, but users can share the structure of a temporary table. Since a user can see and modify only her or his own records, DML locks are not placed on temporary tables. Similarly, the issuing of a truncate command in a session to truncate a temporary table removes only the records of the session. When a session ends, the contents of a temporary table for that session are removed. Since the records held are temporary, the EXPORT and IMPORT utilities capture only the definition of temporary tables.

Indexes and triggers can be created on temporary tables. Views can be created that join both temporary and permanent tables. No partitioning or clustering is permitted. Nor can they be index-organized or defined with referential integrity, though primary key definition is allowed. No tablespace or storage clause can enter their definition; they use temporary segments in the user's assigned or default temporary tablespace. A column in their definition cannot be a nested table or a varray data type. Parallel queries and parallel execution is not supported with temporary tables.

The syntax for creating a session-specific temporary table is as follows:

```
CREATE GLOBAL TEMPORARY TABLE <table_name>
  (<column specifications>
  ) ON COMMIT PRESERVE ROWS;
```

For creating a transaction-specific temporary table, use the following:

```
CREATE GLOBAL TEMPORARY TABLE <table_name>
  (<column specifications>
  ) ON COMMIT DELETE ROWS;
```

With a session-specific temporary table, a session is bound to the temporary table with the first insert statement on the table. The session is unbound at the end of the session or when a TRUNCATE TABLE statement is issued, where the latter removes only the records created in the current session. With a transaction-specific temporary table, a session is bound to the temporary table with the first insert statement on the table and unbound at the end of the transaction. To perform DDL operations on a temporary table, you cannot have any session currently bound to the table.

Transaction-specific temporary tables are useful in applications that must hold a user's state until the user ends the transaction with a commit or rollback statement. For example, order-entry or online-sales applications allow users to fill "shopping carts," changing their items or quantities until the order is placed or canceled. Processing of SQL statements with complex correlated subqueries retrieving records from the same tables multiple times can also experience performance boosts with temporary tables, especially if the results are a greatly reduced or aggregated subset of large tables. Placing the result sets of complex subqueries in temporary tables for either the transaction or session, and then joining against the temporary tables will increase performance by reducing the number of times the smaller set or aggregate is created. A third distributed usage is suggested in the example to follow.

Consider the following example of temporary-table use in a distributed environment. When quoting prices, out-of-office sales representatives are required to use the most current sale prices. Using satellite modems and database links, each representative can access a central database that holds up-to-the-minute prices. The build_current_price_list procedure is created in each laptop database after the session-specific temporary table product_price_list is created with a primary key on product_id. The procedure builds the currently effective price list with product descriptions in the product_price_list table. The example borrows the structures of the product and the price tables from the DEMO schema supplied with some version of Oracle8i. The build script for DEMO can be found in the subdirectory Rdbms as Bdemobld.sql.

```
CREATE GLOBAL TEMPORARY TABLE product_price_list(
   product_id NUMBER (6),
   description VARCHAR2(30),
   list_price NUMBER (8,2),
   min_price NUMBER (8,2),
   end_date DATE,
   max_discount NUMBER
   )ON COMMIT PRESERVE ROWS;

ALTER TABLE product_price_list
   ADD CONSTRAINT product_price_list_pk
   PRIMARY KEY (product_id);

CREATE OR REPLACE PROCEDURE build_current_price_list
AS
BEGIN
```

```
INSERT INTO product_price_list(
    product_id, description, list_price,
    min_price, end_date, max_discount
    )
    SELECT a.product_id, a.description, b.list_price,
           b.min_price, b.end_date,
           ((b.list_price-b.min_price)/b.list_price)*100
      FROM product@oracle.world a, price@oracle.world b
     WHERE a.product_id = b.product_id
       AND b.start_date =(SELECT MAX(b.start_date)
                            FROM price@oracle.world b
                           WHERE NVL(b.end_date, SYSDATE)
                                 >= SYSDATE
                             AND b.start_date <= SYSDATE
                             AND b.product_id =
                                    a.product_id
                          );
   COMMIT;
EXCEPTION
   WHEN OTHERS
   THEN
      -- making sure distributive transaction ends
      ROLLBACK;
      -- handles the case when procedure already has been run
      -- in the session and primary key violation will occur,
      -- effectively the primary key forces the prices
      -- used to be session specific
      -- as required by the business rules
      DBMS_OUTPUT.PUT_LINE(
         'Procedure run already in this session.');
      DBMS_OUTPUT.PUT_LINE(
         'If new price list required create new session.');
END;
```

A database link called "oracle.world" has been created to remotely connect to the corporate database fully specifying the user, password, and the database SID to use with the connection.

The correlated subquery is designed to gather the most recent effective price. The most recent price is given by the MAX function on the start_date from the price table. The effective price is given by the combination of a start_date still in effect—less than or equal to the current date—with an end_date not yet having occurred—greater than or equal to the current date. In actuality, if the product table held a product class field, the foregoing procedure could be passed a product class flag to reduce the product-price list size. In practice, the processing behind the GUI interface of the application would capture the exception now handled with the DBMS_OUTPUT statements and display the appropriate message. When the result set is significant in size using a temporary table to pre-create the product-price list locally, it will enable you to speed performance of application code that otherwise would have joined to the product and the price tables remotely. If you further imagine the product table is local and the price table is remote, performance improvements would certainly be gained with a temporary table of the price data when a significant number of rows are to be returned. A correlated subquery remotely accessing the price data on each iteration would execute more slowly than the initial loading of the price data locally.

# Performance Boosting with Bulk Binding and NOCOPY

New coding alternatives can be used with Oracle's collection data types that can boost the performance of nested tables, varrays, and indexed-by binary-integer tables. Collections can be bulk bound to improve performance when collections are passed between the PL/SQL and SQL engines. This is called bulk binding. The NOCOPY parameter flag can improve performance when collections are passed between PL/SQL routines. Bulk binding and the NOCOPY parameter flag are the topics of this section.

## Bulk Binding Collections Improves Performance

SQL statements embedded in PL/SQL are passed from the PL/SQL engine to the SQL engine for execution. This passing back and forth, sometimes returning records to the PL/SQL engine, is called a *context switch* and degrades performance. In cases in which elements of collections—index-by tables, nested tables, or varrays—would be passed to the SQL engine via a FOR-LOOP for processing, Oracle8i introduces a new method called *bulk binding.* Similarly, bulk binding can be used to bulk fetch records into PL/SQL collections from the SQL engine. With bulk binding, complete collections, not individual records, are passed back and forth. In this way, the number of context switches between the PL/SQL engine and the SQL engine is reduced, and performance is enhanced. As a rule of thumb, if you have five or more records to be passed or fetched, using bulk binds will improve performance. Some of the following examples show processing times reduced by 60 to 90 percent.

Bulk binding should be considered whenever INSERT, UPDATE, or DELETE statements include a collection and operate in a loop. Any SELECT INTO, FETCH INTO, or RETURNING-INTO clause that includes a collection can benefit from bulk binding. Bulk binding improves performance by processing multiple records in a single DML statement.

The collections under discussion—index-by tables, nested tables, and varrays—must be subscripted collections. Collections are like arrays but must be one-dimensional and indexed by integers. A collection can be used to store a column of a table or an instance of an object type. As a column data from a table, a collection can move data between tables, in and out of a table, and between a client application and server-stored procedures. A complete discussion of collections is beyond the scope of this Tip; see the PL/SQL User's Guide and Reference for details. This Tip presents a brief overview of the properties necessary for bulk binds.

Creating a collection type creates a composite data type, which can then be used to declare variables of that type. Nested tables and varrays can be created and stored in the database, while index-by tables are transient. The syntax for creating and declaraing a nested table, varray, and index-by table is as follows:

```
TYPE type_name IS TABLE OF element_type [NOT NULL];
variable_name type_name;

TYPE type_name IS {VARRAY | VARYING ARRAY} (size_limit)
  OF element_type [NOT NULL];
variable_name type_name;

TYPE type_name IS TABLE OF element_type [NOT NULL]
  INDEX BY BINARY_INTEGER;
variable_name type_name;
```

An element_type can be a %TYPE, a %ROWTYPE, most PL/SQL data types, a record type, or an object type. Some examples:

```
-- create a nested table matching deptno from table dept
TYPE dept_type_nt IS TABLE OF dept.deptno%TYPE;
-- declare a variable of nested table type based on the above
nt_dept_tab dept_type_nt;

-- create a varray of 1000 numbers
TYPE number_type_va IS VARRAY(1000) OF NUMBER;
-- declare a variable of varray type based on above
va_number number_type_va;

-- create a index-by table based on the dept table rowtype
TYPE dept_type_ibt IS TABLE OF dept%ROWTYPE
  INDEXED BY BINARY_INTEGER;
-- declare a variable of index-by table type based on the above
ibt_dept dept_type_ibt;
```

Nested tables and varrays must be initialized using constructors; constructors have the same names as their types. For the nested table just discussed,

```
nt_dept_tab := dept_type_nt(1, 2, 10, 23);
```

Bulk Binding Collections Improves Performance

Index-by tables implicitly call their constructors. Elements of a variable are referenced by integer subscripts, so nt_dept_tab(3) equals 10 and so nt_dept_tab(3) := 20 changes the value of the third element to 20.

Finally, collection variables have methods, five of which are of interest: EXTEND, COUNT, FIRST, LAST, and DELETE. The statement nt_dept_tab.EXTEND adds an empty element to the collection nt_dept_tab in preparation for it to be filled. The COUNT method will supply the number of elements in nt_dept_tab and a FOR-LOOP could be written as follows:

```
FOR i IN 1..nt_dept_tab.COUNT LOOP
```

Similarly, a FOR-LOOP could be written with FIRST and LAST:

```
FOR i IN nt_dept_tab.FIRST..nt_dept_tab.LAST LOOP
```

The statement nt_dept_tab.DELETE will remove all elements from the collection and free all memory the collection is holding.

Bulk binds pass entire collections between the PL/SQL and SQL engines. Collections passed to the SQL engine from PL/SQL use a FORALL statement instead of a FOR-LOOP. Returning a collection from the SQL engine to the PL/SQL engine uses a BULK COLLECT clause with a SELECT INTO, FETCH INTO, or RETURNING-INTO clause.

A first example uses a FORALL statement to load 50 records into the test_tab table first introduced in the Tip "Issuing Native Dynamic SQL in PL/SQL." Initially, an index-by binary-integer table is loaded with the records and then passed to the FORALL statement.

```
CREATE OR REPLACE PROCEDURE bulkbind_insert
AS
  TYPE num_ibt IS TABLE OF NUMBER(5)
    INDEX BY BINARY_INTEGER;
  TYPE descr_ibt IS TABLE OF VARCHAR2(20)
    INDEX BY BINARY_INTEGER;
  ibt_x_nums num_ibt;
  ibt_y_nums num_ibt;
  ibt_a_descrs descr_ibt;
  -- two variables to hold cursor attributes
  v_cnt_sqlrow_bulk NUMBER := 0;
  v_cnt_sqlrow NUMBER := 0;
BEGIN
  -- load index-by table
  FOR j IN 1..50
  LOOP
    ibt_x_nums(j) := j;
    ibt_y_nums(j) := j;
```

```
    ibt_a_descrs(j) := 'Test No. ' || TO_CHAR(j);
  END LOOP;
  -- FORALL statement, using bulk binding
  FORALL i IN 1..ibt_x_nums.COUNT
    INSERT INTO test_tab VALUES (ibt_x_nums(i), ibt_y_nums(i),
                                 ibt_a_descrs(i));
    COMMIT;
  v_cnt_sqlrow_bulk := SQL%BULK_ROWCOUNT(10);
  v_cnt_sqlrow := SQL%ROWCOUNT;
  DBMS_OUTPUT.PUT_LINE(
    'FORALL %BULK_ROWCOUNT(10): '||v_cnt_sqlrow_bulk);
  DBMS_OUTPUT.PUT_LINE(
    'FORALL %ROWCOUNT: '||v_cnt_sqlrow);
END;
```

The variables v_cnt_sqlrow and v_cnt_sqlrow_bulk in bulkbind_insert and their respective DBMS_OUTPUT statements are there to demonstrate the behavior of cursor attribute %BULK_ROWCOUNT and the behavior of %ROWCOUNT with a FORALL statement.

```
FORALL %BULK_ROWCOUNT(10): 10
FORALL %ROWCOUNT: 50
```

Fifty records are loaded with the FORALL statement. %ROWCOUNT is reporting the total number of inserted rows with the FORALL statement. %BULK_ROWCOUNT is indexed by an execution number—here 10 for the tenth insert execution—and shows the cumulative total through that execution. Had the execution number been 50, %BULK_ROWCOUNT(50) would have returned 50.

**CAUTION**
*The PL/SQL User's Guide and Reference claims that the ith element of %BULK_ROWCOUNT holds "the number of rows processed by the ith execution of the SQL statement" and if the ith execution "affects no rows, %BULK_ROWCOUNT(i) returns zero." This is not behavior observed. Cumulative totals are reported with insert statements, and with update statements NULLs are returned regardless of whether rows are affected by the update statement.*

The cursor attributes %FOUND and %NOTFOUND also can be used with bulk binds.

The next example demonstrates the use of a BULK COLLECT clause with a FETCH-INTO statement. Here nested tables are loaded with the values from the test_tab table with the FETCH-INTO statement. The example procedure assumes that the test_tab table was loaded in the execution of the previous example.

```
CREATE OR REPLACE PROCEDURE bulkbind_fetch
AS
  -- create two nested table collectors
  TYPE num_nt IS TABLE OF NUMBER(5);
  TYPE descr_nt IS TABLE OF VARCHAR2(20);
  -- declare three collection variables
  -- and initialize as empty
  nt_x_nums  num_nt := num_nt();
  nt_y_nums  num_nt := num_nt();
  nt_a_descrs descr_nt := descr_nt();
  -- a cursor out of which to fetch records
  CURSOR c_test_tab IS
    SELECT x, y, a
      FROM test_tab;
BEGIN
  OPEN c_test_tab;
  FETCH c_test_tab
    BULK COLLECT INTO nt_x_nums, nt_y_nums, nt_a_descrs;
  -- debugging line showing tenth fetch
  DBMS_OUTPUT.PUT_LINE(nt_x_nums(10)||' '||nt_a_descrs(10));
  CLOSE c_test_tab;
END;
```

It is possible to integrate a BULK COLLECT clause in a FORALL statement, as demonstrated by the following procedure, forall_bulkcollect. The procedure selects with a BULK COLLECT clause the first ten rows of test_tab into a nested table and then deletes with a FORALL statement from test_tab based on the value of the 'x' column stored in the nested table. The delete statement uses a RETURNING clause with a BULK COLLECT clause to store the values of the 'a' column of deleted rows in another nested table. The delete statement demonstrates the integration of a BULK COLLECT clause in a FORALL statement. Finally, another FORALL statement inserts these values into a new table test_tab2. Test_tab2 can be created with the statement CREATE test_tab2(deleted VARCHAR2(20));. The procedure also demonstrates the use of a SELECT-INTO statement with a BULK COLLECT clause.

```
CREATE OR REPLACE PROCEDURE forall_bulkcollect
AS
  -- create two nested table collectors
  TYPE num_nt IS TABLE OF NUMBER(5);
  TYPE descr_nt IS TABLE OF VARCHAR2(20);
  -- declare two collection variables
  -- and initialize as empty
  nt_x_nums  num_nt := num_nt();
```

```
      nt_a_descrs descr_nt := descr_nt();
      -- three variables to hold sql%rowcounts for debugging
      v_cnt_sqlrow NUMBER := 0;
      v_cnt_sqlrow2 NUMBER := 0;
      v_cnt_sqlrow3 NUMBER := 0;
BEGIN
      -- select the first ten values of x
      -- into nest table nt_x_nums
      SELECT x BULK COLLECT
        INTO nt_x_nums
        FROM test_tab
       WHERE ROWNUM <= 10;
      -- two debugging lines
      v_cnt_sqlrow := SQL%ROWCOUNT;
      DBMS_OUTPUT.PUT_LINE(v_cnt_sqlrow);
      -- delete from test_tab records where 'x' equals
      -- the values stored in nested table nt_x_nums,
      -- but capture the values in the 'a' column
      -- in nt_a_descrs nested table using the
      -- returning-into clause with a bulk collect clause
      FORALL i in nt_x_nums.FIRST..nt_x_nums.LAST
        DELETE FROM test_tab WHERE x = nt_x_nums(i)
          RETURNING a BULK COLLECT INTO nt_a_descrs;
        COMMIT;
        -- two debugging lines
        v_cnt_sqlrow2 := SQL%ROWCOUNT;
        DBMS_OUTPUT.PUT_LINE(v_cnt_sqlrow2);
      -- insert the values captured in the nested table nt_a_descrs
      -- into the test_tab2
      FORALL i IN nt_a_descrs.FIRST..nt_a_descrs.LAST
        INSERT INTO test_tab2 VALUES(nt_a_descrs(i));
        COMMIT;
        -- two debugging lines
        v_cnt_sqlrow3 := SQL%ROWCOUNT;
        DBMS_OUTPUT.PUT_LINE(v_cnt_sqlrow3);
END;
```

The importance of bulk binding lies in the performance boost that it enables. The following examples were modified to demonstrate the performance gains and to present some suggestive benchmarks. Note that the two procedures, bulkbind_insert and bulkbind_fetch, were modified to gather comparative times. For instance, the following procedure time_bulkbind_insert loads an index-by table and then inserts 50,000 records with a conventional FOR-LOOP and 50,000 records with a FORALL statement into the test_tab table. Similarly, time_bulkbind_fetch measures the performance improvement enabled by a BULK COLLECT clause in a FETCH-INTO statement by comparing execution times of the fetch with and without a BULK COLLECT clause. A function timer has been created to return the seconds since

**Bulk Binding Collections Improves Performance**

midnight, and that allows us to show the performance differences between processing methods.

```
CREATE OR REPLACE FUNCTION timer
  RETURN PLS_INTEGER
AS
BEGIN

  RETURN TO_CHAR(SYSDATE, 'SSSSS');
END;

CREATE OR REPLACE PROCEDURE time_bulkbind_insert
AS
  TYPE num_ibt IS TABLE OF NUMBER(5)
    INDEX BY BINARY_INTEGER;
  TYPE descr_ibt IS TABLE OF VARCHAR2(20)
    INDEX BY BINARY_INTEGER;
  ibt_x_nums num_ibt;
  ibt_y_nums num_ibt;
  ibt_a_descrs descr_ibt;
  -- three variables for the timer function
  v_t1 PLS_INTEGER;
  v_t2 PLS_INTEGER;
  v_t3 PLS_INTEGER;
  -- variable to hold cursor attribute
  v_cnt_sqlrow NUMBER := 0;
BEGIN
  -- load index-by table
  FOR j IN 1..50000
  LOOP
    ibt_x_nums(j) := j;
    ibt_y_nums(j) := j;
    ibt_a_descrs(j) := 'Test No. ' || TO_CHAR(j);
  END LOOP;
  -- get the time from timer and insert via for-loop
  v_t1 := timer;
  FOR i IN 1..ibt_x_nums.COUNT
  LOOP  -- use FOR loop
    INSERT INTO test_tab VALUES (ibt_x_nums(i), ibt_y_nums(i),
                                 ibt_a_descrs(i));
  END LOOP;
  COMMIT;
  -- v_cnt_sqlrow := SQL%ROWCOUNT;
  -- DBMS_OUTPUT.PUT_LINE(
  --    'FOR-LOOP %ROWCOUNT: '||v_cnt_sqlrow);
  -- get the time at end of for-loop and
```

```
-- at start of forall statement
v_t2 := timer;
-- FORALL statement, using bulk binding
FORALL i IN 1..ibt_x_nums.COUNT
  INSERT INTO test_tab VALUES (ibt_x_nums(i), ibt_y_nums(i),
                               ibt_a_descrs(i));
  COMMIT;
-- v_cnt_sqlrow := SQL%ROWCOUNT;
-- get the time via timer at end of forall statement
v_t3 := timer;
-- DBMS_OUTPUT.PUT_LINE(
--    'FORALL %ROWCOUNT: '||v_cnt_sqlrow);
-- generate a report on time differences
DBMS_OUTPUT.PUT_LINE('Execution Time (secs)');
DBMS_OUTPUT.PUT_LINE('--------------------');
DBMS_OUTPUT.PUT_LINE(
  'FOR loop: ' || TO_CHAR(v_t2 - v_t1));
DBMS_OUTPUT.PUT_LINE(
  'FORALL:    ' || TO_CHAR(v_t3 - v_t2));
END;
```

The output of the report shows a significant improvement in performance using a FORALL statement to load the test_tab. A processing time of 41 seconds for the FOR-LOOP was reduced to 3 seconds for the FORALL statement.

```
Execution Time (secs)
--------------------
FOR loop: 41
FORALL:    3
```

The two commented out v_cnt_sqlrow variables in time_bulkbind_insert and their respective DBMS_OUTPUT statements are there to demonstrate the different behavior of the cursor attribute %ROWCOUNT with a FOR-LOOP statement and a FORALL statement.

```
FOR-LOOP %ROWCOUNT: 1
FORALL %ROWCOUNT: 50000
```

Fifty thousand records are loaded by the FOR-LOOP statement and 50,000 by the FORALL statement. %ROWCOUNT is reporting the count on the last iteration in the FOR-LOOP case and showing the total number of inserted rows in the FORALL case. Of course, had the FOR-LOOP contained an UPDATE or DELETE statement, the value returned could have differed from one.

The following procedure time_bulkbind_fetch is designed to measure the performance improvement enabled by adding a BULK COLLECT clause to a FETCH-INTO statement. The script uses two nested tables and three nested-table

**Bulk Binding Collections Improves Performance**

variables, the timer function again, and a FETCH-INTO without and with a BULK COLLECT clause.

```
CREATE OR REPLACE PROCEDURE time_bulkbind_fetch
AS
  -- create two nested table collectors
  TYPE num_nt IS TABLE OF NUMBER(5);
  TYPE descr_nt IS TABLE OF VARCHAR2(20);
  -- declare three collection variables
  -- and initialize as empty
  nt_x_nums  num_nt := num_nt();
  nt_y_nums  num_nt := num_nt();
  nt_a_descrs descr_nt := descr_nt();
  -- four variables for the timer function
  v_t1 PLS_INTEGER;
  v_t2 PLS_INTEGER;
  v_t3 PLS_INTEGER;
  v_t4 PLS_INTEGER;
  -- a counter for loop iteration
  v_cnt PLS_INTEGER := 1;
  -- a cursor out of which to fetch records
  CURSOR c_test_tab IS
    SELECT x, y, a
      FROM test_tab;
  v_cnt_sqlrow NUMBER := 0;
  v_cnt_sqlrow2 NUMBER := 0;
BEGIN
  OPEN c_test_tab;
  -- gather time before loop and fetching
  v_t1 := timer;
  LOOP
    -- create empty nested table elements to hold
    -- fetched values
    nt_x_nums.EXTEND;
    nt_y_nums.EXTEND;
    nt_a_descrs.EXTEND;
    -- fetch without bulk collect
    FETCH c_test_tab
      INTO nt_x_nums(v_cnt), nt_y_nums(v_cnt),
           nt_a_descrs(v_cnt);
      EXIT WHEN c_test_tab%NOTFOUND;
    v_cnt := v_cnt + 1;
  END LOOP;
  -- v_cnt_sqlrow := c_test_tab%ROWCOUNT;
  -- gather time at end of fetching
  v_t2 := timer;
  -- DBMS_OUTPUT.PUT_LINE(v_cnt_sqlrow);
```

```
   CLOSE c_test_tab;
   -- reinitialize
   nt_x_nums := num_nt();
   nt_y_nums := num_nt();
   nt_a_descrs := descr_nt();
   OPEN c_test_tab;
   -- gather time before second fetch with bulk collect
   v_t3 := timer;
   FETCH c_test_tab
     BULK COLLECT INTO nt_x_nums, nt_y_nums, nt_a_descrs;
   -- v_cnt_sqlrow2 := c_test_tab%ROWCOUNT;
   -- gather time at end of second fetch
   v_t4 := timer;
   -- DBMS_OUTPUT.PUT_LINE(v_cnt_sqlrow2);
 CLOSE c_test_tab;
 -- report times
 DBMS_OUTPUT.PUT_LINE('Execution Time (secs)');
 DBMS_OUTPUT.PUT_LINE('---------------------');
 DBMS_OUTPUT.PUT_LINE(
   'Fetch Into: ' || TO_CHAR(v_t2 - v_t1));
 DBMS_OUTPUT.PUT_LINE(
   'Bulk Collect:   ' || TO_CHAR(v_t4 - v_t3));
 END;
```

The execution times under both methods of fetching are reported next.

```
Execution Time (secs)
---------------------
Fetch Into: 17
Bulk Collect:   5
```

Again, a significant improvement is shown with the bulk bind method over a loop. The two commented out DBMS_OUTPUT statements and the v_cnt_sqlrow and v_cnt_sqlrow2 variables, if commented in, would show that both sections of the code fetched 100,000 records each, the number inserted with time_bulkbind_insert. They were left commented out so that their processing would not interfere with the performance results.

## Bulk Binding in Native Dynamic SQL

Native dynamic SQL does not support bulk binding, as the DBMS_SQL package does. There is a work-around that can be implemented by passing anonymous PL/SQL blocks containing the bulk-bind SQL commands to native dynamic SQL. Bulk binding can dramatically enhance performance by minimizing context switches between the PL/SQL and SQL engines. Bulk binding is discussed in detail in the previous Tip, "Bulk Binding Collections Improves Performance." Native dynamic SQL is discussed in detail in the Tip "Issuing Native Dynamic SQL in PL/SQL."

The example procedure copy_col bulk selects into a varray collector variable a VARCHAR2 column from a given table and then inserts the records stored in the varray collector variable into a column of a second table. Both steps rely on a USING clause to reference the collector variable. The copy_col procedure takes two table names as source and destination tables and the column name from the source that is to be copied into the destination. The test tables used have the following form. Column 'a' is copied from test_tab to test_tab2; obviously the data types must be conformable.

```
SQL> DESC test_tab
 Name       Null?     Type
 --------   -------   --------------
 X                    NUMBER
 Y                    NUMBER
 A                    VARCHAR2(20)
SQL> DESC test_tab2
 Name       Null?     Type
 --------   -------   --------------
 DESCR                VARCHAR2(20)
```

The varray collector is created outside the procedure and in the database instance. Attempting to create the varray inside the procedure and then declaring and using a variable of its type causes the PL/SQL engine to raise a compile time error: *PLS-00457: in USING clause, expressions have to be of SQL types.* The native dynamic SQL component of the PL/SQL compiler requires the data type to exist prior to compile time.

```
CREATE TYPE descr_type_va IS VARRAY(100000) OF VARCHAR2(20);
-- if type created internally with procedure
-- PL/SQL error raised
-- PLS-00457: in USING clause,
-- expressions have to be of SQL types

CREATE OR REPLACE PROCEDURE copy_col
  (i_tab1 IN VARCHAR2,
   i_col IN VARCHAR2,
   i_tab2 IN VARCHAR2
  )
AS
  -- declare a varray collector variable to hold bulk select
  -- and initialize it empty
  va_descr_col  descr_type_va := descr_type_va();
  -- three timer variables
```

```
  v_t1 PLS_INTEGER := 0;
  v_t2 PLS_INTEGER := 0;
  v_t3 PLS_INTEGER := 0;
BEGIN
  -- gather time before bulk select
  v_t1 := timer;
  -- bulk select the 'a' column into varray collector
  -- issue dynamic sql with anonymous pl/sql block
  EXECUTE IMMEDIATE
    'BEGIN SELECT '|| i_col ||
          ' BULK COLLECT INTO :descr FROM ' || i_tab1 ||
          '; END;'
    USING OUT va_descr_col;
  -- gather time after select
  v_t2 := timer;
  -- bulk insert the 'descr' column into second table
  -- issue second anonymous pl/sql block
  EXECUTE IMMEDIATE
    'BEGIN FORALL i IN :first .. :last
       INSERT INTO ' || i_tab2 || ' VALUES (:descr(i)); END;'
    USING va_descr_col.first, va_descr_col.last,
          va_descr_col;
    COMMIT;
  -- gather time at end of insert
  v_t3 := timer;
  -- report on times
  DBMS_OUTPUT.PUT_LINE('Execution Time (secs)');
  DBMS_OUTPUT.PUT_LINE('--------------------');
  DBMS_OUTPUT.PUT_LINE(
    'Bulk Collect: ' || TO_CHAR(v_t2 - v_t1));
  DBMS_OUTPUT.PUT_LINE(
    'FORALL:    ' || TO_CHAR(v_t3 - v_t2));
END;
```

The report generated with the timer function presents the times in seconds for the bulk select and the bulk inserts.

```
EXECUTE copy_col('test_tab', 'a', 'test_tab2')
Execution Time (secs)
--------------------
Bulk Collect: 2
FORALL:    11
```

The timer function was first presented in the Tip "Bulk Binding Collections Improves Performance."

## Using NOCOPY to Enhance Performance When Passing Collectors with and without Bulk Binding

When a function or procedure that accepts IN, IN-OUT, or OUT parameters is created, the parameters are called *formal parameters.* The parameters passed at run time are called *actual parameters.* Actual IN parameters always are passed by reference to the formal parameters at run time. Pointers from the actual to the formal parameters are created, with the pointers referencing areas of memory holding the values of actual parameters. NOCOPY is a compiler hint that allows IN-OUT and OUT formal parameters to reference the memory location of the actual parameter passed at run time rather than to make a copy of the actual parameter. The default behavior of an IN-OUT formal parameter at run time is as follows: a copy is made of the actual parameter passed, processing changes are made to the copy, and on completion the processed copy is copied back to the actual parameter. Similarly, the default behavior of an OUT formal parameter is that the processed parameter is copied back to the actual parameter. The alternative with NOCOPY is the processing changes are made directly to the actual parameter and not to its copy. Copying back and forth reduces performance. NOCOPY allows IN-OUT and OUT formal parameters to act like IN formal parameters at run time. The formal parameters reference the actual parameter, not its copy. It is designed for use with collections, records, and object-type data structures that typically can grow large.

To implement NOCOPY, simply pass it as a flag following a formal IN-OUT or OUT parameter declaration, in the following example:

```
CREATE OR REPLACE PROCEDURE xxx
  (o_collector OUT NOCOPY collector_type,
   io_collector IN OUT NOCOPY collector_type) …
```

NOCOPY is only a compiler hint and is not a compiler directive; it may be ignored at run time. Since it is only a hint and can be ignored, exiting with unhandled exceptions or errors can leave the actual parameters in an ambiguous state. Changes made by processing within the routine passed IN-OUT NOCOPY or OUT NOCOPY parameters alter the actual parameters immediately and are not rolled back on routine failure. Whether the actual parameters were changed or their degree of change is not known, since it is not known if the NOCOPY feature was used at run time. The moral here is that only truly bulletproof code should implement NOCOPY

There are some limitations on the use of NOCOPY. If the limitations are ignored in development, the compiler will ignore the NOCOPY hint.

- Entire index-by tables may be passed as actual parameters, but individual elements of an index-by table may not be.

- If the actual and formal parameters are records, constraints on the individual corresponding elements may not differ.

■ The actual parameters passed must not imply implicit data type conversion.

■ Called routines may not be remote procedures or external procedures.

The series of example scripts to follow demonstrate the use of NOCOPY with index-by binary-integer tables, nested tables, and varrays while timing their performance with and without NOCOPY. Further bulk binding is added to the "experiments" to analyze any performance boost that might be gained by using bulk binding with NOCOPY. All the examples that follow time the processing, using the timer function first introduced in the Tip "Bulk Binding Collections Improves Performance." Also used is an enhanced version of the clone_table procedure developed in the Tip "Issuing Native Dynamic SQL in PL/SQL." As the following script indicates, clone_table now drops the clone table if it already exists before the clone is created and has a second parameter indicating whether the records from the original table should be inserted into its clone.

```
CREATE OR REPLACE PROCEDURE clone_table
  (i_table_name IN VARCHAR2,
   i_records_yn IN VARCHAR2
  )
AS
  v_sql_stmt VARCHAR2(2000);
  v_new_tab_name VARCHAR2(30);
  -- cursor select to check if clone already exists
  CURSOR c_tab_clone_exist IS
    SELECT NULL
      FROM user_tables
     WHERE table_name = v_new_tab_name;
BEGIN
  -- if table name greater than 27 characters
  -- truncate it, since tmp is appended
  v_new_tab_name :=
      UPPER(substr(i_table_name,1,27)||'tmp');
  -- debugging line
DBMS_OUTPUT.PUT_LINE(v_new_tab_name);
FOR r_tab_clone_exist IN c_tab_clone_exist
LOOP
    -- if clone already exists drop it
    v_sql_stmt := 'DROP TABLE '||v_new_tab_name;
    EXECUTE IMMEDIATE v_sql_stmt;
    -- debugging line
    DBMS_OUTPUT.PUT_LINE(v_sql_stmt);
END LOOP;
  -- insert original table's records,
  --    if i_records_yn equals 'Y' or 'y'
  IF UPPER(i_records_yn) = 'Y'
  THEN
    v_sql_stmt := 'CREATE TABLE '||v_new_tab_name||
```

```
                   ' AS SELECT * FROM '||i_table_name;
    -- debugging line
    DBMS_OUTPUT.PUT_LINE(v_sql_stmt);
  ELSE
    v_sql_stmt := 'CREATE TABLE '||v_new_tab_name||
                  ' AS SELECT * FROM '||i_table_name||' WHERE 1 = 2';
    -- debugging line
    DBMS_OUTPUT.PUT_LINE(v_sql_stmt);
  END IF;
  EXECUTE IMMEDIATE v_sql_stmt;
  COMMIT;
END;
```

The NOCOPY examples that follow assume an initial empty clone of the test_tab table exist. To create the empty clone, execute clone_table.

```
EXECUTE clone_table('TEST_TAB', 'N')
```

Clone_table will be called multiple times in the scripts that follow.

The first example procedure time_nocopy_ibt uses index-by binary-integer tables to pass an actual IN-OUT parameter to two declared procedures, insert_rec and insert_rec_nocopy. The index-by binary-integer table is passed without NOCOPY to insert_rec and with NOCOPY to insert_rec_nocopy. The insert procedures each insert 100,000 records into the test_tabtmp clone table. The records are passed to the procedures by the binary-integer tables loaded with the 'x' and 'y' values from the test_tab table. Passed out is a modified value of the 'a' column along with the 'x' and 'y' columns. The clone_table procedure is called twice to drop and re-create the test_tabtmp before each insert procedure is called. The timer function is called before and after the procedure calls to gather comparative processing times.

```
CREATE OR REPLACE PROCEDURE time_nocopy
AS
  -- create a index-by binary-integer table datatype
  -- based on the table test_tab
  TYPE test_tab_ibt IS TABLE OF test_tab%ROWTYPE
    INDEX BY BINARY_INTEGER;
  -- declare two variables of test_tab_ibt type
  ibt_test_table test_tab_ibt;
  ibt_test_table2 test_tab_ibt;
  -- declare a cursor from which to load
  -- the two variables above
  CURSOR c_test_tab IS
    SELECT * FROM test_tab;
  -- declare a counter variable to use in variable loads
  v_cnt PLS_INTEGER := 1;
```

```
-- declare four time return variables
-- for the timer functions
v_t1 PLS_INTEGER;
v_t2 PLS_INTEGER;
v_t3 PLS_INTEGER;
v_t4 PLS_INTEGER;
-- declare a procedure to insert into test_tabtmp
-- without nocopy in the in-out parameter specification,
-- the returning clause will modify the ibt_test_table
-- passed in, passing it out with the new values
-- for 'a' along with the original values for 'x' and 'y'
PROCEDURE insert_rec
  (ibt_test_table IN OUT test_tab_ibt)
IS
BEGIN
  FOR i IN ibt_test_table.FIRST..ibt_test_table.LAST
  LOOP
    INSERT INTO test_tabtmp
      VALUES(ibt_test_table(i).x, ibt_test_table(i).y,
             'COPY. '||ibt_test_table(i).x
            )RETURNING A INTO ibt_test_table(i).a;
  END LOOP;
  COMMIT;
END;
-- declare a procedure to insert into test_tabtmp with a
-- nocopy in-out parameter the returning clause acts as
-- in insert_rec
PROCEDURE insert_rec_nocopy
  (ibt_test_table2 IN OUT NOCOPY test_tab_ibt)
IS
BEGIN
  FOR i IN ibt_test_table2.FIRST..ibt_test_table2.LAST
  LOOP
    INSERT INTO test_tabtmp
      VALUES(ibt_test_table2(i).x, ibt_test_table2(i).y,
             'NOCOPY. '||ibt_test_table2(i).x
            )RETURNING A INTO ibt_test_table2(i).a;
  END LOOP;
  COMMIT;
END;
BEGIN
  -- load the ibt_test_table variable with test_tab table
  -- records
  FOR r_test_tab IN c_test_tab
  LOOP
    ibt_test_table(v_cnt) := r_test_tab;
    v_cnt := v_cnt + 1;
  END LOOP;
```

```
-- create test_tabtmp table
clone_table('test_tab', 'N');
-- gather before without-nocopy time
v_t1 := timer;
-- run without-nocopy inserts
insert_rec(ibt_test_table);
-- gather time after processing
v_t2 := timer;
-- reinitialize counter
v_cnt := 1;
-- load second index-by binary-integer variable
FOR r_test_tab IN c_test_tab
LOOP
   ibt_test_table2(v_cnt) := r_test_tab;
   v_cnt := v_cnt + 1;
END LOOP;
-- recreate test_tabtmp table
clone_table('test_tab', 'N');
-- gather time before run of with-nocopy inserts
v_t3 := timer;
-- process with-nocopy inserts
insert_rec_nocopy(ibt_test_table2);
-- gather after processing time
v_t4 := timer;
-- two debugging lines that show in out variable values
DBMS_OUTPUT.PUT_LINE('No NOCOPY x is: '||
   ibt_test_table(1000).x||' a is: '||
   ibt_test_table(1000).a);
DBMS_OUTPUT.PUT_LINE('NOCOPY x is: '||
   ibt_test_table2(1000).x||' a is '||
   ibt_test_table2(1000).a);
-- report on comparative times
DBMS_OUTPUT.PUT_LINE('....Execution Time (secs)....');
DBMS_OUTPUT.PUT_LINE('-------------------------');
DBMS_OUTPUT.PUT_LINE(
   'Without NOCOPY: '|| TO_CHAR(v_t2 - v_t1));
DBMS_OUTPUT.PUT_LINE(
   'With NOCOPY:    ' || TO_CHAR(v_t4 - v_t3));
END;
```

The timer report that follows shows a 36 percent reduction in processing time with the use of NOCOPY.

```
....Execution Time (secs)....
-------------------------
Without NOCOPY: 129
With NOCOPY:    82
```

The following examples adhere to the same strategy just described. The new aspects are the collector types used and the addition of bulk binding.

Three packages have been designed to compare the relative performance of using the NOCOPY flag with an OUT parameter in the cases in which nested tables, varrays, or index-by binary-integer tables are passed. They also compare the use of the NOCOPY parameter without and with bulk-binding the SQL processing. You may conclude from these cases that using NOCOPY increases performance rather dramatically compared to not using NOCOPY. The addition of bulk binding to NOCOPY processing marginally improves performance compared with not bulk binding. These cases also show that without NOCOPY processing, bulk binding dramatically enhances processing compared with not using bulk binding but that the real dramatic gains come from using NOCOPY processing. These conclusions should be taken as suggestive; your mileage may vary.

All packages consist of four procedures that are passed IN parameters—nested tables, varrays, or indexed-by binary-integer tables—which contain the contents of the 'x' and 'y' columns from the test_tab table holding 100,000 records. Within the procedures, these records are inserted into the test_tabtmp table with a newly created value for the 'a' column based on the 'x' value passed. The new 'a' records are passed back to the calling routine as an OUT parameter. It is with the OUT parameter that NOCOPY processing can be specified. The four procedures within each package cover the cases of with or without bulk binding coupled with or without NOCOPY processing. Bulk binding uses the FORALL and RETURNING-BULK COLLECT-INTO syntax, whereas the non-bulk binding procedures use FOR-LOOP and RETURNING-INTO syntax.

The first of the packages investigates nested tables in the context of NOCOPY and bulk binding. The package specification of time_nocopy_nt_pkg is the next listing.

```
CREATE OR REPLACE PACKAGE time_nocopy_nt_pkg
AS
   -- create three nested table datatypes based on the
   -- columns of test_tab and then declare three
   -- variables based on them
   TYPE test_tab_x_nt IS TABLE OF test_tab.x%TYPE;
   TYPE test_tab_y_nt IS TABLE OF test_tab.y%TYPE;
   TYPE test_tab_a_nt IS TABLE OF test_tab.a%TYPE;
   --
   nt_x_nums test_tab_x_nt;
   nt_y_nums test_tab_y_nt;
   nt_a_vars test_tab_a_nt;
   -- cursor to load nested table x and y variables
   CURSOR c_test_tab IS
     SELECT x, y
       FROM test_tab;
```

```
-- counter to subscript nested table variables
v_cnt PLS_INTEGER := 1;
-- timer function variables
v_t1 PLS_INTEGER;
v_t2 PLS_INTEGER;
v_t3 PLS_INTEGER;
v_t4 PLS_INTEGER;
-- for-loop procedure without nocopy
PROCEDURE insert_nt
  (nt_x_nums IN test_tab_x_nt,
   nt_y_nums IN test_tab_y_nt,
   nt_a_vars OUT test_tab_a_nt
  );
-- for-loop procedure with nocopy
PROCEDURE insert_nocopy_nt
  (nt_x_nums IN test_tab_x_nt,
   nt_y_nums IN test_tab_y_nt,
   nt_a_vars OUT NOCOPY test_tab_a_nt
  );
-- bulk binding procedure without nocopy
PROCEDURE insert_bulk_nt
  (nt_x_nums IN test_tab_x_nt,
   nt_y_nums IN test_tab_y_nt,
   nt_a_vars OUT test_tab_a_nt
  );
-- bulk binding procedure with nocopy
PROCEDURE insert_bulk_nocopy_nt
  (nt_x_nums IN test_tab_x_nt,
   nt_y_nums IN test_tab_y_nt,
   nt_a_vars OUT NOCOPY test_tab_a_nt
  );
-- procedure to run test procedures
PROCEDURE run_nt_tests;
END;
```

The package body of time_nocopy_nt_pkg is the next listing.

```
CREATE OR REPLACE PACKAGE BODY time_nocopy_nt_pkg
AS
  PROCEDURE insert_nt
    (nt_x_nums IN test_tab_x_nt,
     nt_y_nums IN test_tab_y_nt,
     nt_a_vars OUT test_tab_a_nt
    )
  IS
  BEGIN
    -- initialize out variable
    nt_a_vars := test_tab_a_nt();
```

```
    FOR i IN nt_x_nums.FIRST..nt_x_nums.LAST
    LOOP
      -- create empty new element in nested table out
      -- variable
      nt_a_vars.EXTEND;
      INSERT INTO test_tabtmp
        VALUES(nt_x_nums(i), nt_y_nums(i),
               'COPY. '||nt_x_nums(i)
              )RETURNING a INTO nt_a_vars(i);
    END LOOP;
    COMMIT;
END;
PROCEDURE insert_nocopy_nt
    (nt_x_nums IN test_tab_x_nt,
     nt_y_nums IN test_tab_y_nt,
     nt_a_vars OUT NOCOPY test_tab_a_nt
    )
IS
BEGIN
    nt_a_vars := test_tab_a_nt();
    FOR i IN nt_x_nums.FIRST..nt_x_nums.LAST
    LOOP
      nt_a_vars.EXTEND;
      INSERT INTO test_tabtmp
        VALUES(nt_x_nums(i),nt_y_nums(i),
               'NOCOPY. '||nt_x_nums(i)
              )RETURNING a INTO nt_a_vars(i);
    END LOOP;
    COMMIT;
END;
PROCEDURE insert_bulk_nt
    (nt_x_nums IN test_tab_x_nt,
     nt_y_nums IN test_tab_y_nt,
     nt_a_vars OUT test_tab_a_nt
    )
IS
BEGIN
    FORALL i IN nt_x_nums.FIRST..nt_x_nums.LAST
      INSERT INTO test_tabtmp
        VALUES(nt_x_nums(i), nt_y_nums(i),
               'COPY. '||nt_x_nums(i)
              )RETURNING a BULK COLLECT INTO nt_a_vars;
      COMMIT;
END;
PROCEDURE insert_bulk_nocopy_nt
    (nt_x_nums IN test_tab_x_nt,
     nt_y_nums IN test_tab_y_nt,
     nt_a_vars OUT NOCOPY test_tab_a_nt
```

```
    )
IS
BEGIN
  FORALL i IN nt_x_nums.FIRST..nt_x_nums.LAST
    INSERT INTO test_tabtmp
      VALUES(nt_x_nums(i), nt_y_nums(i),
            'NOCOPY. '||nt_x_nums(i)
            )RETURNING a BULK COLLECT INTO nt_a_vars;
    COMMIT;
END;
PROCEDURE run_nt_tests
IS
BEGIN
  -- initialize
  nt_x_nums := test_tab_x_nt();
  nt_y_nums := test_tab_y_nt();
  nt_a_vars := test_tab_a_nt();
  v_t1 := 0;
  v_t2 := 0;
  v_t3 := 0;
  v_t4 := 0;
  v_cnt := 1;
  -- load collector (nested table)
  FOR r_test_tab IN c_test_tab
  LOOP
    -- created new empty elements in nested table out
    -- variables
    nt_x_nums.EXTEND;
    nt_y_nums.EXTEND;
    nt_x_nums(v_cnt) := r_test_tab.x;
    nt_y_nums(v_cnt) := r_test_tab.y;
    v_cnt := v_cnt + 1;
  END LOOP;
  clone_table('test_tab', 'N');
  v_t1 := timer;
  insert_bulk_nt(nt_x_nums, nt_y_nums, nt_a_vars);
  v_t2 := timer;
  -- to show in and out variables for debugging
  -- the integer in the variable references the ith
  -- element here the 1000th
  DBMS_OUTPUT.PUT_LINE('Nested Table No NOCOPY: '||
    nt_x_nums(1000)||' '||nt_a_vars(1000));
  -- reinitialize for next run
  nt_x_nums := test_tab_x_nt();
  nt_y_nums := test_tab_y_nt();
  nt_a_vars := test_tab_a_nt();
  v_cnt := 1;
  FOR r_test_tab IN c_test_tab
```

```
LOOP
  nt_x_nums.EXTEND;
  nt_y_nums.EXTEND;
  nt_x_nums(v_cnt) := r_test_tab.x;
  nt_y_nums(v_cnt) := r_test_tab.y;
  v_cnt := v_cnt + 1;
END LOOP;
clone_table('test_tab', 'N');
v_t3 := timer;
insert_bulk_nocopy_nt(nt_x_nums, nt_y_nums, nt_a_vars);
v_t4 := timer;
-- to show in and out variables for debugging
DBMS_OUTPUT.PUT_LINE('Nested Table NOCOPY: '||
  nt_x_nums(2000)||' '||nt_a_vars(2000));
-- report
DBMS_OUTPUT.PUT_LINE(
  '.........Execution Time (secs)..........');
DBMS_OUTPUT.PUT_LINE(
  '------------------------------------------');
DBMS_OUTPUT.PUT_LINE(
  'Bulk-Bind Nested Table No NOCOPY: '||
  TO_CHAR(v_t2 - v_t1));
DBMS_OUTPUT.PUT_LINE(
  'Bulk_bind Nested Table NOCOPY:   ' ||
  TO_CHAR(v_t4 - v_t3));
-- reinitializes
v_t1 := 0;
v_t2 := 0;
v_t3 := 0;
v_t4 := 0;
v_cnt :=1;
nt_x_nums := test_tab_x_nt();
nt_y_nums := test_tab_y_nt();
nt_a_vars := test_tab_a_nt();
FOR r_test_tab IN c_test_tab
LOOP
  nt_x_nums.EXTEND;
  nt_y_nums.EXTEND;
  nt_x_nums(v_cnt) := r_test_tab.x;
  nt_y_nums(v_cnt) := r_test_tab.y;
  v_cnt := v_cnt + 1;
END LOOP;
clone_table('test_tab', 'N');
v_t1 := timer;
insert_nt(nt_x_nums, nt_y_nums, nt_a_vars);
v_t2 := timer;
-- to show in and out variables for debugging
DBMS_OUTPUT.PUT_LINE('Nested Table No NOCOPY: '||
```

Using NOCOPY to Enhance Performance

```
      nt_x_nums(1000)||' '||nt_a_vars(1000));
      -- reinitialize
      nt_x_nums := test_tab_x_nt();
      nt_y_nums := test_tab_y_nt();
      nt_a_vars := test_tab_a_nt();
      v_cnt := 1;
      FOR r_test_tab IN c_test_tab
      LOOP
        nt_x_nums.EXTEND;
        nt_y_nums.EXTEND;
        nt_x_nums(v_cnt) := r_test_tab.x;
        nt_y_nums(v_cnt) := r_test_tab.y;
        v_cnt := v_cnt + 1;
      END LOOP;
      clone_table('test_tab', 'N');
      v_t3 := timer;
      insert_nocopy_nt(nt_x_nums, nt_y_nums, nt_a_vars);
      v_t4 := timer;
      -- to show in and out variables for debugging
      DBMS_OUTPUT.PUT_LINE('Nested Table NOCOPY: '||
        nt_x_nums(2000)||' '||nt_a_vars(2000));
      -- report
      DBMS_OUTPUT.PUT_LINE(
        '.........Execution Time (secs)..........');
      DBMS_OUTPUT.PUT_LINE(
        '-----------------------------------------');
      DBMS_OUTPUT.PUT_LINE(
        'For-Loop Nested Table No NOCOPY: '||
        TO_CHAR(v_t2 - v_t1));
      DBMS_OUTPUT.PUT_LINE(
        'For-Loop Nested Table NOCOPY:    ' ||
        TO_CHAR(v_t4 - v_t3));
    END;
END;
```

Run_nt_tests can be executed.

```
EXECUTE time_nocopy_nt_pkg.run_nt_tests
```

The reports generated by time_nocopy_nt_pkg indicate using NOCOPY with nested tables accelerates performance from 281 to 82 seconds without bulk binding. Adding NOCOPY to bulk binding nested tables increases performance from 135 to 81 seconds with bulk binding. The results also confirm that bulk-bind processing by itself accelerates performance—from 281 to 135 seconds—but real gains can be achieved simply through the use of NOCOPY processing.

```
.........Execution Time (secs).........
------------------------------------------
Bulk-Bind Nested Table No NOCOPY: 135
Bulk_bind Nested Table NOCOPY:    81


.........Execution Time (secs).........
------------------------------------------
For-Loop Nested Table No NOCOPY: 281
For-Loop Nested Table NOCOPY:    82
```

The second package investigates varrays in the context of NOCOPY and bulk binding. The package specification of time_nocopy_va_pkg is the next listing.

```
CREATE OR REPLACE PACKAGE time_nocopy_va_pkg
AS
  TYPE test_tab_x_va IS VARRAY(100000)
    OF test_tab.x%TYPE;
  TYPE test_tab_y_va IS VARRAY(100000)
    OF test_tab.y%TYPE;
  TYPE test_tab_a_va is VARRAY(100000)
    OF test_tab.a%TYPE;
  va_x_nums test_tab_x_va;
  va_y_nums test_tab_y_va;
  va_a_vars test_tab_a_va;
  CURSOR c_test_tab IS
    SELECT x, y
      FROM test_tab;
  v_cnt PLS_INTEGER := 1;
  v_t1 PLS_INTEGER;
  v_t2 PLS_INTEGER;
  v_t3 PLS_INTEGER;
  v_t4 PLS_INTEGER;
  PROCEDURE insert_va
    (va_x_nums IN test_tab_x_va,
     va_y_nums IN test_tab_y_va,
     va_a_vars OUT test_tab_a_va
    );
  PROCEDURE insert_nocopy_va
    (va_x_nums IN test_tab_x_va,
     va_y_nums IN test_tab_y_va,
     va_a_vars OUT NOCOPY test_tab_a_va
    );
  PROCEDURE insert_bulkbind_va
    (va_x_nums IN test_tab_x_va,
     va_y_nums IN test_tab_y_va,
```

```
      va_a_vars OUT test_tab_a_va
    );
  PROCEDURE insert_bulkbind_nocopy_va
    (va_x_nums IN test_tab_x_va,
     va_y_nums IN test_tab_y_va,
     va_a_vars OUT NOCOPY test_tab_a_va
    );
  PROCEDURE run_va_tests;
END;
```

The package body of time_nocopy_va_pkg is the next listing.

```
CREATE OR REPLACE PACKAGE BODY time_nocopy_va_pkg
AS
  PROCEDURE insert_va
    (va_x_nums IN test_tab_x_va,
     va_y_nums IN test_tab_y_va,
     va_a_vars OUT test_tab_a_va
    )
  IS
  BEGIN
    va_a_vars := test_tab_a_va();
    FOR i IN va_x_nums.FIRST..va_x_nums.LAST
    LOOP
      va_a_vars.EXTEND;
      INSERT INTO test_tabtmp
        VALUES(va_x_nums(i),va_y_nums(i),
               'COPY. '||va_x_nums(i)
              )RETURNING a INTO va_a_vars(i);
    END LOOP;
    COMMIT;
  END;
  PROCEDURE insert_nocopy_va
    (va_x_nums IN test_tab_x_va,
     va_y_nums IN test_tab_y_va,
     va_a_vars OUT NOCOPY test_tab_a_va
    )
  IS
  BEGIN
    va_a_vars := test_tab_a_va();
    FOR i IN va_x_nums.FIRST..va_x_nums.LAST
    LOOP
      va_a_vars.EXTEND;
      INSERT INTO test_tabtmp
        VALUES(va_x_nums(i),va_y_nums(i),
               'NOCOPY. '||va_x_nums(i)
              )RETURNING a INTO va_a_vars(i);
    END LOOP;
```

```
   COMMIT;
END;
PROCEDURE insert_bulkbind_va
  (va_x_nums IN test_tab_x_va,
   va_y_nums IN test_tab_y_va,
   va_a_vars OUT test_tab_a_va
  )
IS
BEGIN
  FORALL i in va_x_nums.FIRST..va_x_nums.LAST
  INSERT INTO test_tabtmp
    VALUES(va_x_nums(i),va_y_nums(i),
           'COPY. '||va_x_nums(i)
          )RETURNING a BULK COLLECT INTO va_a_vars;
  COMMIT;
END;
PROCEDURE insert_bulkbind_nocopy_va
  (va_x_nums IN test_tab_x_va,
   va_y_nums IN test_tab_y_va,
   va_a_vars OUT NOCOPY test_tab_a_va
  )
IS
BEGIN
  FORALL i in va_x_nums.FIRST..va_x_nums.LAST
    INSERT INTO test_tabtmp
      VALUES(va_x_nums(i), va_y_nums(i),
             'NOCOPY. '||va_x_nums(i)
            )RETURNING a BULK COLLECT INTO va_a_vars;
    COMMIT;
END;
PROCEDURE run_va_tests
IS
BEGIN
  -- initialize
  v_t1 := 0;
  v_t2 := 0;
  v_t3 := 0;
  v_t4 := 0;
  va_x_nums := test_tab_x_va();
  va_y_nums := test_tab_y_va();
  va_a_vars := test_tab_a_va();
  v_cnt := 1;
  FOR r_test_tab IN c_test_tab
  LOOP
    va_x_nums.EXTEND;
    va_y_nums.EXTEND;
    va_x_nums(v_cnt) := r_test_tab.x;
    va_y_nums(v_cnt) := r_test_tab.y;
```

```
   v_cnt := v_cnt + 1;
END LOOP;
clone_table('test_tab', 'N');
v_t1 := timer;
insert_bulkbind_va(va_x_nums, va_y_nums, va_a_vars);
v_t2 := timer;
-- to show in and out variables for debugging
DBMS_OUTPUT.PUT_LINE('Varray No NOCOPY: '||
  va_x_nums(3000)||' '||va_a_vars(3000));
-- reinitialize
va_x_nums := test_tab_x_va();
va_y_nums := test_tab_y_va();
va_a_vars := test_tab_a_va();
v_cnt := 1;
FOR r_test_tab IN c_test_tab
LOOP
  va_x_nums.EXTEND;
  va_y_nums.EXTEND;
  va_x_nums(v_cnt) := r_test_tab.x;
  va_y_nums(v_cnt) := r_test_tab.y;
  v_cnt := v_cnt + 1;
END LOOP;
clone_table('test_tab', 'N');
v_t3 := timer;
insert_bulkbind_nocopy_va(va_x_nums, va_y_nums, va_a_vars);
v_t4 := timer;
-- to show in and out variables for debugging
DBMS_OUTPUT.PUT_LINE('Varray NOCOPY: '||
  va_x_nums(4000)||' '||va_a_vars(4000));
DBMS_OUTPUT.PUT_LINE(
  '..........Execution Time (secs)..........');
DBMS_OUTPUT.PUT_LINE(
  '----------------------------------------');
DBMS_OUTPUT.PUT_LINE('Bulk Bind Varray No NOCOPY: '||
  TO_CHAR(v_t2 - v_t1));
DBMS_OUTPUT.PUT_LINE('Bulk Bind Varray NOCOPY:   ' ||
  TO_CHAR(v_t4 - v_t3));
-- reinitialize
v_t1 := 0;
v_t2 := 0;
v_t3 := 0;
v_t4 := 0;
va_x_nums := test_tab_x_va();
va_y_nums := test_tab_y_va();
va_a_vars := test_tab_a_va();
.v_cnt := 1;
FOR r_test_tab IN c_test_tab
LOOP
```

```
     va_x_nums.EXTEND;
     va_y_nums.EXTEND;
     va_x_nums(v_cnt) := r_test_tab.x;
     va_y_nums(v_cnt) := r_test_tab.y;
     v_cnt := v_cnt + 1;
   END LOOP;
   clone_table('test_tab', 'N');
   v_t1 := timer;
   insert_va(va_x_nums, va_y_nums, va_a_vars);
   v_t2 := timer;
   -- to show in and out variables for debugging
   DBMS_OUTPUT.PUT_LINE('Varray No NOCOPY: '||
     va_x_nums(3000)||' '||va_a_vars(3000));
   -- reinitialize
   va_x_nums := test_tab_x_va();
   va_y_nums := test_tab_y_va();
   va_a_vars := test_tab_a_va();
   v_cnt := 1;
   FOR r_test_tab IN c_test_tab
   LOOP
     va_x_nums.EXTEND;
     va_y_nums.EXTEND;
     va_x_nums(v_cnt) := r_test_tab.x;
     va_y_nums(v_cnt) := r_test_tab.y;
     v_cnt := v_cnt + 1;
   END LOOP;
   clone_table('test_tab', 'N');
   v_t3 := timer;
   insert_nocopy_va(va_x_nums, va_y_nums, va_a_vars);
   v_t4 := timer;
   -- to show in and out variables for debugging
   DBMS_OUTPUT.PUT_LINE('Varray NOCOPY: '||
     va_x_nums(4000)||' '||va_a_vars(4000));
   DBMS_OUTPUT.PUT_LINE(
     '..........Execution Time (secs).........');
   DBMS_OUTPUT.PUT_LINE(
     '-------------------------------------------');
   DBMS_OUTPUT.PUT_LINE('For-Loop Varray No NOCOPY: '||
     TO_CHAR(v_t2 - v_t1));
   DBMS_OUTPUT.PUT_LINE('For-Loop Varray NOCOPY:    '||
     TO_CHAR(v_t4 - v_t3));
 END;
END;
```

Run_va_tests can be executed.

```
EXECUTE time_nocopy_va_pkg.run_va_tests
```

The reports generated by time_nocopy_va_pkg indicate using NOCOPY with varrays accelerates performance from 281 to 88 seconds without bulk binding. Adding NOCOPY to bulk binding varrays increases performance from 130 to 80 seconds with bulk binding. The results also confirm that bulk-bind processing by itself increases performance—from 281 to 130 seconds—but real gains can be achieved simply through the use of NOCOPY.

```
..........Execution Time (secs)..........
-----------------------------------------
Bulk Bind Varray No NOCOPY: 130
Bulk Bind Varray NOCOPY:     80

..........Execution Time (secs).........
-----------------------------------------
For-Loop Varray No NOCOPY: 281
For-Loop Varray NOCOPY:     88
```

The third package investigates index-by binary-integer tables in the context of NOCOPY and bulk binding. The package specification of time_nocopy_ibt_pkg is the next listing.

```
CREATE OR REPLACE PACKAGE time_nocopy_ibt_pkg
AS
  TYPE test_tab_x_ibt IS TABLE OF test_tab.x%type
    INDEX BY BINARY_INTEGER;
  TYPE test_tab_y_ibt IS TABLE OF test_tab.y%type
    INDEX BY BINARY_INTEGER;
  TYPE test_tab_a_ibt IS TABLE OF test_tab.a%type
    INDEX BY BINARY_INTEGER;
  ibt_x_nums test_tab_x_ibt;
  ibt_y_nums test_tab_y_ibt;
  ibt_a_vars test_tab_a_ibt;
  CURSOR c_test_tab IS
    SELECT x, y
      FROM test_tab;
  v_cnt PLS_INTEGER := 1;
  v_t1 PLS_INTEGER;
  v_t2 PLS_INTEGER;
  v_t3 PLS_INTEGER;
  v_t4 PLS_INTEGER;
  PROCEDURE insert_ibt
    (ibt_x_nums IN test_tab_x_ibt,
     ibt_y_nums IN test_tab_y_ibt,
     ibt_a_vars OUT test_tab_a_ibt
    );
  PROCEDURE insert_nocopy_ibt
```

```
  (ibt_x_nums IN test_tab_x_ibt,
   ibt_y_nums IN test_tab_y_ibt,
   ibt_a_vars OUT NOCOPY test_tab_a_ibt
  );
PROCEDURE insert_bulkbind_ibt
  (ibt_x_nums IN test_tab_x_ibt,
   ibt_y_nums IN test_tab_y_ibt,
   ibt_a_vars OUT test_tab_a_ibt
  );
PROCEDURE insert_bulkbind_nocopy_ibt
   (ibt_x_nums IN test_tab_x_ibt,
    ibt_y_nums IN test_tab_y_ibt,
    ibt_a_vars OUT NOCOPY test_tab_a_ibt
   );
PROCEDURE run_ibt_tests;
END;
```

The package body of time_nocopy_va_pkg is the next listing.

```
CREATE OR REPLACE PACKAGE BODY time_nocopy_ibt_pkg
AS
  PROCEDURE insert_ibt
    (ibt_x_nums IN test_tab_x_ibt,
     ibt_y_nums IN test_tab_y_ibt,
     ibt_a_vars OUT test_tab_a_ibt
    )
  IS
  BEGIN
    FOR i IN ibt_x_nums.FIRST..ibt_x_nums.LAST
    LOOP
      INSERT INTO test_tabtmp
        VALUES(ibt_x_nums(i), ibt_y_nums(i),
               'COPY. '||ibt_x_nums(i)
              )RETURNING a INTO ibt_a_vars(i);
    END LOOP;
    COMMIT;
  END;
  PROCEDURE insert_nocopy_ibt
    (ibt_x_nums IN test_tab_x_ibt,
     ibt_y_nums IN test_tab_y_ibt,
     ibt_a_vars OUT NOCOPY test_tab_a_ibt
    )
  IS
  BEGIN
    FOR i IN ibt_x_nums.FIRST..ibt_x_nums.LAST
    LOOP
      INSERT INTO test_tabtmp
        VALUES(ibt_x_nums(i), ibt_y_nums(i),
```

```
                  'NOCOPY. '||ibt_x_nums(i)
              )RETURNING a INTO ibt_a_vars(i);
    END LOOP;
    COMMIT;
END;
PROCEDURE insert_bulkbind_ibt
  (ibt_x_nums IN test_tab_x_ibt,
   ibt_y_nums IN test_tab_y_ibt,
   ibt_a_vars OUT test_tab_a_ibt
  )
IS
BEGIN
  FORALL i IN ibt_x_nums.FIRST..ibt_x_nums.LAST
    INSERT INTO test_tabtmp
      VALUES(ibt_x_nums(i), ibt_y_nums(i),
             'COPY. '||ibt_x_nums(i)
            )RETURNING a BULK COLLECT INTO ibt_a_vars;
    COMMIT;
  END;
PROCEDURE insert_bulkbind_nocopy_ibt
  (ibt_x_nums IN test_tab_x_ibt,
   ibt_y_nums IN test_tab_y_ibt,
   ibt_a_vars OUT NOCOPY test_tab_a_ibt
  )
IS
BEGIN
  FORALL i IN ibt_x_nums.FIRST..ibt_x_nums.LAST
    INSERT INTO test_tabtmp
      VALUES(ibt_x_nums(i), ibt_y_nums(i),
             'NOCOPY. '||ibt_x_nums(i)
            )RETURNING a BULK COLLECT INTO ibt_a_vars;
    COMMIT;
END;
PROCEDURE run_ibt_tests
IS
BEGIN
  -- initialize
  v_t1 := 0;
  v_t2 := 0;
  v_t3 := 0;
  v_t4 := 0;
  v_cnt := 1;
  FOR r_test_tab IN c_test_tab
  LOOP
    ibt_x_nums(v_cnt) := r_test_tab.x;
    ibt_y_nums(v_cnt) := r_test_tab.y;
    v_cnt := v_cnt + 1;
  END LOOP;
```

```
clone_table('test_tab', 'N');
v_t1 := timer;
insert_bulkbind_ibt(ibt_x_nums, ibt_y_nums, ibt_a_vars);
v_t2 := timer;
-- to show in and out variables for debugging
DBMS_OUTPUT.PUT_LINE('Index By Table No NOCOPY: '||
  ibt_x_nums(3000)||' '||ibt_a_vars(3000));
-- cleanup index-by tables and reinitialize
ibt_x_nums.DELETE;
ibt_y_nums.DELETE;
ibt_a_vars.DELETE;
v_cnt := 1;
FOR r_test_tab IN c_test_tab
LOOP
  ibt_x_nums(v_cnt) := r_test_tab.x;
  ibt_y_nums(v_cnt) := r_test_tab.y;
  v_cnt := v_cnt + 1;
END LOOP;
clone_table('test_tab', 'N');
v_t3 := timer;
insert_bulkbind_nocopy_ibt(ibt_x_nums, ibt_y_nums, ibt_a_vars);
v_t4 := timer;
-- to show in and out variables for debugging
DBMS_OUTPUT.PUT_LINE('Index By Table NOCOPY: '||
  ibt_x_nums(4000)||' '||ibt_a_vars(4000));
DBMS_OUTPUT.PUT_LINE(
  '..........Execution Time (secs)..........');
DBMS_OUTPUT.PUT_LINE(
  '-----------------------------------------');
DBMS_OUTPUT.PUT_LINE(Bulk Bind Index-By No NOCOPY: '||
  TO_CHAR(v_t2 - v_t1));
DBMS_OUTPUT.PUT_LINE('Bulk Bind Index-By NOCOPY:   '
  || TO_CHAR(v_t4 - v_t3));
-- reinitialize and cleanup
v_t1 := 0;
v_t2 := 0;
v_t3 := 0;
v_t4 := 0;
ibt_x_nums.DELETE;
ibt_y_nums.DELETE;
ibt_a_vars.DELETE;
v_cnt := 1;
FOR r_test_tab IN c_test_tab
LOOP
  ibt_x_nums(v_cnt) := r_test_tab.x;
  ibt_y_nums(v_cnt) := r_test_tab.y;
  v_cnt := v_cnt + 1;
END LOOP;
```

Using NOCOPY to Enhance Performance

```
    clone_table('test_tab', 'N');
    v_t1 := timer;
    insert_ibt(ibt_x_nums, ibt_y_nums, ibt_a_vars);
    v_t2 := timer;
    -- to show in and out variables for debugging
    DBMS_OUTPUT.PUT_LINE('Index By Table No NOCOPY: '||
      ibt_x_nums(3000)||' '||ibt_a_vars(3000));
    -- cleanup and reinitialize
    ibt_x_nums.DELETE;
    ibt_y_nums.DELETE;
    ibt_a_vars.DELETE;
    v_cnt := 1;
    FOR r_test_tab IN c_test_tab
    LOOP
      ibt_x_nums(v_cnt) := r_test_tab.x;
      ibt_y_nums(v_cnt) := r_test_tab.y;
      v_cnt := v_cnt + 1;
    END LOOP;
    clone_table('test_tab', 'N');
    v_t3 := timer;
    insert_nocopy_ibt(ibt_x_nums, ibt_y_nums, ibt_a_vars);
    v_t4 := timer;
    -- to show in and out variables for debugging
    DBMS_OUTPUT.PUT_LINE('Index By Table NOCOPY: '||
      ibt_x_nums(4000)||' '||ibt_a_vars(4000));
    DBMS_OUTPUT.PUT_LINE(
      '..........Execution Time (secs)..........');
    DBMS_OUTPUT.PUT_LINE(
      '-------------------------------------------');
    DBMS_OUTPUT.PUT_LINE('For-Loop Index-By No NOCOPY: '||
      TO_CHAR(v_t2 - v_t1));
    DBMS_OUTPUT.PUT_LINE('For-Loop Index-By NOCOPY:   ' ||
      TO_CHAR(v_t4 - v_t3));
  END;
END;
```

Run_ibt_tests can be executed.

```
EXECUTE time_nocopy_ibt_pkg.run_ibt_tests
```

The reports generated by time_nocopy_ibt_pkg indicate using NOCOPY accelerates performance from 149 to 82 seconds without bulk binding. Adding NOCOPY to bulk binding increases performance from 133 to 80 seconds with bulk binding. The results also confirm that bulk-bind processing by itself increases performance—from 149 to 133 seconds—but real gains can be achieved simply through the use of NOCOPY processing.

```
.........Execution Time (secs).........
--------------------------------------
Bulk Bind Index-By No NOCOPY: 133
Bulk Bind Index-By NOCOPY:    80

.........Execution Time (secs).........
--------------------------------------
For-Loop Index-By No NOCOPY: 149
For-Loop Index-By NOCOPY:     82
```

We may conclude from the foregoing "experiments" that using NOCOPY increases performance rather dramatically compared with not using NOCOPY. The addition of bulk binding to NOCOPY processing improves performance compared with not bulk binding but at times only marginally. These examples also show that without NOCOPY processing, bulk binding dramatically enhances processing compared with not using bulk binding but that the real dramatic gains come from using NOCOPY processing. Again, these conclusions should be taken as only suggestive; for each application and usage, experimentation will prove useful.

# New PL/SQL Built-In Packages: DBMS_PROFILER and DBMS_TRACE

Two new PL/SQL built-in packages help track and gauge the run-time performance of PL/SQL routines. DBMS_PROFILER tracks named PL/SQL routines and reports on their execution times and the number of times they are called on a line-by-line basis. DBMS_TRACE can be used as a debugging tool that tracks the exceptions generated and the routine calls of application code at run time. DBMS_PROFILER and DBMS_TRACE are the topics of this section.

## Monitoring the Execution Times of Named Routines with DBMS_PROFILER

DBMS_PROFILER is an Oracle-supplied package new to Oracle8i. With it any user-defined named procedure, function, and package can be monitored for potential processing time bottlenecks. Through the PL/SQL virtual machine and at the session level DBMS_PROFILER collects data on each line of code processed, including

- The total number of times each line of code is executed

- The total amount of time spent executing the line

- Minimum and maximum times spent executing a line

The demonstration scripts supplied with DBMS_PROFILER include a reporting template that generates detailed and summary reports for a profiler session and across all profiler sessions.

DBMS_PROFILER is implemented by running two scripts, profload.sql and proftab.sql, found in the Rdbms subdirectory of ORACLE_HOME. First run the profload.sql script as SYS or as a user granted SYSDBA to build the server-side profiler package. The proftab.sql script builds three tables that hold the timing information (plsql_profiler_runs, plsql_profiler_units, and plsql_profile_data), as well as a sequence (plsql_profile_runnumber) used to create profiler run or session numbers. Two methods are available to continue the implementation. Proftab.sql can be run in each individual schema that will be profiled. Alternatively, it can be run in a central administrative schema if the owner of the administrative schema has been granted SYSDBA with select and insert privileges granted to public on the tables, select privilege on the sequence granted to public, and public synonyms created on the tables and the sequence. Of course, with this second method, individual users could be granted privileges, and then they could create the necessary synonyms rather than use a public configuration.

**CAUTION**

*In proftab.sql, the CREATE TABLE statements for PLSQL_PROFILER_UNITS and PLSQL_PROFILER_DATA have an extra blank line between the last column name and primary key declaration, which must be removed for the tables to be created.*

The three tables created have a parent-to-child-to-child relationship, with PLSQL_PROFILER_RUNS the parent of PLSQL_PROFILER_UNITS and PLSQL_PROFILER_UNITS the parent of PLSQL_PROFILER_DATA. Each profiler session or run in a user session can execute multiple named PL/SQL routines or units, which in turn have multiple lines of code. The structures of the tables are as follows:

```
DESC plsql_profiler_runs
 Name                                      Null?      Type
 ----------------------------------------- ---------- ---------------
 RUNID                                     NOT NULL   NUMBER
 RUN_DATE                                             DATE
 RUN_COMMENT                                          VARCHAR2(2047)
 RUN_TOTAL_TIME                                       NUMBER
 RUN_SYSTEM_INFO                                      VARCHAR2(2047)
 SPARE1                                               VARCHAR2(256)

DESC plsql_profiler_units
 Name                                      Null?      Type
 ----------------------------------------- ---------- ---------------
 RUNID                                     NOT NULL   NUMBER
```

```
UNIT_NUMBER                             NOT NULL  NUMBER
UNIT_TYPE                                         VARCHAR2(32)
UNIT_OWNER                                        VARCHAR2(32)
UNIT_NAME                                         VARCHAR2(32)
UNIT_TIMESTAMP                                    DATE
TOTAL_TIME                              NOT NULL  NUMBER
SPARE1                                            NUMBER
SPARE2                                            NUMBER


DESC plsql_profiler_data
Name                                    Null?     Type
--------------------------------------- --------- --------------

RUNID                                   NOT NULL  NUMBER
UNIT_NUMBER                             NOT NULL  NUMBER
LINE#                                   NOT NULL  NUMBER
TOTAL_OCCUR                                       NUMBER
TOTAL_TIME                                        NUMBER
MIN_TIME                                          NUMBER
MAX_TIME                                          NUMBER
SPARE1                                            NUMBER
SPARE2                                            NUMBER
SPARE3                                            NUMBER
SPARE4                                            NUMBER
```

The spare fields are reserved by Oracle for future use.

The time fields are measured in nanoseconds. Run_total_time in the runs table is the total time for the profiler session. Total_time in the units table is the total time of a PL/SQL routine executed in the profiler session and may include multiple executions for a routine, if it was executed multiple times. Total_time in the units table is, in fact, a derived field and is set to zero after a DBMS_PROFILER session. The value of total_time in the units table is derived by summing by routine the total_time field in the data table. A PL/SQL package presented in forthcoming pages will update the total_time columns in the units table from the total_time values in the data table. Total_time in the data table is the total time a particular line in a routine or unit executed. If the line executed multiple times, those times are summed in total_time of the data table, and the number of times the line executed is recorded in total_occur. Min_time and max_time in the data table give the minimum and maximum execution times for a particular line; if the line was executed only once, they are the same and equal to total_time in this table.

Clarifying column relationships exist between the profiler tables PLSQL_PROFILER_UNITS and PLSQL_PROFILER_DATA and ALL_OBJECTS and ALL_SOURCE or DBA_OBJECTS and DBA_SOURCE tables. Table 8-1 shows the relationships recording only the common columns. It is from a join on ALL_SOURCE with PLSQL_PROFILER_DATA via PLSQL_PROFILER_UNITS that the actual code for a line in a routine or unit can be queried. The code for a line from a routine is contained in the text column of the all_source table.

| PLSQL_PROFILER_ UNITS | DBA_ OR ALL_OBJECTS | DBA_ OR ALL_SOURCE | PLSQL_PROFILER_ DATA |
|---|---|---|---|
| unit_type | object_type | type | NA |
| unit_owner | owner | owner | NA |
| unit_name | object_name | name | NA |
| NA | NA | line | line# |

**TABLE 8-1.** *Relationships between Profiler Tables and DBA_ or ALL_OBJECTS and DBA_ or ALL_SOURCES*

Four functions and one procedure are created with profload.sql. The START_ PROFILER function starts the data collection when executed in a user session. Profiler sessions are referred to as runs, and START_PROFILER can be passed a name for the profiler session or run. It will default to the system date. The STOP_PROFILER function stops the data collection for the current session and flushes the data being collected to the PLSQL_PROFILER_DATA table. The FLUSH_DATA function flushes the data being collected in a profiler session or run to the PLSQL_PROFILER_DATA table and starts a new session or run. The FLUSH_DATA function is effectively a STOP_PROFILER-START_PROFILER function.

**NOTE**
*In future releases, starting with 8.1.6, FLUSH_DATA will simply flush the data to the profiler table PLSQL_PROFILER_DATA and not stop the profiler session and restart a new session.*

The GET_VERSION procedure reports on the version of the DBMS_PROFILER API currently installed. The INTERNAL_VERSION_CHECK function confirms that the version of DBMS_PROFILER installed is compatible with the version of the Oracle database server installed. A return value of zero from any function signals successful completion. A return value of one signals that an incorrect parameter was passed to a subprogram or to START_PROFILER, since only START_PROFILER takes an IN parameter. If a data flush fails, the return value is two. If the internal version check fails, the return value is minus one.

A profiler session could consist of the user starting the profiler, executing application code, and then stopping the profiler session from the SQL*Plus prompt. A second possibility is the functions that are supplied with the DBMS_PROFILER package could be embedded in application code to profile pieces of functionality and run quietly behind the scene in a test or development environment. A third possibility is that the DBMS_PROFILER functions could be embedded in LOGON and LOGOFF database event triggers to automatically profile all named routines executed by all users. Examples of LOGON and LOGOFF triggers are given later in this Tip. All three possible deployment methods will work from a centrally administrated implementation of DBMS_PROFILER. Outside of the centrally administrated implementations, user deployment or application-code deployment requires the proftab.sql script that builds the profiler tables to be run in each schema that will be profiled.

An example of a user running a profiler session will be demonstrated in forthcoming pages. We recommend that the instance be "warmed up" by running the application code of interest before you begin the profiler session. "Warming up" the instance preloads the PL/SQL byte code into shared memory and minimizes distortion of the performance times through disk I/O. The following example relies on the procedure time_bulkbind_insert developed in the earlier Tip "Bulk Binding Collections Improves Performance."

```
-- start the profiling giving the session
-- the name of test_123
SELECT DBMS_PROFILER.START_PROFILER('test_123')
  FROM dual:
-- outputs success signal
DBMS_PROFILER.START_PROFILER('TEST_123')
-----------------------------------------
                                        0


EXECUTE time_bulkbind_insert
PL/SQL procedure successfully completed.

-- execute it a second time
EXECUTE time_bulkbind_insert
PL/SQL procedure successfully completed.

SELECT DBMS_PROFILER.STOP_PROFILER
  FROM dual;
-- signals success
STOP_PROFILER
-------------
            0
```

The Oracle-supplied demonstration report can now be run, if desired. Its code contains a procedure that will update the zero values in the total_time columns of the PLSQL_PROFILER_UNITS table. The updates are sums derived from the values in the total_time field of the PLSQL_PROFILER_DATA table. In a few pages, this chapter will present you with a package that will do the update without requiring that the demonstration report be executed.

```
SET SERVEROUTPUT ON
-- run report supplied with Oracle8i
@D:\Oracle\Ora81\PLSQL\DEMO\profsum.sql
```

Here D:\Oracle\Ora81 is the ORACLE_HOME on a WinNT system containing in its subdirectories the demonstration report script profsum.sql. It generates a file called profsum.out into the ORACLE_HOME\bin directory by default when run at the SQL*PLUS prompt.

The demonstration report contains a series of subreports. Total times for the user are reported for all profiler sessions; the time is also reported for each profiler session and for each routine in each profiler session. Percentages of time in each routine are reported for each session and for all sessions combined. Comparisons are given among the minimum, maximum, and average times for a line of a routine, since a routine may be called multiple times in a profiler session. Lines that take more then 1 percent of the processing time within a routine are highlighted, as are "popular" lines taking more than 1 percent of processing time across routines. Information is also reported on the number of lines for packages and package bodies. Although the times are gathered in nanoseconds, they are reported in seconds, unless otherwise noted.

**CAUTION**
*In early releases of Oracle8i, the times gathered by DBMS_PROFILER appear occasionally to be exaggerated by as much as a factor of a thousand. The factor has been diagnosed by Oracle Language Development Group to be dependent on the megahertz of the chip and is a consequence of how the number of machine cycles is returned to internal query calls. Under rare conditions, Win95 and WinNT will act as if the machine is a 1.19 MHz machine, regardless of what it really is. For a 450 MHz machine, the factor is approximately 378 or 450/1.19. It is on Pentium III 450 MHz WinNT machines that the exaggeration has actually been experienced. For a 550 MHz machine, it is expected to be a factor of approximately 462 or 550/1.19. It is recommended in such cases that the times be examined for their relative strengths, not their absolute values. A query later in this Tip demonstrates how you can return the percentage of total time for the processing of each line in a routine.*

Perhaps the most immediately interesting parts of the supplied reports are two subreports entitled Detailed Report and Summarized Report. These reports highlight areas of code in which bottlenecks may be occurring. Both reports are broken down by routine and show line by line the number of times a line was executed, the total time for all executions of the line, and the average time of execution for the line. The Detailed Report shows this information for each execution of a routine individually; the Summarized Report shows the same information for all executions of a routine. For example, a small piece of the Detailed Report for one execution of time_bulkbind_insert shows the following:

```
<slice of Detailed Report>
14      50,001   11.676871  .00023353
        FOR j IN 1..50000 LOOP  -- load index-by tables
```

The same piece from the Summarized Report shows the following:

```
<slice of Summarized Report>
14      100,002   23.356140  .00023355
        FOR j IN 1..50000 LOOP  -- load index-by tables
```

Both pieces of the reports show the same code segment. The first piece is for one execution of time_bulkbind_insert, where the FOR-LOOP was executed 50,001 times. The second piece is for the FOR-LOOP executed 100,002 times for both executions. The total time is about doubled in the Summarized Report at 23.356140 seconds, but the average time is roughly the same at .00023353 and .00023355 seconds. Scanning these reports for lines showing alarming average times relative to the work done will suggest areas in which performance may be improved.

If you don't wish to run the demonstration report and are interested in the total_time values aggregated over the runs of a routine within a profiler session, then you can use the following package rollup_units to update the total_time zero values in PLSQL_PROFILER_UNITS. Total_time in PLSQL_PROFILER_UNITS would be used to calculate percentage of total time, for example. Rollup_units sums by routine and session the total_time values in PLSQL_PROFILER_DATA and uses them to update total_time in PLSQL_PROFILER_UNITS. To execute this package and its procedures successfully, the user executing them must be granted the privilege of updating the PLSQL_PROFILER_UNITS table or be the table owner.

```
CREATE OR REPLACE PACKAGE rollup_units
AS
   -- package updates plsql_profiler_units.total_time field
   -- from values in plsql_profiler_data.total_time field
   -- plsql_profiler_units.total_time is derived from
   -- plsql_profiler_data.total_time
   --
```

**Monitoring the Execution Times of Named Routines**

```
  -- overloaded procedure to 1)update all
  -- plsql_profiler_units or 2) only update
  -- plsql_profiler_units for a individual run and unit
  PROCEDURE rollup_to_units;
  PROCEDURE rollup_to_units
    (i_run_id IN NUMBER,
     i_unitnumber IN NUMBER
    );
END;

CREATE OR REPLACE PACKAGE BODY rollup_units
AS
  PROCEDURE rollup_to_units
  IS
    -- variable to hold exceptions
    v_sqlerrm VARCHAR2(512);
    -- cursor to capture profiler session id or run id
    -- and pl/sql routine or unit number
    CURSOR c_plsql_units IS
      SELECT runid, unit_number
        FROM plsql_profiler_units;
  BEGIN
    FOR r_plsql_units IN c_plsql_units
    LOOP
      UPDATE plsql_profiler_units
        SET total_time =
          (SELECT SUM(total_time)
             FROM plsql_profiler_data
            WHERE runid = r_plsql_units.runid
              AND unit_number = r_plsql_units.unit_number)
        WHERE runid = r_plsql_units.runid
        AND unit_number = r_plsql_units.unit_number;
    END LOOP;
    COMMIT;
  EXCEPTION
    WHEN OTHERS
    THEN
      v_sqlerrm := SQLERRM;
      DBMS_OUTPUT.PUT_LINE(v_sqlerrm);
  END;
  PROCEDURE rollup_to_units
    (i_run_id IN number,
     i_unitnumber IN number
    )
  IS
    v_sqlerrm VARCHAR2(512);
  BEGIN
    UPDATE plsql_profiler_units
```

```
        SET total_time =
            (SELECT SUM(total_time)
               FROM plsql_profiler_data
              WHERE runid = i_run_id
                AND unit_number = i_unitnumber
            )
      WHERE runid = i_run_id
        AND unit_number = i_unitnumber;
    COMMIT;
  EXCEPTION
    WHEN OTHERS
    THEN
      v_sqlerrm := SQLERRM;
      DBMS_OUTPUT.PUT_LINE(v_sqlerrm);
  END;
END;
```

The package has one overloaded procedure rollup_to_units that can update all total_time values in the plsql_profiler_units table or only the total_time values for a particular routine or unit within a profiler session or run.

A Caution earlier in this Tip warned that the times collected by the DBMS_ PROFILER in early releases of Oracle8i appear at times to be overcalculated. The following query will return the processing time for each line of a routine as a percentage of the total processing time devoted to that routine. Note that if the same routine is run multiple times in a profiler session, the percentages roll up the multiples for both the multiple executions of a routine and the multiple executions of each line within the routine.

```
COLUMN UNIT_NAME FORMAT A12
COLUMN UNIT_TYPE FORMAT A10
COLUMN TEXT FORMAT A80

  SELECT ppu.runid, ppu.unit_name, ppu.unit_type, ppd.line#,
         (ppd.total_time/ppu.total_time)*100
         "Percent of Total",
         a.text
    FROM plsql_profiler_units ppu, plsql_profiler_data ppd,
         all_source a
   WHERE ppd.runid = ppu.runid
     AND ppd.unit_number = ppu.unit_number
     AND ppu.total_time <> 0
     AND ppu.unit_owner = a.owner
     AND ppu.unit_name = a.name
     AND ppu.unit_type = a.type
     AND ppd.line# = a.line
   ORDER BY ppu.runid, ppu.unit_number, ppd.line#;
```

To check that the line-by-line percentages sum to 100 percent of the total routine processing time, you can run the following query:

```
SELECT ppu.runid, unit_type, unit_name, ppd.unit_number,
       SUM(ppd.total_time/ppu.total_time)*100
  FROM plsql_profiler_units ppu, plsql_profiler_data ppd
 WHERE ppd.runid = ppu.runid
   AND ppd.unit_number = ppu.unit_number
   AND ppu.total_time <> 0
 GROUP BY ppu.runid, unit_type, unit_name, ppd.unit_number
 ORDER BY ppu.runid, unit_type, unit_name, ppd.unit_number;
```

We will end this Tip with a few management points. First, we mentioned at the outset that when DBMS_PROFILER was configured to run from a central administrative schema, such as SYSTEM_MANAGER, LOGON and LOGOFF database event triggers could be used to profile all named routines for all users. The following triggers start and stop the profiler sessions as users log on and log off.

```
CREATE OR REPLACE TRIGGER logon_trg
  AFTER LOGON ON DATABASE
DECLARE
  -- the logging-in user and date will be
  -- concatenated and passed to the start_profiler
  -- function. variables declared to hold
  -- user and date
  v_user VARCHAR2(30);
  v_date DATE;
  -- the start_profiler function returns a binary_integer
  -- signaling its success or failure. v_out is used to
  -- capture the signal
  v_out BINARY_INTEGER;
BEGIN
  -- capture the logged in user from system event
  -- attribute function sys.login_user
  v_user := SYS.LOGIN_USER;
  -- capture date
  v_date := TRUNC(SYSDATE);
  -- call start_profiler with user-date string
  -- capturing the success signal in v_out
  v_out :=
       DBMS_PROFILER.START_PROFILER(v_user||'-'||v_date);
END;

CREATE OR REPLACE TRIGGER logoff_trg
  BEFORE LOGOFF ON DATABASE
DECLARE
  -- the stop_profiler function returns a binary_integer
```

```
   -- signaling its success or failure. v_out is used to
   -- capture the signal
   v_out BINARY_INTEGER;
BEGIN
   -- call stop_profiler capturing the success
   -- signal in v_out
   v_out := DBMS_PROFILER.STOP_PROFILER;
END;
```

These triggers are created in a user account granted SYSDBA and fire on logon and logoff of every user.

Second, to execute the GET_VERSION procedure of DBMS_PROFILER, you can execute the following function. GET_VERSION returns two OUT parameters that need to be captured.

```
CREATE OR REPLACE FUNCTION profiler_get_version
   RETURN VARCHAR2
AS
   -- get_version returns two binary integers
   v_major BINARY_INTEGER;
   v_minor BINARY_INTEGER;
BEGIN
   SYS.DBMS_PROFILER.GET_VERSION(v_major, v_minor);
   RETURN  v_major||'.'||v_minor;
END;
```

This function can be run with a SELECT statement against the table DUAL and returns the current version installed.

A third area of management covers cleaning up of the three tables created when DBMS_PROFILER is configured. The contents of the tables persist until they are truncated, and the demonstration report will detail all the profiler sessions contained in the tables each time it is run. The foreign key relationships must be disabled in order to truncate the tables and they must be reenabled after truncation. The following commands will remove all records from all three tables.

```
ALTER TABLE plsql_profiler_data
   DISABLE CONSTRAINT sys_c00917;
ALTER TABLE plsql_profiler_units
   DISABLE CONSTRAINT sys_c00914;
TRUNCATE TABLE plsql_profiler_data;
TRUNCATE TABLE plsql_profiler_units;
TRUNCATE TABLE plsql_profiler_runs;
ALTER TABLE plsql_profiler_units
   ENABLE CONSTRAINT sys_c00914;
ALTER TABLE plsql_profiler_data
   ENABLE CONSTRAINT sys_c00917;
```

The foreign key constraint names beginning with 'sys' are system generated and need to be determined for each schema in which proftab.sql has been run. The USER_ or ALL_CONSTRAINTS views hold the information, where foreign key constraints are of type 'R'.

```
SELECT table_name, constraint_name, constraint_type
  FROM all_constraints
 WHERE table_name IN
       ('PLSQL_PROFILER_UNITS', 'PLSQL_PROFILER_DATA')
   AND constraint_type = 'R';
```

## Monitoring Run-Time PL/SQL Routine Calls and Exceptions with DBMS_TRACE

The DBMS_TRACE Oracle built-in package allows you to do run-time debugging of applications by printing to a trace file either routine calls made by the application code or exceptions raised within the routines. DBMS_TRACE is designed to capture run-time problems, not problems at compile time. The DBMS_TRACE package is created automatically on instance creation with a call to dbmspbt.sql. Tracing can be done (1) for all routine calls, (2) only for enabled routine calls, (3) for all exceptions, or (4) only for exceptions from enabled routines. For enabling routines, they can be created in a session that has been altered with the following ALTER SESSION command:

```
ALTER SESSION SET PLSQL_DEBUG = TRUE;
```

Alternatively, recompiling it with the following ALTER command can enable an individual routine.

```
ALTER [PROCEDURE | FUNCTION | PACKAGE BODY] <routine_name>
  COMPILE DEBUG;
```

Routines that are not individually enabled for DBMS_TRACE can still be traced by tracing all calls or all exceptions, but in a large application this method may generate a very large trace file full of extraneous information. This is particularly true when you are tracing routine execution calls; the trace file will fill with calls to routines owned by the system user SYS.

DBMS_TRACE will not work in a session that is connected to the database instance in multithreaded server (MTS) mode. The session must have a dedicated server connection. If the instance is configured for MTS (as is required for the Java Virtual Machine), a dedicated server connection can be made with an addition of a new network alias in the tnsnames.ora file of the client machine. The following network connection alias generates a dedicated server connection through the addition of the flag SERVER = DEDICATED in its CONNECT_DATA section.

```
ORA81_DED =
  (DESCRIPTION =
    (ADDRESS_LIST =
      (ADDRESS = (PROTOCOL = TCP)
                 (HOST = testnt)
                 (PORT = 1521)
      )
    )
    (CONNECT_DATA =
      (SERVICE_NAME = ora81.testnt)
      (SERVER = DEDICATED)
    )
  )
```

Four levels of tracing correspond to the possibilities discussed earlier. The first of the three procedures supplied with DBMS_TRACE is SET_PLSQL_TRACE and takes one parameter, which must have one of four integer values as listed in Table 8-2 and which corresponds to the four levels of tracing.

Tracing enabled routines is started by executing set_plsql_trace in a session of a user that has execution privileges on the routines.

```
EXECUTE DBMS_TRACE.SET_PLSQL_TRACE(2)
```

As the enabled routines are executed, their execution calls will be written to a trace file in the Udump directory for the instance on the server. Similarly, the tracing of exceptions raised by enabled routines can be traced.

```
EXECUTE DBMS_TRACE.SET_PLSQL_TRACE(8)
```

| SET_PLSQL_TRACE | Integer |
| --- | --- |
| trace all routine calls | 1 |
| trace enabled routine calls | 2 |
| trace all exceptions | 4 |
| trace enabled exceptions | 8 |

**TABLE 8-2.**   *Integer Parameters for SET_PLSQL_TRACE*

Monitoring Run-Time PL/SQL
Routine Calls and Exceptions

The most recently executed SET_PLSQL_TRACE statement determines the trace mode for the session. For discontinuing tracing, a second procedure is supplied with the DBMS_TRACE package. Tracing will end in a session when you issue the following execution command:

```
EXECUTE DBMS_TRACE.CLEAR_PLSQL_TRACE
```

The third procedure supplied with DBMS_TRACE reports on the current version of DBMS_TRACE installed. This procedure returns two OUT binary-integer variables, which can be captured with the following function:

```
CREATE OR REPLACE FUNCTION trace_version_check
  RETURN VARCHAR2
AS
  v_major BINARY_INTEGER;
  v_minor BINARY_INTEGER;
BEGIN
  SYS.DBMS_TRACE.PLSQL_TRACE_VERSION(v_major, v_minor);
  RETURN  v_major||'.'||v_minor;
END;
```

Executing TRACE_VERSION_CHECK with a SELECT statement against the DUAL table will return the current version number.

To see a small example of the usage of DBMS_TRACE, consider a procedure designed to raise exceptions. First, break_except attempts to use a SELECT-INTO statement against a multirecord result set and then in its EXCEPTIONS section attempts to assign a six-character string to a variable defined to hold up to two characters. These features will demonstrate exceptions tracing. Second, the procedure also calls the procedure timer from the earlier Tip "Bulk Binding Collections Improves Performance." It will appear in the trace file of the called routine only if recompiled into debug mode. Timer actually does nothing in the procedure break_except; it is there to show called routine tracing. The trace file for called routines will show calls to both the break_except and timer functions.

To allow the tracing of the procedure timer, the following ALTER PROCEDURE is issued:

```
ALTER PROCEDURE timer compile DEBUG;
```

Next, the following ALTER SESSION command permits all created routines in the user's schema to be enabled for tracing. Break_except is then created in the session that has been altered.

```
ALTER SESSION SET PLSQL_DEBUG=TRUE;

CREATE OR REPLACE PROCEDURE break_except
```

```
AS
  -- variable to hold a character string
  v_dd VARCHAR2(2);
  -- variable to pass to timer function
  v_t1 PLS_INTEGER;
BEGIN
  -- call timer
  v_t1 := timer;
  -- attempt to select a multi-row result set
  -- into a single dimensioned variable
  SELECT a
    INTO v_dd
    FROM test_tab;
EXCEPTION
  -- when above select raise an exception
  -- processing moves to when others
  WHEN OTHERS
  THEN
    -- attempt to assign six characters
    -- to two character variable
    v_dd := 'ABC123';
END;
```

Note that break_except will compile. DBMS_TRACE is designed to capture run-time problems, not compile-time problems. To continue in the same session creating routines that are not enabled for tracing, you could execute the following ALTER SESSION command:

```
ALTER SESSION SET PLSQL_DEBUG=FALSE;
```

Executing DBMS_TRACE.SET_PLSQL_TRACE(8) begins enabled exception tracing. Executing break_except generates records into the Udump trace file on the server.

```
----------- PL/SQL TRACE INFORMATION -----------
Levels set :  8
Trace:     Pre-defined exception - OER 1422 at line 7
              of PROCEDURE SCOTT.BREAK_EXCEPT:
Trace:     Pre-defined exception - OER 6502 at line 11
              of PROCEDURE SCOTT.BREAK_EXCEPT:
```

The routine is listed where the exception was raised, with the line number of the code in the routine where the problem occurs and the error number of the problem. OER 1422 is *ORA-01422 exact fetch returns more than requested number of rows;* the SELECT statement generates it. OER 6502 is *ORA-06502 PL/SQL: numeric or value error;* it is generated by the variable assignment in the EXCEPTIONS section. Executinsg DBMS_TRACE.SET_PLSQL_TRACE(2) begins enabled-routine call tracing. Again, executing break_except generates records into the Udump trace file on the server.

```
------------ PL/SQL TRACE INFORMATION -----------
Levels set :  2
Trace:    PROCEDURE SCOTT.BREAK_EXCEPT:
          BREAK_EXCEPT Stack depth = 2
Trace:    PROCEDURE SCOTT.TIMER:
             TIMER Stack depth = 3
```

The output shows the routines called and the order in which they were called. The stack depth gives the call-order. Finally, to end the tracing session, you can execute the following DBMS_TRACE procedure:

```
EXECUTE DBMS_TRACE.CLEAR_PLSQL_TRACE
```

Although the demonstration is simple, it shows that DBMS_TRACE is useful at tracking both run-time routine calls and run-time exceptions and thus makes a handy addition to the debugging arsenal.

# Tips Review

Oracle8i enables native dynamic SQL to now be issued within PL/SQL with ease. Invoker-rights routines are useful in code management and code sharing. To introduce autonomous transactions, you can use PL/SQL code that audits and tracks database objects and routine usage. Temporary tables are useful as tools for maintaining a user's state, for boosting subquery processing, and for enhancing distributive processing. Bulk binding collectors passed between the PL/SQL engine and the SQL engine can be used to improve performance. You can also bulk bind in native dynamic SQL. In addition, performance boosts can be obtained through the use of the NOCOPY parameter flag to pass collections between PL/SQL routines. Extra performance gains are also possible when bulk binding is used with NOCOPY. The new PL/SQL built-in package DBMS_PROFILER monitors the execution times of named routines on a line-by-line basis. The new package DBMS_TRACE monitors run-time PL/SQL routine calls and exceptions by acting as a debugging tool.

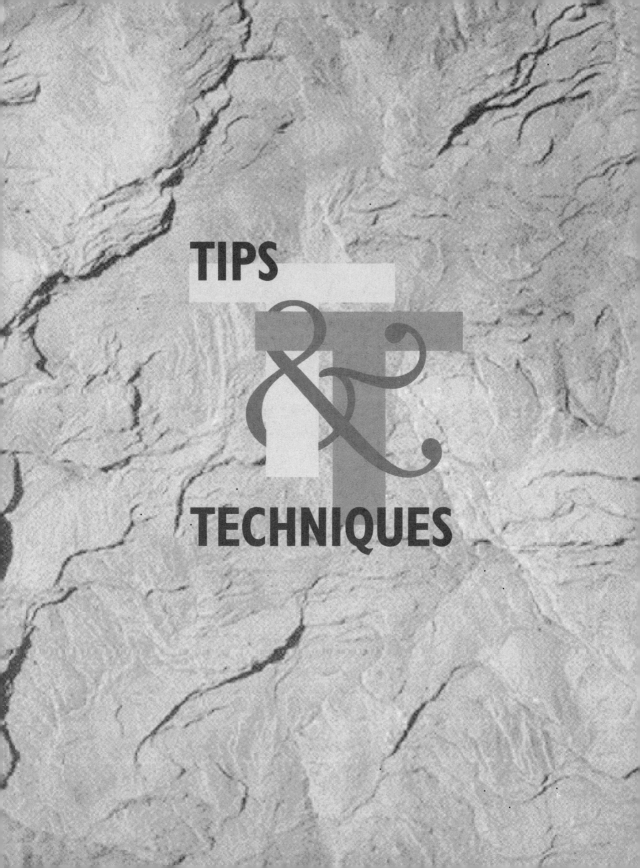

TIPS & TECHNIQUES

# CHAPTER
## 9

## SQLJ and JDBC

The JDBC and SQLJ Tips in this chapter fall into four categories: improvement of JDBC performance; exploiting of Oracle object-relational types and collections; streaming of Oracle LONG and Large Object (LOB) columns; and use of stored procedures with Java.

The following tips on improving JDBC performance are discussed:

■ Casting to the Oracle-Specific Types

■ Logging JDBC Calls

■ SQL Exception

■ Handling SQL Nulls

■ Disabling auto-commit mode to avoid commits after every DML statement

■ Using the `oracle.sql` package for efficiency and precision

■ Speeding up data access with ROWIDs

■ Using prepared statements to avoid unnecessary compilation overhead

■ Reducing network round trips by prefetching rows, batching updates, and defining column types

■ Closing `Connection`, `Statement`, and `ResultSet` objects to free valuable resources

■ Using JDBC connection pooling to avoid frequently creating connections

■ Enhancing concurrency with Java multithreading in client-side Java programs

Oracle8i offers a variety of object-relational features to model complex real-world objects. The following tips on using Oracle collections from JDBC are presented:

■ Retrieving Oracle VARRAYs and nested tables

■ Retrieving Oracle object types

Oracle LONG columns and, more importantly, Large Object (LOB) columns are used for the storing of unstructured data, notably multimedia files. The challenge of streaming these large data types through JDBC is the subject of the third category of tips, which include the following:

■ Caveats on streaming LONG and LONG RAW columns

■ Streaming LOBs

The chapter concludes with the following tips on using stored procedures with Java:

- Using the Server-Side JDBC Driver
- Using `loadjava` to load Java programs into the database
- Writing call specs to publish Java procedures in the Oracle data dictionary
- Calling Java stored procedures from SQL, PL/SQL, and database triggers
- Calling stored procedures from JDBC

No attempt is made to discuss the basics of JDBC and SQLJ; it is assumed that you know how to create connections and statements and to iterate through result sets.

# Preliminary Remarks

The Tips & Techniques used in this chapter exploit Oracle JDBC driver extensions to the standard JDBC API. The extensions are supported by all three Oracle JDBC drivers—Thin, OCI, and Server-Side—with exactly the same syntax, giving you the flexibility of deploying a program as an applet, as a client-side application, or as a stored procedure.

This section provides an overview of these extensions, setting the stage for Tips & Techniques presented later in the chapter. It also includes techniques for trapping exceptions and logging JDBC calls to help in debugging JDBC applications as well as a few comments on treating SQL NULL values in JDBC.

## Standard JDBC Packages versus Oracle JDBC Packages

Standard JDBC classes and interfaces are contained in the `java.sql` package. The JDBC 2.0 API adds another package `javax.sql`, known as the JDBC Standard Extension; the `java.sql` package is now known as the JDBC core API.

Oracle JDBC implementations and extensions are located primarily in three packages: `oracle.jdbc.driver` and `oracle.sql`, for JDBC; and `oracle.sqlj.runtime`, for SQLJ.

**NOTE**
*Currently, Oracle JDBC drivers have implemented some but not all of the JDBC 2.0 interfaces. Those that are supported can be found in the* `oracle.jdbc2` *package.*

**THE ORACLE.JDBC.DRIVER PACKAGE**    This package contains Oracle's connection and performance extensions to JDBC. Classes from this package that are used in this chapter are shown in Table 9-1.

| Oracle-Specific JDBC Class | Features Used in This Chapter |
| --- | --- |
| `OracleConnection` Implements `java.sql.Connection`. | Methods to enable or disable auto-commit mode. |
| `OracleStatement` Implements `java.sql.Statement`. Superclass of `OraclePreparedStatement` and `OracleCallableStatement`. | Methods to set Oracle performance extensions for individual statements. |
| `OraclePreparedStatement` Implements `java.sql.PreparedStatement`. Extends `OracleStatement`. | `setXXX` methods to bind `oracle.sql` objects to a prepared statement. |
| `OracleCallableStatement` Implements `java.sql.CallableStatement`. Extends `OraclePreparedStatement`. | `getXXX` methods to retrieve data in `oracle.sql` objects; `setXXX` methods to bind `oracle.sql` objects to a callable statement (inherited from `OraclePreparedStatement`). Used for calling stored procedures. |
| `OracleResultSet` Implements `java.sql.ResultSet`. | `getXXX` methods to retrieve data in `oracle.sql` format. |
| `OracleTypes` | Defines constants that are used to identify SQL types. |

**TABLE 9-1.**  *Classes in the* `oracle.jdbc.driver` *Package Used in This Chapter*

**THE ORACLE.SQL PACKAGE**    This package contains classes that map to Oracle SQL data types and act as Java wrappers for raw SQL data. The `oracle.sql.Datum` class is parent to all these classes.

The classes can be grouped into two categories:

- The classes CHAR, DATE, and NUMBER substitute for standard JDBC classes, using the methods shown in Table 9-2. In some situations, these classes yield better performance and precision over their standard JDBC counterparts—a topic discussed in the Tip "Using the `oracle.sql` Package for Efficiency and Precision."

- The remaining classes, ARRAY, BFILE, BLOB, CLOB, LONG, RAW, LONG RAW, REF, ROWID, and STRUCT, can be placed in a second category. In addition to acting as wrappers for raw SQL data, they provide methods for manipulating Oracle object types, collections, and LOBs. Table 9-3 shows methods that retrieve data into these types and the Tips that discuss them. With the exception of RAW and ROWID, these classes have corresponding JDBC 2.0 classes. RAW is used to hold the Oracle RAW data type. ROWID is

| Oracle SQL Data Type | Standard Methods for Retrieving SQL Type | OracleResultSet Substitute Methods |
|---|---|---|
| CHAR and VARCHAR2 | `String getString()` | `oracle.sql.CHAR getCHAR()` |
| NUMBER | `java.math.BigDecimal getBigDecimal()` or `int getInt()` or `long getLong()` or `float getFloat()` or `short getShort()` | `oracle.sql.NUMBER getNUMBER()` |
| DATE | `java.sql.Timestamp getTimeStamp()` | `oracle.sql.DATE getDATE()` |

**TABLE 9-2.** *Standard JDBC Methods and their* `oracle.sql` *Substitute Methods for Retrieving Data from a* `ResultSet`

| Oracle SQL Data Type | Standard Methods for Retrieving SQL Type | OracleResultSet Substitute Methods |
|---|---|---|
| VARRAY, Nested Table | `java.sql.Array getArray` (JDBC 2.0) | `oracle.sql.ARRAY getArray()` |
| BFILE | ___ | `oracle.sql.BFILE getBFILE()` See "Tips on Streaming Data with JDBC." |
| BLOB | `java.sql.Blob getBlob` (JDBC 2.0) | `oracle.sql.BLOB getBLOB()` See "Tips on Streaming Data with JDBC." |
| CLOB | `java.sql.Clob getClob` (JDBC 2.0) | `oracle.sql.CLOB getCLOB()` See "Tips on Streaming Data with JDBC." |
| LONG | `byte[] getBytes()` or `InputStream getAsciiStream()` | `byte[] getBytes()` or `InputStream getAsciiStream()` See "Tips on Streaming Data with JDBC." |
| Object Reference | `java.sql.Ref getRef()` (JDBC 2.0) | `oracle.sql.REF getREF()` |

**TABLE 9-3.** *Additional Oracle SQL Types and their* `oracle.sql` *Mappings*

| Oracle SQL<br>Data Type | Standard Methods for<br>Retrieving SQL Type | OracleResultSet<br>Substitute Methods |
|---|---|---|
| RAW, LONG RAW | `byte[] getBytes()`<br>or `InputStream`<br>`getBinaryStream()` | `oracle.sql.RAW getRAW()` |
| REF CURSOR | Materialized as<br>`java.sql.ResultSet` | Materialized as<br>`java.sql.ResultSet.` |
| ROWID | `String getString()` | `oracle.sql.ROWID`<br>`getROWID()` See "Using ROWID<br>as a Speedy Way to Access Rows in<br>a SQL Statement." |
| Oracle Object | `java.sql.Struct`<br>(JDBC 2.0) | `getOracleObject()` returns<br>class specified in type map or<br>`oracle.sql.STRUCT` if no type<br>map. See "Exploiting Oracle<br>Collections and Object Types." |

**TABLE 9-3.** *Additional Oracle SQL Types and their* `oracle.sql` *Mappings* (continued)

used to hold the ROWID data type STRUCT is provided as a default type for storing an arbitrary Oracle database object for which no type map entry is provided.

**THE ORACLE.SQLJ.RUNTIME PACKAGE**   One class in this package is of immediate relevance to this chapter: `oracle.sqlj.runtime.Oracle`. It provides methods for establishing and installing SQLJ database connections through `getConnection` and `connect` methods.

## Casting to Oracle-Specific Types

Use of Oracle-specific extensions requires casting standard JDBC objects to Oracle-specific objects where necessary. As an example, consider the `OracleResultSet` class, which implements the `java.sql.ResultSet` interface. When you execute a SELECT statement using a standard JDBC `Statement` object, a `java.sql.ResultSet` object is returned. `java.sql.ResultSet` will suffice if your needs are limited to standard JDBC methods. However, to use Oracle extensions, you must use `OracleResultSet`. Two approaches are available to you:

■ Create a `java.sql.ResultSet` object and later cast it to an `OracleResultSet` whenever you need to use Oracle extensions.

The following example assumes that a `Statement` object `stmt` is already created.

```
ResultSet rs = stmt.executeQuery ("SELECT * FROM dual");
```

You can cast `rs` to an `OracleOracleResultSet` object as follows:

```
OracleResultSet ors = (OracleResultSet)rs;
```

Note that `rs` is unchanged with the casting; only the type by which the Java compiler identifies the object is changed.

■ Create the object as an `OracleResultSet` from the outset. For example, assume you have already created a `Statement` object `stmt`. Now, you can create an `OracleResultSet` object directly:

```
OracleResultSet ors stmt.executeQuery("SELECT * FROM dual");
```

If you create an Oracle object from the very beginning, you avoid the inconvenience of casting it every time you need Oracle-specific functionality.

## Logging JDBC Calls

To aid in debugging, you can log JDBC calls by using the following line in your JDBC application:

```
java.io.PrintStream.DriverManager.setLogStream(System.out);
```

This sets the logging PrintStream used by the DriverManager.

## SQLException

When an error occurs in JDBC, a `java.sql.SQLException` invariably gets thrown. The `java.lang.Exception` is the superclass of `java.lang.SQLException`, and the superclass's `getMessage` method provides sufficient information about the error in most cases.

Two additional methods can help debug errors:

■ The `printStackTrace` method of the `Exception` class (inherited from `java.lang.Throwable`) prints a trace to a specified output stream.

■ The `getNextException` method of the `SQLException` class allows multiple `SQLException` instances to be chained together—a useful feature as a single error can generate more than one `SQLException`.

The following code uses `getMessage` and then `getNextException` in a loop to process all `SQLException` instances in the chain. It also calls `printStackTrace` to print a trace to the standard output.

```
catch (SQLException e) {
  System.err.println("SQLException caught: " + e.getMessage());
  while((e = e.getNextException()) != null) {
    System.err.println(e.getMessage());
  }
  e.printStackTrace();
```

## Handling SQL NULLs

You often encounter SQL NULL values in columns being retrieved in JDBC. How does JDBC convert SQL NULLs to Java types? Different return values are returned, depending on which `getXXX` method you use:

- **null**   For any `getXXX` method that returns an object, a Java null is returned. If null is used where an object is required, Java will throw the infamous `NullPointerException`.

- **0**   For methods `getShort`, `getInt`, `getFloat`, `getLong`, and `getByte`, which return Java scalar types `short`, `int`, `float`, `long`, and `byte`, respectively, a zero value is returned.

- **false**   In the case of the `getBoolean` method, a false is returned.

The constants zero and false were arbitrarily chosen by the JDBC designers to signify null, since Java scalar types cannot represent null. Methods that return zero or false pose a problem: how can you detect SQL NULLs unambiguously, given that zero and false can be valid data values? JDBC's work-around to the problem is the `ResultSet` class's `wasNull` method, which returns true if the last column read was SQL NULL.

Alternatively, you can substitute a method that returns zero and false with either a `getObject` method (which returns data into a `java.lang.Object`) or a `getOracleObject` method (which returns data into an `oracle.sql.Datum`). Both `getObject` and `getOracleObject` will return a Java null if a SQL NULL is encountered. You can then downcast the `Object` or `Datum` to the required Java or `oracle.sql` object.

# JDBC and SQLJ Performance Tips

To achieve portability of applications among different relational databases, JavaSoft's JDBC specification does not specify the mechanism by which database access should occur. The specification merely defines a set of Java interfaces that vendors must implement in their JDBC drivers. As you saw in Chapter 2, all three flavors of Oracle JDBC drivers (Thin, OCI, and Server-Side) support the 1.22 JDBC specification for relational database support and parts of the 2.0 specification that extend 1.22 to object-relational types, collections, and LOBs. In addition, Oracle JDBC drivers provide Oracle-specific extensions. Together these extensions provide a variety of ways for improving the performance of JDBC and SQLJ applications.

## Disabling Auto-Commit Mode to Avoid COMMITS after Every DML Statement

Auto-commit mode tells the database to issue a commit after every DML statement. Auto-commit is not limited to Java programming; it can be used in PL/SQL or SQL*Plus and is available in other databases, too. Auto-commit mode is a programming convenience, since it frees you from issuing commits manually. However, auto-commit mode incurs the following serious disadvantages:

- Slower performance, because a commit is issued after each INSERT, UPDATE, and DELETE statement.

- An inability to group several DML statements into one transaction and to roll back all changes if any part of the transaction fails.

- An inability to do batch updates, since batch updates require that auto-commit be disabled.

- An inability to perform SELECT FOR UPDATE queries. With auto-commit mode enabled, you will get an "ORA-01002 fetch out of sequence" error as a result of using a SELECT FOR UPDATE cursor after a commit.

For these reasons, you are better off managing transactions using COMMIT and ROLLBACK statements, with auto-commit disabled.

**NOTE**
*The Oracle Server-Side JDBC Driver does not support auto-commits.*

### Auto-Commit Settings
Beware! Auto-commit mode defaults in JDBC differ from those in SQLJ.

**AUTO-COMMIT DEFAULTS IN JDBC**    On a client, when you create a JDBC `Connection` object or an `OracleConnection` object, auto-commit mode is set to true by default, in accordance with the JDBC specification.

You cannot specify the auto-commit mode at the time you create a connection object. Instead, you must change the auto-commit mode using the connection object's `setAutoCommit` method. For example, the following statement turns off auto-commit mode:

```
conn.setAutoCommit(false);
```

where `conn` is a `Connection` object or an `OracleConnection` object.

Do not try to disable auto-commit mode while a transaction is open—that is, when there are outstanding changes that are uncommitted. In fact, it is a good practice to disable auto-commit mode immediately after instantiating a `Connection` or `OracleConnection` object.

**AUTO-COMMIT DEFAULTS IN SQLJ**     To establish a database connection in SQLJ, you typically use one of the `getConnection` methods or one of the `connect` methods of the `oracle.sqlj.runtime.Oracle` class:

- A `connect` method is used when a single, implicitly shared connection context is sufficient.

- A `getConnection` method is used when multiple or explicitly passed connection contexts are required.

Both `connect` and `getConnection` come in many method signatures. You can use a method that does not take the auto-commit parameter as part of its signature—in which case, auto-commit mode is false by default. Alternatively, you can specify the auto-commit parameter explicitly. Notice that the auto-commit `boolean` parameter is always the last parameter in these methods.

Once auto-commit is turned off, you can save changes you have made since the last commit, using the following:

```
#sql { commit };
```

To roll back changes since the last commit, use

```
#sql { rollback };
```

 **CAUTION**
*On a client that has auto-commit disabled, make sure that you explicitly commit changes before you close a connection context object using ctx.close()—that is, the close method without any parameters. If you do not, uncommitted changes will be rolled back. Even if you use ctx.close(KEEP_CONNECTION), it is wise to explicitly commit changes before closing a connection context object.*

# Using the oracle.sql Package
# for Efficiency and Precision

The `oracle.sql` package contains classes that map to all Oracle SQL data types and act as Java wrappers for raw SQL data (see Tables 9-2 and Table 9-3). These classes include `ARRAY`, `BFILE`, `BLOB`, `CHAR`, `CLOB`, `DATE`, `NUMBER`, `RAW`, `REF`, `ROWID`, and `STRUCT`—each extending the abstract class `oracle.sql.Datum`. Noticeably missing are `VARCHAR` and `VARCHAR2`; these string types can be mapped to `CHAR`.

Just as standard JDBC provides a `getXXX` method and `setXXX` method for each standard Java type, `OracleResultSet` and `OracleCallableStatement` classes provide a `getXXX` method and `setXXX` method for each `oracle.sql` type. For example, the `getDATE` method returns an `oracle.sql.DATE` object.

## Benefits

Two benefits can arise from using `oracle.sql` types instead of `java.lang` types: efficiency and precision. All `oracle.sql` objects store SQL data as byte arrays. Unlike `java.lang` objects, they do not reformat the data or perform any character-set conversions. The `oracle.sql` classes are immutable (like `java.lang.String`), allowing for possible optimization of data copying between SQL and Java by Oracle JDBC drivers.

## When to Use `oracle.sql` Objects

With `oracle.sql` objects, you can reap the advantages of efficiency and precision only if you do not need to convert the `oracle.sql` objects to Java objects. If you are moving data in and out of tables without the need for manipulating the data, you stand to gain by using `oracle.sql` objects. On the other hand, if you need to do complicated mathematical operations, to perform string manipulations, or to display data, you will probably want to use standard JDBC classes.

**MATHEMATICAL OPERATIONS**    Consider mathematical operations first. Suppose that an `OracleResultSet` object `ors` has already been created and that four `oracle.sql.NUMBER` objects are declared and assigned as follows:

```
oracle.sql.NUMBER n1, n2, n3, n4;
n1 = ors.getNUMBER(1);
n2 = ors.getNUMBER(2);
n3 = ors.getNUMBER(3);
n4 = ors.getNUMBER(4);
```

The calls to `getNUMBER` do not involve conversions and therefore are fast and suffer no loss of precision.

For arithmetic operations, the `oracle.sql.NUMBER` class contains the methods add, sub, mul, and div for addition, subtraction, multiplication, and division. The following line is equivalent to the formula n5 = (n1 + n2) * n3 / (n4 − n2):

```
oracle.sql.NUMBER n5 = (n1.add(n2)).mul(n3).div(n4.sub(n2));
```

The syntax is unintuitive. It is also error-prone: care must be taken with the sequence of the `add`, `sub`, mul, and div methods, as well as the parentheses. However, the syntax is necessary because Java operators, unlike C++ operators, cannot be overloaded. The following line will give compile errors:

```
oracle.sql.NUMBER n5 = (n1 + n2) * n3 / (n4 − n2); // Bad syntax
```

When the compiler javac encounters the expression (n1 + n2), for example, it gives the error "Incompatible type for +. Can't convert oracle.sql.NUMBER to int."

In addition to the `add`, `sub`, `mul`, and `div` methods, `oracle.sql.NUMBER` has the following features:

- Constructors to construct `oracle.sql.NUMBER` objects from Java types such as `double`, `int`, and `java.math.BigDecimal`. These constructors throw a `SQLException` on over/underflow of the NUMBER exponent and/or mantissa.

- Static methods to convert `oracle.sql.NUMBER` data to Java types `byte`, `short`, `integer`, `long`, `double`, `String`, `BigInteger`, and `BigDecimal`. In many of these methods, a `SQLException` will be thrown if the Oracle NUMBER exponent is out of range.

- Methods for rounding and for performing trigonometric, logarithmic, and square root functions.

- Methods that return constants such as pi and positive infinity.

The following line uses the conversion method `doubleValue` to convert `oracle.sql` objects n1, n2, n3, and n4 into Java doubles:

```
double d = (n1.doubleValue() + n2.doubleValue())
       * n3.doubleValue / n4.doubleValue();
```

The resultant double will be rounded on loss of precision. However, an exponent over/underflow cannot occur with the `doubleValue` method (or the `toDouble` method), since the exponent range of an IEEE double is greater than that of an `oracle.sql.NUMBER`.

A final point: there is no benefit from using `oracle.sql` objects for numeric operations that use `java.lang` or `java.math`, since you will have to convert the objects into Java scalar types (`long`, `double`, `short`, `int`) to make use of the packages.

**STRING MANIPULATIONS**    Unfortunately, `oracle.sql.CHAR` does not provide any methods for concatenating or parsing strings or for formatting numbers into strings. You will have to use standard Java classes to perform such operations.

## Example

The lack of a rich set of methods in `oracle.sql.CHAR` underscores the purpose of `oracle.sql` objects in general. As illustrated in the following example, `oracle.sql` types are intended to be wrappers to hold raw data so that the data can be pumped back into the database.

The example selects the top-five list prices (five largest list prices) from the demo.price table. The corresponding product_id, description, list_price, start_date, and end_date are retrieved into `oracle.sql` objects using `getXXX` methods and then displayed with `System.out.println`.

```
Statement stmt = conn.createStatement();
String q = "SELECT *"
        +  " FROM ("
        +  "      SELECT a.product_id, RPAD(description, 30, '.'),"
        +  "             list_price, start_date, end_date"
        +  "        FROM demo.price a, demo.product b"
        +  "         WHERE a.product_id = b.product_id"
        +  "      ORDER BY list_price DESC)"
        +  " WHERE rownum < 6";
OracleResultSet ors = (OracleResultSet)stmt.executeQuery(q);
// Format as Deutsche Marks
NumberFormat nf = NumberFormat.getCurrencyInstance(Locale.GERMAN);

while (ors.next()) {
  oracle.sql.NUMBER id = ors.getNUMBER(1);
  oracle.sql.CHAR desc = ors.getCHAR(2);
  oracle.sql.NUMBER price = ors.getNUMBER(3);
  oracle.sql.DATE startDate = ors.getDATE(4);
  oracle.sql.DATE endDate = ors.getDATE(5);

  System.out.println(id.intValue() + "..."
          + desc.stringValue()
          + nf.format(price.doubleValue()) + ".."
          + startDate.stringValue() + " - "
          + ((endDate == null) ? "" : endDate.stringValue()));
}
```

Notice that the getCHAR method is used to retrieve the description column, which has a VARCHAR2 SQL type (a getVARCHAR2 method does not exist). Also notice that the SQL function RPAD is used to format the description column in the SELECT statement. Using SQL functions is one way to compensate for the lack of functionality in oracle.sql.CHAR.

If there is a NULL in the end_date column, the oracle.sql.DATE variable endDate will be assigned a null. An invocation of the endDate.stringValue method with endDate equal to null will result in a run time NullPointer Exception—hence the need to test for NULLs with the expression

```
(endDate == null) ? "" : endDate.stringValue()
```

The output is as follows:

```
104352..DUNK BASKETBALL PROFESSIONAL..58,30 DM...6/1/1990 0:0:0 -
100890..ACE TENNIS NET................58,00 DM...1/1/1989 0:0:0 -
100890..ACE TENNIS NET................54,00 DM...6/1/1988 0:0:0 - 12/31/1988 0:0:0
104352..DUNK BASKETBALL PROFESSIONAL..54,00 DM...1/1/1990 0:0:0 - 5/31/1990 0:0:0
104352..DUNK BASKETBALL PROFESSIONAL..50,00 DM...1/1/1989 0:0:0 - 12/31/1989 0:0:0
```

This example is a contrived one. As in any case in which you need to display data, oracle.sql objects are no better than java.lang objects. (It is necessary to use java.lang types when displaying data with System.out.println.) In the example, no conversions were necessary when the data was fetched into oracle.sql objects—id, desc, price, startDate, endDate—using getXXX methods. Later, however, in the System.out.println statement, these performance gains are lost when id, desc, price, startDate, and endDate are converted to the corresponding Java types using the conversion methods shown in Table 9-4.

# Using ROWID as a Speedy Way to Access Rows in a SQL Statement

Each row in an Oracle table has an identification tag called a ROWID. It can be thought of as a pseudo-column that has a unique value for each row. A ROWID gives you the physical address of a row. It is generally the fastest way to access a row in a table, faster even than using a primary key. When used in a WHERE clause, ROWIDs can speed up UPDATE and DELETE operations.

Oracle's JDBC drivers do not support the java.sql.ResultSet. getCursorName and java.sql.Statement.setCursorName JDBC methods. Oracle supports similar functionality through the access of ROWIDs.

| SQL Column and Data Type | Java Variable | Converted to `java.lang` Type with |
|---|---|---|
| product_id NUMBER(6) | `oracle.sql.NUMBER id` | `intValue()` |
| description VARCHAR2(30) | `oracle.sql.CHAR desc` | `stringValue()` |
| price NUMBER(8, 2) | `oracle.sql.NUMBER price` | `doubleValue()` |
| start_date DATE | `oracle.sql.DATE startDate` | `stringValue()` |
| end_date DATE | `oracle.sql.DATE endDate` | `stringValue()` |

**TABLE 9-4.** *Data Type Transformations Performed in the Example in "Using the* `oracle.sql` *Package for Efficiency and Precision"*

**CAUTION**
*ROWIDs can change if data in the table is exported and imported.*

## Retrieving and Binding ROWIDs

To retrieve a ROWID, include the ROWID pseudo-column in the SELECT clause of your query as you would use a normal column. The ROWID can be retrieved into either a `String`, using one of the `getString` methods, or into an `oracle.sql.ROWID`, using one of the `getROWID` methods.

To bind a ROWID to a `PreparedStatement` parameter, use one of the `setROWID` methods. Alternatively, if you use a `String` to hold a ROWID, use one of the `setString` methods.

All `get` and `set` methods discussed here belong to the `OracleResultSet` class.

## A SQLJ Example that Uses ROWID to Do In-Place Updates

This SQLJ example demonstrates how you may access and manipulate ROWID data to do in-place updates. The goal is to convert the column "function" in the demo.job table into mixed-case.

The core of the program is found in the `demoROWID` method. A "SELECT FOR UPDATE" SQL statement retrieves the rowid, job_id, and function columns from the demo.job table into a SQLJ result set iterator. The rowid value is then used in the WHERE clause of an UPDATE statement. The function column is converted to mixed-case by calling `toMixedCase`, a method implemented in the following example. `toMixedCase` capitalizes the first character of a string token, converting the rest of the token to lowercase.

```java
import java.sql.*;
import oracle.jdbc.driver.*;
import oracle.sql.*;
import oracle.sqlj.runtime.Oracle;

public class sqljRowID {

  sqljRowID(String url, String user, String pwd) throws SQLException {
    Oracle.connect(url, user, pwd);
  }

  // Returns a mixed-case version of token.
  String toMixedCase(String token) {
    String s1 = new String("");
    if (token.length() != 0)
      s1 = token.substring(0, 1).toUpperCase() +
      token.substring(1).toLowerCase();
    return s1;
  }

  #sql iterator JobIter (oracle.sql.ROWID rowID, int jobID,
             String jobFunction);

  // Update the function column in demo.job to mixed-case.
  public void demoROWID() throws SQLException {
      JobIter jobs = null;
      #sql jobs = {    SELECT rowid, job_id AS jobID, function as jobFUNCTION
                       FROM demo.job FOR UPDATE
      };

    while (jobs.next()) {
      #sql {   UPDATE demo.job SET function = :(toMixedCase(jobs.jobFunction()))
              WHERE rowid = :(jobs.rowID())
      };

    #sql {COMMIT};
    jobs.close();
  }

  public static void main(String args[]) throws SQLException {
    if (args.length != 3) {
```

```
   System.out.println("Usage: java sqljRowID <url> <user> <pwd>");
   System.exit(0);
 }

 sqljRowID aTester = null;

 try {
  aTester = new sqljRowID(args[0], args[1], args[2]);
  aTester.demoROWID();
 } catch (SQLException e) {
  // Print all the errors in the chain
  do {
   System.err.println("SQLException caught: " +
              e.getMessage());
  } while((e = e.getNextException()) != null);
 } catch (Exception e) {
  e.printStackTrace();
 }
 }
}
```

## Using Prepared Statements to Avoid Unnecessary Compilation Overhead

PreparedStatement is a specialization of the Statement class. Both classes are standard in the JDBC specification. If you frequently execute a particular SQL query, use a PreparedStatement object instead of a Statement object; it will reduce execution time in most cases.

Table 9-5 contrasts the use of the PreparedStatement with that of the Statement class. When you create a PreparedStatement object, you provide a string containing a SQL statement to the object. For example,

```
PreparedStatement ps = conn.prepareStatement("SELECT * FROM dual");
```

where conn is either a Connection or an OracleConnection object.

Typically, the SQL statement will be sent to Oracle right away, where it will be compiled. Whenever you execute the PreparedStatement object, Oracle can run the precompiled SQL statement without the overhead of compiling it each time.

PreparedStatement can be used for SQL statements with or without parameters. You can prepare a query with parameters and use it many times, each time supplying different values for the parameters. You indicate parameters with question mark placeholders, a technique best explained with an example.

| Statement | Prepared Statement |
|---|---|
| `// SQL String. Usually static`<br><br>`String q = "<select statement>";`<br><br>`Statement stmt =`<br>`conn.createStatement();`<br><br>`ResultSet rs =`<br>`stmt.executeQuery(q)` | `// SQL String with optional ?`<br>`// placeholders`<br>`String q = "<select statement>";`<br><br>`PreparedStatement ps =`<br>`   conn.prepareStatement(q);`<br><br>`// Bind placeholders`<br>`ps.setXXX(1);`<br>`ps.setXXX(2);`<br>`   . . .`<br>`ResultSet rs =`<br>`ps.executeQuery();` |

**TABLE 9-5.**   *Using* `PreparedStatement` *Versus* `Statement`

Let's say you frequently use a SQL query that selects the last names of employees who work for a certain manager. In addition, you want to restrict the employees to those whose salary exceeds a certain amount. The following code snippet creates a prepared statement to do just this. It assumes that a `Connection` object `conn` has been successfully created.

```
String q = "SELECT last_name" +
        "  FROM demo.employee" +
        " WHERE manager_id = ? AND salary > ?";
PreparedStatement ps = conn.prepareStatement(q);
```

Note the '?' IN parameter placeholders. Before executing the prepared statement, you must bind these parameters to actual values. Use one of the `setXXX` methods in `PreparedStatement` or `OraclePreparedStatement`, such as `setInt`, `setDouble`, or `setString`.

```
// Bind 7505 to the 1st question mark placeholder
ps.setInt(1, 7505); // The SQL type of the column manager_id is NUMBER(4)

// Bind 500.00 to the 2nd question mark placeholder
ps.setDouble(2, 500.00); // The SQL type of the column salary is NUMBER(7,2)
```

Notice that the host data is bound by position. (SQLJ allows binding by name.)

To use `oracle.sql` types, you would have to cast the `PreparedStatement` object to an `OraclePreparedStatement` object. `OraclePreparedStatement`, a class that extends standard JDBC prepared statement functionality, provides `setXXX` methods, such as `setBLOB`, for binding specific `oracle.sql` types into prepared statements.

Once all parameters are bound to values, you can execute the query. When you reuse the query, you will set one or more parameters that have changed. Once a parameter has been set with a value, it will retain that value until it is reset to another value or the method clearParameters is called.

The following example chooses five managers from the demo.employee table and displays the employees they manage who earn a salary greater than $500.00. In order to simulate user-choices in a real-world application, a randomizer class is used to choose the managers randomly.

```
String q = "SELECT last_name" +
           "  FROM demo.employee" +
           " WHERE manager_id = ? AND salary > ?";
OraclePreparedStatement ops = (OraclePreparedStatement)conn.prepareStatement(q);


ResultSet rs = null;
ManagerRandomizer mr = new ManagerRandomizer();
// Display 5 randomly chosen managers and the employees they manage

// Bind 500.00 to position 2. The salary column is of type NUMBER(7,2)
// No reason for this to be inside the for loop since it doesn't change.
  ops.setDouble(2, 500.00);

for (int i = 0; i < 5; i++) {
  int managerID =  mr.next(); // Get a random Manager ID
  System.out.print("\nManager ID " + managerID + ": ");

  // Bind managerID to position 1. Note: column manager_id is of type NUMBER(4)
  ops.setInt(1, managerID);

  rs = ops.executeQuery();
  while (rs.next())
    System.out.print(rs.getString(1) + " ");
}
. . .
```

Don't concern yourself with the `ManagerRandomizer` class; assume that it holds manager IDs and that its `next` method returns a manager ID randomly. The following output is the result of one of the runs:

```
Manager ID 7569: FISHER ROBERTS
Manager ID 7839: DOYLE DENNIS BAKER JONES ALBERTS BLAKE CLARK
Manager ID 7566: SCOTT FORD
Manager ID 7698: ALLEN WARD MARTIN TURNER JAMES
Manager ID 7505: PETERS SHAW PORTER ROSS JENSEN
```

Had the example used `Statement` rather than `PreparedStatement`, the database would have had to compile the SQL statement five times instead of just once.

## Prefetching Rows into Client-Side Buffers to Reduce Network Round Trips

Standard JDBC pre-JDB 2.0 receives a result set for a query one row at a time, each row reflecting a round trip to the database. Oracle's JDBC drivers, however, support prefetching rows into client-side buffers, thereby reducing the number of round trips to the database.

You can set the number of rows to prefetch for all statements in your connection or for individual statements.

■ To set the number of rows to prefetch for all statements (that is, the default row prefetch value), use an `OracleConnection` object's `setDefaultRowPrefetch` method. If you do not change the default row prefetch value, Oracle will prefetch 10 rows.

**NOTE**
*The number of rows to prefetch is set to 1 whenever an Oracle JDBC Driver encounters a column containing a data stream.*

■ When a `Statement` or an `OracleStatement` object is instantiated, it gets the default row prefetch value from its associated `Connection` or `OracleConnection` object. To override an individual Statement's prefetch value, use the `setRowPrefetch` method. `setRowPrefetch` is analogous to JDBC 2.0's `setFetchSize` method of the `Statement` class and its subclasses.

The following example illustrates the use of the methods `setDefault RowPrefetch` and `setRowPrefetch`. It assumes that a `Connection` object conn has been instantiated.

```
// Set the default row prefetch value of conn to 50 rows
((OracleConnection)conn).setDefaultRowPrefetch(50);
Statement stmt = conn.createStatement(); //stmt gets conn's default. i.e 50
```

```
ResultSet rs1 = stmt.executeQuery("SELECT . . .");

// Override stmt's default row prefetch value. Set it to 25.
((OracleStatement)stmt).setRowPrefetch(25);
ResultSet rs2 = stmt.executeQuery("SELECT . . .");
```

In this example, the first `executeQuery` uses a row prefetch value of 50; the second uses a value of 25.

### Choosing a Row Prefetch Value

Increasing a row prefetch value above a certain cut-off point will yield diminishing returns for a particular query. You can estimate this cut-off point by comparing the performance of your query for different prefetch values as outlined in the following:

```
stmt.setRowPrefetch(N);
long startTime = System.currentTimeMillis();
ResultSet rs = stmt.executeQuery("SELECT . . ."); // Your query
while (rs.next()); // Loop through the result set
long timeTaken = System.currentTimeMillis() - startTime;
```

The larger N is, the more memory will be consumed by the client-side prefetch buffer. There is no maximum value for N.

## Batching Updates to Reduce Network Round Trips

Like row prefetching, batch updating improves performance by reducing the number of round trips to the database. With Oracle's JDBC drivers, you can accumulate UPDATEs and INSERTs at the client and send them to the database as one batch, in one network round trip. The number of executions to process in one batch can be controlled by setting a predefined batch value. Actual execution of all SQL statements occurs when the number of statements in the batch reaches this predefined value.

You can set the batch value for all statements or for individual statements in your connection.

- To set the batch value for all statements in a connection (that is, the default batch value), use the `setDefaultExecuteBatch` method in the `OracleConnection` class.

- To override a batch value for a particular statement, use the `setExecuteBatch` method in the `OraclePreparedStatement` class.

**NOTE**
*The Oracle JDBC drivers will automatically set the batch value to 1 if they encounter any stream bind types.*

You can "flush" a batch at any time (before the number of batched executions reaches the predetermined batch value) by using the `sendBatch` method in the `OraclePreparedStatement` class.

In the following example, the default batch value is overridden for an `OraclePreparedStatement` object named `ops`. The value is set to 50, using `setExecuteBatch(50)`:

```
final int START_ID = 500;
OraclePreparedStatement ops = (OraclePreparedStatement)conn.prepareStatement(
  "INSERT INTO demo.location (location_id, regional_group) VALUES (?,?)");
ops.setExecuteBatch(50);

// Insert 100 rows
for (int i = 1; i <= 100; i++) {
  ops.setInt(1, START_ID + i);
  ops.setString(2, "Region " + Integer.toString(START_ID + i));
  int r = ops.executeUpdate();
  if (r != 0)
    System.out.println("i=" + Integer.toString(i)
    + " : Rows Inserted=" + Integer.toString(r));
}
```

The resulting output shows that the INSERTs are executed only on the 50th and 100th statements.

```
i=50 : Rows Inserted=50
i=100 : Rows Inserted=50
```

Observe that an `executeUpdate` is issued to execute the prepared statement. `executeUpdate` is a versatile method: you can use it to execute prepared INSERT, UPDATE, or DELETE statements as well as to execute statements that return nothing—such as DDL statements. `executeUpdate` returns an int value representing the number of rows inserted, updated, or deleted. A zero is returned if no rows are affected—a feature exploited in the `if` statement of the example.

## Defining Column Types to Reduce Network Round Trips

Standard JDBC performs a query by first determining the data types that it should use for the columns of the result set. This is done by going to the database, resulting in a network round trip. JDBC then issues another query to get the data—in a second round trip. After receiving the data, it converts the data as necessary while populating the result set. Oracle JDBC drivers allow you to specify the types of the columns in an upcoming query, eliminating the first round trip to the database that would otherwise be necessary to describe the table.

You specify the type under which you will fetch data from a column using the following method in the `OracleStatement` class:

```
void defineColumnType(int column_index, int type);
```

For the column_index parameter, use 1 for the first column, 2 for the second column, and so on. For the type parameter, use static constants defined in the following two classes:

- The `java.sql.Types` class, which defines constants for identifying SQL types, including `Types.INTEGER`, `Types.FLOAT`, `Types.VARCHAR`, and `Types.VARBINARY`.

- The `oracle.jdbc.driver.OracleTypes` class, which defines constants for Oracle-specific types, including `OracleTypes.VARCHAR`, `OracleTypes.NUMBER`, and `OracleTypes.ROWID`.

**CAUTION**
*When you specify column types with the* `defineColumnType` *method, you must declare the types of* all *columns in the query. If you miss definitions or provide too many, a call to* `executeQuery` *will fail and a* `SQLException` *will be thrown.*

When you retrieve the data from the result set, use the `getXXX` method corresponding to the SQL type of the defined column. It is not mandatory, but it will give you the best performance because the data has already been converted to the right type.

The following example demonstrates the use of `defineColumnType`. It SELECTs from a random sample of rows in the demo.job table, using a SAMPLE clause in a SELECT statement. SAMPLE is a SQL feature introduced with Oracle8i, and it is particularly useful for data-mining applications.

```
// OracleStatement is required to use the define column type extension
OracleStatement ostmt = (OracleStatement)conn.createStatement();
String q = "SELECT job_id, function FROM demo.job SAMPLE (50)";

ostmt.defineColumnType(1, Types.INTEGER);
ostmt.defineColumnType(2, Types.VARCHAR);

OracleResultSet ors = (OracleResultSet)ostmt.executeQuery(q);
while (ors.next()) {
  int id = ors.getInt(1);
  String s = ors.getString(2);
  System.out.println(id + " " + s);
}
ors.close();
```

In the example, static constants are used from the `java.sql.Types` class for the type parameter in the `defineColumnType` method. Note that you must call `defineColumnType` *before* you instantiate the `OracleResultSet`; if you don't, you will get an exception: "Cannot do new defines until the current `ResultSet` is closed: `defineColumnType`."

## Closing Connection, Statement, and ResultSet Objects to Free Valuable Resources

You must explicitly close the following objects after you finish using them:

- `Connection` and `OracleConnection`
- `ResultSet` and `OracleResultSet` (and subclasses)
- `Statement` and `OracleStatement` (and subclasses)

Oracle JDBC does *not* implement finalize methods on these objects. This means that these objects are not automatically closed when garbage-collected. (Oracle intends to remedy this in a future release of Oracle JDBC.)

If you do not explicitly close these objects, serious memory leaks could occur. You might also get an "ORA-0100: maximum open cursors exceeded" error. The number of cursors a user process can have open at a time is set with the OPEN_CURSORS parameter in the INIT.ORA parameter file (the default value is 50). Closing a result set or statement releases the corresponding cursor in the database.

These objects may be closed via the `close` method.

## Using JDBC Connection Pooling to Avoid Frequently Creating Connections

You were cautioned to close JDBC connections in the section "Closing `Connection`, `Statement`, and `ResultSet` Objects to Free Valuable Resources." However, a different strategy is required for situations in which connections are frequently created and destroyed. Such situations often arise in middle-tier applications that service a large number of users—for example, a servlet that generates HTML pages in response to user requests. Because it takes several seconds to open a connection, opening and closing connections for each user request (or even for each user session) would degrade performance. Instead, the servlet could open a pool of JDBC connections that would remain "alive" and shared among the users.

Support for connection pooling has been added to the JDBC 2.0 API through two interfaces in the `javax.sql` package: `PooledConnection` and `ConnectionPoolDataSource`. A `PooledConnection` object represents a physical connection to a data source. A `ConnectionPoolDataSource` object is a factory for `PooledConnection` objects.

Although Oracle JDBC drivers currently do not have built-in support for JDBC 2.0 connection pooling, you can expect such support in the future. For now, you will have to code such functionality or use third-party packages. You should also be aware of the technologies described in the boxed section "Non-JDBC Connection Sharing Techniques."

## Enhancing Concurrency with Java Multithreading in Client-Side Java Programs

Multithreading enhances functionality and concurrency by allowing two or more simultaneous flows of control to accomplish multiple tasks in less time. This section examines the appropriateness of using Java threading in JDBC and SQLJ in both client-side and server-side (stored procedure) environments. You will see that no concurrency benefits can be derived from using server-side Java multithreading in Oracle8i.

Writing multithreaded applications is inherently difficult, but several features of Java make the process easier. Many threading features are built into the Java language itself; others are required by Java Virtual Machines. Java's threading model provides for threads and monitors. (A *thread* is a program's path of execution; *monitors* are a structured way of using semaphores to control access to shared resources.) In addition, standard Java classes are thread-safe, allowing multiple threads within an application to call the same method without interfering with each other. Finally, the JDBC specification requires that all JDBC class implementations must be thread-safe.

Java Multithreading

## Non-JDBC Connection Sharing Techniques

Here is a brief outline of several non-JDBC technologies that provide some of the capabilities of JDBC connection pooling.

*Oracle multithreaded server (MTS)* configuration enables many user processes to share very few server processes. (Conversely, the dedicated server configuration assigns each user a server process.) Java stored procedures can run either in dedicated server mode or in MTS mode, but EJBs and CORBA servers run only in MTS mode. MTS configures multiple dispatchers that broker user requests, passing them to server processes. MTS is leveraged to allow connections to the JVM to scale well. For more information, please see the section on "Database Connections" in Chapter 2 and the section on "Enabling the Multithreaded Server" in Chapter 3.

*Oracle server's connection pooling* (not to be confused with JDBC connection pooling) allows you to maximize the number of physical network connections to a multithreaded server. With connection pooling, a dispatcher's set of connections is shared among multiple client processes. Through the use of a time-out mechanism, a transport connection that has idled for a specific period of time is temporarily released. The released connection is made available for incoming clients, while a logical network session is still maintained with the previous idle connection. When the idle client needs the connection again, the physical connection is reestablished with the dispatcher.

*Connection concentration*, a feature available through Oracle Connection Manager (CMAN), increases the number of sessions a server can handle. With multiple Connection Managers, it is feasible to have thousands of concurrent users connecting to a server. CMAN leverages Net8's ability to multiplex multiple logical client sessions through a single connection to a multithreaded server. This improves server memory usage by enabling the server to use fewer connection end points for incoming requests. JDBC drivers can communicate to Oracle through Oracle Connection Manager. Details on Oracle's connection pooling and connection concentration can be found in the Oracle Net8 Administrator's Guide.

*Transaction managers* (TP monitors) are typically used in three-tier applications that support an extremely heavy volume of users and transactions. They perform transaction coordination, security functions, and resource scheduling and are often bundled with products that provide distributed component support. Examples of transaction managers include IBM's CICS and Microsoft's MTS (Microsoft Transaction Server).

**CAUTION**
*In Java 2, there is a new set of collection classes that extend java.util.Collection and java.util.Map that are not synchronized (and are therefore not thread-safe) but may be made synchronized externally with "synchronizing wrappers." These wrappers return a new synchronized collection backed by a specified collection. This new mechanism was designed with an eye toward efficiency, since synchronized methods are slower than unsynchronized ones.*

It cannot be overemphasized that, even in Java, complex issues—thread safety being the most important—must be thoroughly understood before you start writing complex multithreaded applications. These issues are beyond the scope of this book. There are several books devoted to Java multithreading. *Java Threads* by Scott Oaks and Henry Wong (O'Reilly, 1999), is as good an introduction as any. *Concurrent Programming in Java: Design Principles and Patterns* by Doug Lea (Addison Wesley, 1997), which is more advanced, is highly recommended.

**SERVER-SIDE JAVA MULTITHREADING**    Support for threading in Oracle's JVM was implemented only to be JDK compliant. Multithreaded Java programs can be loaded and executed on the Oracle8i database server without modification. However, there are no benefits to using Java threads in stored procedures, since threads in the Oracle8i JVM are severely restricted in functionality. Significantly, Java threads are cooperative, not preemptive; and run sequentially, not concurrently. As a result, Java threads in Oracle8i do not increase concurrency.

Most JVMs (the Oracle8i JVM is an exception) were developed as client-side JVMs for single-user environments. To achieve scalability in multiuser environments, these JVMs use threads to fork off user-sessions. This approach presents problems: programming and debugging threads are difficult, and more importantly it does not scale well enough to handle enterprise applications.

Oracle has taken a different approach to multiuser scalability: leveraging the multithreaded server rather than Java threads. In Oracle8i, when a user session is started, the user gets a "Virtual Virtual Machine," which can be thought of as the user's private JVM. Oracle recommends that you write your Oracle8i Java application as if it were to run for a single user, leaving multiuser scalability to be handled automatically by MTS.

**CLIENT-SIDE JAVA MULTITHREADING**    Multithreading can be put to numerous uses in client-side applications. A common one is the improvement of user-interface responsiveness—for example, by allowing a long-running SQL query to be cancelled by the user. The SQL query is started in one thread, and a stop button is monitored in another thread. When the user clicks on the stop button, the query is cancelled by calling the `cancel` method on the `Statement` object.

Another common use of multithreading is having the CPU stay busy during I/O waits. For instance, a Java client application that fetches data and then manipulates and displays the results could improve performance by running two threads concurrently—one to perform database access, the second to manipulate and display the results. While waiting for the data, the CPU is kept busy manipulating data and rendering data onto the screen.

# Exploiting Oracle Collections and Object Types with Java

With Oracle's object-relational features, you can create database objects that closely model complex real-world objects. A key feature of this technology is the ability to encapsulate data and behavior with user-defined data types—what Oracle terms "object types." In Oracle8i, Java can interact with database object types in several ways. You can implement database object type methods in Java (or PL/SQL or C++); generate Java classes from database object types; and access database object type data from Java using JDBC or SQLJ.

In addition to object types, Oracle provides collection structures: PL/SQL tables (index-by-tables), nested tables, and VARRAYs (variable-size arrays). Nested tables and VARRAYs can be used as data types of fields in tables and as attributes of objects and can be directly retrieved with JDBC. However, currently there is no direct way of retrieving PL/SQL tables with JDBC.

## Retrieving Oracle VARRAYs and Nested Tables

This section demonstrates how to retrieve Oracle VARRAYs and nested tables from JDBC. A simple table called varray_test_tab containing a VARRAY column is used as an example. A more complex example can be found in the Tip "Retrieving Oracle Object Types."

Here is how varray_test_tab is created and populated.

```
-- Array of primitive type VARCHAR
CREATE OR REPLACE TYPE varray_of_varchar AS VARRAY(5) OF VARCHAR2(10);
/
CREATE TABLE varray_test_tab (col1 varray_of_varchar);
/
INSERT INTO varray_test_tab
  VALUES (varray_of_varchar('April', 'June', 'September', 'November'));
```

Oracle provides the `oracle.sql.ARRAY` class for holding arrays. An `oracle.sql.ARRAY` object can be used to hold elements of a VARRAY or a nested table.

Three different methods are provided in the `oracle.sql.ARRAY` class for retrieving data:

- **getArray**   Retrieves the array elements into a `java.lang.Object[]` array. The returned elements are of the Java type corresponding to the SQL type.

- **getOracleArray**   Retrieves the array elements into a `oracle.sql.Datum[]` array. The returned elements are of the `oracle.sql` type corresponding to the SQL type.

- **getResultSet**   Returns the array elements into a `ResultSet`. The result set contains one row for each array element, with two columns in each row. The first column stores the index into the array for that element; the second stores the element value.

**NOTE**
*Use `getResultSet` when retrieving a nested table. Nested tables are unbounded in size. `getArray` and `getOracleArray` return the entire contents of a database array at one time. In contrast, `getResultSet` returns the contents as a `ResultSet`, which you iterate through using `next()`.*

The following code retrieves the database array stored in varray_test_tab into an `oracle.sql.ARRAY` object, using the `getArray` method in the `OracleResultSet` class. The elements are retrieved through use of the `getArray` method of the `oracle.sql.ARRAY` class. Note how the result of `getArray` is cast to an array of `String`.

```
public void get() throws SQLException {
   PreparedStatement st = conn.prepareStatement(
     "SELECT col1 FROM demo.varray_test_tab");
   OracleResultSet ors = (OracleResultSet)st.executeQuery();

   while (ors.next()) {
     ARRAY arr = ors.getArray(1);
     // Get the array elements
     String[] elems = (String[]) arr.getArray();
     for (int i = 0; i < elems.length; i++)
       System.out.println(elems[i]);
   }
   ors.close();
   st.close();
```

## Using a Type Map

By default, `getArray` and `getResultSet` map SQL types to Java data types according to the default type mapping (the connection's default type map). Thus, NUMBER SQL types are mapped to `BigDecimal`.

If you do not want the default mapping, you can use one of the following methods to specify a type map to associate a database object to a different class:

```
Object getArray(java.util.Dictionary map)
ResultSet getResultSet(java.util.Dictionary map)
```

For an example of how to use a type map, see the Tip "Retrieving Oracle Object Types."

If the type map does not contain an entry for a particular database object that is retrieved, the database object is returned as an `oracle.sql.STRUCT`.

# Retrieving Oracle Object Types

This section focuses on how to access object type data from Java using JDBC. A "contact" object containing information such as contact name and phone numbers is used as the basis of discussion. A table called cust_contact_tab, having a one-to-one relationship to the demo.customer table, will be created. cust_contact_tab will use a nested table to hold multiple "contact" objects for each customer.

"Contact" is modeled as an Oracle object type "Contact_t" containing six attributes and one method:

```
CREATE OR REPLACE TYPE Contact_t AS OBJECT (
   name    VARCHAR2(30),
   title   VARCHAR2(10),
   email   VARCHAR2(20),
   phone   VARCHAR2(15),
   mobile  VARCHAR2(15),
   fax     VARCHAR2(15),
   MEMBER FUNCTION some_method RETURN VARCHAR2(20)
);
```

You can use an object type wherever a built-in type can be used. Thus, Contact_t can be used as the data type of a column in a table:

```
CREATE TABLE my_table (contact Contact_t);
```

In this example, a named table type called Contact_List_t is created based on the Contact_t object type. Contact_List_t, in turn is used in the cust_contact_tab table as a nested table in the column "contacts." You can see how object types lend themselves to the modeling of complex structures.

```
-- Nested table of Contacts
CREATE OR REPLACE TYPE Contact_List_t AS TABLE OF Contact_t;
/

CREATE TABLE cust_contact_tab (
   customer_id  NUMBER(6) PRIMARY KEY
               REFERENCES demo.customer(customer_id),
   contacts    Contact_List_t)
 NESTED TABLE contacts STORE AS contacts_nt;
```

Object types can be queried and manipulated with SQL. The following INSERT statement inserts two contacts for customer ID 205 into cust_contact_tab:

```
INSERT INTO cust_contact_tab
  VALUES (205, Contact_List_t(
    Contact_t('Jose Saramago', '', 'js@blimunda.com', '', '', ''),
    Contact_t('Maha Chakri Sirindhorn', 'Princess', '', '', '', '') ));
```

Note how the system-defined constructor methods Contact_t() and Contact_List_t() are used to create objects of type Contact_t and Contact_List_t, respectively.

### Struct Versus Custom Java Classes

You have the choice of letting JDBC materialize a database object as a standard JDBC class called Struct or as a class you implement (custom Java class). A Struct object contains a value for each attribute of the database object it represents. Oracle has implemented Struct in two forms: oracle.jdbc2.Struct, which is JDBC 2.0 compliant, and oracle.sql.STRUCT, which can be more efficient and precise.

### Creating Customized Java Classes for Oracle Object Types

Custom Java classes that correspond to a database object type must implement one of two interfaces:

■ The SQLData interface, which is a JDBC 2.0 standard

■ The CustomDatum interface, which is more powerful than SQLData but is Oracle-specific

CustomDatum can provide better performance and precision since it works directly with oracle.sql types, which is the internal format used by the driver to hold Oracle objects (see Tip "Using the oracle.sql Package for Efficiency and Precision"). Oracle provides a tool called JPublisher to help you create classes that implement CustomDatum. For information on implementing the CustomDatum

**Retrieving Oracle Object Types**

interface and the JPublisher utility, refer to the Oracle8i JDBC Developer's Guide and Reference and the Oracle8i JPublisher User's Guide.

A key point to remember about SQLData is that it needs a *type map*. A type map associates a Java class with a database object type. A type map entry to associate the Contact_t database object type to a Java class called Contact could be defined as follows:

```
java.util.Dictionary typeMap = conn.getTypeMap();
typeMap.put("CONTACT_T", Class.forName("Contact"));
```

### Implementing the SQLData Interface with Contact.java

The SQLData interface has three methods, all of which must be implemented by your custom Java class (see Table 9-6). Oracle JDBC places the SQLData interface in the oracle.jdbc2 package.

The following code implements the oracle.jdbc2.SQLData interface methods for the custom class Contact to correspond to the SQL type Contact_t.

```
import java.sql.*;

public class Contact implements oracle.jdbc2.SQLData {
  private String sqlType;
  private String name, title, email, phone, mobile, fax;

  public Contact() {}

  public Contact(String sqlType, String name, String title,
         String email, String phone, String mobile, String fax) {
    this.sqlType  = sqlType;
    this.name = name;
    this.title = title;
    this.email = email;
    this.phone = phone;
    this.mobile = mobile;
    this.fax = fax;
  }

  // Implement methods of the SQLData interface

  public String getSQLTypeName() throws SQLException {
    return sqlType;
  }

  public void readSQL(oracle.jdbc2.SQLInput stream, String typeName)
     throws SQLException {
    sqlType = typeName;
```

```
    name = stream.readString();
    title = stream.readString();
    email = stream.readString();
    phone = stream.readString();
    mobile = stream.readString();
    fax = stream.readString();
  }

  public void writeSQL(oracle.jdbc2.SQLOutput stream) throws SQLException {
    stream.writeString(name);
    stream.writeString(title);
    stream.writeString(email);
    stream.writeString(phone);
    stream.writeString(mobile);
    stream.writeString(fax);
  }

  public String toString() {
    return  "Name:" + name +
            ", Title: " + title +
            ", Email:" + email +
            ", Phone:" + phone +
            ", Mobile:" + mobile +
            ", Fax:" + fax;
  }
}
```

Note how the instance variables `sqlType`, `name`, `title`, `email`, `phone`, `mobile`, and `fax` are initialized with the `Contact` constructor.

| Method | Description |
| --- | --- |
| String getSQLTypeName() | Returns the fully-qualified name of the SQL user-defined type that this object represents. |
| void readSQL(SQLInput stream, String typeName) | Populates this object with data read from the database. |
| void writeSQL(SQLOutput stream) | Writes this object to the given SQL data stream. |

**TABLE 9-6.** *Methods in the `SQLData` Interface*

## Using the Contact Class

Now that the `Contact` custom class has been created, it can be used in Java programs. The `getContact` method shown in the following retrieves contacts for a given customer ID into objects of the custom class `Contact`. It then displays information on each contact by calling the `Contact.getString` method.

```
public void getContacts(int custID)
    throws SQLException, ClassNotFoundException {
  PreparedStatement ps = conn.prepareStatement(
    "SELECT customer_id, contacts" +
    "  FROM demo.cust_contact_tab" +
    " WHERE customer_id = ?");

  ps.setInt(1, custID);
  OracleResultSet ors = (OracleResultSet)ps.executeQuery();

  // Add a new type map entry to map SQL type "CONTACT_T"
  // to Java class "Contact"
  java.util.Dictionary typeMap = conn.getTypeMap();
  System.out.println(Class.forName("Contact"));
  typeMap.put("CONTACT_T", Class.forName("Contact"));

  if (ors.next()) {
    // Get the Contact_List object
    ARRAY contactArray = ors.getArray(2);

    // Get elements in Contact_List
    Object[] contacts = (Object[]) contactArray.getArray(typeMap);
    // Note: you'll get a run time error in the above if you cast it to
    // (Contact[]) instead of (Object[])

    System.out.println("Customer ID: " + ors.getInt(1)
      + " has " + contacts.length + " contacts:");
    for (int i = 0; i < contacts.length; i++)
      System.out.println(Integer.toString(i+1) + ": "
              + contacts[i].toString());
  }

  // displayResultSet(rs);
  ors.close();
  ps.close();
}
```

A `PreparedStatement` is used to get the row from cust_contact_tab for the required customer ID. The contact_list_t object (which is a nested table) is then retrieved using `getArray(2)`.

Elements of the nested table (which consists of Contact_t objects) are extracted into the contacts array using the `getArray(Dictionary typeMap)` method of the `oracle.sql.ARRAY` class. The `getArray` method returns the elements of the ARRAY objects using `typeMap` for type map customizations.

Finally, details of each contact are printed by calling the toString method of the Contact class. The output generated is as follows:

```
Customer ID: 205 has 2 contacts:
1: Jose Saramago Title:null, Email:js@blimunda.com, Ph:null, Cell:null, Fx:null
2: Maha Chakri Sirindhorn Title:Princess, Email:null, Ph:null, Cell:null, Fx:null
```

# Tips on Streaming Data with JDBC

Oracle LONG and LONG RAW columns can hold up to 2GB of data, and LOB objects (BLOB, CLOB, and BFILE) can hold up to 4GB. Oracle JDBC drivers support the streaming of these types in either direction between database and client.

The technique of streaming data involves fetching data into standard Java stream classes belonging to java.io, a package with a bewildering hierarchy of over 60 stream classes. Thankfully, for most tasks involving streaming LONG or LOB data, you can focus on a handful of classes: `InputStream` and `BufferedInputStream` to read a sequence of bytes or characters and `OutputStream` and its subclass `FileOutputStream` to write a sequence of bytes or characters.

**NOTE**
*Oracle strongly recommends that you convert LONG columns to LOB columns. LOB columns are subject to far fewer restrictions than LONG columns. (Information on how to convert LONG columns to LOBs using the TO_LOB function can be found in Chapter 4.)*

## Streaming LONG and LONG RAW Columns

This section provides examples of streaming LONG and LONG RAW columns from JDBC. Also covered in this section are several caveats regarding streaming data when multiple columns are used.

The principal methods used to retrieve data from LONG and LONG RAW columns are found in the `ResultSet` class and are summarized in Table 9-7. Oracle JDBC drivers, unlike PL/SQL, support the streaming of the entire 2GB of LONG or LONG RAW data.

| Method | Return Type | Interpretation of Data |
|---|---|---|
| `getBinaryStream` | `InputStream` | Uninterpreted |
| `getAsciiStream` | `InputStream` | One-byte ASCII characters |
| `getUnicodeStream` | `InputStream` | Two-byte Unicode characters |
| `getBytes` | `byte[]` (fetched in one call—not streamed) | Uninterpreted |

**TABLE 9-7.**   *Methods of* `ResultSet` *for Retrieving LONG and LONG RAW Columns*

As an illustration of the use of these methods, a table named employee_pic will be created under the demo schema:

```
CREATE TABLE employee_pic (
  employee_id    NUMBER(4) PRIMARY KEY
                 REFERENCES employee(employee_id),
  pic            LONG RAW,
  date_inserted DATE
);
```

## An Example That Uses getBinaryStream

The following example illustrates streaming of a LONG RAW column, using `getBinaryStream`. The example reads from the table demo.employee_pic, which contains images of employees in GIF or JPEG graphic format. Assuming `stmt` is a `Statement` object, the following code retrieves the image for employee_id 7369:

```
ResultSet rs =
  stmt.executeQuery("SELECT pic FROM demo.employee_pic WHERE employee_id = 7369");

// Retrieve the first row
if (rs.next ()) {
  // Get the data as an InputStream from the database to the client
  java.io.InputStream instream = rs.getBinaryStream(1);

  // Create a byte array for instream.read()
  byte[] buffer = new byte[1024]; // 1K buffer
  int length; // no. of bytes read

  // Read instream in a loop
```

```
while ((length = instream.read(buffer)) != -1) {
  // Do something with buffer
  . . .
}
instream.close();
```

The `getBinaryStream` method returns a `java.io.InputStream` object without converting the data. In each iteration through the while loop, `instream.read(buffer)` reads a sequence of bytes into buffer and returns the number of bytes read (or –1 if the end of the stream is reached). In each call, `instream.read(buffer)` reads at most `buffer.length` bytes.

## Using getBytes

If you are certain that the size of your LONG data is small, you can avoid streaming LONG or LONG RAW columns by redefining them as CHAR, VARCHAR, or VARBINARY Java types, using the technique described in "Defining Column Types to Reduce Network Round Trips." You can then retrieve the data in one call, using the `getBytes` method rather than incrementally using one of the `getXXXStream` methods. `getBytes` will use more memory but can be faster. Note that the default behavior of Oracle's JDBC drivers is to stream LONG and LONG RAW columns.

There is a positive side effect to redefining the LONG column: the `defineColumnType` method saves the driver a round trip to the database when executing the query. Without `defineColumnType`, the JDBC Driver has to request the data types of the columns.

The following code modifies the example from the previous section. The `Statement` object stmt is cast to the `oracle.jdbc.driver.OracleStatement`, and the column containing LONG RAW data is redefined to be of type VARBINARY. Data is written to the byte array buffer in one sweep, using `getBytes`.

```
// The defineColumnType method requires an OracleStatement object
 OracleStatement ostmt = (OracleStatement)stmt;

// Redefine the LONG column at position 1 to VARBINARY
ostmt.defineColumnType(1, Types.VARBINARY);
ResultSet rs =
 ostmt.executeQuery("SELECT pic FROM demo.employee_pic WHERE employee_id = 7369");

// Retrieve the first row
if (rs.next ()) {
  // Get the entire data in one call instead of streaming it
  byte[] buffer = rs.getBytes(1)
  // Do something with buffer
  . . .
```

### Caveats on Streaming Multiple Columns

You should be aware of a quirk with streaming LONG columns: *if you perform any JDBC operation that communicates with the database other than reading the current stream, Oracle JDBC drivers will automatically discard the stream data.* The implication: columns after a streaming column should be read only after the stream column has been read.

To avoid accidentally losing your stream data, keep the following rules in mind:

- Call a stream column in SELECT list order. If you bypass a stream column and access data in a column that follows it, your stream data will be lost.

- Read and store the stream data immediately after you get it. It is not sufficient to use getBinaryStream or getAsciiStream on the column; you must read and store its contents, or else the contents will be discarded with the next getXXX call.

Both of these rules are adhered to in the following example, which builds on code in the example "An Example That Uses getBinaryStream." It retrieves all three columns of the employee_pic table.

```
ResultSet rs =
  stmt.executeQuery("SELECT employee_id, pic, date_inserted" +
                    "  FROM demo.employee_pic" +
                    "  WHERE employee_id = 7369");

// Retrieve the first row
if (rs.next()) {
  ///////////// 1. Get employee_id
  int id = rs.getInt(1);

  ///////////// 2. Stream pic
  java.io.InputStream instream = rs.getBinaryStream(2);

  // Create a byte array for instream.read()
  byte[] buffer = new byte[1024]; // 1K buffer
  int bytesRead;
  // Read instream data and store it in a file outstream
  FileOutStream fos = new FileOutStream("emp_pic.jpg");
  while ((bytesRead = instream.read(buffer)) != -1)
    fos.write(buffer, 0, bytesRead);

  instream.close();
  fos.close();

  ///////////// 3. Get date_inserted
  java.sql.Date = rs.getDate(3);
}
```

In the example, the sequence of access is the SELECT list order:

1. employee_id

2. emp_pic (the stream)

3. date_inserted

Any other sequence would result in loss of the stream data. The JDBC Driver will raise a "Stream Closed" error when you call the `rs.getBinaryStream` method owing to the lack of data.

## Streaming LOBs

Prior to Oracle8, the only way to store binary data was in LONG RAW columns, which could store up to 2GB of data per row. Because LONG columns are subject to severe restrictions, Oracle now recommends the use of Large Objects (LOBs) instead of LONGs for storing unstructured binary data. LOBs bring new capabilities for manipulating and viewing unstructured data and the ability to store up to 4GB of data. A value in a LOB column holds a LOB locator, not actual data; a LOB locator specifies the location of the data. Multiple LOB columns per table are allowed.

There are two types of LOBs: internal and external. The internal LOB types BLOB (binary), CLOB (character), and NCLOB (multicharacter) are stored in the database; their locators point to either in-line locations or out-of-line locations. External LOBs (BFILEs) are stored externally; their locators point to operating system files.

The primary methods for reading and writing to LOB objects are summarized in Table 9-8. Observe the following from the table:

- LOBs may be read from or written to as a whole using `getXXXStream` methods; alternatively, a given number of bytes may be read from or written to at a specified position.

- The `oracle.sql.CLOB` class provides `getAsciiXXX` methods for ASCII characters and `getCharacterXXX` methods for Unicode characters.

- No methods are provided for writing to BFILEs.

The following methods are common to all oracle.sql LOB classes:

- **`isConvertibleTo`**   Tests if the object can be converted to a specified Java type

- **`length`**   Returns the size of the object

- **`position`**   Finds the position of a given byte or character pattern

- **`toJDBC`**   Converts the object into its default Java object type

**Read entire object as a stream**
`oracle.sql.BLOB.getBinaryStream`
`oracle.sql.CLOB.getAsciiStream` or `getCharacterStream`
`oracle.sql.BFILE.getBinaryStream`

**Read at specified position**
`oracle.sql.BLOB.getBytes`
`oracle.sql.CLOB.getChars` or `getSubString`
`oracle.sql.BFILE.getBytes`

**Write to object from a stream**
`oracle.sql.BLOB.getBinaryOutputStream`
`oracle.sql.CLOB.getAsciiOutputStream` or `getCharacterOutputStream`

**Write to object at specified position**
`oracle.sql.BLOB.putBytes`
`oracle.sql.CLOB.putChars` or `putString`

**TABLE 9-8.** *Methods for Reading and Writing in the oracle.sql Classes BLOB, CLOB, and BFILE*

## Example

BFileViewer.java is a client-side application that illustrates the streaming of LOB objects from an Oracle database. It streams multi-media data stored as a BFILE column, writes the data to a file on the client machine, and invokes an external application to view or play the file. Multi-media data of any format—word processing, spreadsheet, graphic, audio, or video—can be viewed or played, provided that a viewer or player for the format is preinstalled on the client machine. Note that the program will not run as an applet because it accesses the client's hard drive.

What follows is a brief look at the table used by BFileViewer.java.

## Creating and Populating demo.bfile_tab

BFileViewer.java reads the table demo.bfile_tab,which is created as follows:

```
CREATE TABLE demo.bfile_tab (
  id NUMBER(4) PRIMARY KEY,
  bf BFILE NOT NULL,
  mime_type  VARCHAR2(30) NOT NULL
);
```

The column id serves as a unique identifier; bf holds the locator for the external BFILE; and mime_type identifies the MIME type of the BFILE's content.

**NOTE**
*MIME (Multipurpose Internet Mail Extension) types represent a standard way of classifying file types on the Internet. A MIME type has two parts, a type and a subtype, separated by a slash. The MIME types used in this example are "text/plain" for ASCII, "application/ msword" for MS Word, "application/x-msexcel" for MS Excel, and "image/jpeg" for JPEG.*

Populating the table first requires creation of a DIRECTORY object. The following creates a DIRECTORY object called "BFILE_DIR" and grants READ privileges to "demo."

```
CREATE OR REPLACE DIRECTORY BFILE_DIR AS 'D:\TEMP\';
GRANT READ ON DIRECTORY BFILE_DIR TO demo;
```

**CAUTION**
*Failure to grant READ on the DIRECTORY object will result in an ORA-22285 error, "nonexistent directory or file for FILEEXISTS op," when you try to access files in the DIRECTORY.*

The DIRECTORY object BFILE_DIR now serves as an alias for the full pathname to the operating system directory "D:\TEMP\." When creating DIRECTORY objects, be sure to specify the right directory, since Oracle does not verify whether the directory and pathname you specify actually exist. If your operating system uses case-sensitive pathnames and filenames, be sure to specify the appropriate case.

Test data is inserted into the bfile_tab table, using BFILENAME(), a built-in Oracle function that initializes a BFILE column to point to an external file.

```
INSERT INTO demo.bfile_tab
  VALUES (1, BFILENAME('BFILE_DIR', '01.txt'), 'text/plain');

INSERT INTO demo.bfile_tab
  VALUES (2, BFILENAME('BFILE_DIR', 'MyWord.doc'),'application/msword');

INSERT INTO demo.bfile_tab
  VALUES (3, BFILENAME('BFILE_DIR', 'MySpreadsheet.xls'),
    'application/x-msexcel');

INSERT INTO demo.bfile_tab
  VALUES (4, BFILENAME('BFILE_DIR', 'Mandrill.jpg'), 'image/jpeg');
```

Streaming LOBs

The files "01.txt," "MyWord.doc," "MySpreadsheet.xls," and "Mandrill.jpg"—all physically residing in the directory BFILE_DIR—are now associated with the BFILEs in demo.bfile_tab.

## The BFileViewer Class

This section examines important excerpts of `BFileViewer`. The code for `BFileViewer` is listed in its entirety following this section. You can run BFileViewer after compiling it from the command line with the following syntax:

```
java BFileViewer <url> <user> <pwd>
```

where <url> is the JDBC database URL name, <user> is a user that has rights to the demo schema, and <pwd> is the corresponding password.

The BFileViewer class contains an instance variable viewers declared as a Hashtable.

```
private Hashtable viewers = null;
```

The Hashtable `viewers` associates a MIME type with an external application—"text / plain" with "notepad.exe," for instance. The public method `registerViewer` allows other classes to register MIME type into the Hashtable. The `getViewerCommand` method returns the name of the application associated with a given MIME type.

**THE GETBFILE METHOD**    The `getBfile` method in the `BFileViewer` class takes a bfileID as a parameter and queries the bfile_tab table accordingly. It then retrieves data from the "bf" and "mime_type" columns from the `ResultSet` using the `getBFILE` and `getString` methods, respectively:

```
while (ors.next()) {
  bfile = ors.getBFILE(1);
  mimeType = ors.getString(2);
}
```

Next, information about the BFILE is printed, using the `getDirAlias`, `getName`, and `length` methods of the `oracle.sql.BFILE` class:

```
System.out.println("Displaying BFILE"
    + "\n\tDir Alias: " + bfile.getDirAlias()
    + "\n\tFilename : " + bfile.getName()
    + "\n\tMime Type: " + mimeType
    + "\n\tSize      : " + bfile.length() + " bytes\n");
```

**THE DISPLAYCONTENTS METHOD**    The `displayContents` method accepts a BFILE as one of its parameters and displays the BFILE contents. First, it streams the BFILE, using the `getBinaryStream` method (which returns the entire BFILE as an `InputStream`). If a viewer or player for the MIME type has been registered, the `displayContents` method reads the stream and immediately writes it to a temporary output file, using a `FileOutputStream`.

```
// Create a file output stream
String tempFilename = "c:\\_tmp_" + bfile.getName();
File outfile = new File(tempFilename);
FileOutputStream fos = new FileOutputStream(outfile);
```

The outfile references a temporary file that is to be created on the root directory of drive c: of a Windows client. The filename of the temporary file consists of the actual BFILE's name prefixed with "C:\\_tmp_"—the two backslashes are necessary, since the backslash character is the escape character in Java strings. The method `FileOutputStream(File f)` creates a new file output stream, using the information encapsulated in the `File` object, deleting any existing file with that name.

In this example, data streaming is done in 4K chunks in a while loop. In each loop iteration, data is read from instream into buffer, then written from buffer to the file output stream fos:

```
while ((bytesRead = instream.read(buffer)) != -1)
  fos.write(buffer, 0, bytesRead);
```

Finally, the appropriate viewer or player is invoked on the output file in a separate process:

```
Runtime.getRuntime().exec(exeName + " " + tempFilename);
```

If no viewer or player for the file type has been registered, the program uses `System.out.print` to display the bytes of the file to the standard output.

The entire code for BFileViewer.java follows.

```
import java.sql.*;
import oracle.jdbc.driver.*;
import oracle.sql.*;
import java.util.Hashtable;
import java.io.*;

/**
 * Note  First run BFileViewer.sql to create and populate the
 *       table used in this sample.
 */

public class BFileViewer {
  private OracleConnection conn = null;
  private Hashtable viewers = null;
```

```
BFileViewer(String url, String user, String pwd) throws SQLException {
  DriverManager.registerDriver(new OracleDriver());
  conn = (OracleConnection)DriverManager.getConnection(url, user, pwd);
  DatabaseMetaData meta = conn.getMetaData(); // For driver info
  System.out.println("\nConnected as User " + user + " to " + url
   + " using JDBC Driver Version " + meta.getDriverVersion() + "\n");

  viewers = new Hashtable();
}

public void registerViewer(String mimeType, String viewerCommand) {
  viewers.put(mimeType, viewerCommand);
}

//  Returns the viewer command; or null if not found
public String getViewerCommand(String mimeType) {
  return (String)viewers.get(mimeType);
}


void displayContents(  BFILE bfile,
           String mimeType) throws Exception {
  InputStream instream = bfile.getBinaryStream();

  // Temporary buffer for instream.read()
  byte[] buffer = new byte[4 * 1024]; //4K buffer
  int bytesRead;

  String exeName = getViewerCommand(mimeType);

  if (exeName != null) { // Known type
    // Create a file output stream
    String tempFilename = "c:\\_tmp_" + bfile.getName();
    File outfile = new File(tempFilename);
    FileOutputStream fos = new FileOutputStream(outfile);

    // Read instream and write it to the file output stream
    while ((bytesRead = instream.read(buffer)) != -1)
      fos.write(buffer, 0, bytesRead);

    fos.close();

    // Call external application in a separate process
    Runtime.getRuntime().exec(exeName + " " + tempFilename);
  }
  else {
    // Unregistered MIME type. Display as a binary dump
```

```
    // Read and display bytes in blocks
    long byteNum = 0;
    while ((bytesRead = instream.read(buffer)) != -1) {
      System.out.print("\n" + byteNum + ":\t");
      for (int i = 0; i < bytesRead; i++)
        System.out.print(buffer[i] + " ");
      byteNum += bytesRead;
    }
  }

  instream.close();
}


boolean getBfile(int bfileID) throws Exception {

  oracle.sql.BFILE bfile = null;
  String mimeType = null;

  PreparedStatement ps = conn.prepareStatement(
    "SELECT bf, mime_type" +
    "  FROM demo.bfile_tab " +
    " WHERE id = ?");

  ps.setInt(1, bfileID);

  OracleResultSet ors = (OracleResultSet)ps.executeQuery();

  while (ors.next()) {
    bfile = ors.getBFILE(1);
    mimeType = ors.getString(2);
  }

  if (bfile == null) {
    System.out.println("Error: ID not found");
    return false;
  }
  if (!bfile.fileExists()) {
    System.out.println("Error: File doesn't exist");
    return false;
  }

  bfile.openFile();
  System.out.println("Displaying BFILE"
    + "\n\tDir Alias: " + bfile.getDirAlias()
    + "\n\tFilename : " + bfile.getName()
    + "\n\tMime Type: " + mimeType
```

```
              + "\n\tSize   : " + bfile.length() + " bytes\n");


    displayContents(bfile, mimeType);
    return true;
  }


public static void main(String args[]) throws SQLException {
  if (args.length != 3) {
    System.out.println("Usage: java BFileViewer <url> <user> <pwd>");
    System.exit(0);
  }

  BFileViewer aTester = null;

  try {
    aTester = new BFileViewer(args[0], args[1], args[2]);

    // Register viewers
    aTester.registerViewer("application/msword",
      "C:\\Program Files\\Microsoft Office\\Office\\winword.exe");
    aTester.registerViewer("text/plain",
        "notepad");
    aTester.registerViewer("application/x-msexcel",
      "C:\\Program Files\\Microsoft Office\\Office\\excel.exe");
    aTester.registerViewer("image/jpeg",
        "C:\\i386\\iexplore.exe");

    aTester.getBfile(4);

  } catch (SQLException e) {
    // Print all errors in the chain
    do {
      System.err.println("SQLException caught: " + e.getMessage());
    } while((e = e.getNextException()) != null);

    e.printStackTrace();
  } catch (Exception e) {
    e.printStackTrace();
  } finally {
    // Close connection explicitly
    if (aTester.conn != null) aTester.conn.close();
  }
 }
}
```

# Working with Stored Procedures with Java

This section contains tips on using the Server-Side JDBC Driver, loading Java code with loadjava, publishing Java methods with call specs, and calling stored procedures in Oracle8i.

## Using the Server-Side JDBC Driver

Java programs loaded into Oracle8i can use the embedded Server-Side JDBC Driver, which runs within a default session and default transaction context. With this driver, you do not need to create a JDBC connection: you are already connected to the database and all your SQL operations are part of a default transaction.

The following statement gets a handle on the default session in the form of a Connection object:

```
Connection conn = new OracleDriver().defaultConnection();
```

Some points to remember when using the Server-Side Driver:

- The defaultConnection method always returns the same connection object.

- Calling the close method on a connection object established by the Server-Side Driver has no effect.

- Because the Server-Side Driver does not support auto-commits, you must explicitly manage transactions with commits or rollbacks.

### Debugging Java Stored Procedures

In Java stored procedures, System.out and System.err print output is sent to trace files. For debugging, you can be redirected to the output of the SQL*Plus text buffer by issuing the following commands in SQL*Plus before calling a stored procedure:

```
SQL>SET SERVEROUTPUT ON SIZE 5000
SQL>CALL dbms_java.set_output(5000)
```

The output is printed when the stored procedure exits.

Using the Server-Side JDBC Driver

## Using loadjava to Load Java Programs into the Database

After writing a Java program, you must perform two steps before you can call the program as a stored procedure in Oracle8i:

1. Load the program into the database

2. Publish those methods that you want to be callable from SQL or PL/SQL or JDBC

Step 1, the focus of this Tip, is conveniently performed with a tool called `loadjava`. Step 2 is covered in the Tip "Writing Call Specs to Publish Java Procedures in the Oracle Data Dictionary."

The `loadjava` tool uses the built-in LOADLOBS package to upload Java files into a BLOB column in the table CREATE$JAVA$LOB$TABLE, which is created in the logon schema. `loadjava` then uses the SQL CREATE JAVA statement to load the Java files into the database as schema objects.

The `loadjava` tool is run from the command line using the following syntax:

```
loadjava {-user | -u} username/password[@database]
   [-option_name -option_name ...] filename filename ...
where option_name  stands for the following syntax:
{   {andresolve | a}
  | debug
  | {definer | d}
  | {encoding | e} encoding_scheme_name
  | {force | f}
  | {grant | g} {username | role_name}[,{username | role_name}]...
  | {oci8 | o}
  | oracleresolver
  | {resolve | r}
  | {resolver | R} "resolver_spec"
  | {schema | S} schema_name
  | {synonym | s}
  | {thin | t}
  | {verbose | v} }
```

The following is a description of commonly used options in `loadjava` (for a comprehensive discussion of `loadjava`, see the "Oracle8i Java Stored Procedures Developer's Guide"):

- **filename**  Names of Java source, class, resource files, SQLJ input files, and uncompressed .jar and .zip archives—specified in any order. To avoid schema object naming complications, store your files in a .jar or .zip archive. If a .jar or .zip archive works with the JDK, it will also work with `loadjava`.

- **debug**  Generates debug information. Equivalent to `javac -g`.

- **force**  Forces the loading of Java class files whether or not they have been loaded before. By default, previously loaded class files are rejected. If you previously loaded the source file, you cannot force the loading of a class file; you must drop the source schema object first.

- **oci8 | thin**  Specifies which driver is to be used to communicate with the database. oci8 is the default.

- **grant username | role_name**  Grants EXECUTIVE privilege on uploaded classes to the specified database users/roles. (Users must have EXECUTIVE privilege to call methods of a class directly.) This option is cumulative: users and roles are added to the list of those having the EXECUTIVE privilege. To revoke the privilege, either drop and reload the schema object without specifying `-grant` or use the SQL REVOKE statement. You need the CREATE PROCEDURE WITH GRANT privilege to grant the privilege on an object in another user's schema.

- **resolve**  Resolves all external references after all files on the command line are loaded and compiled (if needed). When this option is omitted, files are loaded but not compiled or resolved until run time.

In the following example, `loadjava` connects to a machine called myComputer using the Thin JDBC Driver, and then loads and resolves the TotalSales.class file into the demo schema:

```
loadjava -user demo/demo@myComputer:1521:orcl -thin -resolve
TotalSales.class
```

# Writing Call Specs to Publish Java Procedures in the Oracle Data Dictionary

In order to call Java methods from SQL or PL/SQL or JDBC, you must first publish them into the Oracle dictionary. Publishing does not happen automatically when you load a Java class into the database because Oracle cannot automatically determine which of its methods are safe for calling from within SQL. Instead, you must write call specifications (call specs) which map the class' methods to their SQL representations.

**NOTE**
*There is no need to publish database-loaded Java classes to be accessible from other database-loaded Java classes.*

Once a call spec is created and a method has been published, an application can reference the method as if it were a PL/SQL function or procedure. Oracle's run-time system looks up the call spec in the Oracle data dictionary and runs the appropriate Java method.

To create a call spec, you encase a Java method name within a PL/SQL stored procedure/function or a PL/SQL package or a SQL object type. Methods that return values are published as functions, while void methods are published as procedures.

 **CAUTION**
*Only `public static` Java methods should be published in the Oracle Dictionary. Non-public static methods cannot be called from SQL or PL/SQL or through JDBC.*

A call spec specifies a method name, parameter types, and return types in the following syntax:

```
CREATE [OR REPLACE]
{  PROCEDURE procedure_name [(param[, param]...)]
 | FUNCTION function_name [(param[, param]...)] RETURN sql_type}
 [AUTHID {DEFINER | CURRENT_USER}]
 [PARALLEL_ENABLE]
 [DETERMINISTIC]
 {IS | AS} LANGUAGE JAVA
 NAME 'java_method_fullname (java_type_fullname[, java_type_fullname]...)
   [return java_type_fullname]';
```

A few comments on the call spec syntax:

- `procedure_name` or `function_name` does not have to be the same name as its corresponding Java method name.

- `param` must be in the following form `parameter_name [IN | OUT | IN OUT] sql_type`. Valid types for `sql_type` are shown in Table 9-9 and are discussed in "SQL Data Types in a Call Spec" in this section.

- `java_method_fullname` takes the form `<Java class name>.<Java method name>`

- `java_type_fullname` corresponds to a fully-qualified Java class name in dot notation, for example `java.lang.String`. Java names can be broken into multiple lines wherever "." appears as in the following example:

```
java.lang.
   String
```

- Exceptions declared in the Java method should not be included in the call spec definition.

For information on `AUTHID`, `DEFINER`, `CURRENT_USER`, `PARALLEL_ENABLE`, and `DETERMINISTIC` see the "Oracle8i Java Stored Procedures Developer's Guide."

## SQL Data Types in a Call Spec

Table 9-9 shows valid SQL to Java type mappings that you can use in a call spec. Oracle automatically converts between SQL and Java types.

When mapping Java types to call spec SQL types, be aware of the following:

- A call-spec maps each `java_type_fullname` element by position, so a one-to-one correspondence should exist between Java method arguments and the call spec parameters. However, the Java method `main` is treated as a special case; its `String[]` parameter can be mapped to multiple CHAR or VARCHAR2 call spec parameters (see Example 5 in this section).

- A call spec OUT or IN OUT parameter must map to a one-element Java array (see Example 2 in this section).

- Java numerical types should always be mapped to NUMBER. Subtypes of NUMBER—for instance, INTEGER, REAL, and POSITIVE—are not allowed in a call spec.

- UROWID cannot be used in a call spec.

- PL/SQL BOOLEANs cannot be used in a call spec. Use NUMBER instead. (See Example 3 in this section).

- You cannot specify constraints (such as precision, size, or NOT NULL) on call spec parameters. Thus, in a call spec you specify VARCHAR2, not VARCHAR2(255).

- As a rule of thumb, Java strings should be mapped to VARCHAR2 rather than CHAR. This avoids the problem of CHAR columns being padded with spaces: in PL/SQL, OUT or IN OUT parameters defined as CHAR are returned to a length of 32767 bytes, padded with spaces. If you choose to use CHAR, set the maximum limit on the length that can be returned for any column using the `setMaxFieldSize` method of a `Statement` object before you register an OUT parameter. However, be aware that `setMaxFieldSize` affects the length of all CHAR, RAW, LONG, LONG RAW, and VARCHAR2 columns in that statement.

| SQL Type | Java Type |
|---|---|
| CHAR, NCHAR, LONG, VARCHAR2, NVARCHAR2 | `oracle.sql.CHAR, java.lang.String, java.sql.Date, java.sql.Time, java.sql.Timestamp, java.lang.Byte, java.lang.Short, java.lang.Integer, java.lang.Long, java.lang.Float, java.lang.Double, java.math.BigDecimal byte, short, int, long, float, double` |
| NUMBER | `oracle.sql.NUMBER, java.lang.Byte, java.lang.Short, java.lang.Integer, java.lang.Long, java.lang.Float, java.lang.Double, java.math.BigDecimal byte, short, int, long, float, double` |
| DATE | `oracle.sql.DATE, java.sql.Date, java.sql.Time, java.sql.Timestamp, java.lang.String` |
| RAW, LONG RAW | `oracle.sql.RAW, byte[]` |
| ROWID | `oracle.sql.CHAR, oracle.sql.ROWID, java.lang.String` |
| BFILE | `oracle.sql.BFILE` |
| BLOB | `oracle.sql.BLOB, oracle.jdbc2.Blob` |
| CLOB, NCLOB | `oracle.sql.CLOB, oracle.jdbc2.Clob` |
| OBJECT | `oracle.sql.STRUCT, oracle.sqljData, oracle.jdbc2.Struct` |
| REF | `oracle.sql.REF, oracle.jdbc2.Ref` |
| TABLE, VARRAY | `oracle.sql.ARRAY, oracle.jdbc2.Array` |
| Any of the foregoing SQL types | `oracle.sql.CustomDatum, oracle.sql.Datum` |

**TABLE 9-9.** *Valid SQL to Java Type Mappings in a Call Spec*

## Example 1: Passing an IN Parameter and Returning Parameter

This example illustrates the writing of a call spec for a Java stored function that takes an IN parameter and returns a value. The `getTotalSales` method shown next accepts a customer ID as an argument and returns the total purchases made by the customer.

```java
import java.sql.*;
import oracle.jdbc.driver.*;

public class TotalSales {
  public static double getTotalSales(int custID)
      throws SQLException {
    Connection conn = new OracleDriver().defaultConnection();
    ResultSet rs = null;
    PreparedStatement ps = null;
    double sales = -1;
    try {
      String q = " SELECT SUM(total)" +
                 "  FROM demo.sales_order" +
                 "  WHERE customer_id = ?";
      ps = conn.prepareStatement(q);
      ps.setInt(1, custID);
      rs = ps.executeQuery();
      if (rs.next())
        sales = rs.getDouble(1);
    } catch (Exception e) {
      System.err.println("Exception caught: " + e.getMessage());
    } finally {
      if (rs != null) rs.close();
      if (ps != null) ps.close();
    }
    return sales;
  }
}
```

Before writing the call spec for the `getTotalSales`, it is worth looking at an equivalent PL/SQL version of the method:

```sql
CREATE OR REPLACE FUNCTION total_sales_for_cust_plsql (i_cust_id IN NUMBER) RETURN NUMBER
IS
  o_total_sales NUMBER;
BEGIN
  SELECT SUM(total) INTO o_total_sales
    FROM sales_order
    WHERE customer_id = i_cust_id;
  RETURN o_total_sales;
END;
```

The following call spec publishes the `getTotalSales` Java method as the function total_sales_for_cust:

```
CREATE OR REPLACE FUNCTION total_sales_for_cust (customer_id NUMBER)
  RETURN NUMBER
AS LANGUAGE JAVA
NAME 'TotalSales.getTotalSales(int) return double';
```

Note that the `int` and `double` Java types are mapped to NUMBER SQL types: subtypes of NUMBER are illegal in a call spec.

## Example 2: Passing IN OUT Parameters

An OUT or IN OUT parameter in a call spec must be mapped to a Java array argument. The following class `Swapper` contains the classic `swap` method to swap two numbers. Note how the IN OUT parameters `x` and `y` are represented as arrays of `double`, and how the arrays' first elements `x[0]` and `y[0]` are swapped.

```
public class Swapper {
  public static void swap(double[] x, double[] y) {
    double temp = x[0];
    x[0] = y[0];
    y[0] = temp;
  }
}
```

The following call spec publishes the `swap` method as a procedure called swap_doubles:

```
CREATE PROCEDURE swap_doubles (x IN OUT NUMBER, y IN OUT NUMBER)
AS LANGUAGE JAVA
NAME 'Swapper.swap(double[], double[])';
```

A generic version of the `Swapper` class that swaps any two Java objects is not difficult to create:

```
public class ObjectSwapper {
  private static void swapObjects(Object[] x,  Object[] y) {
    Object temp = x[0];
    x[0] = y[0];
    y[0] = temp;
  }

  // String wrapper for call spec
  public static void swap(String[] x, String[] y) {
    swapObjects(x, y);
  }
```

```
// Double wrapper for call spec
public static void swap(Double[] x, Double[] y) {
    swapObjects(x, y);
}
}
```

Note that the `swapObjects` method in `ObjectSwapper` cannot be accessed from a call spec because `java.lang.Object` types cannot be mapped to SQL types in a call spec. Thus the need for the two `swap` methods which act as wrappers.

Call specs to publish the wrapper methods can be written like this:

```
CREATE OR REPLACE PROCEDURE swap(x IN OUT VARCHAR2, y IN OUT VARCHAR2)
AS LANGUAGE JAVA
NAME 'ObjectSwapper.swap(java.lang.String[], java.lang.String[])';

CREATE OR REPLACE PROCEDURE swap(x IN OUT NUMBER, y IN OUT NUMBER)
AS LANGUAGE JAVA
NAME 'ObjectSwapper.swap(java.lang.Double[], java.lang.Double[])';
```

## Example 3: Passing Boolean Values

JDBC drivers do not support the passing of Boolean parameters to PL/SQL stored procedures because of a restriction in the OCI layer. Two complications arise as a result; each will be examined in this example:

- To publish a Java stored procedure that takes Boolean arguments, the call spec must map each Java Boolean argument to the NUMBER SQL type, *not* the BOOLEAN PL/SQL type.

- To call an existing PL/SQL stored procedure that takes BOOLEAN PL/SQL parameters from JDBC, a PL/SQL wrapper procedure must be written.

First, let's examine the writing call specs for Java stored programs that take Boolean parameters. The following method `echo` simply returns the Boolean value passed to it:

```
public class BooleanExample {
    public static boolean echo(boolean b) { return b; }
}
```

A call spec to publish `echo` must use the NUMBER SQL type as follows:

```
CREATE OR REPLACE FUNCTION echo_boolean (b IN NUMBER)
    RETURN NUMBER
AS LANGUAGE JAVA
NAME 'BooleanExample.echo(boolean) return boolean';
```

As the following tests in SQL*Plus show, a zero passed to the Java stored function is converted into a Java `false`; any non zero is converted to a Java `true`.

```
SQL> select echo_boolean(0) FROM dual;

ECHO_BOOLEAN(0)
---------------
              0

SQL> SELECT echo_boolean(1) FROM dual;

ECHO_BOOLEAN(1)
---------------
              1

SQL> SELECT echo_boolean(2) FROM dual;

ECHO_BOOLEAN(2)
---------------
              1

SQL> select echo_boolean(-1) FROM dual;

ECHO_BOOLEAN(-1)
----------------
              1
```

**CALLING PL/SQL STORED PROCEDURES THAT CONTAIN BOOLEANS FROM JDBC**    How do you call a PL/SQL procedure that contains BOOLEAN parameters from JDBC? Rewriting the stored procedure to use NUMBER instead of BOOLEAN is often not a viable option. Instead, you can wrap the PL/SQL procedure with a second PL/SQL procedure that accepts the argument as an INTEGER and passes it to the first stored procedure. When the second procedure is called, Oracle performs the conversion from INTEGER to BOOLEAN.

The following example contains two stored procedures: proc_1, which accepts two BOOLEAN parameters and proc_1 wrapper, which accepts INTEGER parameters.

```
CREATE OR REPLACE PROCEDURE proc_1(x IN BOOLEAN, y IN BOOLEAN)
AS
BEGIN
  . . .
END;

CREATE OR REPLACE PROCEDURE proc_1_wrapper(x IN INTEGER, y IN INTEGER)
AS
  proc_1(int_to_bool(x), int_to_bool(y));
END;
```

The procedure proc_1_wrapper uses the following PL/SQL function to convert an INTEGER value to a BOOLEAN.

```
FUNCTION int_to_bool(i IN INTEGER) RETURN BOOLEAN
IS
BEGIN
  IF (i > 0) THEN
    RETURN TRUE;
  ELSE
    RETURN FALSE;
  END IF;
END;
```

The proc_1_wrapper can now be called from JDBC:

```
final int TRUE = 1;
final int FALSE = 0;
CallableStatement cs = conn.prepareCall("begin proc_1_wrapper(?, ?); end;");
cs.setInt(1, TRUE);
cs.setInt(2, FALSE);
cs.execute();
```

## Example 4: A Packaged Call Spec

When publishing Java methods, it is a good practice to organize logically related Java methods into a PL/SQL package. A PL/SQL package should not be confused with a Java package. Loosely analogous to a Java class, a PL/SQL package is made up of two parts:

■ A *package specification (spec)*, which serves as an interface to clients. It declares the types, constants, variables, exceptions, cursors, and subprograms that clients can use.

■ A *package body*, which implements the spec. A package body can contain PL/SQL—or in the case of Oracle8i, it can contain a call spec to a Java stored procedure.

Let's create a packaged call spec for the following class' methods:

```
public class Overloader {
  public static String get(String s1) {
    return "get(String) called.";
  }

  public static String get(String s1, String s2) {
```

```
    return "get(String, String) called.";
  }

  public static String get(int i) {
    return "get(int) called.";
  }

  public static String get(double d) {
    return "get(double) called.";
  }
}
```

Note that the foregoing Java class contains overloaded `get` methods. You can also overload published procedure and function names in a call spec. As in Java, overloaded procedures and functions are differentiated by the number and type of the arguments they take.

We will package the first three `get` methods only, omitting the `get(double)` method for reasons that will be made clear presently. The first step is to create a package spec:

```
-- Package spec
CREATE OR REPLACE PACKAGE pkg_overloader AS
  FUNCTION get (s1 IN VARCHAR2) RETURN VARCHAR2;
  FUNCTION get (s1 IN VARCHAR2, s2 IN VARCHAR2) RETURN VARCHAR2;
  FUNCTION get (n1 IN NUMBER) RETURN VARCHAR2;
END pkg_overloader;
```

Next, you create a package body containing call specs for the three Java methods:

```
-- Package body
CREATE OR REPLACE PACKAGE BODY pkg_overloader IS
  FUNCTION get (s1 IN VARCHAR2) RETURN VARCHAR2
  AS LANGUAGE JAVA
  NAME 'Overloader.get(java.lang.String) return java.lang.String';

  FUNCTION get (s1 IN VARCHAR2, s2 IN VARCHAR2) RETURN VARCHAR2
  AS LANGUAGE JAVA
  NAME 'Overloader.get(java.lang.String, java.lang.String)
    return java.lang.String';

  FUNCTION get (n1 IN NUMBER) RETURN VARCHAR2
  AS LANGUAGE JAVA
  NAME 'Overloader.get(int) return java.lang.String';
END pkg_overloader;
```

Tests performed in SQL*PLUS confirm that the three `get` functions are differentiated as distinct functions:

```
SQL> SELECT pkg_overloader.get('New', 'Monastery') FROM dual;

PKG_OVERLOADER.GET('NEW','MONASTERY')
-------------------------------------------------------------------
get(String, String) called.

SQL> SELECT pkg_overloader.get('Flight') FROM dual;
PKG_OVERLOADER.GET('FLIGHT'
-------------------------------------------------------------------
get(String) called.
SQL> SELECT pkg_overloader.get('Syeedas''s', 'Song') From DUAL;

PKG_OVERLOADER.GET('SYEEDAS''S','SONG')
-------------------------------------------------------------------
get(String, String) called.

SQL> SELECT pkg_overloader.get(19) FROM dual;

PKG_OVERLOADER.GET(19)
-------------------------------------------------------------------
SQL> SELECT pkg_overloader.get(2.5) FROM dual;

PKG_OVERLOADER.GET(2.5)
-------------------------------------------------------------------
get(int) called.
```

Note that any number passed to the get function will result in the `get(int)` Java method being called. Oracle will automatically convert the number into a Java `int` as illustrated by the foregoing "SELECT pkg_overloader.get(2.5) FROM dual" statement.

Not surprisingly, if you try to invoke a function or procedure whose signature is not supported in the call spec, you will get an error. Thus:

```
SQL> SELECT pkg_overloader.get('Syeedas''s', 'Song', 'Flute') FROM DUAL;
SELECT pkg_overloader.get('Syeedas''s', 'Song', 'Flute') FROM DUAL
       *
ERROR at line 1:
ORA-06553: PLS-306: wrong number or types of arguments in call to 'GET'
```

A short note on why the `get(double)` Java method was not incorporated in the package call spec. You will recall that subtypes of NUMBER, such as INTEGER and REAL, are not allowed in call specs. This means that the `get(double)` method would have to be represented as FUNCTION get (n1 IN NUMBER)—which is illegal because but such a signature already exists.

## Example 5: Passing Parameters to a main Method

A main method's String[] parameter can be mapped to multiple CHAR or VARCHAR2 call spec parameters. The following class MainArgs, whose main method prints arguments passed to it, will be used as an example:

```
public class MainArgs {
  public static void main(String[] args) {
    for (int i = 0; i < args.length; i++)
      System.out.println(args[i]);
  }
}
```

There is no direct way of passing an array to Java methods from SQL or PL/SQL, so call specs for a different number of arguments need to be written. The following example shows three overloaded call spec procedures. The first is parameter-less; the second takes one VARCHAR2 parameter, the third takes two VARHCAR2 parameters.

```
CREATE OR REPLACE PROCEDURE main_args
AS LANGUAGE JAVA
NAME 'MainArgs.main(java.lang.String[])';

CREATE OR REPLACE PROCEDURE main_args(s2 VARCHAR2)
AS LANGUAGE JAVA
NAME 'MainArgs.main(java.lang.String[])';

CREATE OR REPLACE PROCEDURE main_args(s1 VARCHAR2, s2 VARCHAR2)
AS LANGUAGE JAVA
NAME 'MainArgs.main(java.lang.String[])';
```

As a test, you can call the main_args call spec from SQL*Plus:

```
SQL> CALL main_args('Pueblo', 'Nuevo');
Pueblo
Nuevo
Call completed.
```

If you do not get any output in SQL*PLUS, make sure that you run the following scripts before calling main_args:

```
SQL> SET SERVEROUTPUT ON SIZE 5000;
SQL> CALL dbms_java.set_output(5000);
```

# Calling Java Stored Procedures SQL, PL/SQL, and Database Triggers

Once published into the database, Java stored procedures can be called from a variety of clients including PL/SQL, database triggers, SQL, and JDBC clients (see Table 9-10).

## Calling Java Stored Procedures from SQL and PL/SQL

You use the SQL CALL statement to call Java methods that are published at the top level, in PL/SQL packages, or in SQL object types. In SQL*Plus, you can execute the CALL statement interactively using the syntax:

```
CALL [schema_name.][{package_name | object_type_name}][@dblink_name]
{ procedure_name ([param[, param]...])
 | function_name ([param[, param]...]) INTO :host_variable};

where param stands for the following syntax:
{literal | :host_variable}
```

| Client | Calling Technique |
| --- | --- |
| PL/SQL | PL/SQL in any form—anonymous blocks, stored procedures, stored functions, and packages—can call Java stored procedures using the SQL CALL statement. |
| Database Triggers | Triggers can call Java stored procedures using the SQL CALL statement. :new and :old columns values can be passed to the Java stored procedures. |
| SQL DML | SELECT, INSERT, UPDATE, and DELETE statements can use Java stored methods that are published as functions. The function must pass purity rules and must not declare OUT or IN OUT parameters. |
| JDBC clients | JDBC clients can call Java stored procedures using a `CallableStatement` object. |

**TABLE 9-10.** *How Java Stored Procedures Can Be Called from Various Clients*

## Propagation of Uncaught Java Exceptions to PL/SQL and SQL

When a Java stored procedure is called from PL/SQL, an uncaught Java exception is propagated to PL/SQL as the error "ORA-29532 Java call terminated by uncaught Java exception: <exception string>." The exception can be caught in an EXCEPTION clause.

Host variables (that is, variables declared in a host environment) must be prefixed with ":". A host variable can appear only once in a CALL statement. Thus the CALL statement in the following SQL*Plus script is illegal and gives the error message "ORA-03106: fatal two-task communication protocol error."

```
VAR s VARCHAR2(50)
BEGIN
  :s := 'Impromptu';
END;
CALL main_args(:s, :s) -- Illegal: duplicate host variables
```

A procedure or function that takes no parameters must be called with an empty parameter list:

```
CALL main_args(); -- () required
```

## Calling Java Stored Code from Database Triggers

Consider the following BEFORE INSERT trigger that validates a row before insertion into the demo.item table. If the data inserted passes the validity test, the trigger calculates the total column as `actual_price * quantity`; if not, an application error is raised. In a real-world application, the trigger would be implemented as a BEFORE INSERT OR UPDATE trigger.

```
CREATE OR REPLACE TRIGGER before_line_item_i
  BEFORE INSERT
  ON item
  FOR EACH ROW
DECLARE
  v_err_num NUMBER;
  v_err_msg VARCHAR2(255);
BEGIN
  validate_line_item(:NEW.product_id, :NEW.actual_price, :NEW.quantity,
                v_err_num, v_err_msg);
  IF v_err_num > 0 -- No errors
  THEN
```

```
    :NEW.total := :NEW.actual_price * :NEW.quantity;
  ELSE
    RAISE_APPLICATION_ERROR(v_err_num, v_err_msg);
  END IF;
END;
```

The trigger calls a Java stored procedure to do the validation:

```
import java.sql.*;
import oracle.jdbc.driver.*;

public class PriceValidator {
  public static void validateLineItem(Integer productID,
                                      Double actualPrice,
                                      Integer quantity,
                                      int[] errorNum, // OUT
                                      String[] errorMsg // OUT
                                      ) throws SQLException {
    if (productID != null && actualPrice != null
        && quantity != null) {
      String q = "SELECT NVL(min_price, 0)" +
                 "   FROM demo.price" +
                 " WHERE end_date IS NULL" +
                 " AND product_id = ?";
      ResultSet rs = null;
      PreparedStatement ps = null;
      try {
        Connection conn = new OracleDriver().defaultConnection();
        ps = conn.prepareStatement(q);
        ps.setInt(1, productID.intValue());
        rs = ps.executeQuery();
        if (rs.next())
          if (actualPrice.doubleValue() >= rs.getDouble(1))
            errorNum[0] = 1; // All's well
          else {
            errorNum[0] = -20005;
            errorMsg[0] = "Price lower than min price.";
          }
        else { // No data found
          errorNum[0] = -20000;
          errorMsg[0] = "Product not found in price table.";
        }
      } catch (Exception e) {
          errorNum[0] = -20001;
          errorMsg[0] = e.getMessage();
      } finally {
        if (rs != null) rs.close();
        if (ps != null) ps.close();
      }
```

```
        }
      else {
        errorNum[0] = -20004;
        errorMsg[0] = "Line item incompletely filled out";
      }
   }
}
```

The `validateLineItem` method first checks if `productID`, `actualPrice`, and `quantity` are not null. It then queries the demo.price table to get the minimum price for the given product ID, and compares the minimum price with `actualPrice`. If there are no errors, the method returns a 1 through the `errorNum` variable; otherwise an error number and message is returned through the `errorNum` and `errorMsg` variables.

For readers who know PL/SQL, the following is the PL/SQL version of the `validateLineItem` method:

```
CREATE OR REPLACE PROCEDURE validate_line_item_plsql
  (i_product_id IN item.product_id%TYPE,
   i_actual_price IN item.actual_price%TYPE,
   i_quantity IN item.quantity%TYPE,
   o_err_num OUT NUMBER,
   o_err_msg OUT VARCHAR2
  )
AS
  v_min_price price.min_price%TYPE;
BEGIN
  IF (i_product_id IS NOT NULL
    AND i_actual_price IS NOT NULL
    AND i_quantity IS NOT NULL)
  THEN
    SELECT NVL(min_price, 0)
      INTO v_min_price
      FROM demo.price
     WHERE end_date IS NULL
       AND product_id = i_product_id;

    IF (i_actual_price >= v_min_price)
    THEN
      o_err_num := 1; -- All's well
    ELSE
      o_err_num := -20005;
      o_err_msg := 'Price lower than min price';
    END IF;
  ELSE
    o_err_num := -20004;
```

```
      o_err_msg := 'Line item incompletely filled out';
   END IF;
EXCEPTION
  WHEN NO_DATA_FOUND
  THEN
     o_err_num := -20000;
     o_err_msg := 'Product not found in price table.';
  WHEN OTHERS
  THEN
     o_err_num := -20001;
     o_err_msg := 'Unknown error';
END;
```

The call spec to publish the Java method is shown here. Note that SQLException is not declared in the call spec.

```
CREATE OR REPLACE PROCEDURE validate_line_item
  (i_product_id IN NUMBER,
   i_actual_price IN NUMBER,
   i_quantity IN NUMBER,
   o_err_num OUT NUMBER,
   o_err_msg OUT VARCHAR2
  )
AS LANGUAGE JAVA
NAME 'PriceValidator.validateLineItem(java.lang.Integer,
  java.lang.Double,java.lang.Integer,
  int[],java.lang.String[])';
```

Now we can test the trigger with INSERTs:

```
INSERT INTO item (ORDER_ID, ITEM_ID, PRODUCT_ID, ACTUAL_PRICE, QUANTITY)
  VALUES (1010, 6, 103130, 10, 1);
```

The INSERT succeeds because the actual price (10) is above the minimum price (8) for product 103130. As expected, the following INSERT fails, producing the error "ORA-20005: Price lower than min price:"

```
INSERT INTO item (ORDER_ID, ITEM_ID, PRODUCT_ID, ACTUAL_PRICE, QUANTITY)
  VALUES (1010, 5, 103130, 3, 1);
```

## Using Java Stored Functions in SQL DML

SELECT, INSERT, UPDATE, and DELETE statements can use Java stored methods that are published as functions. The function must pass purity rules and must not declare OUT or IN OUT parameters.

## Purity Rules for Methods That Are Callable from SQL DML Statements

To control side effects, a Java method must conform to certain purity rules when called from SQL DML statements:

- If accessed from an INSERT, UPDATE, or DELETE statement, the method should not query or modify any database tables modified by that statement.

- If accessed from a SELECT statement or a parallelized INSERT, UPDATE, or DELETE statement, the method should not modify any database tables.

- If accessed from a SELECT, INSERT, UPDATE, or DELETE statement, the method should not execute SQL transaction control statements (such as COMMIT), session control statements (such as SET ROLE), or system control statements (such as ALTER SYSTEM). In addition, the method should not execute DDL statements (such as CREATE) because such operations are automatically committed.

A method that violates any of the rules will result in a run-time error when the SQL statement is parsed.

**EXAMPLES**    You have already seen how to call a stored function from SQL*Plus. For example, published stored function echo_boolean was called in the Tip "Writing Call Specs to Publish Java Procedures in the Oracle Data Dictionary" with the following syntax:

```
SQL> SELECT echo_boolean(1) FROM dual;
```

Host variables can also be used in SQL*Plus:

```
SQL> VARIABLE sales NUMBER
SQL> CALL total_sales_for_cust(204) INTO :sales;
```

```
Call completed.

SQL> PRINT sales;

   SALES
---------
  15071.4
```

## Calling Stored Procedures from JDBC

PL/SQL stored procedures and published Java stored procedures can be called from JDBC using a `CallableStatement` object. A `CallableStatement` object is returned by the `prepareCall(String sql)` method of a `Connection` (or `OracleConnection`) class. For the `sql` parameter, use either the SQL92 escape syntax or the Oracle syntax shown in Table 9-11.

IN parameter values are set using `setXXX` methods. OUT parameter types must be registered with the `registerOutParameter` method prior to executing the stored procedure; after execution, their values are retrieved via `getXXX` methods. A `CallableStatement` can return a `ResultSet` object.

The following examples show the techniques used in calling stored procedures from JDBC.

| | | |
|---|---|---|
| **Stored procedure without parameters** | **SQL92** | `"{call procedure_name}"` |
| | **Oracle** | `"begin procedure_name(); end;"` |
| **Stored procedure with parameters** | **SQL92** | `"{call procedure_name(?, ?, . . .)}"` |
| | **Oracle** | `"begin procedure_name(?, ?, . . .); end;"` |
| **Stored function** | **SQL92** | `"{? = call function_name(?, ?, . . .)}"` |
| | **Oracle** | `"begin ? := function_name(?, ?, . . .); end;"` |

**TABLE 9-11.** *SQL 92 and Oracle Syntax for Calling Stored Procedures and Functions from JDBC*

## Example 1: Calling a Stored Function That Takes an IN Parameter from JDBC

The following JDBC method calls the stored function total_sales_for_cust. Recall that total_sales_for_cust is the published name of a Java method developed in the Tip "Writing Call Specs to Publish Java Procedures in the Oracle Data Dictionary."

```
public void callTotalSales(int custID) throws SQLException {
  OracleCallableStatement ocs = (OracleCallableStatement)conn.prepareCall(
    "{ ? = call total_sales_for_cust(?) }" );
  ocs.registerOutParameter(1, Types.DOUBLE);
  ocs.setInt(2, custID);
  ocs.execute();

  double sales = ocs.getDouble(1);
  System.out.println("Total sales:" + sales);
  ocs.close();
}
```

## Example 2: Calling a Stored Procedure That Takes an IN OUT Parameter from JDBC

To bind a '?' placeholder that corresponds to an IN OUT parameter, you must use both `registerOutParameter` and `setXXX`. The following JDBC code excerpt calls the swap stored procedure (created in "Writing Call Specs to Publish Java Procedures in the Oracle Data Dictionary"), which takes two IN/OUT NUMBER parameters and swaps them.

```
OracleCallableStatement ocs = (OracleCallableStatement)conn.prepareCall(
  "{call swap(?, ?) }" );
ocs.registerOutParameter(1, Types.FLOAT);
ocs.registerOutParameter(2, Types.FLOAT);

float x = 1, y =2;
ocs.setFloat(1, x);
ocs.setFloat(2, y);
ocs.execute();

float xx = ocs.getFloat(1);
float yy = ocs.getFloat(2);
System.out.println("x=" + x + "  y=" + y + "  xx=" + xx + "  yy=" + yy);
```

The output generated is

```
x=1.0  y=2.0  xx=2.0  yy=1.0
```

As the foregoing output shows, the values of the variables x and y remain unchanged after the stored procedure call.

## Example 3: Accessing PL/SQL Package Variables

PL/SQL package variables can be declared in a PL/SQL package body or specification. The first time a user references a package element, the entire package is loaded into the SGA. Data declared in the package is unique to a session (that is, the data is private to the session) and remains in the SGA for the duration of the session.

Consider the following package called session_data_pkg which contains two package variables, session-start-time and user-id:

- **session_start_time** is declared in the specification of the package, and as a result, is a global, public variable. This means that programs running outside the package (but running in the same session) can access it.

- **user_id** is declared in the body of the package, and consequently is private to the package. Programs running outside the package cannot change the value of the variable; however, they can read its value through the accessor function get_user_id.

```
CREATE OR REPLACE PACKAGE session_data_pkg
IS
  -- Global public data
  session_start_time CONSTANT DATE := SYSDATE;

  -- Accessor function declaration
  FUNCTION get_user_id RETURN VARCHAR2;
END session_data_pkg;
```

```
CREATE OR REPLACE PACKAGE BODY session_data_pkg
IS
  -- Package-level data (private to the package body)
  user_id CONSTANT VARCHAR2(10) := USER;

  -- Accessor function implementation
  FUNCTION get_user_id RETURN VARCHAR2
  IS
  BEGIN
    RETURN user_id;
  END;
END session_data_pkg;
```

Calling Stored Procedures from JDBC

The following Java stored procedure accesses the two variables using JDBC:

```
import java.sql.*;
import oracle.jdbc.driver.*;

public class PLSQLPackageData {
  public static void test() throws SQLException {
    Connection conn = new OracleDriver().defaultConnection();
    CallableStatement cs = null;
    try {
      // Access private PL/SQL package var through accessor function
      cs = (CallableStatement)conn.prepareCall(
        "{ ? = call session_data_pkg.get_user_id() }" );
      cs.registerOutParameter(1, Types.CHAR);
      cs.execute();
      String userID = cs.getString(1);
      System.out.println("User " + userID);

      // Access public PL/SQL package variable
      cs = (CallableStatement)conn.prepareCall(
        "begin ? := session_data_pkg.session_start_time; end;" );
      cs.registerOutParameter(1, Types.DATE);
      cs.execute();
      java.sql.Date startDate = cs.getDate(1);
      System.out.println("Package instantiated at " + startDate.toString());
    } finally {
      cs.close();
    }
  }
}
```

To test the stored procedure from SQL*Plus, a call spec for the Java method can be written:

```
CREATE OR REPLACE PROCEDURE plsql_package_data
AS LANGUAGE JAVA
NAME 'PLSQLPackageData.test()';
```

The call spec can now be called from SQL*Plus:

```
SQL> CALL plsql_package_data();
User DEMO

Package instantiated at 1999-09-10

Call completed.
```

## Example 4: Retrieving a Record Set from a PL/SQL Stored Procedure

A REF CURSOR (cursor variable type) is a pointer to a query work area. It provides a mechanism for passing query results between different stored procedures and for passing query results from stored procedures to Java, as well.

In JDBC, a REF CURSOR can be retrieved from a PL/SQL stored procedure and materialized as a `ResultSet`. The technique is as follows:

- Use a `CallableStatement` or an `OracleCallableStatement` to call the stored procedure.

- Retrieve the REF CURSOR data with `getObject` if you use a `CallableStatement` or with getCursor if you use `OracleCallableStatement`.

- Cast the REF CURSOR to a JDBC `ResultSet` object.

**NOTE**
*In the current release of Oracle8i, there is no direct way of retrieving a PL/SQL table through JDBC.*

This example illustrates how to use Java to retrieve a REF CURSOR from a PL/SQL stored function.

**CREATING THE PKG_REF_CURSOR PL/SQL PACKAGE**   A PL/SQL package pkg_ref_cursor, which is used at a later stage by the Java example, is depicted in the following sample code. The package specification contains declarations for a REF CURSOR type orders_cursor_t and a function get_orders. The get_orders function returns all the orders placed by a specified customer ID in the form of an orders_cursor_t REF CURSOR.

```
CREATE OR REPLACE PACKAGE demo.pkg_ref_cursor AS
  TYPE orders_cursor_t IS REF CURSOR RETURN demo.sales_order%ROWTYPE;

  FUNCTION get_orders(i_cust_id IN demo.sales_order.customer_id%TYPE)
    RETURN orders_cursor_t;
END pkg_ref_cursor;
```

The package body is

```
CREATE OR REPLACE PACKAGE BODY demo.pkg_ref_cursor AS
   FUNCTION get_orders(i_cust_id IN demo.sales_order.customer_id%TYPE)
     RETURN orders_cursor_t
   IS
     rc orders_cursor_t;
   BEGIN
     OPEN rc FOR SELECT *
                   FROM demo.sales_order
                  WHERE customer_id = i_cust_id;
     RETURN rc;
   END;
END pkg_ref_cursor;
```

**CALLING THE GET_ORDERS STORED FUNCTION FROM JAVA**    The
following Java method `getOrders` takes a `custID` as a parameter, calls the pkg_
ref_cursor.get_orders PL/SQL function, and returns a `ResultSet`.

```
public ResultSet getOrders(int custID) throws SQLException {
  CallableStatement cs = conn.prepareCall(
    "{ ? = call pkg_ref_cursor.get_orders(?) }" );
    // Bind the ? placeholders
  cs.registerOutParameter(1, OracleTypes.CURSOR);
  cs.setInt(2, custID);

  cs.execute();

  // Cast CURSOR to ResultSet
  ResultSet rs = (ResultSet)cs.getObject(1);
   cs.close();
   return rs;
}
```

Two observations:

- In the call to the PL/SQL function, the OUT '?' placeholder is bound through
  the use of `registerOutParameter(1, OracleTypes.CURSOR)`. The
  Oracle type code for a REF CURSOR is `OracleTypes.CURSOR`. The IN '?'
  placeholder is bound through the use of `setInt(2, custID)`. If you do
  not bind all host variables, you will get an "ORA-01008: not all variables
  bound" error.

- After executing the stored function, the `getObject` method is used to retrieve
  the REF CURSOR data as a Java `Object`, which is then casted to a `ResultSet`.

Now that the REF CURSOR has been materialized as a standard JDBC
`ResultSet`, the data can be readily displayed. In the following code, column names
are obtained through use of the `ResultSetMetaData.getColumnName` method.

```
public void displayResultSet(ResultSet rs) throws SQLException {
  ResultSetMetaData rsm = rs.getMetaData();
  final int CC = rsm.getColumnCount();

  // Display column names
  for (int i = 1; i <= CC; i++)
    System.out.print(rsm.getColumnName(i) + " ");

  // Display data
  while (rs.next()) {
    System.out.println();
    for (int i = 1; i <= CC; i++)
      System.out.print(rs.getObject(i) + " ");
  }
}
```

# Tips Review

Four general categories of JDBC and SQLJ Tips & Techniques were presented in this chapter.

Oracle's JDBC drivers provide a variety of ways for improving JDBC performance. Auto-commit mode can be turned off to avoid commits after every DML statement. `oracle.sql` objects can be more precise and efficient than standard JDBC objects in certain situations. Prepared statements avoid unnecessary compilation overhead. Network round trips can be reduced by prefetching rows, batching updates, and defining column types. Closing `Connection`, `Statement`, and `ResultSet` objects after finishing with them will free resources. Certain applications require some form of connection sharing to avoid frequently creating JDBC connections. Although Java multithreading on the client side can enhance concurrency and functionality, no benefit is gained from server-side Java multithreading.

Oracle's object types and collection structures can help in the modeling of complex real world objects in the database, such as retrieving Oracle object types and collections (VARRAYs and nested tables).

Streaming is an important technique for today's multimedia data. Several precautions to observe during the streaming of LONG columns, and tips on streaming LOB are available.

Finally, there are techniques for exploiting stored procedures. The `loadjava` tool can be used to load Java programs into the database, after which call specs can be written to publish them into the Oracle data dictionary. Once published, Java stored procedures can be called from a variety of clients including SQL, PL/SQL, database triggers, and JDBC. REF CURSOR can be used to retrieve a multirow record set from a stored procedure to a JDBC program.

Tips Review

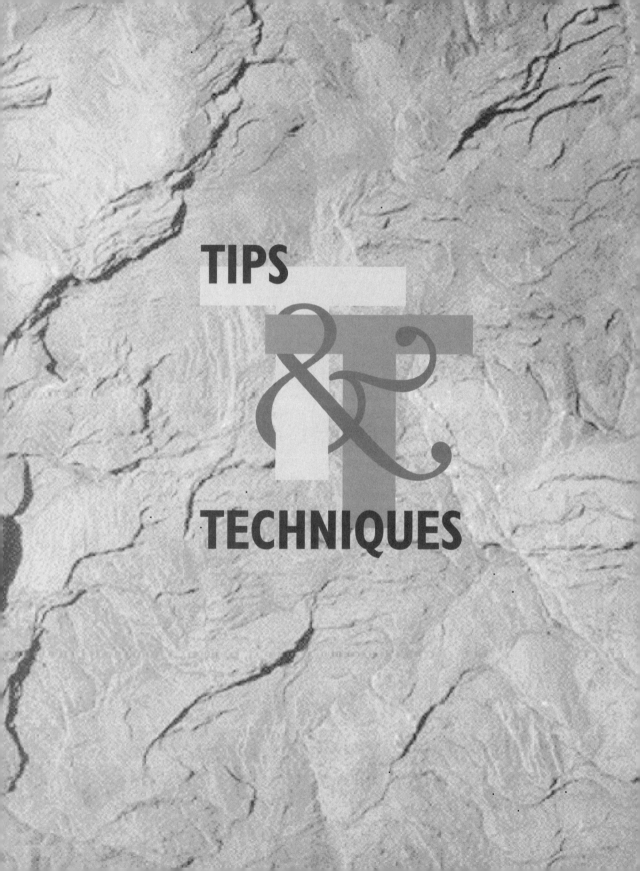

TIPS

&

TECHNIQUES

# CHAPTER
## 10

## Enterprise JavaBeans

Enterprise JavaBeans (EJB) is a powerful cross-platform, server-side component model for Java. In Chapter 2, we examined how the Java enabling architecture of Oracle8i, in particular the embedded JVM and CORBA ORB, supports the EJB component model. We saw that an EJB lives in a container that provides it with transaction, concurrency, data persistence, and security services. This chapter presents Tips & Techniques to help you harness these services in Oracle8i.

First, the basic mechanics for developing EJB components are presented. These techniques include the following:

- Defining the home interface, the remote interface, and the bean class

- Defining the deployment descriptor

- Compiling and packaging the EJB

- Deploying the EJB to Oracle8i

- Writing the EJB client

The EJB transaction model supports container-managed transaction demarcation as well as explicitly managed transaction demarcation. The following tips on EJB transactions are presented:

- Choosing the right declarative attribute for container-managed transaction demarcation

- ShoppingCart: A Stateful Session Bean That Uses Container-Managed Transaction Demarcation

- Saving a session object handle for later reactivation

- Using bean-managed transaction demarcation for fine-grained transaction control

The following tips on designing EJB components are presented:

- Differentiating between session and entity beans

- Designing EJB components when entity beans are not supported

- Choosing between pass-by-value objects and entity beans

- Reducing network traffic with session beans

# Preliminary Remarks

This section describes naming conventions used in this chapter, EJB programming restrictions, sending output to a trace file, overcoming loadjava memory problems, and checking IIOP connections.

## Naming Conventions for EJB Classes, Interfaces, and Packages

When programming EJB components, you often need to work with a large number of interfaces and classes. A good naming convention that clearly delineates the nature of each interface or class is a great help. The examples in this chapter follow the naming convention shown in Table 10-1.

For the text form of the deployment descriptor (described in "Defining the Deployment Descriptor"), this chapter uses a "TDD.ejb" suffix. This distinguishes the text form of the descriptor from the serialized deployment descriptor, with "DD.ser" as the suffix.

It is a good practice to separate interfaces and implementations into different packages. For example, in the ShoppingCart EJB that will be developed in this chapter, the home and remote interfaces are placed in a package called `shoppingCart`, while the bean class is placed in a package called `shoppingCartImpl`.

## EJB Programming Restrictions

The EJB specification places a number of important restrictions on programmers. An EJB is not allowed to do the following:

- Start new threads or attempt to terminate the running thread.

- Use thread synchronization primitives.

- Call the underlying transaction manager directly. This restriction is relaxed for TX_BEAN_MANAGED beans; such beans can use the JTA interface to demarcate transactions (see "Using Bean-Managed Transaction Demarcation for Fine-Grained Transaction Control").

- Use JDBC commit and rollback methods.

- Issue direct SQL commit or rollback statements with SQLJ or JDBC.

- Change its `java.security.Identity`.

| | Class/Interface Name Suffix | Example |
|---|---|---|
| **Remote interface** | ⎯⎯ | `ShoppingCart.java` |
| **Home interface** | Home | `ShoppingCartHome.java` |
| **Bean class** | Bean | `ShoppingCartBean.java` |
| **Client that calls bean methods** | Client | `ShoppingCartClient.java` |
| **Text form of deployment descriptor** | TDD | `ShoppingCartTDD.ejb` |

**TABLE 10-1.**   *EJB Naming Conventions Used in This Chapter*

## Sending Output to a Trace File

For debugging, it is often useful to insert `System.out.println` statements in a bean class. The output goes to a trace file in a directory specified by the USER_DUMP_DEST configuration parameter.

## Overcoming loadjava Problems

You may experience memory problems loading large jar files in Oracle8i. Increasing the value of SHARED_POOL_SIZE will very likely solve this problem. (For a discussion of Java memory issues, see Chapter 2.)

To confirm that loadjava has properly loaded and resolved a class, connect as the user who loaded the class—for instance, demo/demo—and execute the following query:

```
SELECT dbms_java.longname(object_name), status
  FROM user_objects
 WHERE object_type = 'JAVA CLASS';
```

A correctly loaded and resolved class will show a 'VALID' status code.

## Checking Your IIOP Connection with Session Shell

The Session Shell tool can be used to check if your IIOP connection is functioning properly. For example, run it from the command line:

```
sess_sh -u demo/demo -s sess_iiop://localhost:2481:orcl
```

The -s specifies the service URL which has the form

```
sess_iiop://<host>:<lport>:<sid>
```

where <host> is the host server, <lport> is the listener port for IIOP request, and <sid> is the database SID. Note that 2481 is the default listener port for IIOP requests; the listener port can be configured in the listener.ora file.

If the IIOP connection is set up correctly, you will invoke the session shell with the $ prompt:

```
--Aurora/ORB Session Shell--
--type "help" at the command line for help message
$
```

Type "exit" to close the Session Shell tool.

# Basic EJB Techniques in Oracle8i

This chapter will develop EJB components for an online shopping cart application. The first EJB will be a simple stateless session bean named `ProductSearcher`, which will allow a customer to search a catalog of products by description. Developing an EJB involves the following steps:

- Defining home and remote interfaces

- Defining the bean class

- Defining the deployment descriptor

- Compiling and packaging the bean

- Deploying the bean to the database

Much the same mechanics apply to developing a stateful session bean or an entity bean.

## Defining the Home Interface, the Remote Interface, and the Bean Class

You must define a home interface, a remote interface, and a bean class for every EJB you write. This section describes the rules to follow in developing these constructs. This section also walks you through the development of `ProductSearcher`, a stateless session bean that encapsulates the process of an online shopper searching through a catalog of products.

### The Home Interface

The home interface defines the bean's life-cycle methods that clients call to create, find, and remove bean instances. The home interface must extend `javax.ejb.EJBHome`, which in turn extends `java.rmi.Remote`, as shown in the following:

```
public interface javax.ejb.EJBHome extends java.rmi.Remote {
  // Remove an EJB object identified by its primary key
  public abstract void remove(Object primaryKey)
    throws java.rmi.RemoteException, javax.ejb.RemoveException;
```

```
  // Remove an EJB object identified by its handle
  public abstract void remove(Handle handle)
    throws java.rmi.RemoteException, javax.ejb.RemoveException;

  // Obtain the EJBMetaData interface for the EJB. Allows a
  // client to obtain information about the EJB. Used by tools.
  public abstract javax.ejb.EJBMetaData getEJBMetaData()
    throws java.rmi.RemoteException;
}
```

**NOTE**
*The home interface is implemented by the EJB container (see "The Bean Class").*

A client locates the home interface through the Java Naming and Directory Interface (JNDI), then uses the home interface to create a bean object. The home interface specifies one or more `create` methods. A `create` method can take parameters from the client to initialize the state of a newly created bean object.

For each `create` method in the home interface, you must specify a corresponding `ejbCreate` method in the bean class with the same signature. When a client invokes `create` on the home, the container interposes whatever services are required at that point and then calls the corresponding `ejbCreate` method in the bean itself.

**REQUIREMENTS OF A HOME INTERFACE**     For reference, the following is a summary of the requirements of a home interface:

- A home interface must extend `javax.ejb.EJBHome`.

- A home interface must define at least one `create` method. Stateless session beans must define only one `create` method; the method takes no arguments.

- The return type for the `create` methods must be the remote interface.

- The `create` methods must be valid RMI methods: their arguments and return values must be serializable types. They must throw `java.rmi.RemoteException` and `javax.ejb.CreateException`.

- The home interface `create` methods must match the counterpart `ejbCreate` methods defined in the bean class. However, the home interface `create` method must return the remote interface type, whereas the bean class `ejbCreate` methods must return `void`.

**ProductSearcherHome: THE HOME INTERFACE**    Here is the definition of the home interface for the ProductSearcher bean:

```
package productSearcher;

import javax.ejb.*;
import java.rmi.RemoteException;

public interface ProductSearcherHome extends EJBHome {
  public ProductSearcher create()
    throws CreateException, RemoteException;
}
```

As with all home interfaces for stateless session beans, `ProductSearcherHome` has one no-argument `create` method. You cannot define `create` methods with arguments in a stateless session bean. This makes sense because in a stateless session bean there is no conversational state that needs to be initialized.

## The Remote Interface

The remote interface lists all the methods or public interfaces of the bean that clients can call. The remote interface extends `javax.ejb.EJBObject`, which in turn extends `java.rmi.Remote` as shown in the following:

```
public interface javax.ejb.EJBObject extends java.rmi.Remote {
  // Obtain the EJB home interface
  public abstract javax.ejb.EJBHome getEJBHome()
    throws java.rmi.RemoteException;

  // Obtain the primary key of the EJB object
  public abstract java.lang.Object getPrimaryKey()
    throws java.rmi.RemoteException;

  // Remove the EJB object
  public abstract void remove()
    throws java.rmi.RemoteException, javax.ejb.RemoveException;

  // Obtain a handle for the EJB object
  public abstract Handle getHandle() throws java.rmi.RemoteException;

  // Test if a given EJB object is identical to the invoked EJB object
  public abstract boolean isIdentical(javax.ejb.EJBObject obj)
    throws java.rmi.RemoteException;
}
```

Defining Required Interfaces and the Bean Class

**NOTE**
*Like the home interface, the remote interface is implemented by the EJB container (see "The Bean Class").*

**REQUIREMENTS OF A REMOTE INTERFACE**    The following is a summary of the rules you must follow when developing a remote interface:

- A remote interface must extend `javax.ejb.EJBObject`.

- A remote interface can define zero or more business methods. The methods must be declared as `public`; they cannot be `final` and they cannot be `static`. Their names must not begin with "ejb."

- Each method in the remote interface must have a matching method signature (including the exceptions thrown) in the bean class.

These methods must be legal RMI methods: their arguments and return values must be serializable types and they must throw `java.rmi.RemoteException`. In EJB 1.1, an EJB should throw the `javax.ejb.EJBException` or another `RuntimeException` to signal nonapplication exceptions to the container.

### ProductSearcher: THE REMOTE INTERFACE

The `ProductSearcher` remote interface is as follows:

```
package productSearcher;

import javax.ejb.EJBObject;
import java.rmi.RemoteException;
import java.sql.SQLException;
import java.util.Enumeration;

public interface ProductSearcher extends EJBObject {
  public Enumeration searchByDescription(String likeClause)
    throws RemoteException, SQLException;
}
```

The `searchByDescription` method allows clients to search for products by name. For example, to get a list of products with "SOFTBALL" in their descriptions, a client could call the method with "%SOFTBALL%" as the `likeClause` parameter. Since multiple items may be returned, an `Enumeration` is used to hold the results.

**NOTE**
*You can enhance* searchByDescription *by using a text search with interMedia Text, rather than a LIKE search. interMedia Text is described in Chapter 11.*

You can easily envision additional "searchBy" methods for the ProductSearcher interface. For instance, a searchByProductSKU method would be useful to clients.

## The Bean Class
The bean class (also called the bean implementation) implements the bean's business logic. The bean class will reside on the server.

**REQUIREMENTS OF A BEAN CLASS**    Here are some important rules you must follow when writing a bean class:

- For each method signature you expose in the remote interface, there must be a matching method signature in the bean class.

- For each create method you specify in the home interface, there must be a corresponding ejbCreate method in the bean class.

- Bean methods must be legal RMI/IIOP methods: their arguments and return values must be serializable types and they must throw java.rmi.RemoteException.

- An entity bean class must implement javax.ejb.EnityBean. A session bean must implement javax.ejb.SessionBean. (Both javax.ejb.EntityBean and javax.ejb.SesssionBean extend javax.ejb.EnterpriseBean.)

- A bean class should never define constructors.

- A bean class must be defined as public. It cannot be abstract, and it cannot be final.

**ProductSearcherBean: THE BEAN CLASS**    The business logic of ProductSearcherBean is rather simple: it selects products from the demo.product table matching a user's request. ProductSearcherBean

### Who Implements the Home and Remote Interfaces?

Oddly, you are not required to implement the home or remote interfaces in the bean class. That is, your bean class does not have to say `implements Home1, Remote1`, where `Home1` and `Remote1` are the home and remote interfaces. In fact, you are discouraged from implementing the remote interface because of the danger of passing this as a method argument or result.

When a bean is deployed in the database, Oracle8i deployment tools automatically generate classes that implement the remote and home interfaces. The inputs to the tools are the home interface, the remote interface, and the bean class that you write. The outputs are remote Java objects that are accessible from a client through the standard Java API for remote object invocation. A client never interacts with a bean class directly but rather through the generated objects. This scheme enables the EJB container to intercede in client operations on the bean.

implements the `javax.ejb.SessionBean` interface. The fact that the bean is stateless rather than stateful is specified in its deployment descriptor.

```
package productSearcherImpl;

import productSearcher.ProductInfo;
import productSearcherImpl.VectorEnumeration;

import java.sql.*;
import java.rmi.RemoteException;
import javax.ejb.*;
import java.util.Enumeration;
import java.util.Vector;

public class ProductSearcherBean implements SessionBean {

  public Enumeration searchByDescription(String likeClause)
    throws RemoteException, SQLException {

    // This will be sent to a trace file on the server
    System.out.println("From ProductSearcherBean.searchByDescription()");

    PreparedStatement ps = null;
    ResultSet rs = null;
    try {
```

```
      Connection conn =
         new oracle.jdbc.driver.OracleDriver().defaultConnection();
      ps = conn.prepareStatement(
            "SELECT a.product_id, description, list_price" +
            "  FROM demo.product a, demo.price b" +
            " WHERE a.product_id = b.product_id" +
            "    AND description LIKE ? " +
            "    AND end_date IS NULL");
      ps.setString(1, likeClause);
      rs = ps.executeQuery();
      Vector vect = new Vector();
      while (rs.next()) {
        ProductInfo prod = new ProductInfo(rs.getInt(1),
                        rs.getString(2), rs.getDouble(3));
        vect.addElement(prod);
      }

      if (vect.size() > 0)
        return new VectorEnumeration(vect);
      else
        return null;
    } finally {
      if (rs != null) rs.close();
      if (ps != null) ps.close();
    }
  }

  public void ejbCreate() throws CreateException, RemoteException {}

  // SessionBean interface methods
  public void ejbActivate() {}
  public void ejbPassivate() {}
  public void ejbRemove() {}
  public void setSessionContext(SessionContext ctx) {}
}
```

**Defining Required Interfaces and the Bean Class**

Examine the methods in ProductSearcherBean. As a stateless session bean, it has one no-argument ejbCreate method that matches the create method in ProductSearcherHome except for the void return type. The four SessionBean interface methods—ejbActivate, ejbPassivate, ejbRemove, and setSessionContext—are not implemented.

Finally, there is one business method, searchByDescription. Although the bean class does not declare that it implements the ProductSearcher remote interface, the searchByDescription method signatures in ProductSearcherBean and the ProductSearcher (the remote interface) are precisely the same. The searchByDescription method simply queries the database using JDBC and returns the results as a VectorEnumeration collection of ProductInfo objects. The ProductInfo class will be described next.

**ProductInfo: THE SERIALIZABLE CLASS**     `ProductSearcherBean` uses
`ProductInfo` to simplify the passing of product information—product ID,
description, and price—to the client. `ProductInfo` is defined as follows:

```
package productSearcher;

public class ProductInfo implements java.io.Serializable {
  private int id = -1;
  private String description = null;
  private double price = -1;

  public ProductInfo(int id, String description, double currentPrice) {
    this.id = id;
    this.description = description;
    this.price = currentPrice;
  }

  public String toString() {
    return Integer.toString(id) + ": " + description +
      " (Price: " + price + ")";
  }

  public int getID() { return id; }
  public String getDescription() { return description; }
  public double getPrice() { return price; }
}
```

Notice that `ProductInfo` is not a bean: it implements `java.ioSerializable`,
not `javax.ejb.EntityBean`. This means that a `ProductInfo` object created
on the server will be passed by value to the client—the object will be serialized and
a copy of the object (not a remote object reference) will be provided to the client.
The section "Choosing Between Pass-By-Value Objects and Entity Beans" discusses
the design issue of modeling objects as pass-by-value objects versus entity beans.

**RETURNING AN ENUMERATION**     `ProductSearcherBean` uses a class
called `VectorEnumeration` to pass back a collection of `ProductInfo` objects
to the client. `VectorEnumeration` implements `java.io.Serializable` and
`java.util.Enumeration` as follows:

```
package productSearcherImpl;

import java.io.Serializable;
import java.util.Enumeration;
import java.util.NoSuchElementException;
import java.util.Vector;
```

```
public class VectorEnumeration implements Serializable, Enumeration {
  private Vector vect;
  private int count = 0;

  public VectorEnumeration(Vector vect) {
    this.vect = vect;
  }

  public boolean hasMoreElements() {
    return count < vect.size();
  }

  public Object nextElement() {
    if (count < vect.size())
      return vect.elementAt(count++);
    throw new NoSuchElementException();
  }
}
```

If you exclude the implements `Serializable` declaration in the definition of
`VectorEnumeration`, you will get a `java.io.NotSerializableException`
run-time exception, which will be logged in the trace file as follows:

```
org.omg.CORBA.MARSHAL[completed=MAYBE,
  reason=java.io.NotSerializableException: java.util.VectorEnumerator]
```

## Defining the Deployment Descriptor

EJB gives you the ability to specify security and transaction behavior with
declarative attributes—at the bean level or at the method level of the bean.
The specification of attributes is done through deployment descriptor classes.

In EJB 1.0, deployment descriptors are Java `serializable` classes defined
in the `javax.ejb.deployment` package. In EJB 1.1, JavaSoft has changed the
deployment descriptor to XML instead of `serializable` classes.

To simplify the writing of deployment descriptors, Oracle8i can accept a
deployment descriptor in a text form. Oracle8i's deployment tool will automatically
convert the text form descriptor to the serialized form.

The syntax of the text form for a session bean is as follows:

```
SessionBean <EJB class name> {
  <attribute name> = <attribute value>;
  <attribute name> = <attribute value>;
  . . .
}
```

The descriptor begins with the keyword `SessionBean` followed by the fully qualified class name of the bean class. The body of the descriptor contains a list of name-value pairs of the form <attribute name> = <attribute value>. Table 10-2 lists the attributes that you will commonly use.

| Attribute Name | Attribute Value | Required? |
|---|---|---|
| BeanHomeName | Published name of the bean. Note that this name should specify an object name, not a class. | Yes |
| HomeInterfaceClassName | Fully-qualified name of the home interface | Yes |
| RemoteInterfaceClassName | Fully-qualified name of the remote interface | Yes |
| AllowedIdentities | Database users/roles who will be allowed to access the bean. Example: {DEMO, SCOTT} | No |
| SessionTimeout | The number of seconds the session should remain alive after the last bean client disconnects. The default value 0 ends the session immediately after the last client disconnects. | No |
| StateManagementType | STATEFUL_SESSION (default) \| STATELESS_SESSION | No |
| RunAsMode | CLIENT_IDENTITY \| SPECIFIED_IDENTITY \| SYSTEM_IDENTITY | No |
| RunAsIdentity | Database user. Cannot be a role. | Yes, if RunAsMode is used |
| TransactionAttribute | TX_SUPPORTS (default) \| TX_BEAN_MANAGED \| TX_MANDATORY \| TX_NOT_SUPPORTED \| TX_REQUIRED \| TX_REQUIRES_NEW | No |

**TABLE 10-2.** *Commonly Used Deployment Descriptor Attributes*

**NOTE**
*StateManagementType is not relevant in Oracle8i's EJB implementation because stateful and stateless beans are treated the same way in the server. In addition, the current release of Oracle8i does not support the transaction isolation attribute in the deployment descriptor.*

Transaction attributes are discussed in "Choosing the Right Declarative Attribute for Container-Managed Transaction Demarcation."

### ProductBeanTDD.ejb: The Deployment Descriptor
The deployment descriptor for the `ProductBean` class is as follows:

```
SessionBean productSearcherImpl.ProductSearcherBean {
  BeanHomeName = "test/tips/productSearcherBean_1";
  RemoteInterfaceClassName = productSearcher.ProductSearcher;
  HomeInterfaceClassName = productSearcher.ProductSearcherHome;
  AllowedIdentities = {DEMO};
  SessionTimeout = 20;
  StateManagementType = STATELESS_SESSION;
  TransactionAttribute = TX_NOT_SUPPORTED;
}
```

In the preceding example, `AllowedIdentities` and `TransactionAttribute` apply to the entire bean. For information on how to set attributes at the method level, please refer to the Oracle8i Enterprise JavaBeans and CORBA Developer's Guide.

## Compiling and Packaging the EJB
You have now been shown how to write home and remote interfaces, the bean class, and the deployment descriptor for the `ProductSearcher` EJB. The next step shows how to compile the .java files and package them up for deployment.

The following commands use javac to compile the .java files (remote and home interfaces, the bean class, and any other classes required by the bean) to .class files:

```
javac -g productSearcher\ProductSearcher.java
javac -g productSearcher\ProductInfo.java
javac -g productSearcher\ProductSearcherHome.java
javac -g productSearcherImpl\VectorEnumeration.java
javac -g productSearcherImpl\ProductSearcherBean.java
```

Compiling and Packaging the EJB

Packaging involves nothing more than archiving the compiled class files into a standard Java .jar file. The following command uses the standard jar tool to package the .class files into a file named "server.jar":

```
jar cf0 server.jar productSearcher\ProductSearcher.class
   productSearcher\ProductInfo.class
   productSearcher\ProductSearcherHome.class
   productSearcherImpl\VectorEnumeration.class
   productSearcherImpl\ProductSearcherBean.class
```

## Deploying the EJB to Oracle8i

The deployejb tool is used to deploy server.jar into the database according to the deployment descriptor. The deployejb tool can take a long time to run because it performs a great deal of work behind the scenes, including the following:

- Parsing and validating the deployment descriptor
- Generating information that the EJB server requires for declarative security and transactions
- Uploading the server-side run time into the Oracle8i database, a process that is automated by the loadjava tool
- Generating client-side classes
- Populating the JNDI-accessible name service defined in the deployment descriptor
- Enforcing security for the RunAs properties of the bean
- Generating communication support code

The syntax for running deployejb is as follows:

```
deployejb [options] -temp workdir ejbJarFile
```

The following command deploys the classes in server.jar using the deployment descriptor ProductSearcherTDD.ejb:

```
call deployejb -republish -temp temp -u demo -p demo
  -s sess_iiop://localhost:2481:ORCL
   -descriptor ProductSearcherTDD.ejb server.jar
```

If a bean with the same name already exists in the database, the -republish option forces the republishing of the bean. The -temp argument specifies a temporary directory to hold intermediate files that deployejb creates. The -s argument specifies the service URL of the database where the bean is to be published. The `-descriptor` argument specifies the filename of the text form of the deployment descriptor.

Here is a sample of the output produced when deployejb is run. A more detailed status output can be produced using the `-verbose` option.

```
Reading Deployment Descriptor...done
Verifying Deployment Descriptor...done
Gathering users...done
Generating Comm Stubs........................................done
Compiling Stubs...done
Generating Jar File...done
Loading EJB Jar file and Comm Stubs Jar file...done
Generating EJBHome and EJBObject on the server...done
Publishing EJBHome...done
```

# Writing the EJB Client

An EJB client can be a Java applet, a Java application, or another EJB running either in the same or in a different container. Before invoking an EJB's methods, a client must

- Authenticate itself to Oracle8i

- Locate the EJB home interface, using JNDI

- Create an instance of the bean using methods of the home interface

## Authentication Techniques

A client must first authenticate itself with Oracle8i before activating an EJB. Three authentication techniques are available:

- Oracle8i login protocol over a secure socket (SSL) connection

- Oracle8i login protocol over a non-SSL connection

- Credential-based authentication over an SSL connection

A client specifies an authentication type when it creates a JNDI initial context, a topic discussed shortly in "Locating the Bean's Home with JNDI" in this section. The client specifies its authentication type through the `javax.naming.Context.SECURITY_AUTHENTICATION` attribute, which can take on the values shown in Table 10-3. (The SECURITY_AUTHENTICATION attribute can also specify nothing, in which case the client must activate the login protocol directly before it can activate a server-side object.)

**Writing the EJB Client**

| Authentication Type | SECURITY_AUTHENTICATION Value |
| --- | --- |
| Oracle8i login protocol over an SSL connection | `ServiceCtx.SSL_LOGIN` |
| Oracle8i login protocol over a non-SSL connection | `ServiceCtx.NON_SSL_LOGIN` |
| Credential-based authentication over an SSL connection | `ServiceCtx.SSL_CREDENTIAL` |

**TABLE 10-3.** *Client Authentication Techniques and their Corresponding Constants for Setting Up a JNDI Initial Context*

Note that each of the three authentication techniques is secure. In the first technique, the Oracle8i login protocol encrypts the password when sent from client to server; in the second and third, the SSL transport protocol does the encryption.

Oracle recommends the credential-based authentication because it is slightly more efficient than the Login protocol. The password encryption performed by SSL transport protocol eliminates the need for the handshaking that the Login protocol uses.

## Locating the Bean's Home with JNDI

An EJB client—whether an application or another EJB—looks up a bean's home using Java Naming and Directory Interface (JNDI). A standard extension to the Java platform, JNDI is an interface to heterogeneous enterprise naming and directory services. In Oracle8i, JNDI serves as an interface to the OMG COSNaming service.

To locate the bean's home in Oracle8i, you need not grapple with the details of COSNaming service or even JNDI. It is sufficient to understand how to construct a JNDI `javax.naming.InitialContext` object and use its `lookup` method. The initial context is the starting point for resolving names, in much the same way as a root directory is the starting point of a file system. Oracle8i actually stores EJB classes in the database in a file system-like hierarchy called a *publishing context*. The first `Context` object returned by `new InitialContext(...)` will be bound to the root of the Oracle8i publishing context.

The following method, `getInitialContext`, accepts a username and password as input parameters and returns a JNDI `InitialContext` object for Oracle8i:

```
import javax.naming.*;
. . .
  public static Context getInitialContext(String user, String password)
     throws javax.naming.NamingException {
   Hashtable env = new Hashtable();
   env.put(Context.URL_PKG_PREFIXES, "oracle.aurora.jndi");
   env.put(Context.SECURITY_PRINCIPAL, user);
   env.put(Context.SECURITY_CREDENTIALS, password);
   env.put(Context.SECURITY_AUTHENTICATION, ServiceCtx.NON_SSL_LOGIN);
   return new javax.naming.InitialContext(env);
  }
```

The Java Hashtable's context properties are populated in Oracle8i as follows:

- **`Context.URL_PKG_PREFIXES`** Always set this to "oracle.aurora.jndi"

- **`Context.SECURITY_PRINCIPAL`** Set this to the Oracle username. For example, "DEMO".

- **`Context.SECURITY_CREDENTIALS`** Set this to the password for the username. For example, "DEMO".

- **`Context.SECURITY_AUTHENTICATION`** The possible values are `ServiceCtx.NON_SSL_LOGIN`, `ServiceCtx.SSL_CREDENTIAL`, or `ServiceCtx.SSL_LOGIN` (see Table 10-3).

Once a JNDI connection is established and a context is obtained, the context is used to look up the EJB home of the `ProductSearcherBean` using the `Context.lookup` method, whose signature is as follows:

```
Object Context.lookup(String beanName);
```

The published full pathname of the object is `beanName`—that is, the published name used in the deployment descriptor. For `ProductSearchBean`, it is "test/ tips/productSearcherBean_1," as shown in the following excerpt of the EJB descriptor ProductSearcherTDD.ejb:

```
// ProductBeanTDD.ejb
SessionBean productSearcherImpl.ProductSearcherBean {
  BeanHomeName = "test/tips/productSearcherBean_1";
. . .
  }
```

If you specify values for all four of the JNDI attributes (URL_PKG_PREFIXES, SECURITY_PRINCIPAL, SECURITY_CREDENTIALS, and SECURITY_ AUTHENTICATION), a login is attempted when the client calls Context.lookup for the first time.

The following example looks up the ProductSearcher home. It assumes that the client and the server are on the server machine (localhost), the listener IIOP port is 2481, and the database SID is "ORCL."

```
String url = "sess_iiop://localhost:2481:ORCL";
String objectName = "test/tips/productSearcherBean_1";
String user = "demo";
String password = "demo";
Context ic = getInitialContext(user, password);
ProductSearcherHome home = (ProductSearcherHome)ic.lookup(url
+ objectName);
```

The variable home will now contain a remote reference to the ProductSearcher EJB's home. The client is also authenticated in the process.

### Creating an Instance of the Bean and Invoking Its Methods
Now that you have a reference to the home, you can use it to create an instance of the ProductSearcher session bean:

```
ProductSearcher searchBean = home.create();
```

Your client can now call the business methods exposed in the ProductSearcher remote interface.

### ProductSearcherClient
The following is a client application that tests the ProductSearcherBean. It looks up the published ProductSearcherHome on the server, using the InitialContext.lookup method. The lookup call also authenticates the client, using the Oracle8i login protocol over a non-SSL connection. The client application then instantiates a ProductSearcher object through the home interfaces create method, calls the searchByDescription method, and finally displays information on the products that are returned.

```
import productSearcher.ProductSearcher;
import productSearcher.ProductSearcherHome;
import productSearcher.ProductInfo;

import oracle.aurora.jndi.sess_iiop.ServiceCtx;
```

```
import javax.naming.Context;
import javax.naming.InitialContext;
import java.util.Hashtable;
import java.util.Enumeration;

public class ProductSearcherClient {
  public static Context getInitialContext(String user, String password)
      throws javax.naming.NamingException {
    Hashtable env = new Hashtable();
    env.put(Context.URL_PKG_PREFIXES, "oracle.aurora.jndi");
    env.put(Context.SECURITY_PRINCIPAL, user);
    env.put(Context.SECURITY_CREDENTIALS, password);
    env.put(Context.SECURITY_AUTHENTICATION, ServiceCtx.NON_SSL_LOGIN);
    return (new InitialContext(env));
  }

  public static void main(String[] args) {
    try {
      if (args.length != 5) {
        System.out.println("Usage: java ProductSearcherClient " +
          "serviceURL objectName user pwd searchFor");
        System.exit(1);
      }

      String url = args[0];
      String objectName = args[1];
      String user = args[2];
      String password = args[3];
      String searchFor = "%" + args[4] + "%";

      Context ic = getInitialContext(user, password);
      ProductSearcherHome home = (ProductSearcherHome)ic.lookup(url
      + objectName);
      ProductSearcher searchBean = home.create();
      Enumeration e =  searchBean.searchByDescription(searchFor);
      if (e != null) {
        while (e.hasMoreElements())
          System.out.println(e.nextElement());
      } else System.out.println("No products found.");
    } catch (Exception e) {
      System.out.println("Error: " + e.getMessage());
    }
  }
}
```

As a test, let's search for products whose descriptions contain the string "SOFTBALL," using the following command:

```
java ProductSearcherClient sess_iiop://localhost:2481:orcl
  /test/tips/productSearcherBean_1 demo demo "SOFTBALL"
```

A sample of the output produced is as follows:

```
103120: WIFF SOFTBALL BAT I (Price: 25.0)
103121: WIFF SOFTBALL BAT II (Price: 30.0)
103131: WIFF SOFTBALL, LARGE (Price: 4.5)
103140: WIFF SOFTBALL MITT (LH) (Price: 20.0)
103141: WIFF SOFTBALL MITT (RH) (Price: 20.0)
102132: RH: "GUIDE TO SOFTBALL" (Price: 3.4)
```

This completes the discussion of the creation and deployment of a simple stateless session bean and the writing of a client application that accesses the bean.

# EJB Transaction Management

This section describes how you can take advantage of EJB transaction management features available in Oracle8i. The EJB model provides for automatic support for distributed transactions. In theory, EJBs can atomically update data in multiple databases—possibly across multiple sites. The EJB architecture shifts most of the responsibility of transaction management to the EJB container. For example, the container implements low-level transaction features such as two-phase commits and transaction context propagation.

It is impossible to do justice to the topic of EJB transaction management within the scope of this book. For a fuller account on EJB transaction support, including state management and the effect of exceptions on transactions, please refer to the Enterprise JavaBeans Specification, downloadable from www.javasoft.com.

## Forms of Transaction Support in Oracle8i

In the broadest sense, there are two forms of transaction management for EJBs in Oracle8i. The first is container-managed demarcation, which is the simplest and least error prone. The second form is explicit transaction demarcation—either bean-managed or client-demarcated.

### CONTAINER-MANAGED TRANSACTION DEMARCATION

Container-managed transaction control is one of the great strengths of the EJB model. Rather than write code, you take advantage of the declarative transactional capabilities built into Oracle8i's EJB container. Freed from the responsibility of managing transactions, you will be able to focus on the business logic that you are trying to implement.

Container-managed transactional management in the EJB model is extremely powerful. An EJB can choose among six different transaction policies. These policies can be applied at either the bean level or the method level. These policies are specified declaratively rather than programmatically and are explained shortly in "Choosing the Right Declarative Attribute for Container-Managed Transactions" in this section. Thanks to declarative transaction attributes, there is a clear separation of transactional behavior specification from business logic. This helps make your code less prone to error and clutter.

For an example of the use of container-managed transactions, see "ShoppingCart: A Stateful Session Bean That Uses Container-Managed Transactions."

**EXPLICITLY MANAGED TRANSACTION DEMARCATION**   On rare occasions, you may require finer-grained control on transaction behavior than that offered by container-managed transaction demarcation. You can use explicit calls to two transaction APIs that Oracle provides, either on the client side or in the bean classes themselves. On the server side, you set the transaction attribute to TX_BEAN_MANAGED and explicitly manage transactions using the Java Transaction API (JTA). On the client side in Oracle8i, you use the Java Transaction Service (JTS) API.

## Choosing the Right Declarative Attribute for Container-Managed Transactions

An EJB container supports six different transaction policies for a bean. These policies are specified through `TransactionAttribute` in the deployment descriptor. At run time, the EJB container automatically provides appropriate transaction services based on the specified `TransactionAttribute` value.

The following describes the six valid values for the `TransactionAttribute` in a deployment descriptor. (In the description, "client" refers to a client application or another EJB.)

### JTS and JTA for Explicit Transaction Demarcation

JTS is a Java implementation of OMG's Object Transaction Service (OTS). JTS provides an API that allows direct access to transactional managers and the database. However, the JTS API is complex and is best avoided.

Java Transaction API (JTA) is simpler than JTS. The JTA API is implemented by the `javax.transaction` package and consists of two components: a high-level transactional client interface and a low-level X/Open XA interface. The high-level API is what you will call for bean-managed transactions (see "Using Bean-Managed Transaction Demarcation for Fine-Grained Transaction Control"); the low-level XA interface is typically used by the EJB container.

In general, you are cautioned against using explicit transaction demarcation; robust transaction management is complex with either JTA or JTS.

**TX_NOT_SUPPORTED**   The container invokes the bean's method outside the scope of the client's transaction. The client's transactional scope is not propagated to the TX_NOT_SUPPORTED bean or any of the beans it calls. If the client calls within a transactional context, the container suspends the transaction for the duration of the method call. The container resumes the suspended transaction when the TX_NOT_SUPPORTED bean method is completed.

Recall that the `ProductSearcherBean` was deployed with a TX_NOT_SUPPORTED attribute. The rationale: `ProductSearcherBean` is a stateless bean that performs no transactions. Making a bean part of a transactional scope is costly in terms of efficiency. As a TX_NOT_SUPPORTED bean, `ProductSearcherBean` will always be out of transactional scope, thus potentially improving performance.

**TX_SUPPORTS**   The container invokes the bean's method within the client's transaction. If the client is not part of a transaction, no new transaction is started.

**TX_REQUIRES_NEW**   The container always creates a new transaction before invoking a bean's method. It commits the transaction after the bean's method is completed. If the client is part of a transaction, the container suspends that transaction; it resumes the transaction when the bean method is completed.

**TX_REQUIRED**   The container invokes the bean's method within the client's transaction, if one exists. If the client is not part of a transaction, a new transaction is started. The container commits the transaction when the bean's method is completed.

**TX_MANDATORY**   The container invokes the bean's method inside the client's transaction. If the client is not part of a transaction, the container throws a `javax.transaction.TransactionRequired` exception.

**TX_BEAN_MANAGED**   A bean with a TX_BEAN_MANAGED attribute can issue explicit transaction calls through the JTA `UserTransaction` interface (see "Using Bean-Managed Transaction Demarcation for Fine-Grained Transaction Control").

## ShoppingCart: A Stateful Session Bean That Uses Container-Managed Transaction Demarcation

This section develops an EJB called `ShoppingCart`, a stateful session bean that encapsulates the business process of an online shopper placing an order. The `ShoppingCart` object accumulates items the customer selects while browsing. When the shopper is ready to purchase the items, the client can call the `ShoppingCart.commitOrder` method, which inserts the order information into the database. As a TX_REQUIRES_NEW bean, transaction management is left to the container.

## ShoppingCart: The Remote Interface

The `ShoppingCart` remote interface exposes three methods to clients:

- **addItem**   Adds a product to the shopping cart

- **getItems**   Returns a list of items currently in the shopping cart

- **commitOrder**   Inserts the order to the database and returns an order number if successful

The following is the definition of `ShoppingCart`:

```
package shoppingCart;

import javax.ejb.EJBObject;
import java.rmi.RemoteException;
import java.sql.SQLException;

import shoppingCartImpl.OrderItem;

public interface ShoppingCart extends EJBObject {
  public void addItem(int productID, int quantity, double unitPrice)
    throws RemoteException;

  public int commitOrder()  throws SQLException, RemoteException;

  public OrderItem[] getItems() throws RemoteException;
}
```

## ShoppingCartHome: The Home Interface

`ShoppingCartHome` has one create factory method that clients will use to create a `ShoppingCart` object. The `create` method takes a customer ID as a parameter.

```
package shoppingCart;

import javax.ejb.*;
import java.rmi.RemoteException;

public interface ShoppingCartHome extends EJBHome {
  public ShoppingCart create(int customerID)
    throws CreateException, RemoteException;
}
```

The Home Interface

## ShoppingCartBean: The Bean Class

The `ShoppingCartBean` class implements the functionality of adding items to the cart, listing current items in the cart, and purchasing the items in the cart. Its instance variables fall into two categories:

- **`customerID` and `orderTotal`** Caches order header data

- **`itemVect`** A vector of `OrderItem` objects for caching sales order line item data

The cached data is written to the database using JDBC when the client invokes the `commitOrder` method.

Let's focus on container-managed transaction issues by examining closely the `commitOrder` method. On the basis of the TX_REQUIRES_NEW transaction attribute, the container starts a new transaction before giving control to the method. The `commitOrder` method first inserts a row into the demo.sales_order table representing the order header information. Next, it loops through `itemVect`, the vector holding the `OrderItem` objects, and inserts each line item into the demo.item table. If both sets of inserts are successful and no exceptions are thrown, the container commits the transaction. However, if an insert fails (for instance, if there is a primary key violation resulting from a duplicate order ID), an `SQLException` will get thrown, and the container will automatically roll back the transaction.

```
package shoppingCartImpl;

import shoppingCartImpl.OrderItem;

import java.util.Date;
import java.sql.*;
import java.rmi.RemoteException;
import javax.ejb.*;
import java.util.Vector;

public class ShoppingCartBean implements SessionBean {
  SessionContext ctx;

  // Order header
  int customerID;
  double orderTotal;

  // Order line items
  Vector itemVect = new Vector();

  public void addItem(int productID, int quantity, double price)
      throws RemoteException {
    OrderItem oi = new OrderItem(productID, quantity, price,
      quantity * price);
```

```java
    itemVect.addElement(oi);
    orderTotal += (quantity * price);
}

public OrderItem[] getItems() throws RemoteException {
  OrderItem[] items = new OrderItem[itemVect.size()];
  itemVect.copyInto(items);
  return items;
}

// Return an orderID if successful. Else throw an exception
public int commitOrder() throws SQLException, RemoteException {
  Connection conn =
    new oracle.jdbc.driver.OracleDriver().defaultConnection();

  int orderID = -1;
  PreparedStatement ps1 = null, ps2 = null;
  ResultSet rs = null;

  try {
    // Get a unique order ID
    Statement stmt = conn.createStatement();
    rs = stmt.executeQuery("SELECT sales_order_id_seq.NEXTVAL" +
                           " FROM dual");

    if (rs.next())
      orderID = rs.getInt(1);
    else
      throw new SQLException("Error generating unique order ID");

    // Insert header
    String q1 =
      "INSERT INTO demo.sales_order" +
      " (order_id, customer_id, order_date, ship_date, total)" +
      " VALUES (?, ?, sysdate, null, ?)";
    ps1 = conn.prepareStatement(q1);

    ps1.setInt(1, orderID);
    ps1.setInt(2, customerID);
    ps1.setDouble(3, orderTotal);
    ps1.executeUpdate();

    // Insert order items
    String q2 =
      "INSERT INTO demo.item " +
      "(order_id, item_id, product_id, quantity, actual_price, total)" +
      " VALUES (?, ?, ?, ?, ?, ?)";
    ps2 = conn.prepareStatement(q2);

    ps2.setInt(1, orderID);
    for (int i = 0; i < itemVect.size(); i++) {
      ps2.setInt(2, i + 1);
      OrderItem oi = (OrderItem)itemVect.elementAt(i);
```

**The Home Interface**

```
        ps2.setInt(3, oi.getProductID());
        ps2.setInt(4, oi.getQuantity());
        ps2.setDouble(5, oi.getPrice());
        ps2.setDouble(6, oi.getTotal());
        ps2.executeUpdate();
      }
    return orderID;
  } finally {
    if (rs != null) rs.close();
    if (ps1 != null) ps1.close();
    if (ps2 != null) ps2.close();
  }
}

public void ejbCreate() {}

public void ejbCreate(int customerID)
    throws CreateException, RemoteException {
  this.customerID = customerID;
}


// SessionBean interface methods
public void ejbActivate() {}
public void ejbPassivate() {}
public void ejbRemove() {}
public void setSessionContext(SessionContext ctx) {
  this.ctx = ctx;
}
}
```

In the foregoing class, the `commitOrder` method obtains a unique order_id value from a sequence called sales_order_id_seq, which is created as follows:

```
CREATE SEQUENCE sales_order_id_seq INCREMENT BY 1 START WITH 2000
```

The START with value of 2000 was chosen so that it would not conflict existing values of the primary key in the sales_order table.

### Enhancing the ShoppingCartBean

Many elements have been left out of `ShoppingCartBean`, elements necessary to make the bean industrial strength. Some examples:

- The `commitOrder` method could throw an exception if there are no items in the cart.

- Billing and shipping address information could be represented with an `Address` serializable Java class.

- The bean could use a `CreditCardValidator` session bean to validate credit card information before committing an order.

## OrderItem: A Dependent Object Implemented as a Serializable Object

The `ShoppingCartBean` uses a class called `OrderItem` to hold order item (line item) data. In addition, `OrderItem` is used to encapsulate item information when the `getItems` method is invoked by a client. `OrderItem` is defined as a serializable object rather than an entity bean for reasons described in "Choosing Between Pass-By-Value Objects and Entity Beans." The following is the full definition of the `OrderItem` class:

```
package shoppingCartImpl;

public class OrderItem implements java.io.Serializable {
  private int productID;
  private int quantity;
  private double price;
  private double total;

  public OrderItem(int productID, int quantity,
  double price, double total) {
    this.productID = productID;
    this.quantity = quantity;
    this.price = price;
    this.total = total;
  }

  public String toString() {
    return "ProductID " + Integer.toString(productID) +
      " : Qty " + Integer.toString(quantity);
  }
}
```

## ShoppingCartTDD.ejb: The Deployment Descriptor

The deployment descriptor ShoppingCartTDD.ejb specifies a STATEFUL_SESSION value for `StateManagementType` and a `TX_REQUIRES_NEW` value for `TransactionAttribute`:

```
SessionBean shoppingCartImpl.ShoppingCartBean {
  BeanHomeName = "test/tips/shoppingCartBean_1";
  RemoteInterfaceClassName = shoppingCart.ShoppingCart;
  HomeInterfaceClassName = shoppingCart.ShoppingCartHome;
  AllowedIdentities = {DEMO};
  SessionTimeout = 20;
  StateManagementType = STATEFUL_SESSION;
  RunAsMode = CLIENT_IDENTITY;
  TransactionAttribute = TX_REQUIRES_NEW;
}
```

The Home Interface

### ShoppingCartClient: A Client That Tests ShoppingCartBean

ShoppingCartClient is a simple Java application for testing ShoppingCartBean. The client uses the same technique for the authentication and lookup of the home interface as ProductSearchClient. It creates a ShoppingCart session object by invoking the home's create method, passing a customer ID as a parameter. (Customer ID is an input to the client program.) It then adds two items into the shopping cart and calls commitOrder to make the purchase. It ends the session by calling the remove method on the session bean object.

Here is the code for ShoppingCartClient:

```java
import shoppingCart.ShoppingCart;
import shoppingCart.ShoppingCartHome;
import shoppingCartImpl.OrderInfo;

import oracle.aurora.jndi.sess_iiop.ServiceCtx;

import javax.naming.Context;
import javax.naming.InitialContext;
import java.util.Hashtable;
import java.util.Date;

public class ShoppingCartClient {

  public static Context getInitialContext(String user, String password)
      throws javax.naming.NamingException {
    Hashtable env = new Hashtable();
    env.put(Context.URL_PKG_PREFIXES, "oracle.aurora.jndi");
    env.put(Context.SECURITY_PRINCIPAL, user);
    env.put(Context.SECURITY_CREDENTIALS, password);
    env.put(Context.SECURITY_AUTHENTICATION, ServiceCtx.NON_SSL_LOGIN);
    return (new InitialContext(env));
  }


  public static void main(String[] args) {
    if (args.length != 5) {
      System.out.println("Usage: java ShoppingCartClient " +
        "serviceURL objectName user pwd custID");
      System.exit(1);
    }

    String url = args[0];
    String objectName = args[1];
    String user = args[2];
    String password = args[3];
    int custID = (new Integer(args[4])).intValue();

    try {
```

```
    Context ic = getInitialContext(user, password);
    ShoppingCartHome home = (ShoppingCartHome)ic.lookup(url + objectName);
    Date orderDate = null;

    ShoppingCart cart = home.create(custID);
    System.out.println("Shopping cart created.");

    cart.addItem(103130, 2, 99.90);
    System.out.println("First item added to cart.");

    cart.addItem(103131, 6, 10.00);
    System.out.println("Second item added to cart.");

    int orderID = cart.commitOrder();
    System.out.println("Order committed. Your Order # is " +
      Integer.toString(orderID));

    cart.remove();
    System.out.println("Shopping cart removed.");
  } catch (Exception e) {
    System.out.println("Exception caught in client: " + e.getMessage());
  }
 }
}
```

The following is an example of how `ShoppingCartClient` can be run from the command line:

```
java ShoppingCartClient sess_iiop://localhost:2481:orcl
  /test/tips/shoppingCartBean_1 demo demo 202
```

The output produced by the client is as follows:

```
Shopping cart created.
First item added to cart.
Second item added to cart.
Order committed. Your Order # is 2000
Shopping cart removed.
```

## Saving a Session Object Handle for Later Reactivation

In a real-world application, the `ShoppingCartBean` could be used by a JavaServer Pages (JSP) client to generate HTML pages for an online shopper. In such browser-based applications, it is not uncommon for an online shopper to suspend the shopping session temporarily and resume it later. To support such functionality, you can hold a session bean's reference beyond the life of a client session by storing the bean's handle (a serializable reference to the bean) in persistent storage, such as a file or a database table. At some later time, the handle can be deserialized and used to reactivate the bean, provided that the bean is still alive in the EJB container. You can set how long a session object stays active after the last bean client disconnects with the `SessionTimeout` attribute in the deployment descriptor. However, keep in mind that Oracle8i session beans—including the `ShoppingCartBean` implemented in this chapter—will not survive a system crash. If you try to reactivate a bean that no longer exists in the database, you will get the exception `NoSuchObjectException`.

The example that follows enhances `ShoppingCartClient` by adding a "save bean handle" feature. The example also illustrates how a login IOR can be saved, and used at a later point to reestablish a connection to the session. A login IOR is required when a client needs to make a connection to an existing session using NON_SSL_LOGIN authentication.

The example is composed of the following classes:

- **EJBHandleUtil**  A utility class containing methods to save a handle to a file and to restore a bean handle from a file.

- **IORUtil**  A utility class containing methods to save a login IOR to a file and to restore a login IOR from a file.

- **SaveCartHandleClient**  A class that simulates the interruption of a shopping session. It creates a new JNDI context, activates a `ShoppingCart` object, and adds two items to the cart. Before exiting, it calls `EJBHandleUtil` and `IORUtil` methods to write the bean handle and the login IOR to files.

- **RestoreCartHandleClient**  A class that simulates the resumption of a shopping session. It calls methods of `EJBHandleUtil` and `IORUtil` to restore the bean handle and login IOR saved by the `SaveCartHandleClient`. It continues with the shopping session by adding a third item to the cart. Finally, it commits the order and removes the `ShoppingCart` object.

We will now look at the code for these classes.

## EJBHandleUtil

The `EJBHandleUtil` class is comprised of two static methods:

- **save**  Saves a handle to a file, using the `writeObject` method of the `java.io.ObjectOutputStream` class.

- **restore**  Reconstitutes a handle from a file, using the `readObject` method of the `java.io.ObjectInputStream` class. `readObject` returns an `Object` type, so the return value is cast to a `Handle` type.

```
import java.io.*;
import javax.ejb.Handle;

public class EJBHandleUtil {
  public static void save(Handle handle, String fileName)
      throws IOException {
    FileOutputStream fos = new FileOutputStream(fileName);
    ObjectOutputStream oos = new ObjectOutputStream(fos);
    oos.writeObject(handle);
    oos.flush();
    fos.close();
  }

  public static Handle restore(String fileName)
      throws IOException, java.lang.ClassNotFoundException {
    FileInputStream fis = new FileInputStream(fileName);
    ObjectInputStream ois = new ObjectInputStream(fis);
    java.lang.Object obj = ois.readObject();
    fis.close();
    ois.close();
    return (Handle)obj;
  }
}
```

### IORUtil

If a client uses NON_SSL_LOGIN as its authentication mechanism to connect to an existing session, a login IOR must be used. The following class `IORUtil` is a utility class that facilitates working with login IORs. `IORUtil` has three methods:

- **save** Saves a CORBA object to a file.

- **restore** Reads a login IOR from a file and returns it as a `String`.

- **authenticate** Uses a login object to authenticate a client explicitly against the server.

```
import java.io.*;

import org.omg.CORBA.ORB;
import org.omg.CORBA.BindOptions;
import org.omg.CORBA.COMM_FAILURE;

import oracle.aurora.jndi.sess_iiop.ServiceCtx;
import oracle.aurora.client.*;
import oracle.aurora.AuroraServices.LoginServer;
import oracle.aurora.AuroraServices.LoginServerHelper;
```

```
public class IORUtil {
  public static void save(org.omg.CORBA.Object obj, String iorFile)
      throws IOException {
    ORB orb = ORB.init();
    String ior = orb.object_to_string(obj);
    OutputStream os = new FileOutputStream(iorFile);
    os.write(ior.getBytes());
    os.close();
  }

  public static String restore(String iorFile)
      throws IOException, FileNotFoundException {
    InputStream is = new FileInputStream(iorFile);
    byte[] iorbytes = new byte[ is.available() ];
    is.read(iorbytes);
    is.close();
    return new String(iorbytes);
  }

  /**
   * @throws org.omg.CORBA.COMM_FAILURE if the session has timed out
   * or Exception if the login fails
   */
  public static void authenticate(String loginIOR,
                                  String user,
                                  String password)
      throws COMM_FAILURE, Exception {
    // Initialize the CORBA ORB
    ORB orb = ServiceCtx.init(null, null, null, false, null);

    // Authenticate with the login object
    LoginServer lserver =
      LoginServerHelper.narrow(orb.string_to_object(loginIOR));
    lserver._bind_options(new BindOptions(false, false));
    Login login = new Login(lserver);
    login.authenticate(user, password, null);
  }
}
```

In the foregoing class' save method, the call to ORB.init() initializes the
ORB. Note that the input argument obj is an org.omg.CORBA.Object type
rather than a java.lang.Object type, and the OutputStream.write(byte[])
method is used rather than ObjectOutputStream.writeObject(Object). The
authenticate method merits special attention. It first calls the Service.init

method to initialize the ORB. (The reason for the odd looking set of `null` values in the call to `ServiceCtx.init` is that authentication will be done using the `Login` object's authenticate method.) It then calls the `LoginServerHelper.narrow` method, passing it the `loginIOR` string, to get a `LoginServer` object. The `LoginServer` object is used to get a `Login` object, whose `authenticate` method attempts to authenticate the client.

## SaveCartHandleClient

For the most part, `SaveCartHandleClient` resembles `ShoppingCartClient` depicted in the Tip "ShoppingCart: A Stateful Session Bean That Uses Container-Managed Transaction Demarcation." Both clients do a JNDI lookup, both activate a `ShoppingCart` object, and both insert items into the shopping cart. The primary point of difference is that `SaveCartHandleClient` calls the `EJBHandleUtil.save` and `IORUtil.save` methods to save the bean's handle and the login IOR. The saved handle and login IOR can be used at a later point by another client to access the same session and the same bean object.

```
import shoppingCart.ShoppingCart;
import shoppingCart.ShoppingCartHome;
import shoppingCartImpl.OrderInfo;
import IORUtil;
import EJBHandleUtil;

import oracle.aurora.jndi.sess_iiop.ServiceCtx;
import oracle.aurora.client.*;
import oracle.aurora.AuroraServices.LoginServer;

import javax.naming.Context;
import javax.naming.InitialContext;

import java.util.Hashtable;
import java.io.*;


public class SaveCartHandleClient {
  public static Context getInitialContext(String user, String password)
      throws javax.naming.NamingException {
    Hashtable env = new Hashtable();
    env.put(Context.URL_PKG_PREFIXES, "oracle.aurora.jndi");
    env.put(Context.SECURITY_PRINCIPAL, user);
    env.put(Context.SECURITY_CREDENTIALS, password);
    env.put(Context.SECURITY_AUTHENTICATION, ServiceCtx.NON_SSL_LOGIN);
    return (new InitialContext(env));
  }
```

Save Session Object Handle and Reactivate Later

```
public static void main(String[] args) throws Exception {
  try {
    if (args.length != 7) {
      System.out.println("Usage: java SaveCartHandleClient " +
      " serviceURL objectName user pwd custID handleFile IORFile");
      System.exit(1);
    }

    String url = args[0];
    String objectName = args[1];
    String user = args[2];
    String password = args[3];
    int custID = (new Integer(args[4])).intValue();
    String handleFile = args[5];
    String iorFile = args[6];

    Context ic = getInitialContext(user, password);
    ShoppingCartHome home = (ShoppingCartHome)
                      ic.lookup(url + objectName);

    // Get the LoginServer IOR at the well-known name etc/login
    LoginServer lserver = (LoginServer)ic.lookup(url + "/etc/login");

    // Create cart and add two items to it
    ShoppingCart cart = home.create(custID);
    System.out.println("Shopping cart created.");
    cart.addItem(103130, 2, 99.90);
    System.out.println("First item added to cart.");
    cart.addItem(103131, 6, 10.00);
    System.out.println("Second item added to cart.");

    // Save handle and loginIOR
    EJBHandleUtil.save(cart.getHandle(), handleFile);
    System.out.println("Bean handle written to file.");
    IORUtil.save(lserver, iorFile);
    System.out.println("Login IOR written to file.");
  } catch (Exception e) {
    System.out.println("Exception caught in client: "
      + e.getMessage());
  }
  }
}
```

Notice how `lserver` (the login IOR) is obtained with a JNDI lookup at the well-known name "etc/login." Also note that the client exits without invoking `cart.remove()`, so that the session bean will continue running on the server until it times out or the server crashes.

The saved IOR and bean handle can now be used by other clients, as the following section describes.

### RestoreCartHandleClient

`RestoreCartHandleClient` fetches a previously saved login IOR from file, and attempts to authenticate against the server with the `IORUtil.authenticate` method. If authentication succeeds, `RestoreCartHandleClient` calls the `EJBHandleUtil.restore` method, which deserializes the handle from file and returns it in the form of a `Handle` object. It then invokes the `Handle` object's `getEJBObject` method, which returns a remote reference (`EJBObject` type) to the object. A cast is performed on the reference to convert it to a `ShoppingCart` object.

Once the handle to the cart is reestablished, the client adds a third item to the cart, commits the order, and finally invokes the bean's `remove` method to discard the bean.

```
import shoppingCart.ShoppingCart;
import shoppingCart.ShoppingCartHome;
import shoppingCartImpl.OrderInfo;
import EJBHandleUtil;
import IORUtil;

import javax.ejb.Handle;
import java.io.*;

import org.omg.CORBA.COMM_FAILURE;

public class RestoreCartHandleClient {
  public static void main(String[] args) throws java.io.IOException {
    if (args.length != 7) {
      System.out.println("Usage: java RestoreCartHandleClient " +
        " serviceURL objectName user pwd custID handleFile IORFile");
      System.exit(1);
    }

    String url = args[0];
    String objectName = args[1];
    String user = args[2];
    String password = args[3];
    int custID = (new Integer(args[4])).intValue();
    String handleFile = args[5];
    String iorFile = args[6];

    try {
      String ior = IORUtil.restore(iorFile);
      try {
        IORUtil.authenticate(ior, user, password);
        System.out.println("\nAuthenticated with restored IOR.");
      } catch (COMM_FAILURE e) {
        System.out.println("The session has timed out.");
        System.exit(0);
      }
```

```
        Handle handle = EJBHandleUtil.restore(handleFile);
        ShoppingCart cart = (ShoppingCart)handle.getEJBObject();
        System.out.println("Bean handle restored.");

        cart.addItem(103131, 80, 10.00);
        System.out.println("Third item added to cart.");

        int orderID = cart.commitOrder();
        System.out.println("Order commited. Your Order # is "
                    + Integer.toString(orderID));

        cart.remove();
        System.out.println("Shopping cart removed.");
    } catch (Exception e) {
        System.out.println("Exception caught in client: " + e.getMessage());
    }
  }
}
```

### Testing the Clients

The following is an example of how `SaveCartHandleClient` can be called from the command line:

```
java SaveCartHandleClient sess_iiop://localhost:2481:orcl
  /test/tips/shoppingCartBean_1 demo demo 202 _handle.dat _IOR.dat
```

In this case, the client runs on the same machine as the server. The parameters "_handle.dat" and "_IOR.dat" are the name of files in which the cart handle and login IOR will be saved. The output produced is as follows:

```
Shopping cart created.
First item added to cart.
Second item added to cart.
Bean handle written to file.
Login IOR written to file.
```

After the `SaveCartHandleClient` program has exited, the `ShoppingCart` bean object will remain alive in the EJB container for the duration of the `ShoppingCartBean`'s timeout value. Recall that the `SessionTimeout` attribute was set to 20 seconds in the deployment descriptor ShoppingCartTDD.ejb. While the bean is still alive, the second client can be run from the command line:

```
java RestoreCartHandleClient sess_iiop://localhost:2481:orcl
  /test/tips/shoppingCartBean_1 demo demo 202 _handle.dat _IOR.dat
```

Note that the handle and IOR filenames match those that were used to run
`SaveCartHandleClient`. The output from `RestoreCartHandleClient`
is as follows:

```
Authenticated with restored IOR.
Bean handle restored.
Third item added to cart.
Order commited. Your Order # is 2011
Shopping cart removed.
```

# Using Bean-Managed Transaction Demarcation for Fine-Grained Transaction Control

On the rare occasion when container-managed transaction demarcation proves
limiting, you can call JTA methods to explicitly manage transactions, either on the
server-side (bean-managed) or on the client-side. This Tip discusses issues arising
from the use of the JTA for bean-managed transaction demarcation.

### The UserTransaction Interface

In the method implementation of a TX_BEAN_MANAGED bean, you must explicitly
start a transaction using the Java Transaction API (JTA) `UserTransaction`
interface. The interface is made available by the EJB container through the
`EJBContext.getUserTransaction` method.

Here is a basic template of how to work with the JTA in a bean method.
A detailed example will be presented later in this section.

```
SessionContext ctx;
. . .
ctx.getUserTransaction().begin();
. . .
ctx.getUserTransaction().commit();
// or ctx.getUserTransaction().rollback()
```

### TX_BEAN_MANAGED Behavior

When a TX_BEAN_MANAGED bean method is invoked, the EJB container
suspends the client's transaction (if one exists) for the duration of the method call.
Note that this happens even if the TX_BEAN_MANAGED bean method does not
start a transaction.

> **CAUTION**
> *When you use TX_BEAN_MANAGED at the bean
> level, you should not specify other attributes for
> individual methods.*

With stateful session beans, it is possible to maintain the same transactional context across method calls. In other words, you can call `UserTransaction.begin` in one method and call `UserTransaction.commit` in another. The EJB container will associate the same transaction across method calls until the bean commits the transaction. That this is allowed makes sense: a stateful session bean represents the conversational state of only one client. Entity beans and stateless session beans do not allow transaction control across method calls.

**CAUTION**
*Transactional control across methods is generally best avoided because it is difficult to understand and debug. Worse, it can result in long-lived transactions that lock up resources.*

**AN EXAMPLE**    Let's modify the `commitOrder` method of `ShoppingCartBean` to explicitly manage transactions through JTA. First, the transaction attribute in the deployment descriptor is changed to TX_BEAN_MANAGED. Second, `UserTransaction` begin and commit calls are introduced into the code, as follows:

```
// Return an orderID if successful. Else throw an exception
public int commitOrder() throws SQLException, RemoteException {
  Connection conn =
    new oracle.jdbc.driver.OracleDriver().defaultConnection();

  int orderID = -1;
  PreparedStatement ps1 = null, ps2 = null;
  ResultSet rs = null;

  try {
    // First get a unique order id.

    Statement stmt = conn.createStatement();
    rs = stmt.executeQuery("SELECT sales_order_id_seq.NEXTVAL" +
                           "  FROM dual");
    if (rs.next())
      orderID = rs.getInt(1);
    else
      throw new SQLException("Error generating unique order ID");

    // Start transaction
    ctx.getUserTransaction().begin();

    // Insert header
    String q1 =
      "INSERT INTO demo.sales_order" +
```

```
        " (order_id, customer_id, order_date, ship_date, total)" +
        " VALUES (?, ?, sysdate, null, ?)";
      ps1 = conn.prepareStatement(q1);

      ps1.setInt(1, orderID);
      ps1.setInt(2, customerID);
      ps1.setDouble(3, orderTotal);
      ps1.executeUpdate();

      // Insert order items
      String q2 =
        "INSERT INTO demo.item " +
        "(order_id, item_id, product_id, quantity, actual_price, total)" +
        " VALUES (?, ?, ?, ?, ?, ?)";
      ps2 = conn.prepareStatement(q2);

      ps2.setInt(1, orderID);
      for (int i = 0; i < itemVect.size(); i++) {
        ps2.setInt(2, i + 1);
        OrderItem oi = (OrderItem)itemVect.elementAt(i);
        ps2.setInt(3, oi.getProductID());
        ps2.setInt(4, oi.getQuantity());
        ps2.setDouble(5, oi.getPrice());
        ps2.setDouble(6, oi.getTotal());
        ps2.executeUpdate();
      }

      // Commit transaction
      ctx.getUserTransaction().commit();

      return orderID;
    } finally {
      if (rs != null) rs.close();
      if (ps1 != null) ps1.close();
      if (ps2 != null) ps2.close();
    }
  }
```

# Design Tips

A robust EJB application starts with a carefully thought out object-oriented design. In designing EJB components, you should avail yourself of the rich set of features— transactions, data persistence, security, remoting—built into the underlying EJB architecture. You should exhaust EJB high-level functionality before resorting to writing low-level code. For example, first consider the appropriateness of container-managed persistence rather than bean-managed persistence; or using container-managed transactions rather than explicit transaction management.

This section describes design tips for building an effective EJB component architecture.

## Differentiating Between Entity and Session Beans

When designing your EJBs, carefully differentiate between entity beans and session beans. Entity beans are intended to represent persistent business entities that are shared among multiple clients. Session beans are intended to be pure business process beans representing the conversational state of a particular client session; they are not intended to be persistent. Table 10-4 helps make this distinction clear.

Think of a session bean as a database stored procedure, only more powerful because it can take advantage of object services. Think of an entity bean as a "data" bean, representing a row in a database table. Though not perfect in all respects, these analogies are useful in modeling EJB components.

A typical system will have a mixture of entity bean and session bean objects. The following is a bare-bones set of beans for the online shopping cart application:

- **Customer**   An entity bean to model the customer record

- **SalesOrder**   An entity bean to model a sales order

- **ShoppingCart**   A session bean to model the process of taking and committing an order

- **Product**   An entity bean to model a product record

- **ProductSearcher**   A session bean to model the process of a shopper searching for a product

| Entity Bean | Session Bean |
| --- | --- |
| Models a business entity | Models a business task |
| Represents data in a database | Represents a connection/session for a client |
| Accessible to multiple clients concurrently | Accessible to a single client |
| Persistent (once created, it persists until explicitly deleted) | Transient (persists only for the life of the session) |
| Survives system failures | Typically does not survive system failures |
| For fine-grained data handling | For coarse-grained data handling |
| Examples: Customer, Product, Employee, SalesOrder | Examples: ShoppingCart, CreditCardValidator |

**TABLE 10-4.**   *Contrasting Entity Beans and Session Beans*

- **CreditCardValidator**   A session bean to model the process of validating a credit card

- **StockChecker**   A session bean to check the current availability of a product item

In the foregoing list, note how the business processes and business entities are mapped to entity beans and session beans, respectively.

EJBs are meant to model fairly coarse-grained objects. Dependent fine-grained objects, such as Address, CreditCard, and OrderItem, should not be modeled as beans. As you will see in "Choosing Between Pass-By-Value Objects and Entity Beans," dependent fine-grained objects should be modeled as serializable classes.

## Designing EJB Components When Entity Beans Are Not Supported

The previous section portrayed a typical EJB system as consisting of a mixture of entity and session beans. However, the sample code in this chapter includes only a session bean, ShoppingCart, with no entity beans. This is a compromise approach that was required because entity beans are not supported in the current version of Oracle8i. (Entity bean support became mandatory only in the 1.1 version of the EJB specification.)

How should you model the "sales order" business entity and the "shopping cart" business process when entity beans are not an option? This section discusses three different designs, depicted in Table 10-5.

| A.   Ideal Design (Given Entity Bean Support) | B.   Not-Recommended Design (Given Lack of Entity Bean Support) | C.   Recommended Design (Given Lack of Entity Bean Support) |
|---|---|---|
| SalesOrder_A, an entity bean that uses either container-managed or bean-managed persistence. | SalesOrder_B, a session bean that emulates entity bean persistence. It accesses database tables using JDBC. | ___ |
| ShoppingCart_A, a stateful session bean that uses SalesOrder_A. | ShoppingCart_B, a stateful session bean that uses SalesOrder_B. | ShoppingCart, a stateful session bean that directly accesses database tables using JDBC. |

**TABLE 10-5.**   *Modeling the Shopping Cart Application: Three Design Alternatives*

**DESIGN A**   Design A is the ideal design when support for entity beans is available. The business entity "sales order" is represented as an entity bean, `SalesOrder_A`, and the online order taking process is represented as a session bean, `ShoppingCart_A`.

**DESIGN B**   In the absence of entity bean support, design B models the business entity "sales order" as `SalesOrder_B`, a stateful session bean implementing the `SessionSynchronization` interface. `ShoppingCart_B` would then use this stateful session bean as if it were an entity bean.

## The Optional SessionSynchronization Interface

Session beans often maintain a cache of database information. To maintain data consistency across transaction updates, the cache must be synchronized with the database when transactions are started, committed, or aborted. To keep informed of transaction status changes, the bean can implement the `javax.ejb.SessionSynchronization` interface. The EJB container calls methods of this interface whenever transaction status changes.

Only stateful session beans that use container-managed transaction demarcation should implement the `SessionSynchronization` interface. A stateless session bean should not implement it. Also, there is no need to use the `SessionSynchronization` interface with bean-managed stateful session beans. Such beans are in full control of transactions—they know when a transaction is about to be committed and whether the commit succeeded or failed.

The `SessionSynchronization` interface contains the following callback methods:

- **afterBegin**  The container calls this method to notify the bean instance that a new transaction is about to begin. You can implement this method to do any preliminary database work that might be needed for the transaction.

- **beforeCompletion**  The container calls this method when the bean instance's client has completed work on its current transaction but *before* committing the resource managers that are used by the instance. It is in this method that you write out any database updates the instance has cached.

- **afterCompletion**  The container calls this method when the transaction commits. A completion status of `true` means the data committed. A `false` means the transaction rolled back, which may require that you manually reset the bean's state.

Design B's use of session beans to emulate the persistence of entity beans is a risky practice. The main problem is the lack of concurrency control. Unlike entity beans, stateful session beans are not shared. Rather, each client gets a separate instance of a stateful session bean, each instance with a copy of the same data. The danger of reading and using dirty data is high—unless you implement the `SessionSynchronization` interface perfectly. Moreover, the use of the `SessionSynchronization` interface requires that a bean be used in the client's transactional scope.

**DESIGN C**    Design C is the recommended approach when entity bean support is lacking. In design C, a client interacts only with a session bean; the session bean accesses data directly through JDBC rather than through an "emulated entity bean." This is the strategy followed in the section "ShoppingCart: A Stateful Session Bean That Uses Container-Managed Transaction Demarcation." Recall that the `ShoppingCartBean.commitOrder` method uses JDBC to directly insert data into the demo.sales_order and demo.item tables, without using a SalesOrder "emulated entity bean." The `commitOrder` method is transactionally safe because any exception thrown within the method will cause all inserts to be rolled back. Of course, once Oracle8i supports entity beans, it would make sense to modify `ShoppingCartBean` to use a `SalesOrder` entity bean; a `SalesOrder` entity bean will provide a safe and consistent interface for the sales order data.

## Choosing Between Pass-By-Value Objects and Entity Beans

Not all objects should be modeled as EJB components. EJBs are designed to be relatively coarse-grained business objects, such as a sales order, customer, and employee. Business objects that are fine-grained and dependent should be modeled as normal Java classes; or if they need to be passed between client and server, they should be modeled as serialized objects that will be passed by value. Here the term "fine-grained" is used to depict an object that has little or no behavior; a fine-grained object consists primarily of get and set methods. A "dependent object" is one that depends on another object to give it identity and purpose; it has no meaning outside the context of the object with which it is associated.

Recall that `OrderItem` was declared as a serializable object rather than an entity bean. The `OrderItem` is an excellent candidate for pass-by-value because it is both fine-grained and dependent. It is only a structure to hold data, having no real behavior of its own. Without the sales order entity, an order item has no meaning.

Here are portions of the `OrderItem` class definition that are relevant to this discussion:

```
public class OrderItem implements java.io.Serializable {
  private int productID;
  private int quantity;
  private double price;
  private double total;

  public OrderItem(int productID, int quantity, double price, double total) {
    . . .
}
  public int getProductID() { return productID; }
  public int getQuantity() { return quantity; }
  public double getPrice() { return price; }
  public double getTotal() { return total; }
  . . .
}
```

When a client receives an `OrderItem` object from the server, it receives a copy of the object, not a remote object reference. Thus, if the client were to change the `OrderItem` object, those changes would not be reflected on the server. To emphasize the semantic immutability of `OrderItem`, its instance fields are declared private, and no set methods are defined.

**NOTE**

*Oracle8i supports the use of private instance variables for pass-by-value objects. Unfortunately, many vendors' CORBA clients that use RMI over IIOP do not. To make objects accessible from such clients, pass-by-value classes will have to declare their instance fields public. The recent OMG Object By Value specification supports pass-by-value over IIOP. Once this specification is widely adopted by the industry, pass-by-value classes will no longer have to declare fields to be public.*

## Passing Objects by Value

First, a definition: a *remote object* is one that implements the `java.rmi.Remote` interface; remote objects are used for standard Java remote object communication. With EJBs, nonremote objects can be used as parameters in method calls between clients and bean objects, provided that they are of serializable Java types, which include the following:

- Any Java primitive types such as `short`, `int`, `double`, `float`, `boolean`
- Any non–remote object class that implements the `java.io.Serializable` interface

Interestingly, the `Serializable` interface has no methods or fields; it serves only to identify the semantics of being serializable.

Be aware that there is a difference in the way nonremote objects and remote objects are passed between client and server. A remote object is passed by reference: when a remote object is passed as a parameter, the stub for the remote object is passed. In contrast, a nonremote object is passed by copy between client and server.

Also be aware that when nonremote objects are passed between client and server, only nonstatic and nontransient fields are copied. Transient fields are set to their default values when an object is deserialized: a primitive number is set to zero, an object reference to null, and a Boolean object to false.

## Listing Services for Remote Clients

Typically, a listing service queries a large set of data and presents the client with a subset that matches the client's criteria. `ProductSearcher` is an example of a listing service. It provides the client with choices. Recall that the `findByDescription` method returned an enumeration of `ProductInfo` objects. `ProductInfo` was defined as a serialized class, not an EJB. Consider an alternative: returning an enumeration of `Product` remote references, where `Product` is an entity bean. Which is preferred?

The enumeration of `ProductInfo` objects will be less bulky than an enumeration of `Product` remote references. In addition, the collection of remote references alternative requires that the client work with many stubs; each stub will have its own connection to EJB objects on the server, thereby taking up resources on the server. Furthermore, to list the products' descriptions and prices, the client will have to iterate through the enumeration of remote references and make a remote call to the `getDescription` method, each time. The result will be increased network traffic and decreased performance.

The enumeration of pass-by-value objects, then, is the clear winner in terms of speed. However, you should also be aware of the risk of data staleness, always present with pass-by-value objects. A `ProductInfo` object, once present on the client, will no longer represent data in the database.

**Pass-By-Value versus Entity Beans**

### Reducing Network Traffic by Making Remote Client Interact Primarily with Session Beans Rather than Entity Beans

Remote method invocations are slow and generate network traffic. A good EJB component design will seek to minimize the number of remote method invocations needed to accomplish a business task and, at the same time, to minimize the risk of inconsistent data being held by clients. There is a fundamentally important design principle that will help achieve this goal: *remote clients should interact primarily with coarse-grained session beans rather than with entity beans.* By encapsulating the interactions of finer-grained entity beans with coarse-grained session beans, you will significantly reduce network traffic.

## Tips Review

Developing EJB components in Oracle8i first involves the mechanics of writing the home interface, remote interface, bean class, and deployment descriptor; as well as compilation and deployment of EJBs into the Oracle8i database. EJB clients can look up a bean's home with JNDI; the home's `create` methods can then be used to create an instance of the bean.

In managing transactions in an EJB application, a robust technique is to use container-managed transaction demarcation. Of the six available declarative policies, five free the developer from writing code. In addition, the JTA can be used to explicitly demarcate transactions.

In considering the design of EJB components, a clear distinction must be made between a session bean (the business process) and an entity bean (the business entity). When entity bean support is unavailable, care must be taken when session beans are used in lieu of entity beans. For performance, fine-grained dependent objects should be modeled as serializable Java objects. Finally, network traffic can be reduced by having clients interact primarily with session beans rather than entity beans.

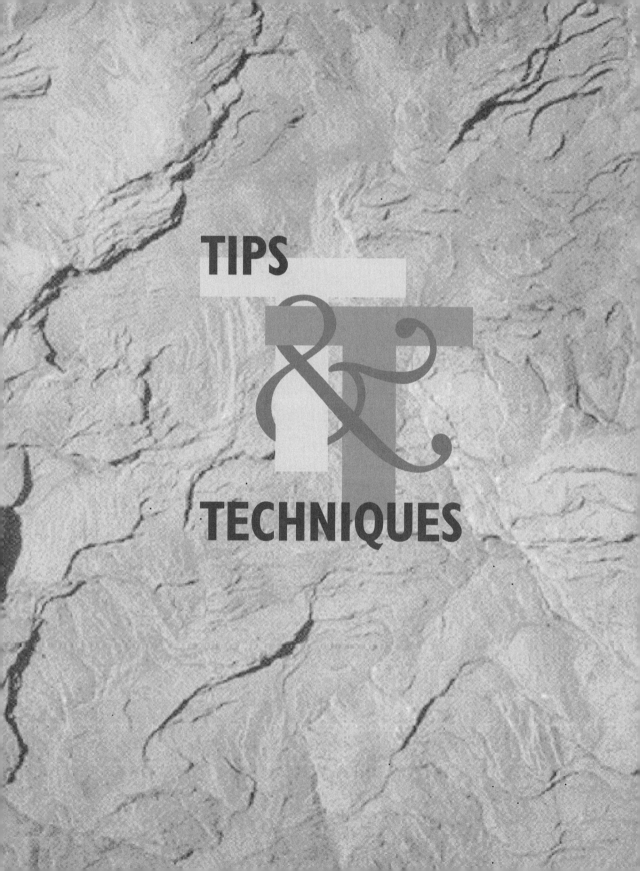

TIPS
&
TECHNIQUES

# CHAPTER
## 11

## interMedia Text

Oracle's interMedia Text is a set of services that provides indexing methods for documents, leading to Text searching techniques that extend the standard SQL language. The Oracle technical white paper *Text Management with Oracle interMedia: Managing Text and Multimedia Content with Oracle8i* (Oracle Corporation, February 1999) describes interMedia Text as a fourth-generation text engine because of its full integration into the database kernel.

Some of the interMedia Text services were originally part of Oracle ConText, an add-on product that was available in conjunction with Oracle7. ConText services are replaced in Oracle8i by interMedia Text, and have been fully integrated into the database. This integration leads to easier creation and management of Text indexes, better performance, and seamless searching through SQL queries. Additional services also have been added, providing easier and faster database access to the search terms. Although some of the techniques described in this chapter are not wholly new to Oracle8i, they have been included because of their central position in Oracle8i's text processing capabilities. Tips discussed include:

- Making LOB storage decisions

- Bulk loading documents with SQL*Loader

- Loading documents using DBMS_LOB

- Loading an external document during INSERT

- Adding additional row data to a Text index with a USER_DATASTORE preference

- Adding XML tags to indexed Text for custom WITHIN searching

- Tracking Text index build with CTX_OUTPUT logging

- Reviewing Text index build errors with CTX_USER_INDEX_ERRORS

- Using INSO_FILTER in an NT installation with multiple ORACLE_HOMEs

- Issuing queries about concepts or themes

- Creating thesauri to increase relevance

- Finding foreign terms with the TR operator

- Finding foreign terms and their synonyms with the TRSYN operator

- Using synonyms for history recasting

- Prefiltering Adobe PDF and Word files outside the database via ctxhx

- Converting stored binary documents into HTML in the database

- Converting stored binary documents into HTML in a SELECT statement

- Accessing a converted HTML document via the PL/SQL cartridge

# Overview

Using interMedia Text entails three basic steps:

1. Load the textual information

2. Index the textual information

3. Issue queries against the textual information

The Oracle-provided schema DEMO will be used for the examples in this chapter. You should grant the CTXAPP role to DEMO, and in the future to an account that will be performing Text indexing. This will give the account the ability to issue all of the necessary interMedia Text calls.

Loading textual information can be as simple as issuing a DML statement, as shown in the following INSERT statement in which a row is added to the product table:

```
INSERT INTO product (product_id, description)
    VALUES (200381, 'YELLOW JERSEY BICYCLE BELL');
```

Indexing the textual information will make it quickly searchable. The description column can be indexed through use of the following CREATE INDEX statement:

```
CREATE INDEX product_description
  ON product (description)
  INDEXTYPE IS CTXSYS.CONTEXT;
```

You can then do querying on the basis of the description column, using the CONTAINS operator in the SQL predicate. CONTAINS returns the relevance value for each row on a scale of 0 to 100, zero meaning the row is completely irrelevant, or, in other words, that no matching text string was found for that row.

```
SELECT product_id, description
  FROM product
 WHERE CONTAINS (description, 'bicycle') > 0
 ORDER BY description;

PRODUCT_ID DESCRIPTION
---------- -----------------------------
    200381 YELLOW JERSEY BICYCLE BELL
    105124 YELLOW JERSEY BICYCLE GLOVES
    105123 YELLOW JERSEY BICYCLE HELMET
```

To see what words were included in the index on product_promotion just created, you can issue the following SELECT statements:

```
SELECT token_text
  FROM dr$product_promotion$i;
```

The "$" included in the view names are part of the interMedia Text naming convention.

Included in interMedia Text is a set of views, tables, and stored code that are owned by CTXSYS and which are used to participate in the three steps. Many of the CTXSYS objects are prefixed with either CTX_ or DR. The CTX_ views are based at least partially on CTXSYS's tables prefixed with DR$. A query against CTXSYS.USER_OBJECTS reveals two interesting objects: CONTAINS, which is an OPERATOR type, and CONTEXT, which is an INDEXTYPE type. How these are used in interMedia text will be shown in the forthcoming sections. The new types are possible because of Oracle8i's extensible framework, which allows the definition and creation of user-defined indirect indexing schemes (*domain indexes*) and custom operators.

### New USER_INDEXES Columns

A domain index is a user-defined index used for complex datatypes. An interMedia Text index is a type of domain index. The USER_INDEXES view contains some new columns that have information about domain indexes. You may wish to review them when issuing a query to see information about the product_description index. The new columns are as follows:

■ **DOMIDX_OPSTATUS**   This shows the status of the CREATE or ALTER operation on the index. Valid values are: "VALID" and "FAILED."

■ **ITYP_NAME**   For interMedia Text indexes, this will contain the index type name, CONTEXT.

■ **ITYP_OWNER**   This shows the account that owns the definition of the indextype specified at index CREATE time. When the indextype is CONTEXT, the owner will be CTXSYS.

■ **PARAMETERS**   Domain indexes can receive a parameter string containing preferences and options that can be specified at CREATE or ALTER time. The PARAMETERS column of USER_INDEXES contains the parameter string.

# Loading and Storing Textual Information

Loading textual information can be as simple as issuing a DML statement. As shown in the Overview section, an INSERT statement can be used to put textual information into a column defined as VARCHAR2, which can then be indexed as a Text index and queried. Loading textual information can also be as sophisticated as loading a Microsoft Word (.doc) or Adobe Acrobat (.pdf) document.

The examples in this section show the more sophisticated ways of loading textual data for querying. For these examples, two columns—promotion, defined as BLOB and promotion_html defined as CLOB—must be added to the product table, as shown in the ALTER TABLE statement to follow. The promotion column will hold the original version of the document—that is, the binary formatted document (for example, in Word or PDF format)—that was used to create the most recent promotional mailing for a product. The promotion_html column will hold an HTML version of the document.

The defaults of EMPTY_CLOB() and EMPTY_BLOB() are specified for the columns because LOBs must contain a locator before they are written to, even if that locator points to a LOB containing nothing. The following statement makes the necessary alterations to the product table.

```
ALTER TABLE product
  ADD (promotion BLOB DEFAULT EMPTY_BLOB(),
       promotion_html CLOB DEFAULT EMPTY_CLOB()
       );
```

## Making LOB Storage Decisions

LOBs work by storing a LOB locator with the table data (in the table's segment and in the same block as the row). The LOB locator is a pointer to the LOB data, which can be stored either *in-line* with the table's data or *out-of-line* from the table data (where the LOB is stored in its own segment). Whether in-line or out-of-line, when a LOB's data or *value* is stored in a segment, it is considered to be an *internal LOB*. The values of *external LOBs* reside outside the database as operating system files and so can never be stored in-line. BFILE is the only external LOB type. A LOB index is created for the LOB data in the same tablespace as the LOB data. LOB storage information can be seen in the USER_LOBS view.

### Internal Versus External LOBs

Both internal LOBs (BLOB, CLOB, NCLOB) and external LOBs (BFILES) can store up to 4GB of data. By setting the storage parameters of the LOB correctly (as discussed in the next section), you can allow both types to perform nearly equally as efficient in performance. Which of the two is appropriate for use in a particular application? The following rules of thumb can be used to help make this decision:

- An **internal LOB**'s advantage is that it receives the same benefits from an ORDBMS, such as security, manageability, backup and recovery, and transaction control as do standard data types. Using the issue of transaction control as an example, if a row is DELETEd from the promotion table, the corresponding Word document is removed with it when the promotion column is defined as BLOB; it is not removed when the column is defined as a BFILE.

■ A **BFILE**, which at its simplest is a pointer to a file outside the database, will be used under one of two special conditions. First, it can be used to promote the inclusion of legacy data that is already stored as a set of documents in the filesystem. BFILEs can be used to quickly make those files accessible to an Oracle database. Second, BFILEs can be employed when there are applications that cannot connect to the database but need access to the documents. In this way, the database can share the document's data with those applications.

## Storage Parameters Affecting Internal LOB Performance

Several storage parameters affect LOB performance. For example, the BLOB column product.promotion can be placed in a separate tablespace from the table data. If all of these parameters were used in the ALTER TABLE statement that adds the additional columns to the product table, then the statement would appear as follows. This statement assumes the existence of two additional tablespaces: User_documents and User_html.

```
ALTER TABLE product
  ADD (promotion BLOB DEFAULT EMPTY_BLOB(),
    promotion_html CLOB DEFAULT EMPTY_CLOB()
    )
  LOB (promotion) STORE AS promotion_seg
    (TABLESPACE user_documents
     STORAGE(INITIAL 4K NEXT 4K PCTINCREASE 0)
     CHUNK 4K NOCACHE LOGGING ENABLE STORAGE IN ROW
    )
  LOB (promotion_html) STORE AS promotion_html_seg
    (TABLESPACE user_html
     STORAGE(INITIAL 2K NEXT 2K PCTINCREASE 0)
     CHUNK 2K NOCACHE NOLOGGING ENABLE STORAGE IN ROW
    );
```

**NOTE**
*The specification of a name for the LOB segment is not required, but it promotes a more manageable schema. If no name is provided for the LOB segment, a system-generated name like SYS_LOB0000013021C00016$$ will be generated. The segment name can be seen in a query against the USER_SEGMENTS view, as can the segment type of LOBSEGMENT.*

- **TABLESPACE**   Specifies the tablespace for an internal LOB column. If a tablespace is not specified, the LOB segment will be stored in the same tablespace as its associated table. Specifying a different tablespace than the table data can avoid troublesome space-management issues and can reduce device contention during DML and SELECT statements. When separate tablespaces are specified for each LOB column individually, device contention can be reduced when, for example, multiple LOB columns are SELECTed at the same time.

- **CACHE | NOCACHE**   Stipulates whether the LOB data will be passed through the Database Buffer Cache. This should be set to NOCACHE unless the LOB data will be used frequently and the LOB data size is inconsequential with respect to the size of the Database Buffer Cache. An example of this is an image of a small company logo that is used at the top of each screen of an application. The default is NOCACHE. Note that if you specify CACHE, any changes to the LOB value will also be passed to the Redo Log Buffer and into the redo logs.

- **LOGGING | NOLOGGING**   Specifies if changes to the data will be passed to the Redo Log Buffer and later to the redo logs. For bulk loads, NOLOGGING should be used, since it will make the load quicker, and the data will be available from the original source in case of data loss. NOLOGGING will always be quicker than LOGGING, but LOGGING must be used if changes to the LOB need to be recorded in the redo log files for recovery purposes. Also, NOLOGGING cannot be specified if CACHE was specified. The default is taken from the default storage parameters of the LOB segment's tablespace.

- **CHUNK**   An INTEGER specifying the number of bytes used for manipulation of the LOB. The value should be a multiple of the datablock size and set as close as possible to the anticipated size of a read or write to the LOB values in that column. It cannot be set larger than 32768 (32K), the largest Oracle datablock size. The value of CHUNK must be less than or equal to the size of the NEXT parameter (to be described). The default is the size of one Oracle datablock.

- **INITIAL, NEXT, PCTINCREASE**   Specify how the extents of the LOB segment will be allocated. (See the discussion of these parameters in Chapter 1.) NEXT must be greater than or equal to CHUNK.

- **ENABLE | DISABLE STORAGE IN ROW**   Specifies whether the LOB value will be stored in-line (ENABLE) or out-of-line (DISABLE). The default is ENABLE. The choice of which option to use involves consideration of many issues. LOBs can be stored in-line only if their value is less than or equal to

4K in size. If ENABLE is specified and a LOB value larger than 4K is INSERTed into the row, or an UPDATE to a LOB causes it to grow larger than 4K, then the LOB value will be moved out-of-line. LOBs that are moved out-of-line in this way still may have better overall performance, since some control information (other than the LOB locator) will continue to be stored in-line. LOBs migrated out-of-line will reside in the LOB segment (user-named or system-named when the column was defined). So, specifying ENABLE even when it is known that the LOB values will definitely be greater than 4K is a good choice since the LOB data will always be stored out-of-line, but the control information will be stored in-line. Using DISABLE will force all LOB values, no matter the size, into their associated LOB segments but without the benefit of keeping the control information in-line. DISABLE is best specified if many UPDATEs or SELECTs involving full table scans are anticipated against the table's non-LOB data.

## Bulk Loading Documents with SQL*Loader

SQL*Loader is a utility provided with the database for loading external data. It should be used for an initial load of data or subsequent bulk loads. It cannot be used for loading document files into rows that already exist. (See "Loading Documents Using DBMS_LOB" next for a method to accomplish this.)

For this example, assume the existence of a comma-delimited file named productload.dat containing information about products to be loaded into the product table. The data will contain the name of the Word document file that holds associated promotional information. The productload.dat file contains lines of information that will be loaded into the product_id, description, and promotion columns:

```
300002,DUNK SNEAKERS,\ORACLE\ADMIN\PRODUCT_PROMOTIONS\300002.DOC,
300003,DUNK LACES,\ORACLE\ADMIN\PRODUCT_PROMOTIONS\300003.DOC,
300004,DUNK POSTERS,\ORACLE\ADMIN\PRODUCT_PROMOTIONS\300004.DOC,
300005,DUNK SHORTS,\ORACLE\ADMIN\PRODUCT_PROMOTIONS\300005.DOC,
```

A control file named productload.ctl used for the load session is shown in the following listing. It specifies that the product_id is in the first position of the file; the description is in the second; and the filename of the promotional document, found in the FILLER field in the third position, will be held temporarily in *external_filename* and then used to populate the promotion column signified by *LOBFILE(external_filename)*.

```
LOAD DATA
INFILE 'productload.dat'
```

```
APPEND
INTO TABLE product
FIELDS TERMINATED BY ','
(product_id,
 description,
 external_filename FILLER,
 promotion LOBFILE(external_filename)
 TERMINATED BY EOF
)
```

Once the productload.dat and productload.ctl files have been created, the following command should be issued at the command line to start the loaded session:

```
sqlldr userid=demo/demo control=productload.ctl log=productload.log
```

SQL*Loader loads the non-LOB data from the productload.dat file by storing each field into a bind array and then performing an array insert on that data. It then loads the corresponding LOB data. This is known as the *conventional path method.* If an error occurred while the LOBFILE data was being processed—for example, if the LOBFILE could not be found—then the promotion field would be left empty, but the non-LOB data in the array insert would remain intact.

**NOTE**
*You cannot use the direct=true parameter (direct path method) for loading LOBs.*

## Loading Documents Using DBMS_LOB

Although SQL*Loader is used for bulk-loading documents, it is not possible to use it for UPDATEs to individual documents or to a small set of existing documents. Use of the DBMS_LOB package will allow a document residing in the filesystem to be loaded into the BLOB columns of an existing row. The package can be extended for use with reloading a small set of documents for existing rows, or it can be included in a trigger to pull a document off of the filesystem during an UPDATE to the row.

DBMS_LOB is not a package that is specific for use with interMedia Text. It is important to remember that there are many other data sources that can be Text indexed, including data entered into a VARCHAR2 column or even an HTML document accessed directly by the database from the Internet. The DBMS_LOB examples are provided here since they may be useful in storing any type of file in the database for any use, including multimedia, spreadsheet, or any other file less than 4GB in size.

Microsoft Word, Adobe PDF, and other binary formatted documents can be loaded into the promotion column through use of the Oracle built-in DBMS_LOB.LOADFROMFILE. This process has two steps:

1. Create a directory object in the database.

2. Load the document into the BLOB column

### Create a Directory Object in the Database as an Alias to a Filesystem

A directory is an Oracle database object that is the logical representation of an operating system filesystem/directory. Directory objects act as aliases to locations in which BFILES (external LOBs) are located. Users can access the filesystem represented by the directory object only if they have been granted READ privilege on the directory object. Use of directory objects also provides flexibility in locating files, since the file is prefixed by the name of the directory object rather than with a hard-coded absolute location. If the file needs to be moved to a different filesystem or directory, the directory object definition is the only database object that needs to change. None of the code referencing the directory object will need to be changed.

Users must have been granted the CREATE ANY DIRECTORY privilege in order to create a directory object. In the default database, SYS and CTXSYS are the only users that can grant that privilege. The HR_SECURITY_MANAGER user discussed in Chapter 7 will create the directory, and so he or she needs to be granted CREATE ANY DIRECTORY.

As HR_SECURITY_MANAGER, issue a command to create a directory object called product_promotions. In the following example, the product_promotions directory object acts as an alias for the NT operating system directory 'E:\ORACLE\ADMIN\PRODUCT_PROMOTIONS'.

```
CREATE OR REPLACE DIRECTORY product_promotions
  AS 'E:\ORACLE\ADMIN\PRODUCT_PROMOTIONS';
```

Next, as HR_SECURITY_MANAGER, grant READ privileges on the directory object to the DEMO user.

```
GRANT READ ON DIRECTORY product_promotions TO demo;
```

**NOTE**
*To see what directories DEMO can access, query the ALL_DIRECTORIES view.*

## Notes About Creating Directories

- Directory names are not associated with schema names. Thus, only one directory of a specified name can exist in each database.

- The Oracle operating system user (the user under which the Oracle background processes run) must have read permission to the filesystem that the directory object aliases.

- An ending slash (/) or backslash (\) does not have to be included in the filesystem specification.

- The physical directory does not have to exist when the directory object is created, but it must exist when the directory object is used.

### Load a Word Document into the Promotion Column

DBMS_LOB.LOADFROMFILE loads a document from an external file into the promotion column, which has been defined as a BLOB. The load_product_promotion procedure, defined next, assumes that files have been placed in the PRODUCT_PROMOTIONS directory and are named <product_id>.doc. For example, the promotional document for the product with product_id 123456 will be named 123456.doc.

The procedure takes two parameters:

- **i_product_id**   This is a product ID.

- **i_file_extension**   This is the extension for the filename. If the promotions were published in Adobe Acrobat rather than in Word, then the extension ".pdf" could be used.

The BFILENAME function returns a BFILE locator. This will be used as the pointer to the Word document that resides in the operating system filesystem.

```
CREATE OR REPLACE PROCEDURE load_product_promotion
  (i_product_id product.product_id%TYPE,
   i_file_extension VARCHAR2 DEFAULT '.doc'
  )
```

```
AS
  -- Initialize the BFILE locator to the external document.
  v_document_source BFILE :=
    BFILENAME('PRODUCT_PROMOTIONS',
              i_product_id||i_file_extension
             );
  -- x-promotion is used to hold the current promotional_document
  --   during the FOR UPDATE row locking.
  v_promotion product.promotion%TYPE;
BEGIN
  IF DBMS_LOB.FILEEXISTS(v_document_source) = 1
  THEN
    -- There is a promotional document for this product
    --   in the filesystem.
    -- Begin a transaction and lock the row in product.
    SELECT promotion
      INTO v_promotion
      FROM product
     WHERE product_id = i_product_id
     FOR UPDATE;
    DBMS_LOB.OPEN(v_document_source, DBMS_LOB.LOB_READONLY);
    -- Pull the file from the file system as indicated
    --   in the BFILE locator v_document_source, into the
    --   local BLOB variable v_promotion and make
    --   the BLOB the same size as the document DBMS_LOB.GETLENGTH.
    DBMS_LOB.LOADFROMFILE(v_promotion, v_document_source,
                          DBMS_LOB.GETLENGTH(v_document_source)
                         );
    -- Trim the BLOB in case this is an UPDATE so that the internal
    --   LOB size will be reflective of this new LOB value.
    DBMS_LOB.TRIM
      (v_promotion, DBMS_LOB.GETLENGTH(v_document_source));
    DBMS_LOB.CLOSE(v_document_source);
  END IF;
EXCEPTION
  WHEN OTHERS
  THEN
    -- In case there is an error, make sure that, if the
    --   the LOB locator is still open, it gets closed.
    IF DBMS_LOB.ISOPEN(v_document_source) = 1
    THEN
      DBMS_LOB.CLOSE(v_document_source);
    END IF;
END;
```

If all of the products are to be updated, the following anonymous PL/SQL block could be run in SQL*Plus:

```
DECLARE
  CURSOR c_product_id IS
    SELECT product_id
      FROM product;
BEGIN
  FOR r_product_ID IN c_product_id
  LOOP
    load_product_promotion(r_product_id.product_id);
  END LOOP;
  COMMIT;
END;
```

## Loading an External Document During INSERT

The easiest way to load a Word document from a filesystem during an INSERT would be to write a trigger that uses DBMS_LOB.LOADFROMFILE to retrieve the Word document and assign it to :NEW.promotion. Unfortunately, :NEW.promotion cannot be used in this way, since the promotion column is a BLOB, and :NEW and :OLD correlation versions of BLOBs for use in database triggers are not allowed.

The next choice would be to call a procedure such as load_product_promotion from an AFTER row level trigger so that an attempt to load the document occurs for each row as it is INSERTed. Unfortunately, this technique also cannot be used, since the call to DBMS_LOB.LOADFROMFILE as used in the load_product_promotion procedure cannot see the newly INSERTed row. Thus, the BLOB must be put into the row using an UPDATE; but putting an UPDATE inside an AFTER row trigger is not allowed since it creates a mutating table situation.

A solution is to use an AFTER statement level trigger, that uses code similar to load_product_promotion, with the addition that it will include an UPDATE statement. The overall technique is not new, but it works well in loading the document at INSERT time and so is included here. The technique involves four steps:

1. Define a PL/SQL table that can store product_id's in a package header.

2. Define an AFTER row level trigger that loads the PL/SQL table with the product_id of the current row.

3. Define an AFTER statement level trigger that LOOPs through the PL/SQL table and UPDATEs the promotion column for each product_id in the PL/SQL table.

4. Define a BEFORE statement level trigger to make sure that the PL/SQL table is empty.

In the DEMO schema, create the package header api_product as follows:

```
CREATE OR REPLACE PACKAGE api_product
AS
  -- Step 1: Define a PL/SQL table that can store
  --  product_id's in a package header.
  TYPE product_id_ibt
    IS TABLE OF product.product_id%TYPE
    INDEX BY BINARY_INTEGER;
  ibt_product_id product_id_ibt;
END;
```

Next create the row- and statement-level triggers:

```
CREATE OR REPLACE TRIGGER product_air
  AFTER INSERT ON product
  FOR EACH ROW
BEGIN
  -- Step 2: Define an AFTER row level trigger that loads
  --  the PL/SQL table with the product_id of the current row.
  api_product.ibt_product_id
    (NVL(api_product.ibt_product_id.LAST, 0) + 1) := :NEW.product_id;
END;
```

The AFTER statement level trigger will involve a call to the built-in DBMS_LOB.CREATETEMPORARY. Temporary LOBs are new with Oracle8i and are necessary in this program since DBMS_LOB.LOADFROMFILE needs to UPDATE an internal LOB structure. Temporary LOBs are empty when created and are deleted at the end of the session that created them. Like their accompanying LOB indexes, they exist in the current user's temporary tablespace.

DBMS_LOB.CREATETEMPORARY takes three parameters:

- **LOB_LOC**  This is the name of a variable defined as BLOB, CLOB, or NCLOB in the calling procedure.

- **CACHE**  This is a Boolean value specifying whether the LOB should be read into the Database Buffer Cache. The default is FALSE.

- **DUR**  There are two valid values specifying the point at which the temporary LOB should be cleaned up. The first is DBMS_LOB.SESSION, specifying that the temporary LOB should be cleaned up at the end of the user's session. The second is DBMS_LOB.CALL, specifying that the temporary LOB should be cleaned up when the procedure that created it is complete.

**NOTE**
*DBAs can see the amount of storage being used by temporary LOBs for each session by querying the V$TEMPORARY_LOBS view.*

```
CREATE OR REPLACE TRIGGER product_ais
  AFTER INSERT ON product
DECLARE
  -- Step 3: Define an AFTER statement level trigger that
  --  LOOPs through the PL/SQL table and UPDATEs the promotion
  --  column for each product_id in the PL/SQL table.
  v_document_source BFILE;
  v_promotion BLOB;
BEGIN
  DBMS_LOB.CREATETEMPORARY(v_promotion, FALSE, DBMS_LOB.SESSION);
  FOR i_product_id IN
    api_product.ibt_product_id.FIRST ..
    api_product.ibt_product_id.LAST
  LOOP
    -- Loop though each record in the PL/SQL table that
    --  was populated by the AFTER row level trigger,
    --  loading promotional documents, if they exist,
    --  from the filesystem into the internal LOB
    v_document_source :=
      BFILENAME('PRODUCT_PROMOTIONS',
              api_product.ibt_product_id(i_product_id)||'.doc'
              );
    IF DBMS_LOB.FILEEXISTS(v_document_source) = 1
    THEN
      DBMS_LOB.OPEN(v_document_source, DBMS_LOB.LOB_READONLY);
      -- Pull the file from the file system as indicated
      --  in the BFILE locator v_document_source into the
      --  local BLOB variable v_promotion and make
      --  the BLOB the same size as the document
      DBMS_LOB.LOADFROMFILE
        (v_promotion, v_document_source,
         DBMS_LOB.GETLENGTH(v_document_source)
         );
      UPDATE product
        SET promotion = v_promotion
```

```
        WHERE product_id = api_product.ibt_product_id(i_product_id);
      DBMS_LOB.CLOSE(v_document_source);
    END IF;
  END LOOP;
EXCEPTION
  WHEN OTHERS
  THEN
    -- In case there is an error, make sure that if the
    --   the LOB locator is still open, it gets closed.
    IF DBMS_LOB.ISOPEN(v_document_source) = 1
    THEN
      DBMS_LOB.CLOSE(v_document_source);
    END IF;
END;

CREATE OR REPLACE TRIGGER product_bis
  BEFORE INSERT ON product
BEGIN
  -- Step 4: Define a BEFORE statement level trigger to
  --   make sure that the PL/SQL table is empty.
  -- Empty the PL/SQL table to avoid spurious results
  api_product.ibt_product_id.DELETE;
END;
```

**CAUTION**
*These triggers should be disabled if documents are
being loaded in bulk through a method such as
SQL\*Loader.*

This technique can be tested by creating a Word document named 300000.doc
and saving it in the PRODUCT_PROMOTIONS directory. Insert a row into the
product table with a product_id of 300000, as follows:

```
INSERT INTO product (product_id)
  VALUES (300000);
COMMIT;
```

Do not include a value for the promotion or promotion_html columns. Last, issue
the following in SQL\*Plus. The script will show the size of the file in the filesystem
and the size of the BLOB column for product_id 300000. If all worked well, the two
should match.

```
SET SERVEROUTPUT ON
DECLARE
    v_document product.promotion%TYPE;
```

```
BEGIN
  SELECT promotion
    INTO v_document
    FROM product
   WHERE product_id = 300000;
  DBMS_OUTPUT.PUT_LINE
    ('* BFILE length is: '||
     DBMS_LOB.GETLENGTH(
     BFILENAME('PRODUCT_PROMOTIONS', '300000.doc'))
    );
  DBMS_OUTPUT.PUT_LINE('*  BLOB length is: '||
  DBMS_LOB.GETLENGTH(v_document));
END;
.
/

* BFILE length is: 4608
*  BLOB length is: 4608
```

**NOTE**
*The interMedia Web Agent, an interMedia component
that supports Web access to multimedia types, can
also be used to upload documents into the database.
Chapter 12 contains an example of an application
written for the interMedia Web Agent and the PL/SQL
cartridge, which allows the insertion of hand-entered
data along with an uploaded document from a
browser.*

# Indexing Textual Information

The key to speedily querying a large amount of text lies in the capabilities of Text
indexing. Text indexing is powerful because of its many options. Some of those
options will be explored here. In the simple example of a Text index creation
statement that follows, a Text index called product_description is created on the
description column of the product table. The INDEXTYPE clause states that a
domain index is being created of type CTXSYS.CONTEXT.

```
CREATE INDEX product_description
  ON product (description)
  INDEXTYPE IS CTXSYS.CONTEXT;
```

A Text index is characterized as an *inverted index*. It is "inverted" because it is
considered to be used inversely to the way that people usually look at documents.

Normally, users view a document as containing a set of words. The inverse index takes a list of words and turns them into locators for documents. To see this, consider how a text search might be done without a Text index. If a query were written that searched for all of the descriptions that contained the word "BICYCLE," a non-Text query would probably use the INSTR function or a LIKE operator, as in the following examples:

```
SELECT product_id
  FROM product
 WHERE INSTR(UPPER(description), 'BICYCLE') > 0;
```

```
SELECT product_id
  FROM product
 WHERE UPPER(description) LIKE '%BICYCLE%';
```

Neither of these examples uses an index and probably will result in poor response time. These queries would search the entire text of each description looking for the word "BICYCLE". Since descriptions may be mixed case, the UPPER function would also have to be used on the description column in order to find the word no matter how it was capitalized, further ensuring that no index will be used to optimize these queries.

A search against a Text index occurs very quickly. This is because the index is itself a list of words with pointers to the original document. The same query against a column with a Text index would appear as follows:

```
SELECT product_id
  FROM product
 WHERE CONTAINS (description, 'bicycle') > 0;
```

There are some restrictions to creating a Text index:

- Parallel Text index creation is not supported.

- Only one column may be included in a Text index column list. The column must be one of the following types: CHAR, VARCHAR, VARCHAR2, LONG, LONG RAW, BLOB, CLOB, or BFILE. Nested table columns cannot be indexed.

Unlike standard types of indexes, Text indexes are not updated automatically when values in the column are changed. The ALTER INDEX <indexname> REBUILD PARAMETERS ('SYNC') command must be used to refresh the index. Use of the SYNC parameter synchronizes the index for values that have undergone change since the last index rebuild, as shown in Table 11-1. You can rebuild the

| DML Type Against the Indexed Column | Synchronization Status |
|---|---|
| INSERT | Document will not be included in any Text search results until the next synchronization |
| UPDATE | Document will not be included in any Text search results until the next synchronization |
| DELETE | Document will immediately be excluded from all Text searches |

**TABLE 11-1.**  *Text-Indexed Document Availability*

Text index entirely by not including the PARAMETERS ('SYNC') clause, although it will take much longer.

There are several ways to keep the index synchronized automatically. Use of the ctxsrv program is the primary method. Once configured, the ctxsrv process can be run in the background to synchronize the index as often as every few seconds, depending on the size of the documents stored in the indexed column. Alternatively, the DBMS_JOB Oracle built-in or the Oracle Enterprise Manager job queue can be used to schedule periodic refreshes of the Text index. These two methods support the ability to perform batch synchronization during hours of low database usage and avoid the fragmentation that can occur in the index when the ctxsrv program is used to keep it synchronized.

## Stages in Text Index Creation

A Text index is created in four stages. Each stage is considered a class. Associated with each class is a set of options, which are considered objects. Each of those objects has a set of attributes. The four stages are as follows:

1. **Datastore**   This specifies how text to be indexed is stored. For example, one of the datastore options is FILE_DATASTORE. FILE_DATASTORE has one attribute PATH.

2. **Filter**   This specifies how text is filtered for indexing. The filter takes the document data and turns it into a text representation. For example, the INSO_FILTER (so called because the technology is licensed by Oracle from the Inso Corporation) is used to turn formatted binary documents, such as ones created in Word, into textual data. The output of the process is HTML, XML, and plain text.

3. **Section**   This specifies how HTML and XML tags that are received as output from a filter will be broken into groups. The text can then be searched according to group. For example, if there is text inside the tag <TITLE>Yellow Jersey Bicycle Bell</TITLE>, it could be searched as

```
SELECT product_id, description
  FROM product
 WHERE CONTAINS (description, 'bicycle WITHIN TITLE') > 0;
```

If the input to the Section stage is plain text, the output is unchanged.

4. **Lexer**   This specifies how the text that the index receives from the Section stage is split into words.

## Preferences

A *preference* is a set of classes, objects, and attributes that governs the behavior of the four stages of Text index creation. The Database Configuration Assistant configures interMedia Text to use default preferences when the database is installed. The preference system allows for the customization and creation of these preferences via the CTX_DDL.CREATE_PREFERENCE and the CTX_ADMIN.SET_PARAMETER procedures.

### When Good Text Index Creation Goes Bad

The creation of a Text index works differently from b-tree and other previously available Oracle index types. If an error occurs during the creation of a Text index, the index will still be created, but it will be created with errors. If the problem occurred during the creation of indexes on the DR$ tables that are built in the background in support of Text indexes, then the command ALTER INDEX <index_name> REBUILD PARAMETERS ('RESUME') should be used after the physical problem is investigated and resolved. This will allow the index rebuild to continue from the point it stopped rather than your having to drop the Text index and build it again. If the problem was due to some other reason, the Text index will have to be dropped before attempts to recreate it. This can be done with a standard DROP INDEX statement.

When dropping the index, if the message *ORA-29868: cannot issue DDL on a domain index marked as LOADING* is returned, then you should use the DROP INDEX <index_name> FORCE; command.

The CTX_PARAMETERS view holds information about the default parameters, as shown in the following query:

```
COLUMN par_value FORMAT A35
SELECT *
  FROM ctx_parameters;


PAR_NAME                            PAR_VALUE
----------------------------------  -----------------------------------
DEFAULT_DATASTORE                   CTXSYS.DEFAULT_DATASTORE
DEFAULT_FILTER_BINARY               CTXSYS.INSO_FILTER
DEFAULT_FILTER_FILE                 CTXSYS.INSO_FILTER
DEFAULT_FILTER_TEXT                 CTXSYS.NULL_FILTER
DEFAULT_INDEX_MEMORY                12582912
DEFAULT_LEXER                       CTXSYS.DEFAULT_LEXER
DEFAULT_SECTION_HTML                CTXSYS.HTML_SECTION_GROUP
DEFAULT_SECTION_TEXT                CTXSYS.NULL_SECTION_GROUP
DEFAULT_STOPLIST                    CTXSYS.DEFAULT_STOPLIST
DEFAULT_STORAGE                     CTXSYS.DEFAULT_STORAGE
DEFAULT_WORDLIST                    CTXSYS.DEFAULT_WORDLIST
LOG_DIRECTORY                       E:\ORACLE\ADMIN\PRODUCT_PROMOTIONS
MAX_INDEX_MEMORY                    52428800
```

**NOTE**
*The list of objects, classes, and attributes can be seen in the view CTX_OBJECT_ATTRIBUTES.*

## Adding Additional Row Data to a Text Index with a USER_DATASTORE Preference

The USER_DATASTORE object allows data to be added to the value in an indexed column, effectively supporting the synthesis of a document at index time from a combination of data from other sources. This could be useful for including values from other columns in the same row to the index, or for adding custom tags that can then be seen by the XML_SECTIONER for use in WITHIN searches, as is described in the Tip "Adding XML Tags to Indexed Text for Custom WITHIN Searching."

The USER_DATASTORE is configured with four steps:

1. Create a procedure to synthesize the document.

2. Create a USER_DATASTORE preference, and set the procedure attribute of that USER_DATASTORE preference to refer to the procedure in Step 1.

3. Create an index using the new USER_DATASTORE preference.

4. Perform a search to test the index.

## Create a Procedure to Synthesize the Document

This first step creates a procedure that will be called once for each row in the indexed table. Its purpose is to concatenate additional information onto the indexed column to be included in the Text index. That information can come from other columns in the row or from columns from other tables, or it can be hard-coded into the procedure. Hard-coding it into the procedure can be useful for adding XML tags into the indexed information.

The procedure must be defined with two parameters in the format (IN ROWID, IN OUT CLOB) and must be executable by the user creating the index. The procedure must be owned by CTXSYS and executable by the index owner. Be aware that even though the CLOB column is an IN OUT, the only value that will be passed out, and subsequently indexed, is the data supplied in this procedure. Even the data that was originally in the indexed column needs to be SELECTed and attached to the IN OUT CLOB, as shown in the following code sample, if it is to be included in the Text index.

### CREATE A PROCEDURE AS CTXSYS
### TO PERFORM THE CONCATENATION

```
CREATE OR REPLACE PROCEDURE index_customer_region
  (i_rowid IN ROWID, io_clob IN OUT CLOB)
AS
  v_comments VARCHAR2(32767);
  v_regional_group demo.location.regional_group%TYPE;
BEGIN
  -- get the comments and the region for the customer
  --   whose ROWID is passed in via i_rowid
  SELECT c.comments, l.regional_group
    INTO v_comments, v_regional_group
    FROM demo.customer c, demo.employee e,
         demo.department d, demo.location l
  WHERE c.ROWID = i_rowid
    AND c.salesperson_id = e.employee_id
    AND e.department_id = d.department_id
    AND d.location_id = l.location_id;
  -- Set up the LOB locator
  DBMS_LOB.TRIM(io_clob, 0);
  -- add the region to the synthesized document
  DBMS_LOB.WRITEAPPEND
```

```
    (io_clob,length(v_regional_group)+1, v_regional_group||' ');
  IF v_comments IS NOT NULL
  THEN
    -- add the comments to the synthesized document
    DBMS_LOB.WRITEAPPEND
      (io_clob, length(v_comments), v_comments);
  END IF;
END;
```

## Create a USER_DATASTORE Preference and Set the Procedure Attribute

In this step, a preference is created that will be used to tell Oracle to get the data for the index from the procedure instead of directly from the column being indexed. The preference is configured as DEMO in two steps shown in the following PL/SQL block:

**1.** Issue the CTX_DDL.CREATE_PREFERENCE procedure to name the preference and associate it with a preference object.

**2.** Assign a value to an attribute in that object.

```
BEGIN
    CTX_DDL.CREATE_PREFERENCE
       ('CUST_COMMENTS_DATASTORE_PREF', 'USER_DATASTORE');
    CTX_DDL.SET_ATTRIBUTE('CUST_COMMENTS_DATASTORE_PREF',
                          'PROCEDURE', 'INDEX_CUSTOMER_REGION'
                          );
END;
```

## Create an Index Using the New USER_DATASTORE Preference

Issuing this statement with the parameter specification tells the Text index engine to use the USER_DATASTORE that is specified in the procedure attribute of the CUST_COMMENTS_DATASTORE_PREF preference. Finally, it calls the index_customer_region procedure to get the data for the Text index. The index, then, is built on a synthesized document rather than on the customer.comments column.

**CAUTION**
*The synthesized document will not be refreshed with current regional group information unless the comments column is UPDATEd.*

Issue the following CREATE INDEX statement as DEMO:

```
CREATE INDEX customer_comments
  ON customer (comments)
  INDEXTYPE IS CTXSYS.CONTEXT
  PARAMETERS('DATASTORE CUST_COMMENTS_DATASTORE_PREF');
```

### Perform a Search to Test the Index

This query will now find comments for customers whose sales representative is in the Dallas region or whose comments include the word "triathletes."

```
SELECT customer_id, name, comments
  FROM customer
 WHERE CONTAINS (comments, 'triathletes, dallas') > 0;
```

# Adding XML Tags to Indexed Text for Custom WITHIN Searching

The query in the foregoing technique is not as precise as it could be. It does perform a valid simple test of the USER_DATASTORE process, but the addition of custom tags will allow it to support a true representation of the data. For example, the query

```
SELECT customer_id, name, comments
  FROM customer
 WHERE CONTAINS (comments, 'triathletes, dallas') > 0;
```

will find rows for customers whose sales representatives are in the Dallas region or whose comments include the word "triathletes." However, it will also find rows for customers whose sales representatives are in New York but whose comments already include the word "Dallas." The way to explicitly state that the desired rows will be for customers whose sales representatives are in Dallas is to use the XML_SECTIONER instead of the DEFAULT_SECTIONER and then perform a WITHIN search. The search will look as follows:

```
SELECT customer_id, name, comments
  FROM customer
 WHERE CONTAINS (comments, 'triathletes, dallas WITHIN REGION') > 0;
```

There are four steps for enabling this search:

1. Create an XML_SECTION_GROUP and define field definitions.

2. Finalize the index_customer_region procedure to include the creation of the XML sections.

3. Create the Text index with the new XML_SECTION_GROUP.

4. Issue a query to test the index

## Create an XML_SECTION_GROUP and Define Field Definitions

To create an XML_SECTION_GROUP, you make a call to CTX_DDL.CREATE_
SECTION_GROUP, which takes two parameters:

- **Group_name** VARCHAR2 containing the name of the section group
to create

- **Group_type** VARCHAR2 containing a type of section group to create.
In this case, an XML section group will be created with the name of
CUSTOMER_COMMENTS_SECTIONS.

The second call is to CTX_DDL.ADD_FIELD_SECTION, where fields/sections and tags
are defined for the group. This works like the HTML_SECTION_GROUP, which has
predefined tags such as <TITLE>. With the XML_SECTION_GROUP, it is possible to
create custom tags. CTX_DDL.ADD_FIELD_SECTION takes the following four
parameters:

- **Group_name** VARCHAR2 containing the name of the group defined in
the call to CREATE_SECTION_GROUP

- **Section_name** VARCHAR2 containing the name of the section to use for
the WITHIN clause

- **Tag** VARCHAR2 containing the XML tag that will represent the
section_name in documents

- **Visible** A BOOLEAN representing whether or not you should reveal the
contents of the section for general indexing or whether you should restrict
the contents of the section to a WITHIN search. The default is FALSE—don't
allow the contents to be searchable outside of the WITHIN clause.

**NOTE**
*Field sections are for nonrepeating groups. Thus, for
example, you could not have two <REGION> entries
in the document. You may also want to investigate
CTX_DDL.ADD_ZONE_SECTION, which defines
sections that can be repeated and nested, and
CTX_DDL.ADD_SPECIAL SECTION, which defines
sections consisting of searchable sentences and
paragraphs.*

```
BEGIN
  CTX_DDL.CREATE_SECTION_GROUP
    ('CUSTOMER_COMMENTS_SECTIONS', 'XML_SECTION_GROUP');
  CTX_DDL.ADD_FIELD_SECTION
    ('CUSTOMER_COMMENTS_SECTIONS', 'REGION', '<REG>');
END ;
```

### Finalize the index_customer_region Procedure to Include the Creation of the XML Sections

There is one line that needs to be altered; it is represented in bold. In that line, the tags for the region section are added onto the text.

```
CREATE OR REPLACE PROCEDURE index_customer_region
  (i_rowid IN ROWID, io_clob IN OUT CLOB)
AS
  v_comments demo.customer.comments%TYPE;
  v_regional_group demo.location.regional_group%TYPE;
BEGIN
  -- get the comments and the region for the customer
  --   who's ROWID is passed in via i_rowid
  SELECT c.comments, l.regional_group
    INTO v_comments, v_regional_group
    FROM demo.customer c, demo.employee e,
         demo.department d, demo.location l
   WHERE c.ROWID = i_rowid
     AND c.salesperson_id = e.employee_id
     AND e.department_id = d.department_id
     AND d.location_id = l.location_id;
  -- Set up the LOB locator
  DBMS_LOB.TRIM(io_clob, 0);
  -- add the region to the synthesized document,
  --   including XML tags <REG></REG> defining
  --   a REGION section
  DBMS_LOB.WRITEAPPEND
    (io_clob,length(v_regional_group)+12,
    '<REG>'||v_regional_group||'</REG> '
    );
IF v_comments IS NOT NULL
   THEN
     -- add the comments to the synthesized document
     DBMS_LOB.WRITEAPPEND(io_clob, 5, v_comments);
   END IF;
END;
```

### Create the Text Index with the New XML_SECTION_GROUP

Having added the <REG> tags to the synthesized document, you can now use the following CREATE INDEX statement to support searches for text in the REGION field:

```
CREATE INDEX customer_comments
  ON customer(comments)
  INDEXTYPE IS ctxsys.context
  PARAMETERS('SECTION GROUP CUSTOMER_COMMENTS_SECTIONS
            DATASTORE CUST_COMMENTS_DATASTORE_PREF'
            ) ;
```

### Issue a Query to Test the Index

The creation of the customer_comments Text index enables you to perform a WITHIN search, as follows:

```
SELECT customer_id, name, comments
  FROM customer
 WHERE CONTAINS (comments, 'triathletes, dallas WITHIN REGION') > 0;
```

## Tracking Text Index Build with CTX_OUTPUT Logging

A log file can be created so that you can see the progress of Text index creation. The CTX_OUTPUT.START_LOG('*<filename>*') procedure begins logging to the file specified in '<filename>' and CTX_OUTPUT.END_LOG stops logging. By default, CTX_OUTPUT.START_LOG creates the specified log file in the ORACLE_HOME/ctx/log directory. The user creating the index would start logging with the following command:

```
BEGIN
  ctxsys.CTX_OUTPUT.START_LOG('textindex.log');
END;
```

If a message similar to "DRG-11101: failed to open file textindex.log" is received, it means that the log directory was not created by the Installer during installation. The ORACLE_HOME\ctx\log directory should be created, and the CTX_OUTPUT.START_LOG command can be attempted again. Alternatively, the default location for Text index log files can be changed with the CTX_ADM procedure when connected as CTXSYS, as follows:

```
BEGIN
  ctxsys.CTX_ADM.SET_PARAMETER
```

```
('LOG_DIRECTORY',
    'E:\ORACLE\ADMIN\PRODUCT_PROMOTIONS'
   );
END;
```

The first argument to CTX_ADM.SET_PARAMETER is the name of the parameter to be changed; the second argument is the new value for that parameter.

After correcting any directory problems and issuing a call to CTX_LOG.START_LOG as the user creating the index, you should issue the CREATE INDEX statement, as follows:

```
CREATE INDEX product_description
  ON product (description)
  INDEXTYPE IS CTXSYS.CONTEXT;
```

While the index is being created, the file textindex.log can be reviewed for errors and completion status. A sample set of log entries appears as follows:

```
Oracle ConText Option: Release 8.1.5.0.0 - Production on Mon Jul 5 00:09:26 1999

(c) Copyright 1999 Oracle Corporation.  All rights reserved.

00-09-26 07/05/99 begin logging
00-09-32 07/05/99 populate index: DEMO.PRODUCT_DESCRIPTION
00-09-32 07/05/99 Begin document indexing
00-09-33 07/05/99 Errors reading documents: 0
00-09-33 07/05/99 Index data for 34 documents to be written to database
00-09-33 07/05/99    memory use: 263867
00-09-33 07/05/99    index data written to database.
00-09-33 07/05/99 End of document indexing. 34 documents indexed.
```

After Text index creation is completed, the CTX_OUTPUT.END_LOG command should be issued by the user who began index logging. At that time, the following lines will be added to the Text index log file:

```
00-11-56 07/05/99 log
00-11-56 07/05/99 logging halted
```

**NOTE**
*If more than one Text index is created between calls to CTX_OUTPUT.START_LOG and CTX_OUTPUT.END_LOG, the messages for both Index creations will be appended to the existing log file. After CTX_OUTPUT.END_LOG is called, subsequent CTX_OUTPUT.START_LOG calls that specify an existing file will overwrite that file.*

## Reviewing Text Index Build Errors with CTX_USER_INDEX_ERRORS

CTX_USER_INDEX_ERRORS is a view that shows information about errors that occurred during the creation of a Text index. Unlike CTX_OUTPUT, entries in the CTX_USER_INDEX_ERRORS view cannot be seen until Text index creation has completed.

CTX_USER_INDEX_ERRORS shows only the errors that occurred during the creation of indexes by the currently connected user. Another view, CTX_INDEX_ERRORS, shows all of the Text indexing errors that have occurred in the database. Table 11-2 shows the columns of CTX_USER_INDEX_ERRORS.

If the following statement were issued to create a Text index,

```
CREATE INDEX product_promotion
  ON product (promotion)
  INDEXTYPE IS CTXSYS.CONTEXT;
```

and an error occurs, then a query against CTX_USER_INDEX_ERRORS might reveal the following:

```
ERR_INDEX_NAME      ERR_TIMES ERR_TEXTKEY        ERR_TEXT
------------------- --------- ------------------ --------------------
PRODUCT_PROMOTION   05-JUL-99 AAACqzAABAAAHRMAAb DRG-11101: failed to
                                                 open file \drgit9
PRODUCT_PROMOTION   05-JUL-99 AAACqzAABAAAHRMAAc DRG-11101: failed to
                                                 open file \drgit9
```

**NOTE**
*The messages shown in the err_text column in the preceding query are common to Oracle8i on the NT platform. The way to fix this error will be discussed in the next section, "Using INSO_FILTER in an NT Installation with Multiple ORACLE_HOMEs."*

To find the rows in the product table that had problems, you could use the following query:

```
SELECT product_id, err_text
  FROM product, ctx_user_index_errors
 WHERE product.ROWID = ctx_user_index_errors.err_textkey;
```

The rows corresponding to the listed product IDs could then be investigated for problems.

| Name | Type | Description |
|---|---|---|
| ERR_INDEX_NAME | VARCHAR2(30) | Name of the Text index in which the error occurred |
| ERR_TIMESTAMP | DATE | The date and time when the error occurred |
| ERR_TEXTKEY | VARCHAR2(18) | The ROWID for the row in the indexed table on which the error occurred |
| ERR_TEXT | VARCHAR2(4000) | The error message |

**TABLE 11-2.**   *The Columns of the CTX_USER_INDEX_ERRORS View*

The errors can vary greatly depending on what preferences are used. After the cause is found and corrected, the index can be rebuilt. Depending on the type of error, it may be possible to use the ALTER INDEX statement to rebuild the index, otherwise, the index may first have to be dropped and completely recreated. Once the index is successfully created or is dropped, the rows in the CTX_USER_INDEX_ERRORS view for that index are DELETEd automatically. Rows can also be removed from CTX_USER_INDEX_ERRORS manually by the issuing of a DELETE statement.

```
DELETE ctx_user_index_errors
 WHERE err_index_name = 'PRODUCT_PROMOTION';
```

## Using INSO_FILTER in an NT Installation with Multiple ORACLE_HOMEs

The preference in the following example is created to deal with the Text index error shown in the previous section, "Reviewing Text Index Build Errors with CTX_USER_INDEX_ERRORS." By default, the INSO_FILTER is relegated the job of turning a binary formatted document held in product.promotion into text that can be broken into words for use in the Text index. The error (DRG-11101: failed to open file \drgit9) occurs when the INSO_FILTER operation fails in databases that were installed on NT systems with more than one ORACLE_HOME. Thus, in order to create the product_promotion Text index, you need to configure a preference.

### Create and Configure the Preference

In the following example, a preference named "INSO_FILTER_PREFERENCE" is being created and associated with the object "USER_FILTER". The "USER_FILTER" preference allows the use of external programs for performing of the Filtering stage operations. Next, the USER_FILTER attribute COMMAND is given the value "inso_filter.cmd." This statement specifies that a program inso_filter.cmd will be used to perform the Filter stage of Text indexing.

```
BEGIN
  CTX_DDL.CREATE_PREFERENCE
    ('INSO_FILTER_PREFERENCE', 'USER_FILTER');
  CTX_DDL.SET_ATTRIBUTE
    ('INSO_FILTER_PREFERENCE', 'COMMAND', 'inso_filter.cmd');
END;
```

### Create the inso_filter.cmd Program
Next, the inso_filter.cmd program must be written as follows and placed in the ORACLE_HOME\ctx\bin directory:

```
set oracle_home=e:\oracle\ora81
ctxhx.exe %1 %2
```

The first line sets up the ORACLE_HOME environment variable. In your implementation, set it to your ORACLE_HOME location. The second line calls the ctxhx.exe executable. There are two parameters, with the first indicating the source of the document being filtered and the second indicating the resulting text being passed back. The database will pass the document to, and receive the output from, the ctxhx program via inso_filter.cmd.

### Setting the PATH Variable
The operating system PATH variable that is seen by the database kernel must include the location of ORACLE_HOME\ctx\bin. The PATH should be set under the Environment tab in the System Properties dialog, as shown in Figure 11-1; then the database should be shut down and the machine should be restarted.

### Create the Index Using the INSO_FILTER Preference
To specify a preference for Text index creation, you need to add the PARAMETERS clause to the CREATE INDEX statement. In the following example, a PARAMETERS clause indicates that the FILTER to be used when creating the Text index product_promotion is INSO_FILTER_PREFERENCE:

```
CREATE INDEX product_promotion
  ON product (promotion)
  INDEXTYPE IS CTXSYS.CONTEXT
  PARAMETERS('FILTER INSO_FILTER_PREFERENCE');
```

**INSO_FILTERs in NT with Multiple ORACLE_HOMEs**

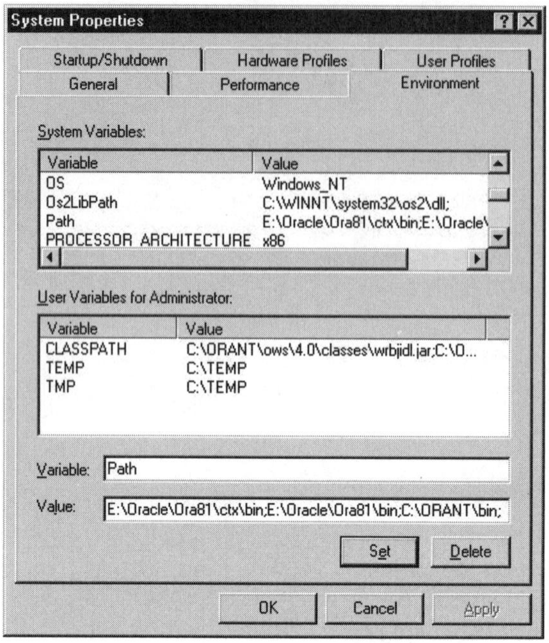

**FIGURE 11-1.** *The NT System Properties dialog*

After this statement has been issued, the words that are contained in Word or PDF documents are searchable through the Text index:

```
SELECT product_id, description
  FROM product
 WHERE CONTAINS (promotion, 'SALE') > 0;
```

The CTX_USER_PREFERENCES view that follows contains the list of preferences created by the currently logged on user:

```
SELECT *
  FROM ctx_user_preferences;

PRE_NAME                 PRE_CLASS  PRE_OBJECT
---------------------    ---------- -----------
INSO_FILTER_PREFERENCE   FILTER     USER_FILTER
```

### Dropping a Preference

CTX_DDL.DROP_PREFERENCE is used to drop a preference. To drop the
INSO_FILTER_PREFERENCE preference, you would issue the following command:

```
BEGIN
  CTX_DDL.DROP_PREFERENCE('INSO_FILTER_PREFERENCE');
END;
```

# Issue Queries Against the Textual Information

The reason, of course, why you need to perform the work of loading documents and
creating Text indexes is so you can use them in queries.

There are two types of Text queries:

■ Word queries match an exact word or phrase.

■ ABOUT queries match documents containing a specified concept. The
concepts or *themes* are generated automatically during the creation of a
Text index.

Examples of simple Word queries using the CONTAINS operator have been
shown in the preceding sections. For the remaining examples, assume that the
product information shown in Table 11-3 has been loaded into the product table
and that a Text index has been created in the product.promotion column.

## Issuing Queries About Concepts or Themes

An ABOUT query finds documents that match a concept or theme. The concepts
are created by default when a Text index is created. When you issue an ABOUT
query, you are essentially saying to the Oracle database, "I will give you a list of
terms I think are relevant to my search; you supply me with the documents that
meet those criteria."

Each of the following queries will return the same result set:

```
SELECT product_id, description
  FROM product
 WHERE CONTAINS (promotion, 'ABOUT(serve)') > 0;
```

```
SELECT product_id, description
  FROM product
 WHERE CONTAINS (promotion, 'ABOUT(serves)') > 0;
```

Issuing Queries
About Concepts or Themes

```
SELECT product_id, description
  FROM product
 WHERE CONTAINS (promotion, 'ABOUT(serving)') > 0;

PRODUCT_ID DESCRIPTION
---------- ------------------------
    100860 ACE TENNIS RACKET I
    100870 ACE TENNIS BALLS-3 PACK
```

Notice that the promotional text for product 100860 includes the word "serve," not "serves." The promotional text for product 100870 includes the word "serves," but not the word "serve." Neither of the promotional texts includes the word "serving," although they both were determined to be about serving.

An about search can be done for more than one theme at a time. The query that follows will find promotions that are about serving or players (nonexclusive or). Even though the search will find all the documents about either of the themes serving or players, documents that contain both of the terms will normally receive a higher score. To retrieve documents that have a higher score, rather than just ones that are about one of the themes, you should increase the value after the > sign in the query:

| PRODUCT_ID | Promotiona Product Text (product.promotion) |
|---|---|
| 100860 | Solde! The French-engineered lightweight style of the racket will knock the socks off of your opponent. Your serve will never be the same. |
| 100861 | Sconto! The ACE Racket II comes to you from Italy. These rackets are molto bene. Hurry in now! They will not last beyond this weekend. |
| 100870 | ACE tennis balls are the best by far. On sale now through the end of the month, they'll increase the speed of your serves big time. |
| 100871 | The ACE tennis balls sold in the six packs are made for even the toughest player. |
| 100890 | ACE tennis nets adjust automatically to the height of each player in your family. |
| 101860 | Come to our SP Tennis Racket sale on July 4th. |
| 101863 | The SP Junior Racket is for the young tennis player in your family. |
| 104362 | The Sports Corporation of America offers the finest selection of used tennis nets. |

**TABLE 11-3.** *Promotional Text for Each Product*

```
SELECT product_id, description
  FROM product
 WHERE CONTAINS (promotion, 'ABOUT(serving players)') > 0;

PRODUCT_ID DESCRIPTION
---------- --------------------------------
    100890 ACE TENNIS NET
    100860 ACE TENNIS RACKET I
    101863 SP JUNIOR RACKET
    100870 ACE TENNIS BALLS-3 PACK
```

## Creating Thesauri to Increase Relevance

Thesauri are used in interMedia Text to map words to other words that are similar or equivalent in definition. In this example, the word "youth" will be defined as a synonym for the word "junior". There are many other uses for the capability of relating terms. This example will also define the phrases "american corporate entropy" and "sports corporation of america" as synonyms for the word "ace". They will act as the expanded version of the company name and the former/legacy version of the company name respectively.

Thesauri can also be used to map translation words between languages. For instance, if a promotional document were written in Italian and contained the word "sconto," you could find that document by doing a search for the word "discount."

A thesaurus is created in three steps:

1. Create a plain text file holding the thesaurus definition.

2. Load the thesaurus.

3. Check thesaurus creation.

### Create a Plain Text File Holding the Thesaurus Definition

For this example, a plain text file called pt.in (promotion thesaurus input) will be created in the E:\ORACLE\ADMIN\PRODUCT_PROMOTIONS directory. The file will contain the lines shown:

```
sale
  italian: saldo
  spanish: oferta
  german: verkauf
  french: solde
  syn discount
    italian: sconto
    spanish: descuento
    german: rabatt
    french: escompte
```

```
ace
  syn american corporate entropy
  syn sports corporation of america
junior
  syn youth
```

The lines can be interpreted as meaning the following:

- The terms discount and sale are synonyms.

- The words listed under sale and discount can be used as foreign terms. For example, "saldo" can be used as the Italian translation for "sale," and "sconto" can be used as the Italian translation for "discount."

- A search against any of: "ace," "american corporate entropy," and "sports corporation of america" will return the same result set.

### Load the Thesaurus

After the file is created, the ctxload program is used to load the thesaurus list into the DEMO user account, as follows:

```
ctxload -user demo/demo -thes -name promotion_thesaurus -file pt.in -log pt.log
```

**NOTE**

*All of these operations can be performed using the procedures and functions in the CTXSYS.CTX_THES package.*

### Check Thesaurus Creation

After the ctxload terminates, you should check the pt.log file to see if any errors occurred during the load. A list of thesauri can be seen with the following query:

```
SELECT *
  FROM ctx_thesauri;

THS_NAME
--------------------
PROMOTION_THESAURUS
```

Another way to check thesaurus creation—and to keep the thesaurus file up-to-date in case individual entries were made directly in the database with CTX_THES—is to dump the thesaurus out of the database to a plain text file, using the following command:

```
ctxload -thesdump -user demo/demo -name promotion_thesaurus -file pt.out
```

The output may not look exactly the same as the original input. It probably will look more like the following because the ctxload utility dumps it out with more detail. UF in the following thesaurus listing means that the *Used For* term will be a synonym (used for) its higher-level term.

```
ACE
   UF   AMERICAN CORPORATE ENTROPY
   UF   SPORTS CORPORATION OF AMERICA
AMERICAN CORPORATE ENTROPY
   UF   ACE
   UF   SPORTS CORPORATION OF AMERICA
DISCOUNT
   UF   SALE
   FRENCH: ESCOMPTE
   GERMAN: RABATT
   ITALIAN: SCONTO
   SPANISH: DESCUENTO
JUNIOR
   UF   YOUTH
SALE
   UF   DISCOUNT
   FRENCH: SOLDE
   GERMAN: VERKAUF
   ITALIAN: SALDO
   SPANISH: OFERTA
SPORTS CORPORATION OF AMERICA
   UF   ACE
   UF   AMERICAN CORPORATE ENTROPY
YOUTH
   UF   JUNIOR
```

To drop a thesaurus, use the CTX_THES.DROP_THESAURUS procedure, as follows:

```
BEGIN
   CTX_THES.DROP_THESAURUS('PROMOTION_THESAURUS');
END;
```

# Finding Foreign Terms with the TR Operator

The TR operator expands a term so that the query will return rows that include the term or foreign term equivalents that have been defined for that term. In the first example, a search is done for the word "discount." The query finds product 100861, which does not include the word "discount" but its Italian equivalent, "sconto," as defined in promotion_thesaurus.

```
SELECT product_id, description
  FROM product
 WHERE CONTAINS (promotion,
                'TR(discount, ITALIAN, PROMOTION_THESAURUS)'
                ) > 0
 ORDER BY product_id;


PRODUCT_ID DESCRIPTION
---------- ------------------------------
    100861 ACE TENNIS RACKET II
```

The second example retrieves three rows; two for the English word "sale" and another for product 100860, which contains the word "solde," the French equivalent of "sale," as defined in promotion_thesaurus.

```
SELECT product_id, description
  FROM product
 WHERE CONTAINS (promotion,
                'TR(sale, FRENCH, PROMOTION_THESAURUS)'
                ) > 0
 ORDER BY product_id;

PRODUCT_ID DESCRIPTION
---------- ------------------------------
    100860 ACE TENNIS RACKET I
    100870 ACE TENNIS BALLS-3 PACK
    101860 SP TENNIS RACKET
```

## Finding Foreign Terms and Their Synonyms with the TRSYN Operator

The TRSYN operator returns rows matching

- The term
- Foreign equivalents of the term
- Synonyms of the term

In this first example, three rows are returned: product 100861 contains "sconto," the Italian equivalent for discount, and products 100870 and 101860 contain the word "sale," the synonym for the word discount.

```
SELECT product_id, description
  FROM product
 WHERE CONTAINS (promotion,
```

```
                    'TRSYN(discount, ITALIAN, PROMOTION_THESAURUS)'
                 ) > 0
  ORDER BY product_id;


PRODUCT_ID DESCRIPTION
---------- ------------------------------
    100861 ACE TENNIS RACKET II
    100870 ACE TENNIS BALLS-3 PACK
    101860 SP TENNIS RACKET
```

The second example shows a result set unchanged from when the same query was issued in the example using the TR operator. Rows are found with the word "sale" as well as rows containing "solde", the French equivalent for the English word "sale".

```
SELECT product_id, description
  FROM product
  WHERE CONTAINS (promotion,
                 'TRSYN(sale, FRENCH, PROMOTION_THESAURUS)'
                 ) > 0
  ORDER BY product_id;


PRODUCT_ID DESCRIPTION
---------- ------------------------------
    100860 ACE TENNIS RACKET I
    100870 ACE TENNIS BALLS-3 PACK
    101860 SP TENNIS RACKET
```

This next example is more interesting. The same rows are retrieved as in the previous example, but the word "discount" is used in place of the word sale. The query is retrieving promotions that contain the French word "solde", the foreign equivalent of the English word "sale", along with other documents containing the English word "sale". Thus, it is picking up "sale", the synonym for discount as defined in promotion_thesaurus, along with its French foreign equivalents.

```
SELECT product_id, description
  FROM product
  WHERE CONTAINS (promotion,
                 'TRSYN(discount, FRENCH, PROMOTION_THESAURUS)'
                 ) > 0
  ORDER BY product_id;


PRODUCT_ID DESCRIPTION
---------- ------------------------------
```

**Find Foreign Terms Plus Synonyms w/TRSYN Operator**

```
100860 ACE TENNIS RACKET I
100870 ACE TENNIS BALLS-3 PACK
101860 SP TENNIS RACKET
```

## Using Synonyms for History Recasting

The promotion_thesaurus thesaurus has been loaded with synonyms for the word "ace". Thus, documents can be searched using the current name of the company, ACE, while finding documents containing company names "american corporate entropy" or "sports corporation of america". The following query, made while performing a search for "ACE", will also return product 104362, which contains the phrase "Sports Corporation of America". This is done through use of the SYN operator for specifying the name of the thesaurus.

```
SELECT product_id, description
  FROM product
 WHERE CONTAINS (promotion, 'SYN(ACE,PROMOTION_THESAURUS)') > 0;

PRODUCT_ID DESCRIPTION
---------- ----------------------------
    100890 ACE TENNIS NET
    100871 ACE TENNIS BALLS-6 PACK
    100861 ACE TENNIS RACKET II
    100870 ACE TENNIS BALLS-3 PACK
    104362 DUNK NETS - RAINBOW
```

# Other Tips

The Tips presented in this section do not fall within any of the three main categories, yet they are still useful.

### Prefiltering Adobe PDF and Word Files Outside the Database via ctxhx

The job of the ctxhx program is primarily to take in a file of almost any document type (the list of supported document types can be found in Appendix C of the Oracle document, Oracle8i interMedia Text Reference) and return the text of that document in HTML. The default filter preference calls the ctxhx program to perform the filtering actions. When ctxhx is called in this way from the database via the CREATE INDEX statement, it takes an input string from the database and passes output back to the database.

The inso_filter.cmd program (described in the section "Using INSO_FILTER in an NT Installation with Multiple ORACLE_HOMEs") calls the ctxhx program, which is located in ORACLE_HOME\ctx\bin. The ctxhx program takes five parameters that must be supplied in the proper position. Table 11-4 lists those parameters.

As shown by the inso_filter.cmd script, it is possible to call the ctxhx program directly from an operating system command. This can be useful, for example, when you wish to prefilter a document before it is loaded or indexed into the database or if you want to see its filtered contents separately from a set of indexed documents that show unexpected results. Seeing the filtered contents of the document outside the database would help you avoid having to create a separate table to hold the document, load the document, create the index, and perform a search.

**CAUTION**
*The INSO filtering technology, as found in the ctxhx program, can be used only in relation to work with interMedia Text. It is a violation of the license to use it otherwise.*

| Position | Parameter Name | Description |
|---|---|---|
| 1 | InputFile | The name of the file to be Filtered/Converted. |
| 2 | OutputFile | The target/output filename. |
| 3 | FallbackCharacterSet | The character set of the InputFile. Default is ascii8. Valid values are: ascii8, shiftjis, chinesegb, chinesebig5, hangeul. |
| 4 | OutputCharacterSet | The character set of the OutputFile. Default is iso8859-1. Valid values are iso8859-1, iso8859-2, iso8859-3, iso8859-4, iso8859-5, iso8859-6, iso8859-7, iso8859-8, iso8859-9, macroman, maclatin2, macgreek, maccyrillic, macromanturkish, gb2312, big5, shiftjis, koi8r, windows1250, windows1251, windows1252, windows1253, windows1254, windows1255, windows1256, windows1257, koreanhangul, koreanjohab, unicode. |
| 5 | H/T | The format of the OutputFile. Default is H. Valid values are: H—HTML, T—plain text. |

**TABLE 11-4.** *Positional Parameters to the ctxhx(.exe) Program*

Start by making a copy of the program inso_filter.cmd to a directory such as Oracle\admin\orcl\adhoc\my_inso_filter.cmd and practice changing the parameters. For example, copy a Word or Adobe PDF file to the ORACLE_HOME\admin\ orcl\adhoc directory, then issue the following:

```
my_inso_filter <word.doc> <word.htm>
```

in which word.doc is the name of the Word or Adobe PDF file copied to the adhoc directory and word.htm is the name of the destination file. After running the my_inso_filter.cmd program, you can open the word.htm file in a text editor or browser and review the results.

## Converting Stored Binary Documents into HTML in the Database

The same mechanism that allows the Filter stage of Text index creation to convert binary documents such as Word or Adobe PDF files into text for the Section stage of Text indexing can also allow the HTML version of a document to be stored for use in an HTML application. For this example, the Word document shown in Figure 11-2 will be stored in the product.promotion column for product 105123.

The CTX_DOC.FILTER procedure will be used to do the conversion. The procedure takes five parameters as shown in Table 11-5.

| Parameter Name | Description |
| --- | --- |
| index_name | Name of the Text index associated with the column to be converted. In this example: product_promotion. |
| textkey | The unique identifier for the row containing the document. In this example: 105123. |
| restab | Name of the result table that will hold the converted version of the document. In this example: ctx_filter_results. |
| query_id | Unique number for a particular run of CTX_DOC.FILTER. This parameter is necessary, since the table could be used for multiple runs of the CTX_DOC.FILTER procedure. |
| plaintext | BOOLEAN designating whether the result is to be in plain text or in HTML format. The default of FALSE signifies HTML format. |

**TABLE 11-5.** *Parameters of CTX_DOC.FILTER*

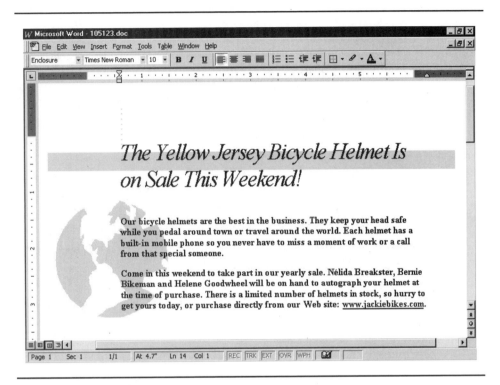

**FIGURE 11-2.** *A promotional document in Word format*

There are three steps to the conversion:

1. Create a result table to hold the converted document. CTX_DOC.FILTER will store its output in a result table, not in the product table. For this example, in which one document will be converted, the table promotion_filter_results will be used.

2. Execute CTX_DOC.FILTER, which produces output in the result table.

3. Move the text from the result table to the appropriate row in the product table.

The result table should be created as shown:

```
CREATE TABLE promotion_filter_results
  (query_id NUMBER,
   document CLOB
   );
```

Steps 2 and 3 will be performed inside an anonymous PL/SQL block that can be run to convert a specific row. This will be helpful when a new version of a promotion is released and that row's document needs to be converted. The block truncates the result table to make sure it's empty.

```
PROMPT Enter a Product ID:
ACCEPT sv_product_id
DECLARE
  cons_product_id CONSTANT product.product_ID%TYPE := &&sv_product_id;
BEGIN
  -- Clean up before starting just in case the table
  --   was not emptied
  EXECUTE IMMEDIATE 'TRUNCATE TABLE promotion_filter_results';
  CTX_DOC.FILTER('PRODUCT_PROMOTION', cons_product_id,
                 'promotion_filter_results',
                 SYS_CONTEXT('USERENV', 'SESSION_USERID')
                );
  UPDATE product
    SET promotion_html =
        (SELECT document
           FROM promotion_filter_results
        )
   WHERE product_id = cons_product_id;
  COMMIT;
END;
```

After the block is run, you can query the product table to make sure that the promotion_html column was populated. In SQL*Plus, set the LONG parameter to a value large enough to make sure the entire page is seen.

```
SET LONG 5000
SELECT promotion_html
  FROM product
 WHERE product_id = 105123;
```

## Converting Stored Binary Documents into HTML in a SELECT Statement

Storing the HTML version of a binary document as described in the previous Tip will promote quick retrieval of the HTML document. That HTML document is static, though, and must be regenerated any time the binary form of the document (which is stored in the BLOB) is UPDATEd. It is possible to create the HTML version of the document on the fly by including a conversion function directly in the column list of a SELECT statement. For example, the following query could be issued, which would bring back the product ID, the product description, and the run time–created

HTML version of the binary document. The SELECT statement uses a procedure called html_conversion.to_html, as follows:

```
SELECT product_id, description,
       html_conversion.to_html('PRODUCT_PROMOTION', product_id)
  FROM product
 WHERE product_id = 105123;
```

The to_html function converts the Word document into an HTML document and returns it as a CLOB data type. It gets passed the name of a Text index and the primary key value in that Text index. Before the package body can be created, a result table must be created, as shown:

```
CREATE TABLE generic_filter_results
  (query_id NUMBER,
   document CLOB
  );
```

```
CREATE OR REPLACE PACKAGE html_conversion
AS
  FUNCTION to_html
    (i_index_name user_indexes.index_name%TYPE,
     i_pk_value VARCHAR2 -- will allow a numeric
                         --   or char primary key
                         --   via implicit conversion
    )
    RETURN CLOB;
  PRAGMA RESTRICT_REFERENCES (to_html, WNDS);
END;
```

```
CREATE OR REPLACE PACKAGE BODY html_conversion
AS
  -- create an anonymous transaction function to
  --   call CTX_DOC.FILTER so that WNDS is not violated
  FUNCTION ctx_doc_to_html
    (i_index_name user_indexes.index_name%TYPE,
     i_pk_value VARCHAR2 -- will allow a numeric
                         --   or char primary key
                         --   via implicit conversion
    )
    RETURN CLOB
  IS
    PRAGMA AUTONOMOUS_TRANSACTION;
    v_document CLOB := EMPTY_CLOB();
    cons_session_id NUMBER :=
      SYS_CONTEXT('USERENV', 'SESSION_USERID');
```

```
BEGIN
    CTX_DOC.FILTER(i_index_name, i_pk_value,
                   'generic_filter_results', cons_session_id
                   );
    SELECT document
      INTO v_document
      FROM generic_filter_results
     WHERE query_id = cons_session_id;
    DELETE generic_filter_results
     WHERE query_id = cons_session_id;
    COMMIT;
    RETURN v_document;
END;
FUNCTION to_html
   (i_index_name user_indexes.index_name%TYPE,
    i_pk_value VARCHAR2
   )
   RETURN CLOB
  IS
  BEGIN
    RETURN ctx_doc_to_html(i_index_name, i_pk_value);
  END;
END;
```

## Accessing a Converted HTML Document via the PL/SQL Cartridge

The HTML in the product.promotion_html column can be displayed in a browser using the Oracle Application Server and the PL/SQL cartridge. Installing and configuring these two components is beyond the scope of this chapter; however, for this example a *database access descriptor (DAD),* which contains information used by the Oracle Application Server to establish a database connection, must be created for the DEMO account, along with a cartridge that accesses it. The DAD will be used to connect to the DEMO account, and the cartridge will have a virtual path of /demo. The HTP calls made in the product_demo procedures are part of the Oracle Application Server's PL/SQL Web Development Toolkit.

A simple application called Product Demo will be built in a package called product_demo. Table 11-6 shows the components, along with the associated procedure in product demo.

| Component | Procedure |
|---|---|
| Search for a product by the contents of its promotional document | product_demo.promotion_search |
| Choose a document from the list returned by the search | product_demo.promotion_list |
| See the HTML form of the promotional document that's stored in the product.promotion_html column | product_demo.promotion_show |

**TABLE 11-6.** *The Product Demo Package Components*

An additional procedure, product_demo.head, is called by the three procedures to write header and title information to the browser in a standardized format.

The syntax for a URL calling a PL/SQL application is as follows:

```
http://hostname[:port]/virtual_path/[^package.]proc_name[?QUERY_STRING]
```

The entry point to the application is the product_promotion.promotion_search procedure. Thus, the first screen will be called with the URL

```
http://cesaria:80/demo/^product_demo.promotion_search
```

Figure 11-3 shows how the search screen looks in a browser. The word "sale" has been entered in the text box. When the Start Search button is clicked, the product_demo.promotion_list procedure will be called with "sale" as the input parameter.

The product_demo.promotion_list procedure performs a Text search on the product.promotion column and shows the results as a list in the browser screen shown in Figure 11-4. Each product is listed with its description (product.description) and product_id (product.product_id). Each listing is anchored, so that if it is clicked, the product_demo.promotion_show is called, showing the promotional document taken from product.promotion_html.

The promotional document shown in Figure 11-5 that was created using CTX_DOC.FILTER is the HTML version of the Word document shown in Figure 11-2. The product_demo.promotion_show procedure contains a loop that passes the

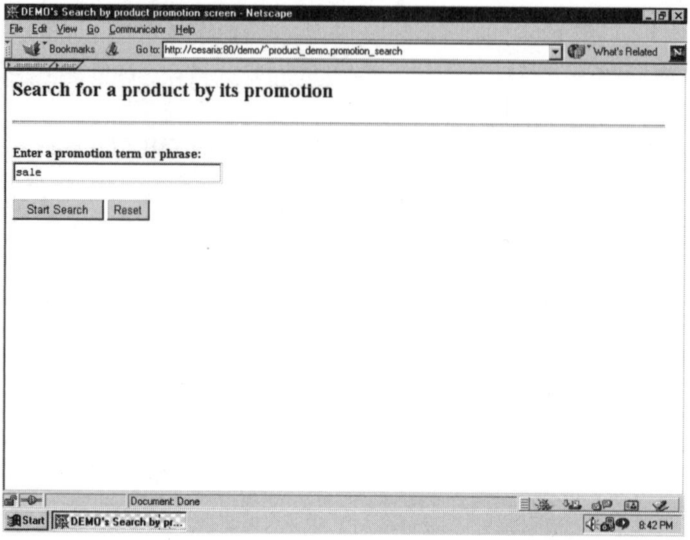

**FIGURE 11-3.** *Promotional search screen for the Product Demo application*

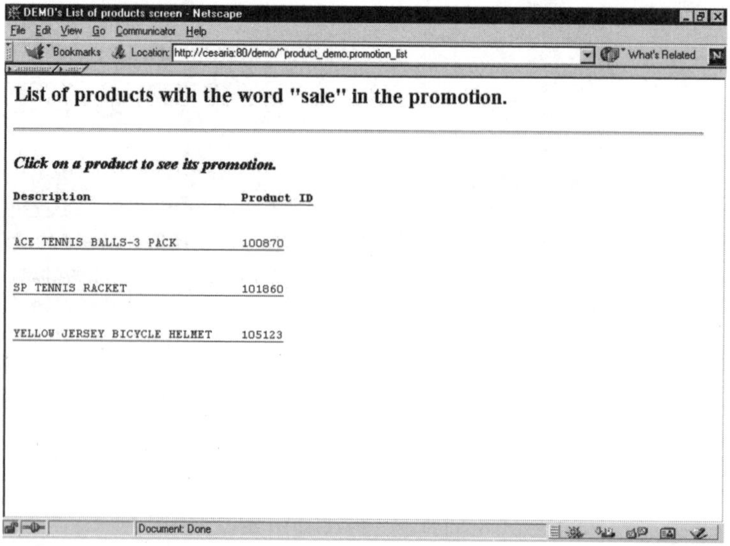

**FIGURE 11-4.** *Product Demo list of products with "sale" in the promotion*

**FIGURE 11-5.** *Promotional material as seen in a browser*

HTML page 4K at a time. This is done because there is no call in the PL/SQL Web Development Toolkit to directly send the contents of a CLOB to the browser. The HTP.PRINT command takes a VARCHAR2 as its parameter data type. Using DBMS_LOB.SUBSTR, the document is created 4K at a time, since that is the maximum size of a VARCHAR2.

The code for product_demo is as follows:

```
CREATE OR REPLACE PACKAGE product_demo
AS
  PROCEDURE head
    (i_title VARCHAR2, i_head VARCHAR2);
  PROCEDURE promotion_search;
  PROCEDURE promotion_list
    (i_search_string VARCHAR2);
  PROCEDURE promotion_show
    (i_product_id product.product_id%TYPE);
END product_demo;
```

```
CREATE OR REPLACE PACKAGE BODY product_demo
AS
  -- head will create a standard looking title and
  --   heading for each screen in the application.
```

```
PROCEDURE head
  (i_title VARCHAR2, i_head VARCHAR2)
IS
BEGIN
  HTP.HTMLOPEN;
  HTP.HEADOPEN;
  HTP.TITLE(i_title);
  HTP.PRINT('<H2>'||i_head||'</H2>');
  HTP.HR;
  HTP.HEADCLOSE;
END;
--
-- promotion_search will accept a search word in a text field
--    then call the procedure that performs the query when the
--    user presses the "Start Search" button.
PROCEDURE promotion_search
IS
BEGIN
  -- Put an informational header on the browser screen.
  head('DEMO''s Search by product promotion screen',
       'Search for a product by its promotion'
       );
  HTP.BODYOPEN;
  -- Create an HTML form that accepts a search word.
  HTP.FORMOPEN('http://cesaria:80/demo/^product_demo.promotion_list');
  HTP.PRINT('<B>Enter a promotion term or phrase:</B>');
  HTP.BR;
  HTP.FORMTEXT('i_search_string', 30);
  HTP.BR;
  HTP.BR;
  HTP.FORMSUBMIT(NULL, 'Start Search');
  HTP.FORMRESET;
  HTP.FORMCLOSE;
  HTP.BODYCLOSE;
  HTP.HTMLCLOSE;
END;
--
-- promotion_list takes in a search word and performs a Text
--    search on the promotion. The result set is shown as HTML
--    anchors that when clicked, will call the procedure that
--    displays the promotional document.
PROCEDURE promotion_list
  (i_search_string VARCHAR2)
IS
  -- c_product defines a result set based on a Text search
  --    of product.promotion for i_search_string.
  CURSOR c_product IS
    SELECT description, product_id
      FROM product
     WHERE CONTAINS(promotion, i_search_string) > 0
     ORDER BY description;
```

```
BEGIN
  -- Put an informational header on the browser screen.
  head('DEMO''s List of products screen',
       'List of products with the word "'||i_search_string||
       '" in the promotion.'
       );
  HTP.BODYOPEN;
  HTP.PRINT('<H3><I>Click on a product to see its promotion.</H3></I>');
  HTP.PRINT('<B><U><PRE>Description                    '||
            'Product ID</PRE></U></B>'
            );
  HTP.BR;
  FOR r_product IN c_product
  LOOP
     HTP.PRINT('<PRE><A HREF="http://cesaria:80/demo/'||
               '^product_demo.promotion_show?i_product_id='||
               r_product.product_id||'">'||
               RPAD(r_product.description,32)||
               r_product.product_id||
               '</A></PRE>'
               );
     HTP.BR;
  END LOOP;
END;
--
-- promotion_show shows the promotional document
--   in HTML format based on a product_id.
PROCEDURE promotion_show
  (i_product_id product.product_id%TYPE)
IS
  v_description product.description%TYPE;
  v_promotion_html product.promotion_html%TYPE;
  v_promotion_length INTEGER := 0;
  cons_buffer_size CONSTANT INTEGER := 4096;
  v_promotion_offset INTEGER := 0;
BEGIN
  -- Retrieve the HTML promotional document
  SELECT description, promotion_html
    INTO v_description, v_promotion_html
    FROM product
   WHERE product_id = i_product_id;
  -- Put an informational header on the browser screen.
  head('DEMO''s Most recent promotion for Product '||
       i_product_id||' screen',
       'Product ID '||i_product_id||': '||v_description
       );
  -- since the HTML document may be greater than 4K (the
  --   maximum size of a VARCHAR2) break the CLOB into 4K
  --   pieces that will work with HTP.PRINT
  v_promotion_length := DBMS_LOB.GETLENGTH(v_promotion_html);
  v_promotion_offset := 1;
```

```
      IF v_promotion_length != 0
      THEN
        -- There was a document in promotion_html.
        FOR i_buffer IN 1 .. CEIL(v_promotion_length / cons_buffer_size)
        LOOP
          -- Loop the number of times there are 4K pieces in the CLOB
          --   plus one more if there is a remaining piece that is under 4K.
          HTP.PRINT(DBMS_LOB.SUBSTR(v_promotion_html, cons_buffer_size,
                              v_promotion_offset
                              )
                   );
          v_promotion_offset := (cons_buffer_size * i_buffer) + 1;
        END LOOP;
      ELSE
        HTP.PRINT('There is currently no promotion information'||
                  ' available for product '||i_product_id||'.'
                 );
      END IF;
    END;
END;
```

# Tips Review

Oracle's interMedia Text services provide the ability to index, format, and retrieve documents stored internally, externally as BFILEs or URLs, or synthesized at index creation time. This chapter has reviewed techniques that help utilize that functionality in three main categories: loading text, indexing text, and querying text. Some of the techniques can be used outside of the scope of interMedia Text. For example, the procedures for loading BFILEs into BLOBs work the same way whether the file being loaded is an image file or a document.

Thesaurus creation has been explored as a means of providing foreign language term translation, synonym definition and history recasting. It was also demonstrated that interMedia Text creates themes automatically for databases configured in the English language.

The final techniques dealt with searching the use of the CTX_DOC.FILTER procedure to create HTML versions of Word documents. There, documents were stored in the database, then retrieved in a PL/SQL cartridge application into a browser.

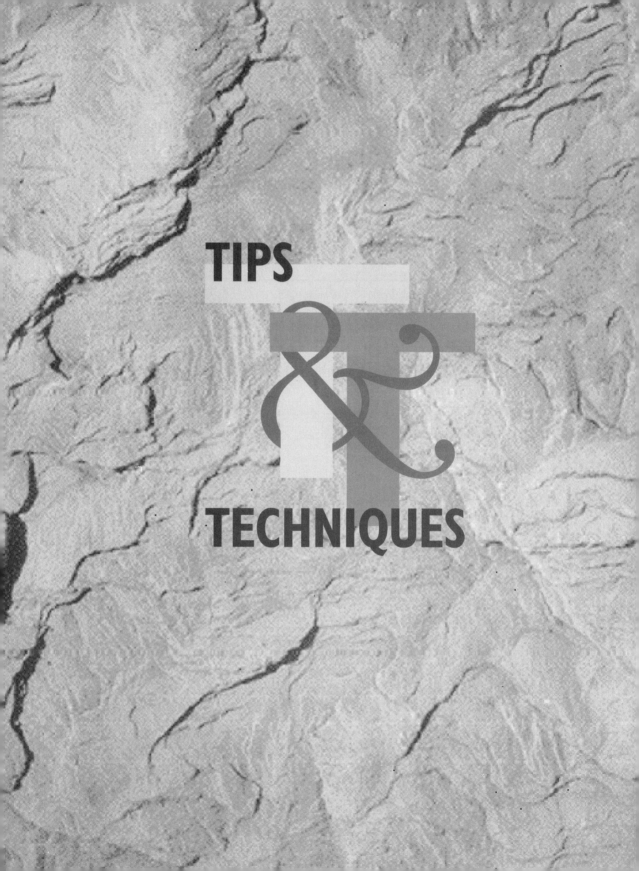

TIPS & TECHNIQUES

# CHAPTER
# 12

## interMedia: Multimedia

TIPS
&
COVERED

Oracle's interMedia provides a set of services that strategically support work with content-rich data for Web-enabled applications. It supports the storage, management, and manipulation of multimedia data types leading to their reuse (also called *re-purposing* in the digital assets disciplines) in a secure and recoverable environment. Oracle can be the central searchable repository for all types of data using interMedia multimedia services with interMedia Text. The interMedia multimedia components can also interact with media servers such as the RealNetworks RealServer G2, which streams RealAudio and RealVideo to a browser or a stand-alone G2 client. The focus in this chapter will be on services provided primarily by the interMedia Web Agent in association with interMedia data types.

- Defining the storage for interMedia multimedia object types

- Adding a default value for an interMedia type column

- INSERTing into an interMedia multimedia type

- SELECTing from an interMedia multimedia type

- Defining multimedia object views on columns of standard data types

- Creating a Put procedure to perform interMedia Web Agent transactions

- Creating a Set procedure to handle interMedia Web Agent transactions

- Creating a Get procedure to handle retrieval of multimedia data

- Creating an application that uses the interMedia Web Agent with the PL/SQL cartridge

- Using the interMedia Web Agent with non-interMedia types

The examples will be built against the tables owned by DEMO, one of the schemas installed with the default database.

# Introduction to interMedia Multimedia Types

Oracle's interMedia comes with three predefined object relational types, each of which stores the multimedia data as BLOBs, BFILEs, URLs, or streaming audio and video data from servers such as Oracle Video Server and the RealNetworks RealServer G2 Servers. The three predefined types, prefixed with ORD (ObjectRelationalData type), are shown here with example formats and file extensions:

- **ORDAudio**   Supports the storage and management of audio data such as AIFF (.aif) and WAVE (.wav)

- **ORDImage**   Supports the storage and management of image data such as GIFF (.gif) and TIFF (.tif)

- **ORDVideo**   Supports the storage and management of video data such as AVI (.avi) and Quicktime (.mov)

## Oracle interMedia Types Attributes

The interMedia multimedia data types are owned by the ORDSYS schema. All three types store data in the ORDSource object relational type, also owned by ORDSYS. Custom types can be defined that also store data in the ORDSource type. Each of the types contains methods and attributes that are detailed in the *Oracle8i interMedia Audio, Image, and Video User's Guide and Reference*. It also contains lists of all of the interMedia native multimedia types (standard multimedia types that interMedia knows about). Table 12-1 shows the attributes of the ORDSource type. The attribute column shows the attribute name and its data type.

Note that, where interMedia multimedia data is stored in LOB types, the LOB storage issues described in Chapter 11 apply.

Table 12-2 shows the attributes of the three interMedia provided types. The key for the table is as follows:

- **OA**   Contained in ORDAudio
- **OI**   Contained in ORDImage
- **Ovd**   Contained in ORDVideo

| Attribute | Description |
|---|---|
| localData<br>BLOB | If the value is stored in a BLOB (internal/local), it contains the value. |
| srcType<br>VARCHAR2(4000) | Type of data storage for nonlocal data. Valid values: "FILE" for BFILE, "HTTP" for HTTP Server, "<name>" for a user-defined data storage type (this is a string that is used to derive a PL/SQL package name). |
| srcLocation<br>VARCHAR2(4000) | Location of the data if nonlocal. For srcType of "FILE"—<DIR> or name of directory object. For "HTTP"—<SourceBase> or URL (for example the base portion of URL less the filename at the end). For "<name>"—<iden> or access string. |
| srcName<br>VARCHAR2(4000) | Name of the data object. For srcType of "FILE"—name of the file. For "HTTP"—<Source> or name of the object (for example, the filename at the end of a URL). For "<name>"—name of the object. |
| updateTime<br>DATE | Last modified timestamp. |
| local<br>NUMBER | Indicates whether the object is stored internally. 1 or NULL = BLOB, 0 = external source. |

**TABLE 12-1.** *Attributes of the ORDSource Object-Relational Type*

| Attribute | Description | OA | OI | Ovd |
|---|---|---|---|---|
| description<br>VARCHAR2(4000) | Description of the audio or video object. Free-form text (not taken from metadata in the header of the object data). | X | | X |
| source<br>ORDSource | The ORDSource storing the data. | X | X | X |
| format<br>VARCHAR2(31) | Audio or video format of the stored data. Example for ORDAudio—WAV. | X | | X |
| mimeType<br>VARCHAR2(4000) | mimeType of the stored data. Example for ORDImage—image/tiff. | X | X | X |

**TABLE 12-2.** *List of ORDAudio, ORDImage, and ORDVideo Attributes*

| Attribute | Description | OA | OI | Ovd |
|---|---|---|---|---|
| comments<br>CLOB | Comment information about the object. Free form text (not taken from metadata in the header of the object data). May be taken or shared for use by Oracle in future versions. It is recommended that you do use this attribute. | X | | X |
| encoding<br>VARCHAR2(256) | Encoding type of the data. Example: ADPCM_G721. Note: this will contain the same value contained in the compressionType attribute. | X | | |
| numberofChannels<br>INTEGER | Number of audio channels. Range: 1 (mono)—6 (AC3 encoded surround sound). | X | | |
| samplingRate<br>INTEGER | Rate at which the data was recorded in samples per second. Range: 5500 (1/4 of Mac sampling rate)—48000 [Digital Audio Tape (DAT)]. | X | | |
| sampleSize<br>INTEGER | Sample width (number of bits per sample). Valid values: 8 (8-bit), 16 (16-bit). | X | | |
| compressionType<br>VARCHAR2(4000) | Compression type. Note that for Audio this will have the same value as the encoding attribute. | X | | X |
| audioDuration<br>INTEGER | Time it takes to play the entire audio clip. | X | | |
| height<br>INTEGER | ORDImage: height of image in pixels; ORDVideo: height of each frame. | | X | X |
| width<br>INTEGER | ORDImage: width of image in pixels; ORDVideo: width of each frame. | | X | X |
| contentLength<br>INTEGER | Size of the on-disk image file in bytes. This value is the same as the one returned by DBMS_LOB.GET_LENGTH. | | X | |
| fileFormat<br>VARCHAR2(4000) | File type. Example: TIFF. | | X | |

**TABLE 12-2.** *List of ORDAudio, ORDImage, and ORDVideo Attributes* (continued)

| Attribute | Description | OA | OI | Ovd |
|-----------|-------------|----|----|----|
| contentFormat VARCHAR2(4000) | Type of image. Example: 8-bit grayscale | | X | |
| compressionFormat VARCHAR2(4000) | Image compression format. Example: JPEG | | X | |
| frameResolution INTEGER | Number of pixels per inch of frames in video data | | | X |
| frameRate INTEGER | Number of frames per second | | | X |
| videoDuration INTEGER | Time it takes to play the entire video clip | | | X |
| numberOfFrames INTEGER | Number of frames in the video data | | | X |
| numberOfColors INTEGER | Number of colors in the video data | | | X |
| bitRate INTEGER | Bit rate of the video data | | | X |

**TABLE 12-2.** *List of ORDAudio, ORDImage, and ORDVideo Attributes* (continued)

The order of the attributes in the type definitions is important for DML statements, such as that shown in the Tip "INSERTing into a Multimedia Type." Following is the attribute definition section of each type:

```
CREATE OR REPLACE TYPE ORDsource
AS OBJECT
( -- ATTRIBUTES
  localData BLOB, srcType VARCHAR2(4000), srcLocation VARCHAR2(4000),
  srcName VARCHAR2(4000), updateTime DATE, local NUMBER,
  -- METHODS ...
```

```
CREATE OR REPLACE TYPE ORDAudio
AS OBJECT
( -- ATTRIBUTES
  description VARCHAR2(4000), source ORDSource,
  format VARCHAR2(31), mimeType VARCHAR2(4000), comments CLOB,
  encoding VARCHAR2(256), numberOfChannels INTEGER,
  samplingRate INTEGER, sampleSize INTEGER,
  compressionType VARCHAR2(4000), audioDuration INTEGER,
  -- METHODS ...
```

```
CREATE OR REPLACE TYPE ORDImage
AS OBJECT
( -- ATTRIBUTES
  source ORDSource, height INTEGER, width INTEGER,
  contentLength INTEGER, fileFormat VARCHAR2(4000),
  contentFormat VARCHAR2(4000), compressionFormat VARCHAR2(4000),
  mimeType VARCHAR2(4000),
  -- METHODS ...
```

```
CREATE OR REPLACE TYPE ORDVideo
AS OBJECT
( -- ATTRIBUTES
  description VARCHAR2(4000), source ORDSource, format VARCHAR2(31),
  mimeType VARCHAR2(4000), comments CLOB, width INTEGER,
  height INTEGER, frameResolution INTEGER, frameRate INTEGER,
  videoDuration INTEGER, numberOfFrames INTEGER,
  compressionType VARCHAR2(4000), numberOfColors INTEGER,
  bitRate INTEGER,
  -- METHODS ...
```

**NOTE**
*PL/SQL is case insensitive. Mixed case is used in the object definitions for clarity only.*

Each of the three multimedia types includes methods for manipulating the data. The complete list of methods can be found in the Oracle document *Oracle8i interMedia Audio, Image, and Video User's Guide and Reference*. Table 12-3 shows the methods that are used in this chapter.

| Method | Description |
| --- | --- |
| getContent() | Returns the content of the local data |
| getContentLength() | Returns the size of the image in bytes (contentLength) |
| getMimeType() | Returns the mime type of the stored image (mimeType) |
| getUpdateTime() | Returns the time the image object was last updated (source.updateTime) |
| setProperties | Fills in the attributes for an image if it is one of the native image types |

**TABLE 12-3.** *List of ORDImage Methods Used in This Chapter*

### Adding an interMedia Type to the DEMO Product Table

In Chapter 11, two columns (promotion_html CLOB, promotion BLOB) were added to DEMO's product table to hold a product's promotional information. That information, stored in a Word document, was then indexed and made searchable. That example will now be extended by the addition of a multimedia column, named product_img, to the product table. The product_img column will be used to hold an image of the product. In its simplest form, the DDL to add this column is as follows:

```
ALTER TABLE product
  ADD(product_img ORDSYS.ORDImage);
```

If the columns defined in Chapter 11 and the product_img columns have been added to the product table, a DESCRIBE in SQL*Plus will show:

```
Name                   Null?     Type
----------------       --------  --------------
PRODUCT_ID             NOT NULL  NUMBER(6)
DESCRIPTION                      VARCHAR2(30)
PROMOTION                        BLOB
PROMOTION_HTML                   CLOB
PRODUCT_IMG                      ORDSYS.ORDIMAGE
```

## Defining the Storage for interMedia Multimedia Object Types

Oracles's interMedia multimedia types can store data in BLOBs, in BFILEs, or as a reference to a URL. The storage choice can be made for each instance of the object type. In other words, the storage choice for the column's value can be made on a row-by-row basis. When you are defining the product_img column as an ORDSYS.ORDImage (or any of the other multimedia types), a LOB segment is created, whether or not the value of the column will be stored internally. The storage parameters for the LOB segment can be specified similarly to the method described in Chapter 11, where a column is defined as a BLOB. The following ALTER TABLE statement shows how the product_img column can be added to the product table with storage parameters specified.

```
ALTER TABLE product
  ADD(product_img ORDSYS.ORDImage)
  LOB(product_img.source.localData)
     STORE AS product_img_seg
       (TABLESPACE user_images
         STORAGE(INITIAL 500K NEXT 500K PCTINCREASE 0)
         CHUNK 50K NOCACHE NOLOGGING ENABLE STORAGE IN ROW
     );
```

Notice that the LOB segment is created for the localData attribute, the attribute of ORDSource that stores internal LOBs.

## Adding a Default Value for an interMedia Type Column

LOBs need to have the LOB locator initialized before they can be used. If the data will be stored internally, the localData attribute can be given a default value. In the ALTER TABLE statement that follows, the product_img column will be defaulted to an ORDImage type that contains an EMPTY_BLOB() when no data is provided for this column at INSERT time. Notice that the EMPTY_BLOB() function is in the localData attribute position, SYSDATE is in the updateTime attribute position, and 1 is in the local position, signifying that the data is stored internally.

```
ALTER TABLE product
  ADD(product_img ORDSYS.ORDImage
     DEFAULT ORDSYS.ORDImage
        (ORDSYS.ORDSource(EMPTY_BLOB(),NULL, NULL, NULL,
                          SYSDATE, 1
                         ),
           NULL, NULL, NULL, NULL, NULL, NULL, NULL
        )
     )
  LOB(product_img.source.localdata)
     STORE AS product_img_seg
        (TABLESPACE user_images
          STORAGE(INITIAL 100K NEXT 100K PCTINCREASE 0)
          CHUNK 50K NOCACHE NOLOGGING ENABLE STORAGE IN ROW
     );
```

## INSERTing into a Multimedia Type

Providing a value to a multimedia type in INSERT or UPDATE statements requires the data to be in the format of the object type. This issue is the same as when you are using standard data types, where columns must receive values of the same type as their definition. The following statement shows an INSERT into the product table, with values provided for the product_id and product_img columns. Note that this example is working with a BFILE, not a local value.

```
INSERT INTO product (product_id, product_img)
  VALUES (300001,
          ORDSYS.ORDImage
            (ORDSYS.ORDSOURCE(NULL,'FILE',
                              'PRODUCT_PROMOTIONS', '300001.jpg',
                              SYSDATE, 0
                             ),
              NULL, NULL, NULL, NULL, NULL, NULL, NULL
            )
         );
```

INSERTing into a Multimedia Type

## SELECTing from a Multimedia Type

SELECTing from a multimedia type is simply a matter of calling a method or attribute from the type as if it were a column. In the following example, the mimeType and ContentFormat of the product_img column are SELECTed from the product table, along with the product_id, using the getMimeType() and getContentFormat() methods.

**NOTE**

*While column aliases are used in the example, they are there for clarity only and are not required. Conversely, you must use table aliases when calling object methods and attributes in SELECT statements.*

```
COLUMN pi_mimeType FORMAT A11
COLUMN pi_ContentFormat FORMAT A16

SQL> SELECT p.product_id,
  2         p.product_img.getMimeType() pi_MimeType,
  3         p.product_img.getContentFormat() pi_ContentFormat
  4    FROM product p
  5   WHERE product_img.getContentLength() IS NOT NULL;

PRODUCT_ID PI_MIMETYPE     PI_CONTENTFORMAT
---------- --------------- --------------------
300001     image/jpeg      24BITRGB
```

## Defining Multimedia Object Views on Columns of Standard Data Types

There may be times in which more flexibility is needed in multimedia storage than can be provided by the standard multimedia types. For example, tables with columns defined as object types cannot participate in Oracle replication. To overcome this, a table can be created (or altered) to contain columns whose data types are conformable to the data types of attributes of the ORDSYS multimedia types. These columns can then be used in an object view against the table. In this way, the table containing standard data types can be used in the replication, and the object view, with its attributes and methods, is available for all other processing as required.

In the following example, the first SQL statement adds columns to DEMO's employee table to store a scanned copy of the employee's resume. The second

creates an object view through which methods can be called to affect the
underlying base columns.

```
ALTER TABLE employee
  ADD (resume_localData BLOB DEFAULT EMPTY_BLOB(),
       resume_srcType VARCHAR2(4000), resume_srcLocation VARCHAR2(4000),
       resume_srcName VARCHAR2(4000), resume_updateTime DATE,
       resume_local NUMBER, resume_height INTEGER,
       resume_width INTEGER, resume_contentLength INTEGER,
       resume_fileFormat VARCHAR2(4000),
       resume_contentFormat VARCHAR2(4000),
       resume_compressionFormat VARCHAR2(4000),
       resume_mimeType VARCHAR2(4000)
       )
  LOB (resume_localData) STORE AS resume_localData_seg
      (TABLESPACE user_images
       CHUNK 32K CACHE ENABLE STORAGE IN ROW
       );
```

```
CREATE OR REPLACE VIEW employee_complete AS
   SELECT employee_id, last_name, first_name, middle_initial,
          job_id, manager_id, hire_date, salary, commission,
          department_id,
          ORDSYS.ORDImage
            (ORDSYS.ORDSource (e.resume_localData,
                               e.resume_srcType,
                               e.resume_srcLocation,
                               e.resume_srcName,
                               e.resume_updateTime,
                               e.resume_local
                               ),
             e.resume_height, e.resume_width,
             e.resume_contentLength, e.resume_fileFormat,
             e.resume_contentFormat, e.resume_compressionFormat,
             e.resume_mimeType
             ) resume
      FROM employee e;
```

To test the object view, issue a SELECT against it:

```
COLUMN resume_mimeType FORMAT A15

SQL> SELECT ec.employee_id, d.name,
  2         ec.resume.getMimeType() resume_mimeType
  3     FROM employee_complete ec, department d
  4    WHERE ec.department_id = d.department_id;

EMPLOYEE_ID NAME            RESUME_MIMETYPE
----------- --------------- ---------------
       7569 RESEARCH        image/tiff
```

# The interMedia Web Agent

The interMedia Web Agent works with Web servers to provide HTTP access to interMedia types managed by the database. The interMedia Web Agent performs retrieval and manipulation of multimedia data managed by the Oracle server on behalf of HTTP clients. It works with most Web/Application servers, including Oracle Application Server (OAS), Netscape Enterprise Server, Netscape FastTrack Server, and Microsoft Internet Information Server. The interMedia Web Agent is optimized for use with multimedia data and is multithreaded so that it will automatically scale to accommodate concurrent requests.

The interMedia Web Agent uses Database Agents for access to the database. A *Database Agent* contains the description of how the database will be accessed. It specifies, for example, the name of the database user to connect as; whether to prompt the user for that information when a request is made; and whether the interMedia Web Agent can be used to perform transactions, only to retrieve data, or to both manipulate and retrieve data from the database. The interMedia Web Agent, the admin Web Agent (a Web Agent used for administration of the interMedia Web Agent), and the Database Agent all keep their configuration information in the same file called ORACLE_HOME/ord/web/admin/wsc.cfg. For detailed configuration and installation information, see the Oracle document *Using Oracle8i interMedia with the Web*.

The focus of the remaining sections will be on building your own application using the interMedia Web Agent with the PL/SQL cartridge. It is worthwhile to note, though, that the interMedia Web Agent has a companion client-side tool called the interMedia Clipboard. The Clipboard provides an interface for directly inserting, retrieving, and editing multimedia types.

**NOTE**

*As part of its work, the interMedia Clipboard generates procedures similar, but more complex than the ones shown in this chapter, in support of its work with the interMedia Web Agent. A good way to learn more about the interMedia Web Agent, the Clipboard, building your own applications, and even working with object types, is to review the generated Clipboard procedures. The Clipboard generated procedures can also be used as templates to your custom procedures.*

## The interMedia Web Agent and URLs

URLs addressed to the interMedia Web Agent include a request to perform either a mediaput (uploads to the database) or a mediaget (retrieval of multimedia data from the database). Both mediaputs and mediagets perform COMMITs and ROLLBACKs against the database. For debugging of Gets, ~mediagets can be used. A ~mediaget functions the same as a mediaget, except that it returns additional error related information when there is a processing problem. For debugging of Puts, appmediaput can be used. It functions the same way as a mediaput, except that an appmediaput returns error information in a format that is easier to use for non-browser applications (such as ones written in C++ or Java). Both Puts and Gets are implemented with the support of PL/SQL procedures. An overview of the parameters along with examples of those procedures will be presented throughout the remainder of this chapter.

The default virtual directory assigned to the interMedia Web Agent is intermedia. Thus, a URL that retrieves multimedia data might appear in the format shown next. In this example, a request is being made to an OAS listener at a host called cesaria on port 80. The virtual directory is intermedia, which has been mapped in the OAS to the interMedia Web Agent. Next, the Database Agent is specified as my_database_agent. A mediaget request is being made to retrieve from the database. The procedure, my_get_procedure, is being used by the interMedia Web Agent to retrieve the data in accordance with the information provided in the last position. The information in the last position is called the *path information,* and it includes the key value with which you can find the correct row in a table storing the data. Thus, in this example, data from the product table for product_id 105123 will be retrieved.

```
http://cesaria:80/intermedia/my_database_agent/mediaget/my_get_procedure/105123
```

If this URL were entered simply as an address in a browser and the data to be returned were an image, the image would be brought back as the sole item in the browser window. The URL can also be used as an image source on a more complex HTML page by including the URL in an <IMG> tag as shown here:

```
<IMG SRC =
"http://cesaria:80/intermedia/my_database_agent/mediaget/my_get_procedure/105123"
>
```

**NOTE**
*Although the ORDImage type will be used as the primary exemplar in this chapter, it is important to remember that the interMedia Web Agent can work with any of the interMedia types. In fact, once you have command over creating the mediaget and mediaput procedures that support the interMedia Web Agent calls to the database, it is possible to use the interMedia Web Agent for multimedia types of your own definition. The interMedia Web Agent can act upon CLOBs, BLOBs, and VARCHAR2s in addition to the multimedia types as described in the Tip "Using the interMedia Web Agent with Non-interMedia Types."*

## Overview of the Processing Common to All interMedia Web Agent Requests

After receiving and decoding a mediaget or mediaput request, the interMedia Web Agent must first assign a database connection and a user session to the request. For optimal performance, the interMedia Web Agent maintains a cache of unassigned database connections and user sessions for each Database Agent. The interMedia Web Agent manages this cache based on how the Database Agent is defined in the configuration file.

When the interMedia Web Agent receives a request for a Database Agent for which a username and password have been specified in the configuration file, the interMedia Web Agent checks the cache for an unassigned database connection and logged-on user session. If found, processing of the request proceeds immediately. If not found, the interMedia Web Agent attaches a new connection to the database and starts a new user session using the username and password specified for the interMedia Web Agent in the configuration file, after which processing of the request can proceed. When a request ends, the interMedia Web Agent returns the database connection and logged-on user session to the cache for use by other requests.

When the interMedia Web Agent receives a request for a Database Agent for which a username and password have not been specified in the configuration file, the interMedia Web Agent checks the cache for an unassigned database connection and idle user session. If not found, the interMedia Web Agent attaches a new connection to the database and creates an idle user session. Once a database connection has been assigned to the request, the interMedia Web Agent attempts to start a database session using the username and password supplied with the request. If successful, processing of the request can proceed immediately. If no username or password were supplied or if an incorrect username and password were supplied, the interMedia Web Agent uses the HTTP Basic Authentication scheme to obtain a valid username and password. When a request ends, the interMedia Web Agent logs out the user session, then returns the database connection and idle session to the cache for use by other requests.

## Overview of a Mediaget and ~mediaget Request

In a mediaget request the interMedia Web Agent will return data to the requestor. A ~mediaget request performs the same functionality, but has the added feature that it will provide additional information to the user in case of an error. This is useful for debugging.

As Figure 12-1 shows, when a mediaget or ~mediaget request is sent to the interMedia Web Agent, it assigns a database connection and a user session, then executes the procedure or SQL statement that was specified in the URL. After the execution of the procedure or SQL statement, the status is handled by the routing shown in Figure 12-3 and is described in more detail in the forthcoming section "Post Execution Processing Common to All Mediaget and Mediaput Requests."

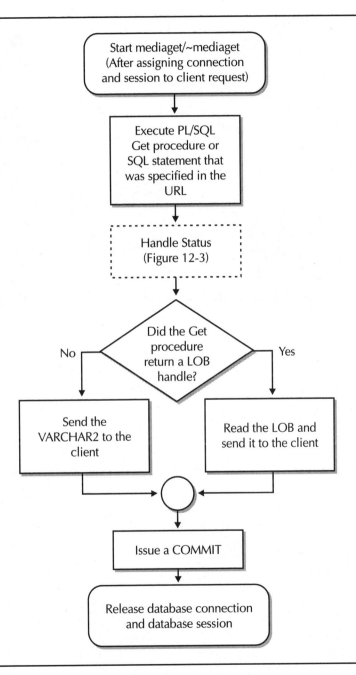

**FIGURE 12-1.**   *Flow of mediaget request*

> ### Overview of the HTTP Basic Authentication Scheme
>
> The HTTP Basic Authentication scheme employs a challenge-response mechanism to obtain, from the user, valid credentials consisting of a username and a password. If the interMedia Web Agent determines that a user has not supplied any credentials or has supplied invalid credentials, it challenges the user to provide valid credentials by completing the request with an HTTP 401 (Unauthorized) status message. On receipt of HTTP 401 (Unauthorized) status message, a client program, such as a Web browser, displays a dialog. The dialog prompts the user to enter a valid username and password. At this point, the user can choose to respond with a username and password, in which case the client program re-sends the original request, accompanied by the username and password, back to the interMedia Web Agent. If the user chooses to cancel the dialog, the client typically displays some form of error message. For example, a browser displays an error message formatted as an HTML page that accompanies the HTTP 401 (Unauthorized) status message.

If the database request completes successfully with an HTTP 200 (Success) status (200 is used as the default if no HTTP status is returned), the interMedia Web Agent acts the same way for a mediaget as it does a ~mediaget. If the database request returned a LOB handle, the interMedia Web Agent reads the LOB and sends the content to the client. Otherwise, if the database request returned some textual content in the ord_content_varchar2 parameter, the interMedia Web Agent sends the text to the client. In both cases, the interMedia Web Agent issues a COMMIT after sending the data. Failure to return any content is considered an error.

### Overview of a Mediaput and Appmediaput Request

A mediaput request is used to upload data to the database. An appmediaput functions the same way as a mediaput, except that an appmediaput returns error information in a format that is easier to use for non-browser applications (such as ones written in C++ or Java). The mediaput consists of two steps. The first one is the Put procedure and is required. The second is the Set or Post-put procedure and is optional.

As shown in Figure 12-2, the first step of mediaput execution is a check to see if the configuration file has been configured to allow mediaputs. If not, an error status is sent to the client.

If the interMedia Web Agent is configured to allow uploads, the interMedia Web Agent next executes the Put procedure or SQL statement that was specified in the URL. After the execution of the procedure or SQL statement, the status is handled by

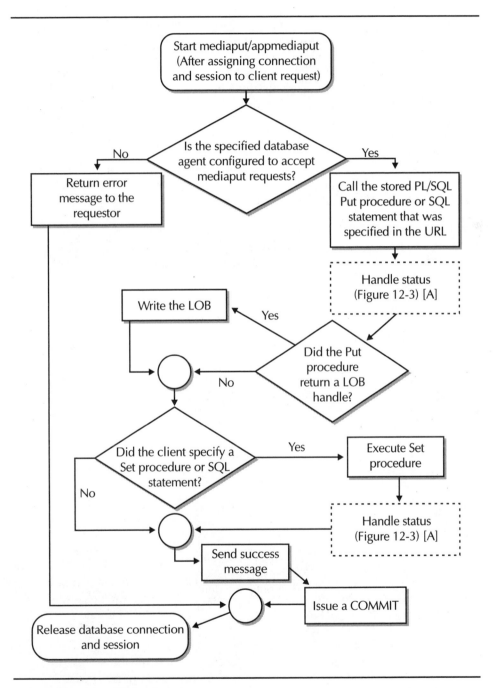

**FIGURE 12-2.** *Flow of mediaput request*

the routing shown in Figure 12-3 and is described in more detail in the next section "Post Execution Processing Common to All Mediaget and Mediaput Requests."

In the case where processing is returned to the mediaput routine as designated in Figures 12-2 and 12-3 with "[A]", the next step is for the interMedia Web Agent to check if it received a LOB handle from the Put procedure. If it did, then the interMedia Web Agent writes the LOB to database. If it did not, it may be because the value passed to the database was a VARCHAR2 rather than a LOB, or an error may have occurred. If an error occurred, the interMedia Web Agent sends an error message to the client.

If there were no errors in the Put procedure, mediaput processing continues by checking to see if a Set procedure or SQL statement was specified by the client. If not, then the interMedia Web Agent sends a success message to the client. Otherwise, the Set procedure or SQL statement is executed and followed by the same status handling routine that came after the Put procedure (as shown in Figure 12-3). If processing is returned to the main mediaput flow (as indicated in figures 12-2 and 12-3 with "[A]", the interMedia Web Agent sends a success message to the client, then issues a COMMIT.

## Post Execution Processing Common to All Mediaget and Mediaput Requests

**NOTE**

*For an example of the mediaput request, see the next tip "Creating a Put Procedure to Perform interMedia Web Agent Transactions."*

Figure 12-3 portrays the status handling algorithm for mediaput and mediaget requests. The markings such as "<1>" in Figure 12-3 indicate that there are additional notes discussed after the figure.

Any unhandled exceptions or errors generated by the database request are handled by an algorithm common to both mediaget and mediaput requests, as are any HTTP status codes other than 200 (Success). For example, a mediaget procedure may retrieve an ORDImage object and determine that the data is actually located on a remote Web server. In this situation, the procedure sets the HTTP status to 302 (Moved Temporarily) and returns the URL of the data in the http_redirect argument. In another example, a mediaget procedure may determine that the contents of a client's local cache is up to date so there is no need to return the content. In this situation, the procedure simply sets the HTTP status to 304 (Not Modified). In a final example, a mediaput or mediaget procedure may perform an application-specific authorization check and determine that the user is not authorized to access the requested information. In this situation, the procedure simply sets the HTTP status to 403 (Forbidden).

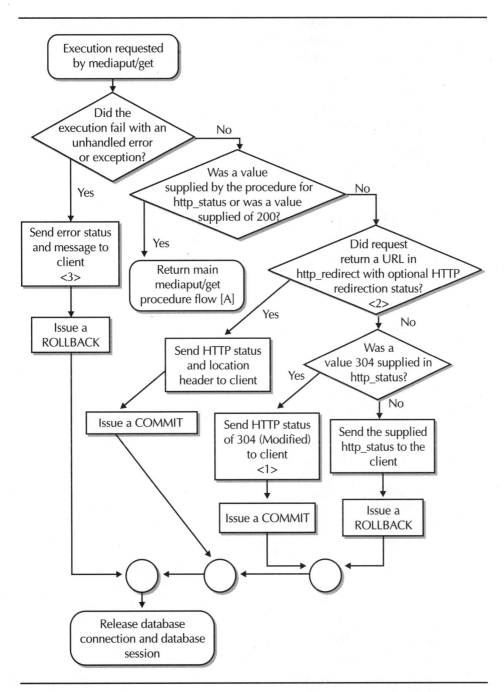

**FIGURE 12-3.** *Status handling part of interMedia Web Agent processing*

There are three markers in Figure 12-3 indicating associated note as follows. **<1>** The HTTP status defaults to 302 if the http_status parameter is not specified and the http_redirect parameter contains a value. **<2>** This step is not included in mediaput processing. **<3>** If any mediaget or mediaput database request completes with an unhandled error or an exception, the interMedia Web Agent processes the error condition based on the type of request being processed and error condition that occurred as follows:

- **mediaget requests**   map error to appropriate HTTP status then return HTTP error to client. For example:

  - Database not available errors are mapped to HTTP 503 (Unavailable)

  - Authorization errors errors are mapped to HTTP 403 (Forbidden)

  - Data not found errors are mapped to HTTP 404 (Not Found)

  - All other errors errors are mapped to HTTP 500 (Internal Server Error)

- **~mediaget requests**   the error message is formatted as an HTML page and sent to the client with the HTTP 200 (Success) status

- **mediaput requests**   the error message is formatted as an HTML page and sent to client with the HTTP 200 (Success) status

- **appmediaput requests**   the error message is formatted as text/plain and sent to client with the HTTP 200 (Success) status

The reason why errors from ~mediaget, mediaput and appmediaput requests are sent with an HTTP 200 (Success) status is that not all Web servers allow application-specific error message text to be sent along with an explicit HTTP error status.

When a mediaget or mediaput database request completes successfully, the interMedia Web Agent next checks the returned HTTP status. If the database request returns 200 (Success), then request processing continues as normal based on the request type. The same is true if the database request does not return an HTTP status. The interMedia Web Agent processes HTTP status codes other than 200 (Success) in the same manner, regardless of the request type.

- **Redirection to a URL**   301 (Moved Permanently) and 302 (Moved Temporarily) [303 is a redirection status that was introduced in HTTP/1.1, but is not yet supported by all browsers]: The interMedia Web Agent sends the specified HTTP status together with the URL in the Location header.

- **Redirection to cache**   304 (Not Modified): The interMedia Web Agent sends only the specified HTTP 304 (Not Modified) status.

- **All other errors, typically either client (400-499) or server (500-599) class errors**   The interMedia Web Agent sends only the specified HTTP status.

# An HTML Application Using the PL/SQL Cartridge and the interMedia Web Agent

In Chapter 11, a PL/SQL Web application was created to retrieve products by performing text searches against DEMO's product table. In this chapter, that application will be extended to include INSERTing and retrieving an image of the product stored in the product table. In addition, procedures will be added for uploading Word documents into the promotion column via a browser using the interMedia Web Agent.

For both scenarios, the first step is to create the stored PL/SQL procedures that will be called by the interMedia Web Agent for mediagets and mediaputs. All of the interMedia Web Agent procedures created in this section act upon the product table in support of the interMedia Web Agent and should be coded in one PL/SQL package. For clarity, however, they will be written as individual stored procedures in this chapter. Assume that the same PL/SQL cartridge (demo) used in Chapter 11 will be used in these examples.

## Creating a Put Procedure to Perform interMedia Web Agent Transactions

A Put procedure is the first one called by the interMedia Web Agent during a mediaput request. The main job of the Put procedure is to pass back the LOB locator if the value is stored internally and NULL for the LOB locator if the value is stored as a BFILE, URL or user-defined data storage type. An individual Put procedure must be defined for each multimedia column in the table. Table 12-4 shows a list of parameters used in Put procedures for multimedia data that is stored as a BLOB. For the full list of parameters see the Oracle Document *Using Oracle8i interMedia with the Web*.

> **NOTE**
> *The parameters prefixed with http_ are particular to the interMedia Web Agent. When used in the procedures, they* must *have the names specified in Table 12-4.*

The procedure wa_product_img_put, for which the main purpose is to pass a valid LOB locator to the Web Agent, will be used to UPDATE the product_img column. This procedure takes two parameters:

- **ord_procedure_path**   Contains a product_id
- **ord_content_blob**   Contains the LOB locator that the interMedia Web Agent will use to populate the BLOB data

| Parameter Name | Data Type | Required | Description |
|---|---|---|---|
| ord_content_blob | OUT BLOB | Y | Returns the LOB locator |
| ord_content_path | IN VARCHAR2 | Y | Contains the identifying key value for the data |
| ord_content_type | OUT VARCHAR2 | N | Specifies the mimetype of the multimedia data |
| http_status | OUT INTEGER | N | Returns an interMedia Web Agent predefined status code, based on standard HTTP status codes. Code ranges: 200–299: success; 300–399: redirection and cache; 400–499: client-side error; 500–599: server-side error |
| http_redirect | OUT VARCHAR2 | N | Returns the URL to be used instead of what the user originally requested |

**TABLE 12-4.** *BLOB Parameters of an interMedia Web Agent Put Procedure*

```
CREATE OR REPLACE PROCEDURE wa_product_img_put
  (ord_procedure_path IN VARCHAR2,
   ord_content_blob OUT BLOB
  )
AS
BEGIN
  SELECT p.product_img.getContent()
    INTO ord_content_blob
    FROM product p
   WHERE product_id = ord_procedure_path
   FOR UPDATE;
END;
```

**NOTE**
*In order for the wa_product_img_put procedure to return a valid LOB locator, the table must be defined with EMPTY_BLOB() as the default for the product_img column as shown in the tip "Adding a Default Value for an interMedia Type Column."*

## Creating a Set Procedure to Handle interMedia Web Agent Transactions

The Set procedure populates the attributes of the ORDSYS.ORDImage column so that they are synchronized with the data value. For example, if a TIFF that was contained in the product_img column was subsequently UPDATEd to contain a JPEG, the Set procedure would make sure that the change was reflected in the object. The Set procedure does this by calling the ORDImage.setProperties method.

After the Set procedure runs, the interMedia Web Agent returns the success message shown in Figure 12-4 to the browser. The procedure wa_product_img_set that follows uses the http_redirect parameter to return an application-specific success message. The http_redirect parameter is assigned the value of a URL that makes use of the product_demo.head procedure created in Chapter 11. Upon success, the requestor will see the page shown in Figure 12-5. The success page is the result of calling through use of the interMedia Web Agent to upload an image for product 100860.

```
CREATE OR REPLACE PROCEDURE wa_product_img_set
  (ord_procedure_path VARCHAR2,
   http_redirect OUT VARCHAR2
  )
AS
  ob_product_img product.product_img%TYPE;
  v_rowid UROWID;
BEGIN
  SELECT ROWID, product_img
    INTO v_rowid, ob_product_img
    FROM product
   WHERE product_id = ord_procedure_path
   FOR UPDATE;
  ob_product_img.setproperties();
  UPDATE product
     SET product_img = ob_product_img
   WHERE ROWID = v_rowid;
  http_redirect := 'http://natalie:80/demo/^product_demo.head'||
                   '?i_title=DEMO''s+product+image+screen:+success.'||
                   '&i_head=The+image+for+product+id+'||
                   ord_procedure_path||
                   '+has+been+updated+successfully.';
END;
```

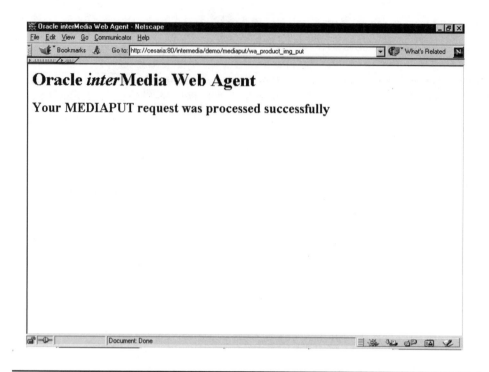

**FIGURE 12-4.** *The default interMedia Web Agent success page*

## Creating a Get Procedure to Handle Retrieval of Multimedia Data

The Get procedure retrieves the multimedia object from the database. Using the wa_product_img_get procedure shown next, it will retrieve the image of a product stored in product_img column. The wa_product_img procedure takes seven parameters. The ord_procedure_path parameter contains the product_id, while the three parameters that begin with ord_content_ pass out information about the object. The three parameters beginning with http_ are used in determining the status of that object in the client's cache. If the most recent version of the object is in the cache, the object data does not need to be retrieved.

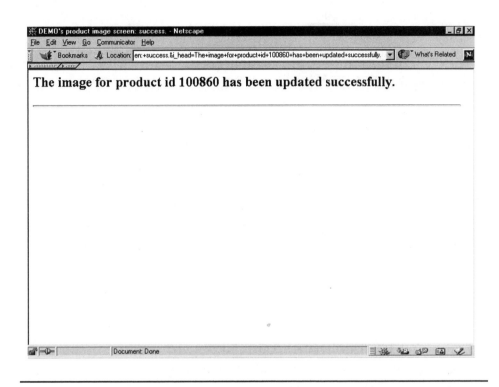

**FIGURE 12-5.**  *A custom success screen*

  **NOTE**
*The SELECT statement in wa_product_img_get does not
need a table alias since the entire column, rather than
an individual attribute, is being SELECTed.*

```
CREATE OR REPLACE PROCEDURE wa_product_img_get
  (ord_procedure_path VARCHAR2,
   ord_content_type OUT VARCHAR2,
   ord_content_length OUT NUMBER,
   ord_content_blob OUT BLOB,
   http_if_modified_since IN VARCHAR2,
   http_status OUT VARCHAR2,
   http_last_modified OUT VARCHAR2
  )
```

```
AS
  ob_product_img ORDSYS.ORDIMAGE;
BEGIN
  SELECT product_img
    INTO ob_product_img
    FROM product
   WHERE product_id = ord_procedure_path;
   http_status := ORDWEBUTL.CACHE_STATUS
     (ob_product_img.getupdatetime(), http_if_modified_since,
       http_last_modified
     );
   IF http_status != 304
   THEN
     -- The client's cache does not contain the most
     --   recent data, the cache must be reloaded. If the
     --   cache were up-to-date the program could return
     --   immediately.
     ord_content_type := ob_product_img.getmimetype();
     ord_content_length := ob_product_img.getcontentlength();
     ord_content_blob := ob_product_img.getcontent();
   END IF;
END;
```

## Creating an Application That Uses the interMedia Web Agent with the PL/SQL Cartridge

Applications using the PL/SQL cartridge can be created to upload and retrieve the multimedia data managed by the database. In this section, two simple applications will be created to work with the images of products held in the product_img column. These procedures will be contained in a package called product_upload.

### An Application Using the PL/SQL Cartridge for Uploading a Product Image

The HTML form used to upload an image using the interMedia Web Agent must contain the specification for the action that calls the Web Agent's Put procedure; the variable ord_post_put_call, which contains the name of the Set procedure; ord_procedure_path, which contains the key value (for example, the product ID input by the user); and ord_content, which contains the specification of the file to be uploaded. The HTML to produce the form for the sample application is shown next. The method of the form action must be `post`, and the enctype must be `multipart/form-data`. For these examples, a Database Agent named demo_da will be used.

```
<HTML>
<HEAD>
<TITLE>DEMO's Upload product image screen</TITLE>
<H2>Upload a Product Image</H2>
<HR>
</HEAD>
<BODY>
<FORM
   ACTION="http://cesaria:80/intermedia/demo_da/mediaput/wa_product_img_put"
   METHOD="POST" ENCTYPE="multipart/form-data"
>
<BR>
<B>Product ID: </B>
<INPUT TYPE="text" NAME="ord_procedure_path" SIZE="6">
<INPUT TYPE="hidden" NAME="ord_post_put_call"
   VALUE="wa_product_img_set"
>
<B>Product Image: </B>
<INPUT TYPE="file" NAME="ord_content" size=35>
<BR>
<BR>
<INPUT TYPE="submit" VALUE="Upload Image Now">
<INPUT TYPE="reset" VALUE="Reset">
</FORM>
</BODY>
</HTML>
```

The product_upload package header will contain a call to the procedure upload_product_img shown here. Upload_product_img will contain calls to the PL/SQL Web development toolkit to produce a form similar to the one preceding.

```
CREATE OR REPLACE PACKAGE product_upload
AS
  PROCEDURE upload_product_img;
END;

CREATE OR REPLACE PACKAGE BODY product_upload
AS
  PROCEDURE upload_product_img
  IS
  BEGIN
    -- Put an informational header on the browser screen.
    product_demo.head('DEMO''s Upload product image screen',
                      'Upload a Product Image'
                      );
    HTP.BODYOPEN;
    -- Create an HTML form to accept a product image.
    HTP.FORMOPEN('http://cesaria:80/intermedia/demo_da/'||
                 'mediaput/wa_product_img_put', 'POST',
```

```
                    cenctype => 'multipart/form-data'
                );
    HTP.BR;
    HTP.PRINT('<B>Product ID: </B>');
    HTP.FORMTEXT('ord_procedure_path', 6);
    HTP.FORMHIDDEN('ord_post_put_call', 'wa_product_img_set');
    HTP.PRINT('<B>Product Image: </B>');
    HTP.FORMFILE('ord_content', cattributes => 'size=35');
    HTP.BR;
    HTP.BR;
    HTP.FORMSUBMIT(NULL, 'Upload Image Now');
    HTP.FORMRESET;
    HTP.FORMCLOSE;
    HTP.BODYCLOSE;
    HTP.HTMLCLOSE;
  END;
END;
```

The product_upload.upload_product_img procedure can be retrieved as a Web page with the following URL:

```
http://cesaria:80/demo/^product_upload.upload_product_img
```

Once the page is retrieved, it will contain two fields: one to enter the product_id and the second specifying the file from the local filesystem to upload in the product_img column. Figure 12-6 shows the page with data entered into the fields.

When the Upload Image Now button is pressed and the image is successfully uploaded, the screen shown in Figure 12-6 will appear.

## An Application Using the PL/SQL Cartridge for Viewing a Product Image

Once the image has been stored in the database, PL/SQL procedures can retrieve it via the interMedia Web Agent. Two procedures will be added to the product_upload package. Review_product_img will show a field in a browser that accepts a product_id for which the user wants to see the product image. Retrieve_product_img will return a Web page containing the product's ID and description along with an image of that product. Retrieve_product_img takes one parameter—i_product_id—which will contain the ID of the product to display. Additions to the code are shown in bold.

```
CREATE OR REPLACE PACKAGE product_upload
AS
  PROCEDURE upload_product_img;
  PROCEDURE review_product_img;
  PROCEDURE retrieve_product_img
    (i_product_id product.product_id%TYPE);
END;
```

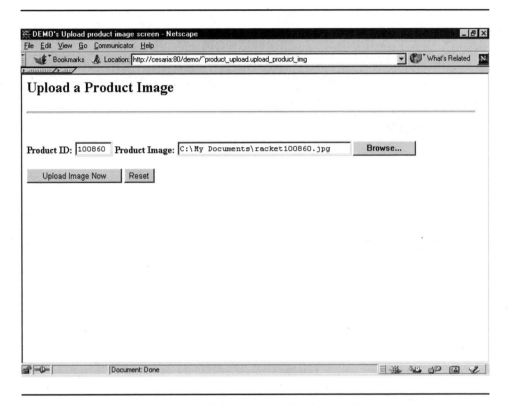

**FIGURE 12-6.**   *Page produced by product_upload.upload_product_img*

```
CREATE OR REPLACE PACKAGE BODY product_upload
AS
  PROCEDURE upload_product_img
  IS
  BEGIN
    -- Put an informational header on the browser screen.
    product_demo.head('DEMO''s Upload product image screen',
                      'Upload a Product Image'
                      );
    HTP.BODYOPEN;
    -- Create an HTML form to accept a product image.
    HTP.FORMOPEN('http://cesaria:80/intermedia/demo_da/'||
                 'mediaput/wa_product_img_put', 'POST',
                 cenctype => 'multipart/form-data'
                 );
    HTP.BR;
```

```
      HTP.PRINT('<B>Product ID: </B>');
      HTP.FORMTEXT('ord_procedure_path', 6);
      HTP.FORMHIDDEN('ord_post_put_call', 'wa_product_img_set');
      HTP.PRINT('<B>Product Image: </B>');
      HTP.FORMFILE('ord_content', cattributes => 'size=35');
      HTP.BR;
      HTP.BR;
      HTP.FORMSUBMIT(NULL, 'Upload Image Now');
      HTP.FORMRESET;
      HTP.FORMCLOSE;
      HTP.BODYCLOSE;
      HTP.HTMLCLOSE;
END;
PROCEDURE review_product_img
IS
BEGIN
   -- Put an informational header on the browser screen.
   product_demo.head('DEMO''s Review product image screen',
                     'Review a Product Image'
                     );
   HTP.BODYOPEN;
   -- Create an HTML form to accept a product id.
   HTP.FORMOPEN('http://cesaria:80/demo/^product_upload.'||
                'retrieve_product_img'
                );
   HTP.PRINT('<B>Enter a product id:</B>');
   HTP.BR;
   HTP.FORMTEXT('i_product_id', 6);
   HTP.BR;
   HTP.BR;
   HTP.FORMSUBMIT(NULL, 'Get Image Now');
   HTP.FORMRESET;
   HTP.FORMCLOSE;
   HTP.BODYCLOSE;
   HTP.HTMLCLOSE;
END;
PROCEDURE retrieve_product_img
   (i_product_id product.product_id%TYPE)
IS
   v_description product.description%TYPE;
BEGIN
   SELECT description
     INTO v_description
     FROM product
    WHERE product_id = i_product_id;
```

```
   -- Put an informational header on the browser screen.
   product_demo.head('Demo''s retrieve product image screen:',
                     'Review image for product '||
                      i_product_id||': '||v_description||'.'
                     );
   -- Create an <IMG> tag that uses the interMedia
   --   Web Agent as the image source.
   HTP.IMG('http://cesaria:80/intermedia/demo_da/mediaget/'||
           'wa_product_img_get/'||i_product_id
          );
   HTP.HTMLCLOSE;
 EXCEPTION
   WHEN NO_DATA_FOUND
   THEN
     -- Provide a custom error message to the user when a product
     --   does not exist for the user-provided product_id.
     product_demo.head('Demo''s retrieve product image screen:'||
                       'failure', 'Product ID '||i_product_id||
                       ' does not exist.'
                      );
   HTP.HTMLCLOSE;
   WHEN OTHERS
   THEN
     -- Provide a custom error message to the user for all
     --   other errors.
     product_demo.head('Demo''s retrieve product image screen:',
                       ' failure', 'Product ID '||i_product_id||
                       ' retrieval failed with Oracle Error '||
                       SQLCODE||'.'
                      );
   HTP.HTMLCLOSE;
 END;
END;
```

The product_upload.review_product_img procedure is called with the following URL:

```
http://cesaria:80/demo/^product_upload.review_product_img
```

It brings up the page shown in Figure 12-7. The figure shows that a search will be performed for product 100860's image.

Figure 12-8 shows the page retrieved for the product, with the description included in the header and with the image pulled from the database via the interMedia Web Agent.

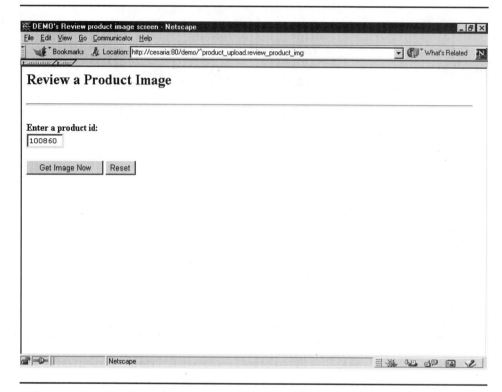

**FIGURE 12-7.** *The review product image page*

# Using the interMedia Web Agent with Non-interMedia Types

In Chapter 11, the product.promotion column (BLOB) was added to the product table to hold Word documents containing material for the most recent promotion of each product. The data was loaded via SQL*Loader and triggers. Through use of the interMedia Web Agent, the document can now be uploaded via a browser. The mediaput and mediaget procedures are similar to the ones shown earlier, which work on the ORDSYS.ORDImage type. In this case, though, the column is simply a BLOB and does not contain the additional attributes of the interMedia types.

## Put Procedure

Wa_promotion_put will be called by the interMedia Web Agent to perform the Put phase of the mediaput. It takes two parameters: ord_procedure_path and

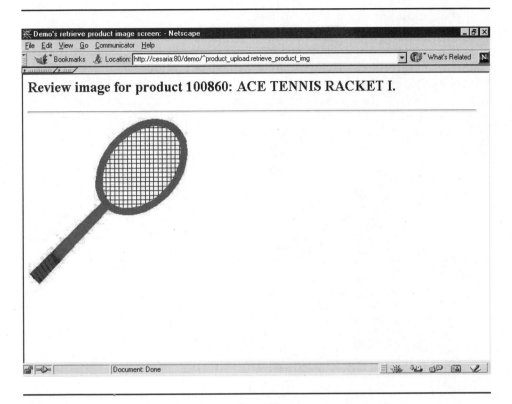

**FIGURE 12-8.** *Retrieve product image page*

ord_content_blob. Its sole purpose is to pass a valid BLOB locator to the interMedia
Web Agent, which will then load the BLOB value into the database.

```
CREATE OR REPLACE PROCEDURE wa_promotion_put
  (ord_procedure_path IN VARCHAR2,
   ord_content_blob OUT BLOB
  )
AS
BEGIN
  -- Return a valid BLOB locator
  SELECT p.promotion
    INTO ord_content_blob
    FROM product p
   WHERE product_id = ord_procedure_path
   FOR UPDATE;
END;
```

## Set Procedure

The wa_promotion_set procedure is used differently than a regular Set procedure. Normally, a Set procedure would be used to set the attributes of a multimedia type column. Since product.promotion is not a multimedia type, the Set procedure has nothing to do. Thus, it is used solely to pass a redirect to the interMedia Web Agent so that the user will see a success message with a standard look and feel. When the interMedia Web Agent sees the redirect, it will consider it a success and issue a COMMIT. Wa_promotion_set takes two parameters: ord_procedure_path and http_redirect.

```
CREATE OR REPLACE PROCEDURE wa_promotion_set
  (ord_procedure_path VARCHAR2,
   http_redirect OUT VARCHAR2
  )
AS
BEGIN
  -- Return the location of an alternate success URL. The
  --   interMedia Web Agent will consider this a success
  --   and issue a commit.
  http_redirect :=
    'http://natalie:80/demo/^product_demo.head'||
    '?i_title=Promotion+Document+Upload+Success+'||
    TO_CHAR(SYSDATE,'MON-DD-YYYY')||
    '&i_head=The+Product+Promotion+Document+has+been'||
    '+updated+for+product+id+'||ord_procedure_path||'.';
END;
```

## Get Procedure

Wa_promotion_get simply passes a BLOB locator to the interMedia Web Agent, which then retrieves the promotion Word document and passes it to the requestor. It also passes back the mimetype, which is hardcoded as 'application/msword'. When a browser sees the mimetype, it will either open the Word document or present a dialog to the user asking whether to save or open the Word document.

Wa_promotion_get takes four parameters: ord_procedure_path, ord_content_type, ord_content_length, and ord_content_blob.

```
CREATE OR REPLACE PROCEDURE wa_promotion_get
  (ord_procedure_path VARCHAR2,
   ord_content_type OUT VARCHAR2,
   ord_content_length OUT NUMBER,
   ord_content_blob OUT BLOB
  )
```

```
AS
BEGIN
   -- Since the promotion documents in Word will not likely be
   --    accessed frequently, it is unlikely that they will
   --    be in the client's cache. So, a check for
   --    the cache status is not done.
   SELECT promotion, DBMS_LOB.GETLENGTH(promotion)
     INTO ord_content_blob, ord_content_length
     FROM product
    WHERE product_id = ord_procedure_path;
   -- set the mimetype
   ord_content_type := 'application/msword';
END;
```

# Tips Review

In Oracle8i interMedia, the interMedia Web Agent is used for uploading and retrieving multimedia data stored in multimedia types. The Web Agent may also be used to upload and download files stored in BLOB columns. Object views are used as a means for supporting Oracle Replication of interMedia object types. Methods are usual for creating, INSERTing, and SELECTing multimedia types.

Tips Review

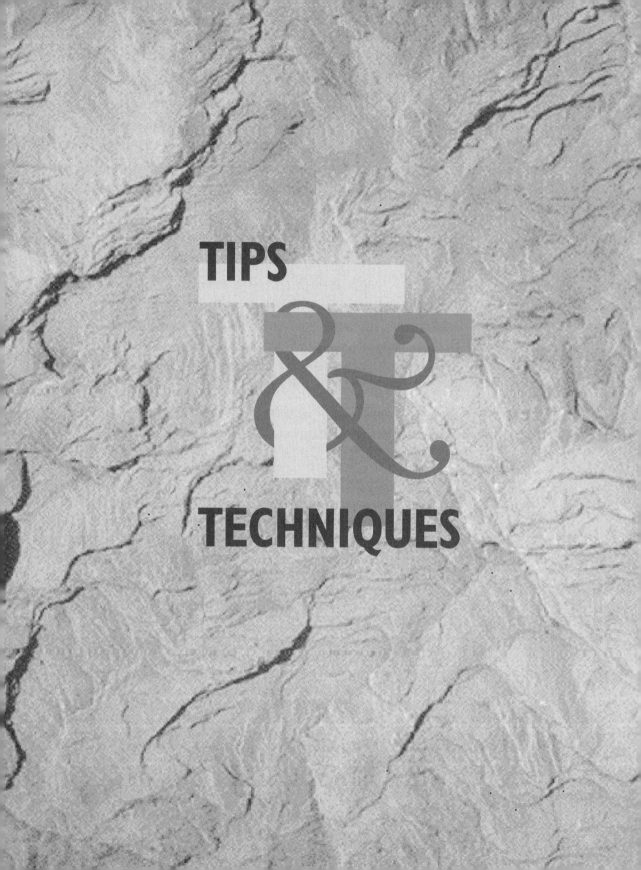

TIPS
&T
TECHNIQUES

APPENDIX

This appendix contains one table that shows a concordance between the chapters. A cell containing an "S" represents a Strong relationship between the chapters. That means the chapter in the leftmost column references or can directly use some information contained in the chapter on the right. A "W" represents a Weak relationship, meaning the chapter in the leftmost column could creatively and practically use some information from the chapter on the right, but the relationship is more subtle and not directly expressed. For clarity, relationships that are either obvious or inconsequential are not noted in the table. For example, Chapter 1, "Oracle ORDBMS Overview," can be used in some way by every chapter in the book.

| For each chapter below ↓, see also Chapter → | 1 | 2 | 3 | 4 | 5 | 6 | 7 | 8 | 9 | 10 | 11 | 12 |
|---|---|---|---|---|---|---|---|---|---|---|---|---|
| Chapter 1: Oracle ORDBMS Overview | | S | S | | | | | | | | S | |
| Chapter 2: Java Enabling Infrastructure | S | | S | | | | | W | S | S | S | |
| Chapter 3: Installation | S | S | | | W | | | | W | W | | |
| Chapter 4: System Management | | | | | W | S | | | | | W | |
| Chapter 5: Performance | | | | S | | W | | | | | | |
| Chapter 6: Data Warehousing | | | | W | W | | | | | | | W |
| Chapter 7: Security | | | | | | | | W | | | | |
| Chapter 8: PL/SQL | | | | | S | | S | | | | W | W |
| Chapter 9: SQLJ and JDBC | S | S | S | | W | W | W | | | S | W | W |
| Chapter 10: Enterprise JavaBeans | | S | S | | W | W | W | | S | | W | W |
| Chapter 11: interMedia Text | S | | | S | W | W | S | W | | | | S |
| Chapter 12: interMedia: Multimedia | | | | S | W | W | W | W | | S | | |

# Glossary

**ACTUAL PARAMETER**   Parameter value passed at run time to PL/SQL routine. Compare with *formal parameter,* when a function or procedure that accepts IN, IN-OUT, or OUT parameters is created. Actual parameters are run-time formal parameters.

**APPLET**   Java program that can be included in an HTML page with the <APPLET> tag. When a browser views the page, the applet is transferred to the client and executed by the browser. For security reasons, applets loaded over a network are subject to several restrictions. For instance, an applet cannot ordinarily access files on the client and cannot make network connections other than to the host that it was downloaded from.

**BULK BINDING**   PL/SQL collections passed as units to improve performance when collections are passed between the PL/SQL and SQL engines.

**COMMON OBJECT REQUEST BROKER ARCHITECTURE (CORBA)**
Standard defined by the Object Management Group (OMG) for building a distributed application based on components. CORBA allows applications to communicate with one another regardless of network location, operating system, or implementation language.

**CONTEXT NAMESPACE**     Type of namespace. A context namespace with an accompanying PL/SQL package will hold application security attributes.

**CONTEXT SWITCH**     Part of SQL statement processing occurring when SQL statements embedded in PL/SQL are passed from the PL/SQL engine to the SQL engine for execution, sometimes returning records to the PL/SQL engine.

**DATABASE**     Set of physical files on disk required to manage storage (datafiles), behavior (control files), and data integrity (redo logs and archive logs). A database and started instance constitute an operating Oracle Object Relational Database Management System.

**DATABASE EVENT TRIGGER**     Holds code that fires as the result of specified non-DML actions such as server startup and shutdown, server error messages, logon and logoff, and DDL operations.

**DATA WAREHOUSE**     Repository for corporate or organizational data. It usually contains historical data and is populated at regular intervals with data from one or more online transaction processing (OLTP) systems.

**DECISION SUPPORT SYSTEM**     Analyzes data for making strategic business decisions. The analysis typically entails summarizing large amounts of data, which can compromise a system's resources, taking minutes or even hours to process.

**DEDICATED SERVERS**     Server that interacts with the database on behalf of a client. With dedicated server processing, each user process connecting to a database instance is assigned an exclusive-use server process.

**DEFINER-RIGHTS ROUTINE**     Routine bound to the schema of the definer; it executes with the privileges of the creator or definer of the routine.

**EJB HOME INTERFACE**     Means by which a client creates a bean instance.

**EJB REMOTE INTERFACE**     Specifies methods you want to expose to clients. The signature for each method you expose in the remote interface must match the signature of the bean implementation. The bean implementation is the area in which you implement the business logic using standard Java.

**ENTERPRISE JAVABEANS (EJB)**     Server-side component model for Java applications.

**ENTITY BEAN**    Also known as *persistent bean.* Represents specific data or collections of data, such as a row in a relational database. Entity bean methods provide operations for acting on the data represented by the bean. An entity bean is persistent; it survives as long as its data remains in the database.

**FORMAL PARAMETER**    Name for a parameter that occurs when a function or procedure that accepts IN, IN-OUT, or OUT parameters is created. Compare with *actual parameter,* the parameter passed at run time.

**GLOBAL INDEX**    Created on an attribute or attributes of a partitioned table; it may or may not be partitioned. If it is partitioned, it should not be equipartitioned with the base table, that is, share the same number of partitions and partition breaks.

**INIT.ORA FILE**    Initialization file holding parameter that an instance uses at startup time to determine configurable instance processes, memory areas, and their sizes—for example, the size of the SGA.

**INSTANCE**    Set of memory areas and set of background processes created when a specific database starts up.

**INTERNET INTER-ORB PROTOCOL (IIOP)**    The CORBA 2.0 standard added the IIOP protocol—mandatory for all ORB vendors—to guarantee a minimum level of interoperability among different ORBs and applications using ORBs. IIOP uses TCP/IP as the underlying transport protocol.

**INVOKER RIGHTS ROUTINE**    Routine that executes with the privileges of the invoker or current user of the routine. It can be created in one schema and then run in another without recompiling the routine in the second schema.

**JAVA ACCELERATOR**    Oracle8i's native Java compiler.

**JAVA DATABASE CONNECTIVITY (JDBC)**    API that provides connectivity to a wide range of SQL databases.

**JAVA POOL**    Memory area holding session-specific Java code and data used by the Java Virtual Machine (JVM). It is sized by the JAVA_POOL_SIZE init.ora parameter.

**JAVA VIRTUAL MACHINE (JVM)**    Interprets Java bytecode (the output of compiling a Java program) into machine-dependent instructions that will run on the computer's processor.

**JSERVER**    Commercial name used for the Oracle8i JVM.

**LARGE POOL**    Memory area created at instance start up, if the optional init.ora parameter LARGE_POOL_SIZE is used. Setting the Large Pool allows a user's memory structures created when the multithreaded server is implemented—which, without use of a Large Pool, would be allocated to the Shared Pool—to be allocated to the Large Pool. In this manner, the Shared Pool is not reduced by the private user-MTS structures, and the allocated memory is available to hold shared SQL representations.

**LOCAL INDEX**    Created on an attribute or attributes of a partitioned table, it is equipartitioned with its underlying table. That is, the index has the same number of partitions and partition keys as the base table.

**MULTIPURPOSE INTERNET MAIL EXTENSION (MIME)**    Extends the format of Internet mail to allow non–US-ASCII textual messages, nontextual messages (including multimedia types), multipart message bodies, and non–US-ASCII information in message headers. Clients can select an appropriate "player" application for a file by looking at its MIME header.

**MULTITHREADED SERVER (MTS)**    Architecture allowing a small number of shared server processes and dispatchers to each handle multiple user processes, reducing system resource usage.

**NAMESPACE**    Area in which no two objects can have the same name. For example, standard namespaces include those that prohibit a table and view from having the same name within the same schema.

**NATIVE DYNAMIC SQL**    Allows any schema-object name to be passed at PL/SQL run time to a Data Manipulation Language (DML) or SELECT statement. In addition, it allows the issuing from within PL/SQL of Data Definition Language, Data Control Language, Session Control Language, and PL/SQL anonymous blocks such as BEGIN . . . END PL/SQL statements. Native dynamic SQL is simpler to use than its earlier implementation, a dynamic SQL.

**OBJECT REQUEST BROKER (ORB)**    Middleware that facilitates communication between distributed objects. Using an ORB, a client can transparently invoke a method on a server object residing on the same machine or on a remote machine. The ORB intercepts the call, finds an object that can implement the request, invoke its method, and returns the results.

**ONLINE TRANSACTION PROCESSING (OLTP)**     Systems (such as order-entry systems) that work with small, well-defined transactions and result sets that must be processed in real-time.

**OPTIMUM FLEXIBLE ARCHITECTURE (OFA)**     Enforces a consistent naming convention—the separation of Oracle homes and their executables for different software versions, the separation of the datafiles of different databases, and the separation of the administrative files of different databases.

**ORACLE DATABASE CONFIGURATION ASSISTANT (DBCA)**     GUI tool used to create and delete database instances.

**PARTITIONING**     Method of physically dividing large tables and indexes into smaller, more manageable pieces called *partitions*. A partitioned object is logically the same as an object that is not partitioned. Physically, each partition is stored in its own segment. Oracle8i supports three types of partitioning: range, hash, and composite. All three types of partitioning support three techniques that optimize performance for retrieving data from partitioned tables and for managing these tables: equipartitioning, partition-wise joining, and partition pruning.

**REMOTE METHOD INVOCATION (RMI)**     Technology developed by JavaSoft intended for Java-to-Java communications across JVMs.

**SERVLET**     Java code that a Web server loads to handle client requests. Servlets offer efficiency and security gains over other server-side coding techniques. Servlet code stays alive in memory when the request ends. A servlet can connect to a database when it is initialized and retain its connection across requests.

**SESSION BEAN**     Logical extension of the client's session, running processes on the client's behalf remotely on the server.

**SHARED POOL**     Area of memory in the SGA. It is sized by the SHARED_POOL_SIZE init.ora parameter. It holds nonsession-specific code and data when either the Java Virtual Machine or the multithreaded server is implemented and when SQL and PL/SQL are used. Session-specific data in the form of response and request queues can also be found in the Shared Pool.

**SHARED SERVERS**     The multithreaded server (MTS) architecture allows a small number of shared server processes to handle multiple user processes, reducing system resource usage. Many user processes can share one server process.

**SQLJ**    Standard way of embedding SQL in Java that is simpler to use than JDBC.

**STAR SCHEMA**    Data warehouse normally built using a dimensional data model. It contains two types of tables—fact tables, which are generally large tables that contain the quantitative data (facts) about a business, and dimension tables, which are usually much smaller and contain descriptive data about the business.

**SUMMARY MANAGEMENT**    Includes capabilities that address two serious problems in managing a data warehouse: (1) how to get data out of the warehouse, in terms of complex queries, involving aggregations and summaries, potentially across many tables and millions of rows, and (2) how to keep the data in the warehouse updated in a timely manner. The techniques and methods employed by summary management include materialized views, dimensions, and query rewriting.

**SYSTEM GLOBAL AREA (SGA)**    Memory area allocated to an instance at startup.

**TRANSPORTABLE TABLESPACE**    It is a tablespace like any other instance tablespace, except it can be moved or copied from one database to another.

**TWO-TASK COMMON (TTC)**    Presentation layer that manages character set, format, and data type conversions between clients and servers. It is the default presentation layer for Net8.

**VIRTUAL PRIVATE DATABASE FEATURE**    Feature that associates a security policy with a specific table or view.

# Index

# C

## Q

## R

## S

**T**

# Think you're
# smart?

You're an Oracle DBA. You're implementing a backup and recovery plan. Which component stores the synchronization information needed for database recovery?

a. redo log files
b. control file
c. parameter file
d. trace file

## Think you're ready to wear this badge?